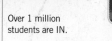

POLICE 2012–2013 Edition
John S. Dempsey and Linda S. Forst

Vice President, Career and Professional Editorial:
Dave Garza

Director of Learning Solutions: Sandy Clark

Senior Acquisitions Editor: Shelley Esposito

Managing Editor: Larry Main

Product Manager: Anne Orgren

Editorial Assistant: Diane Chrysler

Vice President, Career and Professional Marketing:
Jennifer Baker

Marketing Director: Deborah S. Yarnell

Senior Marketing Manager: Mark Linton

Marketing Coordinator: Erin DeAngelo

Production Director: Wendy Troeger

Production Manager: Mark Bernard

Senior Content Project Manager: Betty Dickson

Production Service: Integra Software Services Pvt. Ltd.

Photo Credits: Inside Front Cover: © iStockphoto.com/
sdominick, © iStockphoto.com/A-Digit,
© iStockphoto.com/alexsl; Inside Back Cover: ©
Cengage Learning 2011; Back Cover: © iStockphoto.
com/René Mansi; Page i: © iStockphoto.com/CostinT,
© iStockphoto.com/photovideostock, © iStockphoto.
com/Leontura

For product information and technology assistance, contact us at
Cengage Learning Customer & Sales Support, 1-800-354-9706
For permission to use material from this text or product,
submit all requests online at **www.cengage.com/permissions**
Further permissions questions can be emailed to
permissionrequest@cengage.com

Library of Congress Control Number: 2011932364

SE ISBN-13: 978-1-133-01665-6
SE ISBN-10: 1-133-01665-0

IE ISBN-13: 978-1-133-01666-3
IE ISBN-10: 1-133-01666-9

Delmar
5 Maxwell Drive
Clifton Park, NY 12065-2919
USA

Cengage Learning is a leading provider of customized learning solutions with office locations around the globe, including Singapore, the United Kingdom, Australia, Mexico, Brazil, and Japan. Locate your local office at: **international.cengage.com/region**

Cengage Learning products are represented in Canada by
Nelson Education, Ltd.

To learn more about Delmar, visit **www.cengage.com/delmar**
Purchase any of our products at your local college store or at our preferred online store **www.CengageBrain.com**

Notice to the Reader
Publisher does not warrant or guarantee any of the products described herein or perform any independent analysis in connection with any of the product information contained herein. Publisher does not assume, and expressly disclaims, any obligation to obtain and include information other than that provided to it by the manufacturer. The reader is expressly warned to consider and adopt all safety precautions that might be indicated by the activities described herein and to avoid all potential hazards. By following the instructions contained herein, the reader willingly assumes all risks in connection with such instructions. The publisher makes no representations or warranties of any kind, including but not limited to, the warranties of fitness for particular purpose or merchantability, nor are any such representations implied with respect to the material set forth herein, and the publisher takes no responsibility with respect to such material. The publisher shall not be liable for any special, consequential, or exemplary damages resulting, in whole or part, from the readers' use of, or reliance upon, this material.

Printed in the United States of America
1 2 3 4 5 6 7 15 14 13 12 11

Brief Contents

© Rob Howard/Corbis

© Joel Gordon

Kentucky Office of Homeland Security

AP Photo/Paul Saneya

Contents

© AP Photo/Al Goldis

Chapter 3
Organizing the Police Department   33

Part 2

The Personal Side of Policing 52

© Photo By Mario Tama/Getty Images

Chapter 4
Becoming a Police Officer 53

© iStockphoto/WH1600

Chapter 5
The Police Role and Police Discretion 67

Chapter 6
Police Culture, Personality, and Police Stress   81

Chapter 7
Minorities in Policing   97

Chapter 8
Police Ethics and Police Deviance   107

Part 3

Police Operations 122

© AP Photo/Michael Conroy

Chapter 9
Patrol Operations   123

Chapter 10
Investigations   139

Chapter 11
Police and the Community   153

Chapter 12
Community Policing: The Debate Continues   165

Chapter 13
Police and the Law   177

Part 4

Critical Issues in Policing   192

1

Police History

LO1 Discuss the Early Police

The word *police* comes from the Latin word *politia*, which means "civil administration." The word *politia* goes back to the Greek word *polis*, "city." Etymologically, therefore, the police can be seen as those involved in the administration of a city. *Politia* became the French word *police*. The English took it over and at first continued to use it to mean "civil administration." The specific application of *police* to the administration of public order emerged in France in the early eighteenth century. (Ayto 402)

After studying this chapter, the student should be able to:

LO1 Discuss the early police

LO2 Discuss English policing: our English heritage

LO3 Discuss American policing: the colonial experience

LO4 Discuss American policing: eighteenth and nineteenth centuries

LO5 Discuss American policing: twentieth and twenty-first centuries

© iStockphoto/Roma Oslo

Roman Emperor Caesar Augustus.

Log onto www.cengagebrain.com to practice your vocabulary with flash cards and more.

The reference to the police as a "civil authority" is very important. The police represent the civil power of government, as opposed to the military power of government. We use the military in times of war. The members of the military, of necessity, are trained to kill and destroy. That is appropriate in war. However, do we want to use military forces to govern or patrol our cities and towns?

We do not know much about the very early history of the police. Policing—maintaining order and dealing with lawbreakers—had always been a private matter. Citizens were responsible for protecting themselves and maintaining an orderly society. Uniformed, organized police departments as we think of them today were rare.

Around the fifth century B.C.E., Rome created the first specialized investigative unit, called *questors*, or "trackers of murder." (Dempsey 2003) Around the sixth century B.C.E. in Athens and the third century B.C.E. in Rome, unpaid magistrates (judges), appointed by the citizens, were the only people we would consider law enforcement professionals. The magistrates adjudicated cases, but private citizens arrested offenders and punished them. In most societies, people in towns would group together and form a watch, particularly at night, at the town borders or gates to ensure that outsiders did not attack the town.

At about the time of Christ, the Roman emperor Augustus picked special, highly qualified members of the military to form the **Praetorian Guard**, which could be considered the first group of police officers. Their job was to protect the palace and the emperor. At about the same time, Augustus also established the Praefectus Urbi (Urban Cohort) to protect the city. The Urban Cohort had both executive and judicial powers. Augustus also established the Vigiles of Rome. The **Vigiles** began as firefighters and were eventually also given law enforcement responsibilities patrolling Rome's streets day and night. The Vigiles could be considered the first civil police force designed to protect citizens. They were quite brutal, and our words *vigilance* and *vigilante* come from their name. (Ayto 559)

LO2 Discuss English Policing: Our English Heritage

The American system of law and criminal justice was borrowed from the English. Therefore, we will now concentrate on the English police experience, which is colorful and related to the development of English society.

Early History

Sir Robert Peel is generally credited with establishing the first English police department, the London Metropolitan Police, in 1829. However, the first references to an English criminal justice or law enforcement system appeared some 1,000 years earlier, in the latter part of the ninth century, when England's king, Alfred the Great, was preparing his kingdom for an impending Danish invasion. Part

Sir Robert Peel.

© Photo By Time Life Pictures/Mansell/Time Life Pictures/Getty Images

of King Alfred's strategy against the Danes was maintaining stability in his own country and providing a method for people living in villages to protect one another. To achieve this stability, King Alfred established a system of **mutual pledge** (a form of "society control" where citizens grouped together to protect each other), which organized the responsibility for the security of the country into several levels. At the lowest level were tithings, 10 families who grouped together to protect one another and to assume responsibility for the acts of the group's members. At the next level, 10 tithings (100 families) were grouped together into a hundred; the hundred was under the charge of a constable. People were supposed to police their own communities. If trouble occurred, a citizen was expected to raise the **hue and cry** (yell for help), and other citizens were expected to come to that citizen's assistance. The **constable**, who might be considered the first form of English police officer, was responsible for dealing with more serious breaches of the law.

Groups of hundreds within a specific geographic area were combined to form *shires* (the equivalent of today's county). The shires were put under the control of the king and were governed by a **shire-reeve**, or sheriff.

Over the centuries, as formal governments were established, early, primitive forms of a formal criminal justice system evolved in England. In 1285 C.E., the Statute of Winchester was enacted in England and established a rudimentary criminal justice system in which most of the responsibility for law enforcement remained with the people themselves. The statute formally established (1) the watch and ward, (2) the hue and cry, (3) the parish constable, and (4) the requirement that all males keep weapons in their homes for use in maintaining the public peace.

The **watch and ward** required all men in a given town to serve on the night watch. The watch, therefore, can be seen as the most rudimentary form of metropolitan policing. The watch was designed to protect against crime, disturbances, and fire. The watchmen had three major duties:

- Patrolling the streets from dusk until dawn to ensure that all local people were indoors and quiet and that no strangers were roaming about
- Performing duties such as lighting street lamps, clearing garbage from streets, and putting out fires
- Enforcing the criminal law

Persons serving on the watch would pronounce the hue and cry, if necessary, and all citizens would then be required to leave their homes and assist the watchmen. The Statute of Winchester made it a crime not to assist the watch. The statute also established the office of parish constable, who was responsible for organizing and supervising the watch. The parish constable was, in effect, the primary urban law enforcement agent in England.

A night watchman on his rounds in early England.

© Mary Evans Picture Library/Alamy

Seventeenth Century and Thief-Takers

In seventeenth-century England, as before, law enforcement was seen as the duty of all the people even though more and more officials were being charged with enforcing the law and keeping the peace.

The seventeenth-century English policing system used a form of individual, private police. Called **thief-takers**, these private citizens with no official status were paid by the king for every criminal they arrested—similar to the bounty hunter of the American West. The major role of the thief-takers was to combat highway robbery committed by highwaymen, whose heroes were the likes of such legendary outlaws as Robin Hood and Little John. By the seventeenth century, highwaymen had made traveling through the English countryside so dangerous that no coach or traveler was safe. In 1693, an act of Parliament established a monetary reward for the capture of any road agent, or armed robber. A thief-taker was paid upon the conviction of the highwayman and also received the highwayman's horse, arms, money, and property.

Peel's Police: The Metropolitan Police for London

In 1828, Sir Robert Peel, England's home secretary, drafted the first police bill, the Act for Improving the Police in and near the Metropolis (the Metropolitan Police Act). Parliament passed it in 1829. This act established the first large-scale, uniformed, organized, paid, civil police force in London. More than 1,000 men were hired. Although a civil—rather than a military—force, it was structured along military lines, with officers wearing distinctive uniforms.

Peel has become known as the founder of modern policing; however, it must be noted that he was never a member of a police department. His link to policing comes from his influence in getting the new police bill passed. The early London police were guided by **Peel's Nine Principles**, as described by the New Westminster Police Service.

watch and ward
A rudimentary form of policing designed to protect against crime, disturbances, and fire. All men were required to serve on it.

thief-takers
Private English citizens with no official status who were paid by the king for every criminal they arrested. They were similar to the bounty hunter of the American West.

Peel's Nine Principles
Basic guidelines created by Sir Robert Peel for the London Metropolitan Police in 1829.

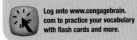 Log onto www.cengagebrain. com to practice your vocabulary with flash cards and more.

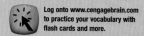
The Metropolitan Police was organized around the **beat system**, in which officers were assigned to relatively small permanent posts and were expected to become familiar with them and the people residing there, thereby making the officer a part of neighborhood life.

Peel's **Nine Principles**

1. The basic mission for which the police exist is to prevent crime and disorder.

2. The ability of the police to perform their duties is dependent upon public approval of police actions.

3. Police must secure the willing co-operation of the public in voluntary observance of the law to be able to secure and maintain the respect of the public.

4. The degree of co-operation of the public that can be secured diminishes proportionately to the necessity of the use of physical force.

5. Police seek and preserve public favour not by catering to public opinion but by constantly demonstrating absolute impartial service to the law.

6. Police use physical force to the extent necessary to secure observance of the law or to restore order only when the exercise of persuasion, advice and warning is found to be insufficient.

7. Police, at all times, should maintain a relationship with the public that gives reality to the historic tradition that the police are the public and the public are the police, the police being only members of the public who are paid to give full-time attention to duties which are incumbent on every citizen in the interests of community welfare and existence.

8. Police should always direct their action strictly towards their functions and never appear to usurp the powers of the judiciary.

9. The test of police efficiency is the absence of crime and disorder, not the visible evidence of police action in dealing with it.

SOURCE: New Westminster Police Service

LO3 Discuss American Policing: The Colonial Experience

The North: The Watch

By the seventeenth century, the northern colonies had started to institute a civil law enforcement system that closely replicated the English model. The county sheriff was the most important law enforcement official. In addition to law enforcement, however, he collected taxes, supervised elections, and had much to do with the legal process. Sheriffs were not paid a salary but, much like the English thief-taker, were paid fees for each arrest they made. Sheriffs did not patrol but stayed in their offices.

In cities, the town marshal was the chief law enforcement official, aided by constables and night watchmen. Night watch was sometimes performed by the military. The city of Boston created the first colonial night watch in 1631 and three years later created the position of constable. In 1658, eight paid watchmen replaced a patrol of

A British "bobby" on his beat.

© Maurice Crooks/Alamy

citizen volunteers in the Dutch city of New Amsterdam. The British inherited this police system in 1664 when they took over the city and renamed it New York.

The South: Slave Patrols

Many police historians and scholars indicate that **slave patrols** in the American South were the precursor to the modern American system of policing. Studies of this early form of policing indicate that the southern colonies developed a formal system of social control, particularly in rural areas, to maintain the institution of slavery by enforcing restrictive laws against slaves. Slave patrols were prominent in many of the early colonies as a means of apprehending runaway slaves and protecting the white population from slave insurrections or crimes committed by slaves.

Slave codes were laws enforced by developing southern police departments to directly support slavery and the existing economic system of the South. These codes were adopted by colonial and, later, state legislatures. Slave patrols became the police mechanism to support the southern economic system of slavery. The codes were designed to ensure the economic survival of southern society— the use of slave labor to produce goods. Slaves were valuable property, and the codes were meant to prevent them from running away or engaging in insurrection. Simply put, these early slave codes were intended to preserve the social order in which whites dominated and subjugated blacks.

© iStockphoto/Charles Schug

LO4 Discuss American Policing: Eighteenth and Nineteenth Centuries

Historically, American policing attempted to control crime and disorder in urban and frontier environments. Although the urban and frontier experiences differed in many ways, both could be classified as brutal and corrupt.

The Urban Experience

During the eighteenth century, the most common form of American law enforcement was the system of constables in the daytime and the watch at night. Crime, street riots, and drunkenness were very common, and law enforcement personnel were incompetent.

Early Police Departments The tremendous migration to large American cities and the poverty and discrimination these new residents encountered led to enormous social problems, including crime and disorder. In response, many large cities began to create formal police departments using the Peelian model. The first organized American police department in the North was created in Boston in 1838. In 1844, the New York state legislature authorized communities to organize police forces and gave special funds to cities to provide 24-hour police protection. In New York City, a London-style police department was created on May 23, 1845.

Philadelphia started its police department in 1854. By the outbreak of the Civil War, Chicago, New Orleans, Cincinnati, Baltimore, Newark, and a number of other large cities had their own police departments. The new police departments replaced the night watch system. As a result, constables and sheriffs were relieved of much of their patrol and investigative duties.

The Early Police Officer's Job Police work was primitive. The role of the American urban police in the eighteenth and nineteenth centuries was varied and often not limited to law enforcement. The early police performed many duties they do not perform today, including cleaning streets, inspecting boilers, caring for the poor and homeless, operating emergency ambulances, and performing other social services.

The Southern Experience

As discussed earlier, slave patrols were an early form of American southern policing and perhaps the first police departments in the United States.

Atlanta, Georgia, was a major railroad hub and supply center for Confederate forces, with troops and refugees flooding into and out of the city from late 1861 through the end of the Civil War in 1865. The Atlanta Police Department was challenged by the problems brought by the war, as well as by having to maintain the traditional social order through the slave code at the same time. However, the most serious crime problem in Atlanta was white rowdyism, vandalism, and theft. The Fulton County court dealt with more cases involving whites than cases

slave patrols
Police-type organizations created in the American South during colonial times to control slaves and support the southern economic system of slavery.

 Log onto www.cengagebrain.com to practice your vocabulary with flash cards and more.

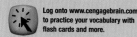
involving bonded slaves and black refugees. Larceny and burglary were the most popular crimes in Atlanta and often involved Confederate soldiers on post in Atlanta.

After the Civil War, from 1867 to 1877, some law enforcement duties were provided by the military in the military districts created from the Confederacy. U.S. marshals in occupied southern states often called on federal troops to form a posse to enforce local laws. Also, the army guarded polling places and curbed the actions of the Ku Klux Klan. Once southern states regained representation in Congress, they tried to prevent such practices.

After the war, many police departments across the South reorganized to meet Reconstruction standards. However, in many cases, police officials under the prewar system simply returned to their posts, and the militia-like nature of slave patrols and volunteer companies survived the war in the newly reorganized police departments. In addition to maintaining public order, police continued to be the upholders of white supremacy in their communities.

Some police departments reluctantly hired blacks on their forces to satisfy demands brought on by Reconstruction. These black officers made whites extremely nervous, and whites taunted black policemen and often paid them no heed.

The Frontier Experience

Life on the American frontier was not easy. Early settlers faced tremendous problems from the weather, the terrain, Native Americans, and the criminals within their own ranks. Formal law enforcement on the frontier was rare. What little law enforcement existed in the Old West consisted mainly of the locally elected county sheriff and the appointed town marshal.

Sheriffs and Town Marshals The locally elected county sheriffs and the appointed town marshals (appointed by the mayor or city council) were usually the only law enforcement officers available on the frontier. Most of the sheriff's time was spent collecting taxes and performing duties for the courts.

If a crime spree occurred or a dangerous criminal was in an area, the sheriff would call upon the **posse comitatus**, a common-law descendent of the old hue and cry. (The Latin term *posse comitatus* means "the power of the county.") No man above the age of 15 could refuse to serve as a member of a legally constituted posse. The posse was

A Western town marshal.

© Rob Howard/Corbis

often little more than a legalized form of vigilantism. Vigilantism and lynch mobs were common in the Old West because of the lack of professional law enforcement.

State Police Agencies Some states and territories created their own police organizations. In 1823, Stephen Austin hired a dozen bodyguards to protect fellow "Texicans" from Native Americans and bandits. Austin's hired guns were officially named the Texas Rangers upon Texas's independence in 1835. The Texas Rangers served as a border patrol for the Republic of Texas, guarding against marauding Native Americans and Mexicans. When Texas was admitted to the Union in 1845, the Texas Rangers became the first U.S. state police agency.

Unlike present-day state police, the Texas Rangers and their counterparts, the Arizona Rangers (1901) and the New Mexico Mounted Patrol (1905), were primarily border patrols designed to combat cattle thievery and control outlaw activities on the Rio Grande. With Pennsylvania leading the way in 1905, other states outside the Southwest began to create their own state police agencies.

Private Police Private police were much more effective than public law enforcement agencies on the frontier. Allan Pinkerton, a native of Scotland, was a former police detective who established a detective agency in Chicago in 1850. The Pinkerton Agency first gained notoriety just before the Civil War, when it thwarted the alleged "Baltimore Plot" to assassinate president-elect Abraham Lincoln. By the 1880s, Pinkerton's National Detective Agency had offices in nearly two dozen cities. In the West, Pinkerton's customers included the U.S. Department of Justice, various railroad companies, and major land speculators.

LO5 Discuss American Policing: Twentieth and Twenty-First Centuries

The first half of the twentieth century saw such dramatic negative events as the Boston police strike and National Prohibition. However, innovation and an increase in professionalism grew to characterize the American police.

Policing from 1900 to 1960

As we have seen, American policing has historically been characterized by ineptness, corruption, and brutality. At the start of the twentieth and twenty-first centuries, serious attempts were made to reform the police.

Technology In the twentieth century, the use of technology grew phenomenally in American police departments. By 1913, the police motorcycle was being used by departments in the Northeast. The first police car was used in Akron, Ohio, in 1910, and the police wagon was first used in Cincinnati in 1912. By the 1920s, the

A police officer on motorcycle in 1923.
© The Library of Congress

patrol car was in widespread use. The patrol car began to change police work by allowing the police to respond quickly to crimes and other problems, as well as by enabling each officer to cover much more territory.

The widespread use of the one-way radio in the 1930s and the two-way radio in the 1940s, combined with the growing use of the patrol car, began to revolutionize police work. A person could call police headquarters or a precinct, and a police car could be dispatched almost immediately, providing rapid response to calls for service and emergencies.

The Boston Police Strike The Boston police strike of 1919 was one of the most significant events in the history of policing, and it increased interest in police reform. While other professions were unionizing and improving their standards of living, police salaries lagged behind, and the police were becoming upset with their diminished status in society. The fraternal association of Boston police officers, the Boston Social Club, voted to become a union affiliated with the American Federation of Labor (AFL). On September 9, 1919, 70 percent of Boston's police officers—1,117 men—went on strike. Rioting and looting immediately broke out, and Governor Calvin Coolidge mobilized the state militia. Public support went against the police, and the strike was broken. All the striking officers were fired and replaced by new recruits. The

© Bettmann/Corbis

During the September 1919 Boston police strike, one of the few policemen who remains on duty (there were only 427 out of 1,544) speaks to a member of the National Guard (on horseback). The National Guard were called in to control lawlessness.

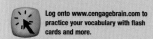
strike ended police unionism for decades. Coolidge became a national hero and went on to become president of the United States. Many say that his action in firing the Boston police propelled him to the presidency.

National Prohibition Another significant event in twentieth-century policing, and one that stirred up another police reform movement, was the experiment with the prohibition of alcohol in the United States. The **Volstead Act** (National Prohibition) was passed in 1919 and became law in 1920 with the adoption of the Eighteenth Amendment to the Constitution. It forbade the sale and manufacture of alcohol, attempting to make America a dry nation. Traditional organized crime families received their impetus during this period as gangsters banded together to meet the tremendous demand of ordinary Americans for alcohol. When the Eighteenth Amendment was repealed in 1933 with the adoption of the Twenty-first Amendment, the organized crime families funneled the vast amount of capital that they had received in the alcohol trade into other vice crimes, such as illegal gambling, prostitution, loan sharking, labor racketeering, and, later, drug dealing.

Local law enforcement was unable to stop the alcohol and vice operations of organized crime and became even more corrupt as many law enforcement officers cooperated with organized crime.

Photo © iStockphoto/Clayton Hansen. Photo illustration by Spitting Images for Cengage Learning.

A barrel of liquor is poured out during Prohibition.

Library of Congress

Policing in the 1960s and 1970s

The 1960s and 1970s, times of great tension and change, probably formed the most turbulent era ever for policing in U.S. history. Numerous social problems permeated these decades, and the police were at the center of each problem. In this era, the struggle for racial equality reached its peak, accompanied by marches, demonstrations, and riots. These riots burned down whole neighborhoods in U.S. urban centers. The Vietnam War was reaching its height, soldiers were dying, and students across the United States were protesting the war and governmental policies. The Supreme Court decided in case after case to protect those who had been arrested from oppressive police practices. The police seemed to be more the targets of radical groups than the respected protectors of the people. In short, during this time of dramatic social change in the United States, the police were not only right in the middle, but often were the focus of it all.

The police, because of their role, were caught between those fighting for their civil rights and the government officials (the employers of the police) who wanted to maintain the status quo, and between demonstrating students and college and city administrators. The police received much criticism during these years. Some of it was deserved, but much of it was for circumstances beyond their control.

Supreme Court Decisions The 1960s saw the Warren Court at its peak—a U.S. Supreme Court that focused dramatically on individual rights. Police actions ranging from arrests to search and seizure and custodial interrogation were being declared unconstitutional. The Court made dramatic use of the exclusionary rule, a 1914 Supreme Court ruling that declared that evidence seized by the police in violation of the Constitution could not be used against a defendant in federal court, thus leading to the possibility that a guilty defendant could go free because of procedural errors by the police.

The Civil Rights Movement Legal segregation of the races finally ended with the landmark Supreme Court case of *Brown v. Board of Education of Topeka* (1954), which desegregated schools all over the nation. However, equal treatment of the races did not occur overnight. Numerous marches and demonstrations occurred before the Civil Rights Act of 1964 was passed.

In the 1960s, African Americans and other civil rights demonstrators participated in freedom marches throughout the United States, particularly in the South. Because the police are the enforcement arm of government, they were used to enforce existing laws, which in many cases meant arresting and inhibiting the freedom of those marching for equality.

During the 1960s, the Reverend Martin Luther King, Jr., was at the forefront of the civil rights marches. In 1963, King led 25,000 demonstrators on a historic march on Washington that culminated in his "I have a dream" speech. During this speech, a defining moment of the movement, a white uniformed police officer stood behind King in a highly visible position, perhaps as a symbolic representation of the new role of the police in America's social history—as defenders rather that oppressors.

The civil rights movement continued and succeeded partly by enrolling more minorities as voters, by outlawing forms of government-sanctioned segregation, and by ensuring that more minorities participated in government. Today, many of our large-city mayors and politicians are members of minority groups. The civil rights movement thus led to efforts to increase the recruitment and hiring of blacks and other minorities in our nation's police departments and other agencies of the criminal justice system.

Although the civil rights movement was necessary in the evolution of our nation, the use of the police by government officials to thwart the movement left a wound in police-community relations that has still not healed.

Assassinations In the 1960s, three of the most respected leaders in the United States were assassinated: President Kennedy in 1963 in Dallas, his brother Robert Kennedy in 1968 in Los Angeles, and Dr. Martin Luther King, Jr., also in 1968, in Memphis. These assassinations clearly reflected the turbulence of the decade.

Anti-Vietnam War Demonstrations The Vietnam War was another turbulent, heartrending experience in American history, and again the police were used in a manner that tarnished their image. There were numerous and violent confrontations between opponents of the Vietnam War and the government's representatives—the police—on college campuses and city streets.

Campus Disorders In addition to the civil rights movement of the 1960s, demonstrations, marches, and civil disobedience also took place on college campuses across the nation. These events protested a perceived lack of academic freedom, the Vietnam War, the presence of Reserve Officers' Training Corps (ROTC) units on campuses, and many other issues. Again, the police were used to enforce the law.

Teach-ins, rallies, student strikes, takeovers of campus buildings, and the burning of draft cards were some of the tactics used on campuses. The campus protests caused college administrators to call in local police departments to maintain order. That, in turn, caused students to complain about the actions of the police. Again, the police became the focus of anger and attention.

Urban Riots Major riots erupted in the ghettos of many U.S. cities during the 1960s. Most started

© AP Photo/File

Rev. Dr. Martin Luther King, Jr., giving his "I have a dream" speech at the Lincoln Memorial in Washington, D.C., on August 28, 1963.

Police departments were challenged by urban riots during the 1960s.

directly following a police action. This is not to say that the riots were the result of the police; rather, a police action brought to the surface numerous underlying problems that many say were the actual causes of the riots.

In the summer of 1964, an off-duty white New York City police lieutenant shot an African American youth who was threatening a building superintendent with a knife. This shooting precipitated the 1964 Harlem riot. Riots also occurred that summer in Rochester, New York; Jersey City, New Jersey; and Philadelphia. In 1965, riots occurred in Los Angeles (the Watts district), San Diego, and Chicago. In 1966, riots again occurred in Watts, as well as in Cleveland, Brooklyn, and Chicago. In 1967, major riots occurred in Boston's Roxbury section, in Newark, and in Detroit.

In 1968, riots occurred in cities all over the United States—including Baltimore, Boston,

The corruption that permeated American policing in the past has continued into the present.

Chicago, Detroit, Kansas City, Newark, New York City, Washington, D.C., and scores of other cities—following the murder of Dr. King. The worst riot occurred in Washington, D.C., with 12 people killed, 1,200 people injured, 7,600 people arrested, and nearly $25 million in property damage. Nationwide, 55,000 federal troops and National Guard members were called out. Forty-six deaths resulted from the riots, and 21,270 people were arrested.

Again, the efforts of the police to maintain order during these massive shows of civil disobedience and violence caused wounds in police-community relations that have yet to heal. Problems between the minority communities and the police continued, as did the riots. Several radical groups, including the Black Panther party and the Black Liberation Army, waged urban warfare against the police, resulting in many deaths among their members and the police.

Corruption The corruption that has historically permeated American policing in the past has continued into the present. Approximately every 20 years, the nation's largest and most visible police department, the New York City Police Department (NYPD), is the subject of a major scandal involving police corruption and governmental hearings: the Seabury Hearings in the 1930s, the Gross Hearings in the 1950s, and the Knapp Commission in 1970.

Policing in the 1980s and 1990s

The tremendous turmoil that permeated society and policing during the decades of the 1960s and 1970s gave way to somewhat more peaceful times in the 1980s and 1990s. The police, as always, were confronted by a myriad of issues and events that severely tested their professionalism and ability. Prominent among those events were the first terrorist bombing of New York City's World Trade Center in 1993 and the bombing of the Federal Building in Oklahoma City, Oklahoma, in 1995. In these cases, police agencies from all over the nation performed numerous heroic and successful actions that saved lives and resulted in the eventual criminal prosecution of the offenders.

Some of the many positive developments of the 1980s and 1990s included the development of a computer revolution in policing involving communications, record keeping, fingerprinting, and criminal investigations; a drastic reduction in violent crime; and the birth of two new major concepts of police work: community policing and problem-solving policing. Community policing and problem-solving policing can be seen either as new approaches to policing or as a return to the policing of the past—the cop on the beat.

Some believe that the highlight of recent developments in policing is the significant crime reductions that occurred throughout the nation in the late twentieth century. This decrease in violent crime was the largest in 36 years. The homicide rate was the lowest it had been nationwide since 1969. These crime decreases continued throughout the decade and into the twenty-first century.

Some criminologists attributed this decline to a number of factors, including community policing, problem-solving policing, and aggressive, zero-tolerance policing. Other factors mentioned were increased jail and prison populations, demographic changes in the numbers of crime-prone young people, and community efforts against crime.

However, the explanation that has gained the most popularity among some law enforcement officials, politicians, and criminologists is that the reduced crime rates are the result of aggressive police tactics like those introduced in New York City by its former commissioner, William J. Bratton. Bratton completely reengineered the NYPD to make reducing crime its primary objective. The keynote behind Bratton's reengineering was a process known as CompStat.

CompStat was originally a document, referred to as the "CompStat book," that included current year-to-date statistics for criminal complaints and arrests developed from a computer file called Comparative Statistics—hence, CompStat. Central to CompStat are the semiweekly crime-strategy sessions conducted at police headquarters. At each CompStat meeting, sophisticated computer-generated maps addressing a seemingly unlimited variety of the latest crime details confront and challenge the precinct commanders. The commanders are held responsible for any increases in crime and must present innovative solutions to address their precincts' crime problems. In these sessions, crime-fighting techniques are developed for implementation. The four-step process that is the essence of CompStat is

1. Timely and accurate intelligence
2. Use of effective tactics in response to that intelligence
3. Rapid deployment of personnel and resources
4. Relentless follow-up and assessment

In 1991, the **Rodney King incident** in Los Angeles shocked the public and may have set the police back 30 years in the progress they had made in improving relationships with the community. A citizen captured on video the police beating of Rodney King, an African American. King had taken the police on a 115-mile-per-hour chase throughout Los Angeles and, when finally stopped by the police, allegedly lunged at one of the officers. The videotape shows four Los Angeles police officers beating King with 56 blows from nightsticks while a dozen other officers stood by and watched. King seemed to be in a defenseless, prone position on the ground. Four of the officers were arrested and charged with the assault of King. They were originally acquitted in a criminal trial but were subsequently convicted in a federal trial.

Perhaps the worst riot in our nation's history occurred in 1992 following the not-guilty verdicts against the officers in the Rodney

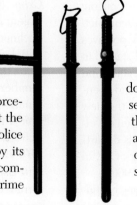

The videotape shows four Los Angeles police officers beating King with 56 blows from nightsticks while a dozen other officers stood by and watched.

© Den Sorokin/www.shutterstock.com

King case. The riot began in Los Angeles and spread to other parts of the country. By the second day of the riot, at least 23 people had been killed, 900 injured, and 500 arrested. Hundreds of buildings burned as the violence spread from south-central Los Angeles to other areas. Entire inner-city blocks lay in ruin. The riot quickly spread to Atlanta; San Francisco; Madison, Wisconsin; and other cities. Fighting between African Americans and whites was reported at high schools in Maryland, Tennessee, Texas, and New York. By the end of the second day, more than 4,000 National Guard troops, as well as more than 500 U.S. Marines, had entered Los Angeles. Nearly a week after the riot had started, calm finally began to appear. The final toll of the Los Angeles riot revealed that 54 people had been killed; 2,383 people had been injured; 5,200 buildings, mostly businesses, had been destroyed by arson; and over $1 billion in property damage had occurred. The riot resulted in the loss of approximately 40,000 jobs. Almost 17,000 arrests were made.

Policing in the 2000s

As the world welcomed a new millennium, some of the same myriad of issues that had influenced policing since the creation of the first organized police forces in the early nineteenth century continued to dominate the policing landscape. Among these issues were police misconduct, corruption, and brutality. There were also many positives for the police as the crime rate decline that had started in the 1990s continued into the 2000s, and as local, state, and federal law enforcement agencies reorganized and reengineered themselves to address the concerns of the new millennium. The CompStat program that had been developed in New York City was adopted by numerous departments throughout the nation. Crime in New York City, in particular, dropped to levels not seen since the 1960s.

In the first half of the 2000s, crime reductions continued to occur nationwide as the police adopted or continued aggressive crime-fighting techniques. Notable crime reductions occurred in many of our nation's largest cities,

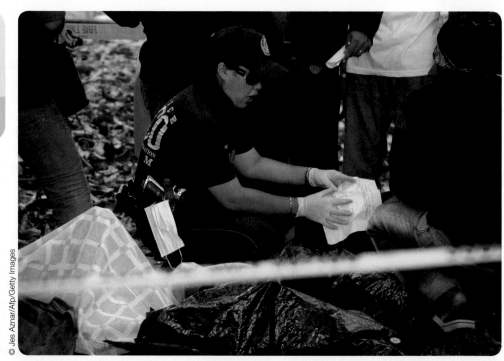

© Jes Aznar/Afp/Getty Images

A crime scene investigator tries to identify a burnt body found at a blast site that leveled several buildings in January 2009.

including New York, Los Angeles, and Chicago. (Federal Bureau of Investigation [FBI], *Uniform Crime Reports*, 2008)

However, for the first time in many years, violent crime increased nationwide in 2005 and 2006. Crime began to drop again in 2007. According to the FBI's Uniform Crime Reports released in 2008, violent crime for 2007 decreased by 0.7 percent, with murder decreasing by 0.6 percent, rape by 2.5 percent, robbery by 0.5 percent, and aggravated assault by 0.6 percent. Larger cities—those with 250,000 or more inhabitants—saw the sharpest drop in violent crime. Property crime showed a decrease of 1.4 percent. New York City's and Chicago's 2007 homicide totals were the lowest in more than 40 years. (Federal Bureau of Investigation [FBI], *Uniform Crime Reports*, 2008) Crime continued to drop in 2008 as violent crime decreased 2.5 percent and property crimes declined 1.6 percent. (Federal Bureau of Investigation [FBI], 2009) Crime has continued to decrease as of 2010 when the nation experienced a 5.5 percent decrease in the number of violent crimes and a 2.9 percent decline in the number of property crimes. (Federal Bureau of Investigation [FBI], *Uniform Crime Reports*, 2011)

9/11 and Its Aftermath Paramount to the new issues facing the police in the 2000s were the tragic terrorist attacks against the United States of America on September 11, 2001. As the twin towers of New York City's World Trade Center's Buildings 1 and 2 were struck by planes within minutes of each other, caught on fire, and then imploded, a massive emergency response that included the New York City Police Department, the New York City Fire Department, the police and rescue operations of the Port Authority of New York and New Jersey, and the city's emergency medical service was immediate. These people entered the buildings in an attempt to rescue those within them. Many of these brave rescuers were lost forever, including much of the high command of the fire and Port Authority departments. Medical, law enforcement, and emergency response personnel from around the world also responded. Almost 3,000 innocent people were murdered that day. Twenty-three New York City police officers, 37 Port Authority of New York and New Jersey officers, 3 New York City court officers, and more than 300 New York City firefighters paid the ultimate price to their professions that day.

Within minutes of the attacks on the World Trade Center, another plane slammed into the five-sided, five-story, concrete-walled structure of the U.S. Pentagon in northern Virginia—the headquarters and command center of the U.S. military forces. The swiftness, scale, and sophisticated coordinated operations of the terrorists, coupled with the extraordinary planning required, made most people realize that terrorism and mass murder had hit the United States.

Following the tragic events of 9/11, many large police departments throughout the nation started specialized antiterrorism units and trained their members in disaster control and antiterrorism duties.

In addition to changes in policing in the wake of 9/11, a major reorganization of the federal government created the massive **Department of Homeland Security**. After 9/11, Congress passed Public Law No. 107-56, the **USA Patriot Act**—Uniting and Strengthening America by Providing Appropriate Tools Required to Intercept and Obstruct Terrorism. The law gives law enforcement new abilities to search, seize, detain, or eavesdrop in their pursuit of possible terrorists. The law has proven controversial, however, and many Americans believe it may threaten their civil liberties.

Hurricane Katrina As we reached the second half of the first decade of the twenty-first century, concerns about terrorism were temporarily replaced by a natural disaster, Hurricane Katrina, which hit the Gulf Coast states of Louisiana, Mississippi, and Alabama in late August and early September 2005. The disaster caused by Katrina led to the realization that local, state, and federal government agencies, despite the creation of the Department of Homeland Security, were ill-equipped to handle a major natural disaster. It also brought to public attention the heroic efforts of the National Guard forces, the U.S. Coast Guard, and police officers throughout the United States who aided the victims and evacuees of the tragedy. In addition, the events of Katrina brought shame to some members of the New Orleans Police Department (NOPD), who were reported in the press to have abandoned their duty when Katrina hit their city and to have watched looters without taking action.

As we have seen in this chapter, the history of policing from early times to today shows that policing is a demanding and unique occupation.

Department of Homeland Security
Federal cabinet department established in the aftermath of the terrorist attacks of September 11, 2001.

USA Patriot Act
Public Law No. 107-56 passed in 2001 giving law enforcement new abilities to search, seize, detain, or eavesdrop in their pursuit of possible terrorists; full title of law is Uniting and Strengthening America by Providing Appropriate Tools Required to Intercept and Obstruct Terrorism.

Log onto www.cengagebrain. com to practice your vocabulary with flash cards and more.

Plane striking the World Trade Center on September 11, 2001.

© Photo By Peter C. Brandt/Getty Images

Log onto www.cengagebrain.com for additional resources including videos, flash cards, games, self-quizzing, review exercises, web exercises, learning checks, and more.

CHAPTER 1 Police History **15**

2

Organizing Security in the United States

LO1 Explain the U.S. Public Security Industry

The public security industry—those institutions and people who maintain law and order in the United States—is enormous. We can almost say that it is a growth industry, expanding every year. Since 9/11, this industry has flourished even more.

This industry spends an immense amount of money and provides jobs for millions of people. The industry operates on all governmental levels: the local level (villages, towns, counties, tribes, and cities), the state level, and the federal level. The public agencies are funded by income taxes, sales taxes, real estate taxes, and other taxes.

Ensuring the safety of U.S. citizens by providing law enforcement services is an extremely complex and expensive undertaking. In 2006, the Bureau of Justice Statistics (BJS) of the U.S. Department of Justice (DOJ) reported that, for the latest reporting year, local, state, and federal agencies spent approximately $185 billion for criminal justice agencies, including police, corrections, and judicial services—an increase of 418 percent from 20 years ago. Local, state, and federal criminal justice agencies employed about 2.4 million people—58 percent at the local level, 31 percent at the state level, and 11 percent at the federal level. Police protection spending amounted to about $83.1 billion of the total national criminal justice budget, up 240 percent from 20 years ago, and local policing expenditures alone accounted for about 45 percent of the nation's entire criminal justice budget. (Hughes 1)

Law enforcement is primarily the responsibility of local governments; 77 percent of the nation's police employees work at the local level. Fourteen percent of police employees work for the federal government, and state governments employ the remaining 9 percent. (Hughes 6)

U.S. law enforcement has developed over the years based on a philosophy of **local control**, the formal and informal use of local or neighborhood forms of government to deter abhorrent behaviors.

After studying this chapter, the student should be able to:

LO1 Explain the U.S. public security industry

LO2 Discuss local law enforcement

LO3 Describe state law enforcement

LO4 Discuss federal law enforcement

LO5 Explain international police

local control
The formal and informal use of local or neighborhood forms of government and measures to deter abhorrent behaviors.

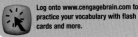
Log onto www.cengagebrain.com to practice your vocabulary with flash cards and more.

TABLE 2.1 Employment by State and Local Law Enforcement Agencies

Type of Agency	Number of Agencies	Full-time Employees			Part-time Employees		
		Total	Sworn	Civilian	Total	Sworn	Civilian
Total	15,636	1,040,728	696,346	344,382	75,581	34,124	44,457
Local police	12,575	601,027	463,147	137,880	54,310	25,202	29,108
Sheriff	3,012	346,337	172,241	174,096	22,747	8,831	13,916
Primary state	49	93,364	60,958	32,406	1,524	91	1,433

SOURCE: Reaves, Brian A. *Local Police Departments, 2007.* Washington, D.C.: Bureau of Justice Statistics, 2010, p. 8.

To understand why, remember that the United States was built on the fear of a large central government, as had existed in England when the colonists came here. The primary responsibility for police protection still falls to local governments (cities, towns, tribes, and counties). Although we have state and federal law enforcement agencies, they are minuscule in size and importance when compared with the law enforcement agencies of local government.

In 2007, state and local governments in the United States operated almost 15,636 full-time law enforcement agencies. These included 12,575 local police departments (mostly municipal and county departments); 3,012 sheriff's offices; and 49 primary state police departments. (See Table 2.1.) (Reaves, *Local Police Departments* 8)

In addition to state and local law enforcement agencies and personnel, 2006 statistics regarding employment for federal law enforcement agencies indicate that the federal government employed about 105,000 full-time personnel authorized to carry firearms and make arrests. (Reaves, *Federal* 1)

LO2 Discuss Local Law Enforcement

When we use the term *local law enforcement*, or *local police*, we are talking about the vast majority of all the law enforcement employees in the United States, including metropolitan police and sheriff's offices. Metropolitan police departments are operated by cities, certain very large counties, villages, and towns, and are generally led or managed by a police commissioner or police chief who is appointed by the executive of the locality. Sheriff's offices are generally operated by counties and are led or managed by a popularly elected sheriff. Officers in police departments are generally called *police officers*, whereas officers in sheriff's offices are generally termed *deputy sheriffs* or *deputies*. Jobs in these agencies increase yearly. Police protection is primarily a local responsibility—local

governments spent 69 percent of the total police expenditures in the United States for the latest reporting year, and local police spending represented about 45 percent of the nation's total justice expenditures. Local expenditures for police protection increased by 305 percent in the past 20 years, for an average annual increase of 6.6 percent. (Hughes 4)

For the latest reporting period, 2007, it was reported that local police departments employed about 601,027 full-time employees, including about 463,147 sworn personnel (see Chapter 3 for an explanation of "sworn personnel"). Local departments also employ about 54,310 people on a part-time basis, about half of whom are sworn officers. (Reaves, *Local Police Departments* 8)

Most local law enforcement agencies are small, but most local police officers work for larger agencies. In 2007, departments with fewer than 10 full-time officers accounted for 50 percent of all agencies, but

Local police form the vast majority of all the law enforcement employees in the United States.

© Image copyright Denise Kappa, 2009. Used under license from www.Shutterstock.com

Most academic and professional studies of policing focus on municipal departments, because this is where the "action" is in the law enforcement world. This action includes problems with crime, budgeting and funding, politics, and population changes, as well as social problems, including homelessness, unemployment, drug addiction, alcoholism, and child abuse. Additionally, after the terrorist bombings of September 11, 2001, these metropolitan departments have had to deal increasingly with the problems of terrorism facing their cities. Also, large municipal departments are highly visible because of their size, complexity, budgets, and innovative programs. In addition to attempting to control crime, municipal police have significant problems maintaining public order and solving quality-of-life problems that bother neighborhood residents. The police handle social problems that other public and private agencies either cannot or will not handle. In a big city, when there is a problem, citizens generally do not call the mayor's office; they call 911.

employed just 5 percent of all officers. About 600 local police departments (4.7 percent) employed 100 or more full-time sworn personnel. These agencies employed 61 percent of all local police officers. (Reaves, *Local Police Departments* 4)

In 2007, racial and ethnic minorities constituted approximately 25 percent of full-time sworn personnel in local departments and women constituted about 12 percent. In particular, the number of African American local police officers increased by 10 percent during the past three years, Hispanic officers by 16 percent, officers from other minority groups by 2.8 percent, and female officers by 8 percent (see Table 2.2). (Reaves, *Local Police Departments* 14)

Metropolitan Law Enforcement

Municipal or city governments operate the vast majority of the nearly 12,575 local police departments in the United States. The rest are operated by county, tribal, or regional (multijurisdictional) jurisdictions. (Reaves, *Local Police Departments* 8)

Most police officers today work for these metropolitan police departments. Metropolitan police departments generally provide the duties and services we typically associate with the police. These include arresting law violators, performing routine patrol, investigating crimes, enforcing traffic laws (including parking violations), providing crowd and traffic control at parades and other public events, and issuing special licenses and permits. Since 9/11, many metropolitan departments have been spending more and more time on antiterrorism duties.

TABLE 2.2 Gender and Race of Local Police Departments and Sheriff's Offices	
Local Police Departments	
Total	100%
Total Male	88.1%
Total Female	11.9%
Total Whites	75.1%
Total Black/African American	11.9%
Total Hispanic/Latino	10.3%
Total Other	2.7%
Sheriff's Offices	
Total	100%
Total Male	87.1%
Total Female	12.9%
Total Whites	81.2%
Total Black/African American	10.0%
Total Hispanic/Latino	6.9%
Total Other	1.9%

Other category includes Asians, Native Hawaiians or other Pacific Islanders, American Indians, Alaska Natives, and any other race.

SOURCES: Reaves, Brian A. *Local Police Departments, 2007.* Washington, D.C.: Bureau of Justice Statistics, 2010, p. 7; and Hickman, Matthew J. and Brian A. Reaves. *Sheriff's Offices, 2003* Washington, D.C.: Bureau of Justice Statistics, 2006, p. 7.

CHAPTER 2   Organizing Security in the United States   **19**

Municipal or city governments operate the vast majority of the nearly 12,575 local police departments in the United States.

© iStockphoto/Stuartb

Some Interesting FACTS about Local Police Departments

55% of departments use foot patrol routinely.

32% use regular bicycle patrol.

91% participate in a 911 emergency system.

35% assign full-time officers to a special unit for drug enforcement, and nearly a quarter assign officers to a multi-agency drug task force.

53% maintain a written community policing plan, and **53%** use full-time community policing officers.

31% have problem-solving partnerships or written agreements with community groups.

38% use full-time school resource officers.

Nearly all departments have a written policy on pursuit driving, and **60%** restrict vehicle pursuits according to specific criteria.

97% have a written policy on the use of deadly force, and **90%** have a policy on the use of nonlethal force.

54% have a written plan specifying actions to be taken in a terrorist attack.

97% authorize use of chemical agents such as pepper spray, up from **51%** in 1990.

61% use video cameras in patrol cars.

SOURCE: Reaves, Brian A. *Local Police Departments, 2007.* Washington, D.C.: Bureau of Justice Statistics, 2010, p. iii.

County Law Enforcement

Most counties in the United States are patrolled by a sheriff's department under the leadership of an elected sheriff (several very large counties in New York, California,

Nevada, Florida, and other states have county police departments).

The role of sheriff has evolved in several stages since the early English sheriff (shire-reeve). During the development of the West in the United States and until the development of municipal departments, the sheriff often served as the sole legal authority over vast geographical areas.

Today, the duties of a county sheriff's office vary according to the size and urbanization of the county. The sheriff's office may perform the duties of coroners, tax assessors, tax collectors, keepers of county jails, court attendants, and executors of criminal and civil processes, as well as law enforcement officers.

According to an impressive article by Lee P. Brown, a former big-city police commissioner, there are several different types of sheriff's departments. Some are oriented exclusively toward law enforcement, and some carry out only court-related duties. Some deal exclusively with correctional and court matters and have no law enforcement duties; others are full-service programs

Some Interesting FACTS about Sheriffs' Offices Today

25% of departments use foot patrol routinely.

10% use regular bicycle patrol.

94% participate in a 911 emergency system compared with **28%** in 1987, and **71%** employ enhanced 911.

36% have officers assigned full time to a special unit for drug enforcement, and nearly a quarter assign officers to a multi-agency drug task force.

10% maintain a written community policing plan, and **51%** use full-time community policing officers.

60% have problem-solving partnerships or written agreements with community groups.

47% use full-time school resource officers.

Nearly all have a written policy on pursuit driving, and about half of them restrict vehicle pursuits according to specific criteria.

97% have a written policy on the use of deadly force, and **89%** have a policy on the use of nonlethal force.

Nearly half have a written plan specifying actions to be taken in a terrorist attack.

96% authorize use of chemical agents such as pepper spray, up from **52%** in 1990.

Two-thirds use video cameras in patrol cars.

SOURCE: Hickman, Matthew J. and Brian A. Reaves, *Sheriff's Offices, 2003.* Washington, D.C.: Bureau of Justice Statistics, 2006, pp. iii, iv.

that perform court, correctional, and law enforcement activities. (Brown 237–240)

In the latest reporting year, sheriff's offices had about 346,337 full-time employees (172,241 sworn). Racial and ethnic minorities composed almost 19 percent of full-time sworn personnel, up from about 13.4 percent in 1987. Women constituted about 12.9 percent, about the same as in 1987. In particular, the number of African American deputy sheriffs increased by 13 percent between 2000 and 2003, Hispanic deputies by 20 percent, deputies from other minority groups by 20 percent, and female deputies by 5 percent. (Hickman and Reaves, *Sheriff's Offices* 111; Reaves, *Local Police Departments* 8)

Ninety-six percent of sheriff's offices are responsible for traditional law enforcement functions, such as responding to citizen requests for assistance, providing routine patrol services, and conducting traffic enforcement. In addition to patrol and traffic duties, about 78 percent of the offices operate one or more jails, and nearly 96 percent are responsible for the serving of civil process and 97 percent for court security. (Reaves, *Local Police Departments* 5)

Rural and Small-Town Law Enforcement

Eighty-seven percent of police departments have 25 or fewer officers and they serve in rural and small-town law enforcement. Often, rural and small-town police face the same problems as large metropolitan and county police. They also face other serious problems because of their size. The state of Wyoming, for example, has the lowest population in the United States and has vast, open areas where one can drive over 100 miles between small towns. The law enforcement officers in this state

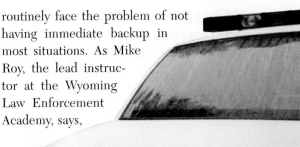

routinely face the problem of not having immediate backup in most situations. As Mike Roy, the lead instructor at the Wyoming Law Enforcement Academy, says,

© iStockphoto/Ron Bailey

"We deal with great distances out here and there is a different mentality. Every other pickup truck you stop out here has a rifle in a gun rack or a pistol in the glove box. Most of the problems we have in law enforcement center around people—where you have people you will have problems." (Hoffman 20–24)

Regarding the lack of readily available backup, Roy says, "Everyone completing our academy is instructed not to get stupid by acting alone in known volatile situations. Officers are instructed to get used to waiting for the closest help to arrive even if it's 60 miles away." (Hoffman 20–24)

Rural and small-town law enforcement agencies engage in mutual assistance programs with neighboring agencies and come to one another's aid when necessary. Limited resources, rising crime trends, and geographic barriers severely impair the ability of rural law enforcement agencies to effectively combat crimes in their communities. To ensure that they can meet the challenge of law enforcement in the twenty-first century, rural executives are increasingly seeking opportunities to provide more education and training for their staffs and to maximize their effectiveness through new and improved technology.

Many small, remote towns and villages cannot afford to hire local police officers and often rely on state troopers based in areas far away. As an example, in 2006 it took four hours for Alaska state troopers to arrive at the 200-person Eskimo village of Nunam Iqua after a man choked and raped his 13-year-old stepdaughter in front of three younger children, beat his wife with a shotgun, and pistol-whipped a friend after an evening drinking home brew. During the attack, residents called troopers in Bethel, Alaska, 155 miles away. But the troopers' aircraft was being serviced, so they had to charter a plane to get to Nunam Iqua. In 2008, it was reported that the village had hired a single public safety officer, but she has no law enforcement training and is unarmed. (Associated Press, "Many Villages")

Many small, remote towns and villages cannot afford to hire local police officers and often rely on state troopers.

© Ronald Karpilo/Alamy

Indian Country and Tribal Law Enforcement

Laurence French, professor at the University of New Hampshire, writes that policing American Indians in the United States has always been contentious, especially from the tribal perspective. First, American Indians were regulated by the U.S. Army and the Department of War, and then later by the Bureau of Indian Affairs and the Department of the Interior. Today the controversy continues with federal, state, and local jurisdictions attempting to intervene in tribal policing. This has caused jurisdictional confusion, tribal discontent, and litigations in Indian country. (French 69–80)

M. Wesley Clark, a senior attorney in the U.S. Drug Enforcement Administration (DEA), says, "Policing in and adjacent to land within Indian country is often a complex and, at times, confusing jurisdictional puzzle. Solving this puzzle depends on a variety of factors, including whether the crime is a felony or misdemeanor, whether the subjects and victims are Indians, and whether the crime violates tribal, state, or federal law." (Clark 22–31)

A 2005 report for the National Institute of Justice offers detailed information gathered on tribal law enforcement agencies, tribal courts and services, and criminal records systems from continental American Indian jurisdictions. More than 92 percent (314) of the 341 federally recognized American Indian tribes in the continental 48 states responded to the census. Relative to policing, the report reveals that 165 of the responding 314 tribes employ one or more full-time sworn officers with general arrest powers; almost all (99 percent) have cross-deputization agreements with another tribal or public agency; and 56 percent of the tribes that employ one or more full-time sworn officers with general arrest powers are also recognized by their state governments to possess arrest authority. (Perry 1–5)

The governmental power to make or enforce laws in Indian country is divided among federal, state, and tribal governments. Jurisdiction in a specific incident depends on the nature of the offense, whether the offender or victim is a tribal member, and the state in which the crime occurred. Public Law 83-280 (commonly called PL 280) confers criminal jurisdiction in Indian country to six state governments (mandatory PL 280 states)—California, Minnesota, Nebraska, Oregon, Wisconsin, and Alaska—and the federal government. It also permits other states to acquire jurisdiction at their option (optional PL 280 states). The optional PL 280 states—Nevada, Idaho, Iowa, Washington, South Dakota, Montana, North Dakota, Arizona, and Utah—assume jurisdiction either in whole or in part over Indian country within their boundaries. In states where PL 280 does not apply, the federal government retains criminal jurisdiction for major crimes.

The 1994 Crime Act expanded federal criminal jurisdiction in Indian country in such areas as guns, violent juveniles, drugs, and domestic violence. Thus, law enforcement in Indian country is dispersed among federal, state, local, and tribal agencies. The tribes have inherent powers to exercise criminal jurisdiction over all tribal members and the authority to arrest and detain non-Indians for delivery to state or federal authorities for prosecution. These tribal police powers are generally limited to the reservation. The work of tribal police is often critical to resolving criminal cases referred to state and federal agencies because tribal police usually discover the crime, interview witnesses, and investigate the circumstances involved in the crime. Often tribal police refer cases to U.S. attorneys' offices for investigation because tribal courts generally hear only misdemeanor cases. (FBI, *Indian Country Crime*)

Cross-deputization agreements have been used to enhance law enforcement capabilities in areas where state and tribal lands are contiguous and intermingled. Under some agreements, federal, state, county/local, and/or tribal law enforcement officers have the power to arrest Indian and non-Indian wrongdoers whenever a violation of law occurs. States, in some cases, have recognized tribal police to have peace officer authority to arrest tribal offenders off the reservation or detain nontribal offenders on the reservation. About 45 percent of the tribes with law enforcement personnel have arrest authority over tribal members off the reservation. About 62 percent of the tribes with at least one sworn officer report having arrest authority over non-Indians on tribal reservations.

Very real problems affect tribal police as they provide law enforcement services in the country's most remote and undeveloped areas. These tribal police officers are stretched thin over large and diverse geographical territories. As an example, in Arizona, the Hualapal nation has only one police chief and 10 commissioned officers to cover the reservation's one million acres and population

> ... Indian reservations are plagued by a systematic breakdown in the delivery of justice.

A Navajo Nation police officer and his canine during a drug-detecting practice session.

Local Law Enforcement and Illegal Immigration

A controversial issue in current law enforcement is the cooperation and escalating involvement of local police with federal immigration officials in enforcing immigration laws. Immigration advocates and some local officials fear that this cooperation will further erode an already tense relationship between minority and immigrant communities and local officers entrusted with serving local residents. It has become routine for some police agencies to assist immigration authorities during arrests and to call immigration officials if a criminal suspect appears to be an undocumented alien. Also, some local police have been deputized as immigration agents at the request of federal authorities under signed agreements. On the other hand, some departments generally prohibit officers from asking people they stop about their immigration status.

Many police departments in cities, counties, and states have policies that restrict enforcement of federal immigration laws by local authorities. These policies, which can be termed as "don't ask," are favored by many police chiefs when dealing with undocumented residents who haven't committed crimes other than being in the country illegally. Chiefs say that these policies are an effective crime-fighting tool because they encourage illegal immigrants to report crimes without fear of deportation. They feel that the police can better fight crime by building trust with residents and encouraging them to help identify suspects and report problems. As an example, the Phoenix Police Department

of 2,800 residents. The Stillaguamish Tribal Police of Arlington, Washington, have only seven patrol officers to cover 650 square miles of fish and game territory, as well as a casino. They face severe community problems and high unemployment, with drugs and substance abuse their greatest challenges. They also experience a lack of funding to build the type of infrastructure needed to accomplish their mission of policing. (Falk 20–27)

In 2007, the *Denver Post* produced a series of articles on criminal justice in Indian country. It reported that Indian reservations are plagued by a systematic breakdown in the delivery of justice. Noting that the sole authority to prosecute felony crimes on reservations lies with the federal government, it reported that U.S. attorneys and FBI investigators face huge challenges fighting crime on reservations because they are mistrusted and viewed as outsiders. The high levels of alcohol use among victims, suspects, and witnesses that accompany many serious crimes can make them very difficult to prove. Additionally, federal law enforcement officials are burdened by competing federal priorities such as immigration and terrorism. (Riley, "Promises, Justice Broken")

These problems are reflected in the statistics: Between 1997 and 2006, federal prosecutors rejected nearly two-thirds of the reservation cases brought to them by FBI and Bureau of Indian Affairs investigators, more than twice the rejection rate for all federally prosecuted crimes. Of the nearly 5,900 aggravated assaults reported on reservations in 2006, only 558 were referred to federal prosecutors, who declined to prosecute 320 of them. Of the more than 1,000 arson complaints reported in 2006, only 24 were referred to U.S. attorneys, who declined to prosecute 18 of them. Commenting on the federal justice system, a Navajo tribal prosecutor stated, "They've created a lawless land." (Riley, "Promises, Justice Broken")

A Border Patrol agent processes a group of illegal immigrants in Arizona.

bars its officers from stopping people for the sole purpose of determining immigration status. It also forbids officers to call the federal Immigration and Customs Enforcement department (ICE) about people who are crime victims or witnesses or people who have committed only minor civil offenses, such as driving without a license. However, officers automatically notify ICE whenever illegal immigrants are booked into jail. (Gonzalez, "Illegal-Immigration") Some anti-illegal-immigration advocates say these policies create "sanctuary cities" for illegal immigrants, shield foreign criminals from deportation, and hamper federal efforts to combat illegal immigration and terrorism.

As of 2008, frustrated with ineffective immigration enforcement and often under considerable political pressure, a growing number of states, counties, and cities are requiring their law enforcement officers to help detect and deport illegal immigrants rather than just rely on federal agents. Some law enforcement agencies are training their officers to perform immigration checks themselves as part of ICE's 287(g) program. This program refers to Section 287(g) of the 1996 Immigration and Nationality Act. The 287(g) program deputizes local officers to help enforce federal immigration laws. ICE provides local officers with access to its immigration database and trains them in identifying illegal immigrants and ordering deportations with ICE's approval. ICE officials report that, under this program, local law enforcement officers have helped detect 32,000 illegal immigrants over the past four years who otherwise may have remained in the country. Approximately 55 state, county, and local law enforcement departments have taken the ICE training and more than 70 others are on the ICE waiting list for training. (Taylor, "Local Police") Officers undergo a five-week training course in the 287(g) program. The training includes instruction on civil rights and immigration laws, federal prohibitions on racial profiling, cross-cultural issues, and treaty obligations that require officers to notify foreign consulates about certain arrests. (Volk, "Police Join Feds")

In 2009, the Police Foundation issued the report *Role of the Local Police: Striking a Balance Between Immigration*

Forty-nine of the 50 U.S. states have a primary state law enforcement agency.

© Tim Graham/Getty Images

Enforcement and Civil Liberties. The overall conclusion of the report was that the costs in lost community support for local and state police and their general public safety mission, along with increased financial costs to state and local law enforcement agencies, outweigh the benefits of the 287(g) program. (Khashu, *Role of the Local Police*)

In 2010, the Department of Homeland Security's inspector general issued a special report stating that the state and local police officers who enforce federal immigration laws through the ICE's 287(g) program are not adequately screened, trained, or supervised, and that the civil rights of the immigrants they deal with are not consistently protected. (Preston, "Report Faults Training")

LO3 Describe State Law Enforcement

Forty-nine of the 50 U.S. states have a primary state law enforcement agency. The only state without a primary state police agency is Hawaii, although it has several law enforcement agencies with statewide jurisdiction.

In the latest reporting year, the 49 primary state law enforcement agencies had about 93,364 full-time employees and more than 60,958 full-time sworn personnel. (Reaves, *Local Police Departments* 8) State expenditures for police protection increased nearly 293 percent from 20 years ago, with an average annual change of 6.4 percent. (Hughes 3)

The largest state law enforcement agency is the California Highway Patrol, which has about 7,085 sworn officers, followed by the New York State Police, with 4,667 sworn employees; the Pennsylvania State Police, with 4,200 sworn officers; and the Texas Department of Public Safety, with 3,437 sworn employees. The smallest state police agencies are the North Dakota Highway Patrol, with 135 sworn employees; the Wyoming Highway Patrol, with 188 sworn personnel; and the South Dakota Highway Patrol, with 154 sworn employees. (Reaves, *Census* 6)

Historically, state police departments were developed to deal with growing crime in nonurban areas of the country, which was attributable to the increasing mobility of Americans, the proliferation of cars, and the ease of travel. The state police agencies were formed by governors and legislators to lessen reliance on metropolitan and county police departments, which were more closely linked with politics and urban and county corruption.

Generally, state police patrol small towns and state highways, regulate traffic, and have the primary responsibility to enforce some state laws. The state police also carry out many duties for local police agencies, such as managing state training academies, criminal identification systems, and crime laboratories.

At the state level, there are two distinct models of law enforcement agencies. The **centralized model of state law enforcement** combines the duties of major criminal investigations with the patrol of state highways. The centralized state police agencies generally assist local police departments in criminal investigations when requested and provide the identification, laboratory, and training functions for local departments.

The second state model, the **decentralized model of state law enforcement**, has a clear distinction between traffic enforcement on state highways and other state-level law enforcement functions. The states that use this model—many southern and Midwestern, and some western states—generally have two separate agencies, one a highway patrol and the other a state bureau of investigation. California, for example, has the California Highway Patrol and the California Division of Law Enforcement.

Although the duties of the various state-level police departments may vary considerably, the most common duties include highway patrol, traffic law enforcement, and the patrol of small towns.

LO4 Discuss Federal Law Enforcement

Although the U.S. Constitution created three branches of government—executive, legislative, and judicial—it did not create a national police force; but it did give the national government power over a limited number of crimes. Traditionally in the United States, the creation of laws and the power to enforce them have been matters for the states. The states have given much of their enforcement powers to local police agencies. In recent years, however, the number of crimes included in the U.S. Criminal Code has multiplied greatly, as has the number of people assigned to enforce these crimes. By the latest reporting year, there were about 105,000 full-time federal law enforcement employees authorized to make arrests and carry firearms. These numbers do not include officers in the U.S. armed forces (Army, Navy, Air Force, Marines, and Coast Guard) and do not include federal air marshals or Central Intelligence Agency (CIA) security protective service officers because of classified information restrictions. (Reaves, *Federal* 1) With the increased attention to border security and homeland defense following the terrorist attacks of 9/11, the number of federal law enforcement officers increases daily.

For the latest reporting period, women accounted for 16 percent of federal law enforcement employees, and a third of federal officers were members of a racial or ethnic minority (17.7 percent were Hispanic and 11.4 percent were African American). Nationwide, there were 36 federal law enforcement officers for every 100,000 citizens. Thirty-eight percent of federal officers' duties included criminal investigation; 21 percent police response and patrol; 16 percent corrections and detention; 16 percent inspections; 5 percent court operations; and 4 percent security and protection.

The total number of criminal justice system employees in the nation grew 86 percent between 1982 and the latest reported year, and the number of federal criminal justice employees increased the most, with a 168 percent increase. Federal expenditures increased 692 percent, with an annual increase of 9.9 percent. Additionally, federal expenditures for police protection increased 708 percent, for an annual percentage increase of 10 percent. (Hughes 1)

Four major U.S. cabinet departments administer most federal law enforcement agencies and personnel: the Department of Justice, the Department of the Treasury, the Department of Homeland Security, and the Department of the Interior. Numerous other federal agencies have law enforcement functions. Each of the agencies discussed in this section has a presence on

centralized model of state law enforcement
Combines the duties of major criminal investigations with the patrol of state highways.

decentralized model of state law enforcement
A clear distinction between traffic enforcement on state highways and other state-level law enforcement functions.

Log onto www.cengagebrain.com to practice your vocabulary with flash cards and more.

the Web, and students are urged to access these sites to obtain information regarding these agencies, their duties, and the many jobs they have available.

Department of Justice

The U.S. Department of Justice is the primary legal and prosecutorial arm of the U.S. government. The Department of Justice is under the control of the U.S. Attorney General and is responsible for (1) enforcing all federal laws, (2) representing the government when it is involved in a court action, and (3) conducting independent investigations through its law enforcement services. The department's Civil Rights Division prosecutes violators of federal civil rights laws, which are designed to protect citizens from discrimination on the basis of their race, creed, ethnic background, or gender. These laws apply to discrimination in education, housing, and job opportunities. The Justice Department's Tax Division prosecutes violators of the tax laws. The Criminal Division prosecutes violators of the *Federal Criminal Code* for such criminal acts as bank robbery, kidnapping, mail fraud, interstate transportation of stolen vehicles, and narcotics and drug trafficking.

Also, the Justice Department maintains administrative control over the Federal Bureau of Investigation (FBI), the Drug Enforcement Administration (DEA), the U.S. Marshals, and the Bureau of Alcohol, Tobacco, Firearms, and Explosives (ATF).

Federal Bureau of Investigation The FBI is the best known of the federal law enforcement agencies. It is the primary agency charged with the enforcement of all federal laws not falling under the purview of other federal agencies. By 2010, the FBI had more than 12,560 special agents. The main headquarters of the FBI is in Washington, D.C., but it also has field offices in major American cities and abroad. The head of the FBI is known as the director and is appointed by the president of the United States, subject to confirmation by the Senate.

In addition to the special agents, the FBI employs almost 18,000 nonenforcement support personnel such as intelligence specialists, language specialists, scientists, information technology specialists, and other staff who perform such duties as fingerprint examinations, computer programming, forensic or crime laboratory analysis, and administrative and clerical duties. All special agents must attend the FBI Academy, located in Quantico, Virginia. In addition to the special agents, other law enforcement officers and officers from some foreign governments attend the academy.

Contrary to popular opinion, the FBI is not a national police force. Rather, it is an investigative agency that may investigate acts that violate federal law. The FBI investigates more than 200 categories of federal crimes and also has concurrent jurisdiction with the DEA over drug offenses under the Controlled Substances Act. The FBI may also assist state and local law enforcement agencies and investigate state and local crimes when asked to do so by those agencies.

Traditionally the FBI focused its investigations on organized crime activities, including racketeering, corruption, and pornography; bank robbery; and white-collar crime, including embezzlement, stock, and other business fraud. The FBI is also at the forefront of our government's efforts against domestic terrorist activity and trains special antiterrorist teams to prevent and respond to terrorist attacks. In addition, it maintains surveillance on foreign intelligence agents and investigates their activities within this country.

Realizing that both international and domestic terrorism were serious national concerns, the federal government had taken several law enforcement measures to deal with terrorism even before September 11, 2001. However, in May 2002, following massive criticism that the FBI had failed to properly handle information that could have led to the prevention of the 9/11 attacks, Director Robert S. Mueller issued a press release outlining the FBI's complete reorganization and creating a new strategic focus for the agency. The FBI's new focus placed the following as its three priorities: (1) protecting the United States from terrorist attack, (2) protecting the United States against foreign intelligence operations and espionage, and (3) protecting the United States against

cyber-based attacks and high-technology crimes. The main organizational improvements Mueller enacted were:

- A complete restructuring of the counterterrorism activities of the bureau and a shift from a reactive to a proactive orientation
- The development of special squads to coordinate national and international investigations
- A reemphasis on the Joint Terrorism Task Forces
- Enhanced analytical capabilities with personnel and technological improvements
- A permanent shift of additional resources to counterterrorism
- The creation of a more mobile, agile, and flexible national terrorism response
- Targeted recruitment to acquire agents, analysts, translators, and others with specialized skills and backgrounds. (FBI, 2002)

Drug Enforcement Administration The DEA is at the vanguard of the nation's "war on drugs" by engaging in drug interdiction, conducting surveillance operations, and infiltrating drug rings and arresting major narcotics violators. The agency also tracks illicit drug traffic; registers manufacturers, distributors, and dispensers of pharmaceutical drugs and controlled substances; tracks the movement of chemicals used in the manufacture of illegal drugs; and leads the nation's marijuana eradication program.

U.S. Marshals Service The U.S. Marshals Service performs many functions. Its primary functions are the transportation of federal prisoners between prisons and courts and the security of federal court facilities. The marshals also protect witnesses at federal trials, apprehend federal fugitives, execute federal warrants, operate the Federal Witness Security Program, and are in charge of the federal government's asset seizure and forfeiture programs, handling the seizure and disposal of property resulting from criminal activity.

Bureau of Alcohol, Tobacco, Firearms, and Explosives The ATF is the nation's primary agency for enforcing federal laws relating to alcohol, tobacco, firearms, and explosives violations. The ATF enforces laws pertaining to the manufacture, sale, and possession of firearms and explosives; attempts to suppress illegal traffic in tobacco and alcohol products; collects taxes; and regulates industry trade practices regarding these items.

The ATF assists other domestic and international law enforcement agencies as the nation's primary agency for tracing of weapons and explosives. The ATF traces these weapons through its records of manufacturers and dealers in firearms. The ATF also investigates cases of arson and bombing at federal buildings or other institutions that receive federal funds, as well as investigating arson-for-profit schemes.

Department of the Treasury

The Department of the Treasury has administrative control over the Criminal Investigation Division of the Internal Revenue Service as well as several very important offices related to the financial aspects of crime, drug trafficking, and terrorism.

Internal Revenue Service (IRS) The IRS, the nation's primary revenue-collection agency, is charged with the enforcement of laws regulating federal income tax and its collection. The investigative arm of the IRS is its Criminal Investigation Division (CID). CID agents investigate tax fraud, unreported income, and hidden assets.

Department of Homeland Security (DHS)

After much study following the terrorist attacks of September 11, 2001, the cabinet-level DHS was established in March 2003. See Chapter 15 for a complete description of the DHS and other government efforts to prevent terrorism and ensure homeland defense.

© stephen Mulcahey/Alamy

© AP Photo/Nati Harnik

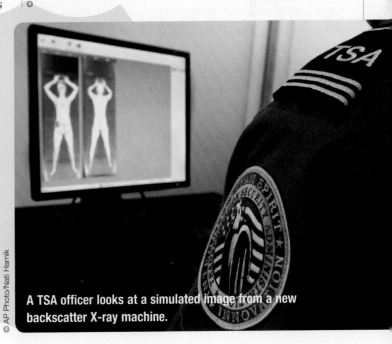

A TSA officer looks at a simulated image from a new backscatter X-ray machine.

The new agency merged 22 previously disparate domestic agencies into one department to protect the nation against threats to the homeland. At its inception, the new agency consisted of more than 170,000 employees, and its creation was the most significant transformation of the U.S. government since 1947, when President Harry S. Truman merged the various branches of the U.S. armed forces into the Department of Defense to better coordinate the nation's defense against military threats.

The DHS represents a similar consolidation, both in style and substance. The DHS assumed the former duties of the U.S. Coast Guard, the U.S. Customs Service, Immigration and Naturalization Service, the Transportation Security Administration, and numerous other federal communications, science, and technology agencies. The DHS does not include the FBI, CIA, or National Security Agency, however. The major enforcement agencies within the DHS include Customs and Border Protection (CBP) and Immigration and Customs Enforcement (ICE). Each of the separate units of the DHS and its functions will be fully discussed in Chapter 15.

The department's major priority is the protection of the nation against further terrorist attacks. The department's units analyze threats and intelligence, guard our borders and airports, protect our critical infrastructure, and coordinate the responses of our nation to future emergencies. The U.S. Secret Service was also placed under the administration of the DHS in 2003.

U.S. Secret Service The U.S. Secret Service has as its primary mission the protection of the president and his or her family, and other government leaders and foreign dignitaries, as well as the security of designated national events. The Secret Service is also the primary agency responsible for protecting U.S. currency from counterfeiters and safeguarding Americans from credit card fraud, financial crimes, and computer fraud. The Secret Service also preserves the integrity of the nation's critical infrastructures. It uses prevention-based training and methods to combat cybercriminals and terrorists who attempt to use identity theft, telecommunications fraud, and other technology-based crimes to defraud and undermine American consumers and industry.

In its role of protecting the president, vice president, and other government officials and their families, along with former presidents and presidential and vice presidential candidates, the Secret Service coordinates all security arrangements for official presidential visits, motorcades, and ceremonies with other federal government agencies and state and local law enforcement agencies. The Secret Service has uniformed and nonuniformed divisions. The uniformed division provides protection for the White House complex and other presidential offices, the Main Treasury Building and Annex, and foreign diplomatic missions.

Department of the Interior

The Department of the Interior's myriad law enforcement agencies provide law enforcement services for the property under its purview including the National Park Service, the U.S. Park Police, the Bureau of Indian Affairs, the Fish and Wildlife Service, the Bureau of Land Management, and the Bureau of Reclamation. The agencies are responsible for protecting most of the nation's historic icons, such as Mount Rushmore, the Washington Monument, the Hoover and Grand Coulee Dams and 350 other dams, and millions of acres of uninhabited wilderness in national parks, preserves, and other lands controlled by the federal government.

Enforcement agents for the National Park Service are known as commissioned park rangers. They are responsible for law enforcement, traffic control, fire control, and search and rescue operations in the 30 million acres of the National Park Service. Additional rangers serve seasonally as part-time commissioned rangers. In addition to park rangers, the Park Service

© stephen Mulcahey/Alamy

© AP Photo/Charles Dharapak

U.S. Secret Service agents stand watch as President Barack Obama gets out of his limousine (known as "the Beast"), to board Air Force One.

also uses Park Police officers, mainly in the Washington, D.C., area. The Park Police also serve at the Statue of Liberty in New York and the Golden Gate Bridge in San Francisco. Enforcement agents for the Department of the Interior's Fish and Wildlife Service are called wildlife law enforcement agents. They investigate people who are illegally trafficking in government-protected animals and birds, such as falcons.

Department of Defense

Each branch of the U.S. military has its own law enforcement agency. The military police agencies are organized in a manner similar to that of the civil police, using uniformed officers for patrol duties on military bases and investigators to investigate crimes. The Army's investigative arm is the Criminal Investigation Division (CID); the investigative arm of the Navy and Marines is the Naval Criminal Investigative Service (NCIS); and that of the Air Force is the Air Force Office of Special Investigations (OSI).

U.S. Postal Service

The Postal Inspections Division of the U.S. Postal Service is one of the oldest of the federal law enforcement agencies, having been created in 1836. Postal inspectors investigate illegal acts committed against the Postal Service and its property and personnel, such as cases of fraud involving the use of the mails; use of the mails to transport drugs, bombs, and firearms; and assaults upon postal employees while exercising their official duties. Postal inspectors are responsible for criminal investigations covering more than 200 federal statutes related to the postal system. Postal police officers provide security for postal facilities, employees, and assets; escort high-value mail shipments; and perform other protective functions.

Other Federal Enforcement Agencies

Many other federal agencies have law enforcement responsibilities. The Department of Agriculture has enforcement officers in its U.S. Forest Service, and its Office of Investigation investigates fraud in the areas of food stamps and subsidies to farmers and rural home buyers. The Department of Commerce has enforcement divisions in its Bureau of Export Enforcement and the National Marine Fisheries Administration. The Department of Labor has the Office of Labor Racketeering as an enforcement division. (Reaves, *Federal* 5)

The Food and Drug Administration (FDA) oversees the enforcement of the laws regulating the sale and distribution of pure food and drugs. Criminal law enforcement divisions are also found in the Securities and Exchange Commission (SEC), the Interstate Commerce Commission (ICC), the Federal Trade Commission (FTC), the Department of Health and Human Services, the Tennessee Valley Authority (TVA), the Environmental Protection Agency (EPA), the Veterans Health Administration (VHA), and the Library of Congress. The Department of State has the Bureau of Diplomatic Security to investigate matters involving passport and visa fraud. The U.S. Supreme Court has its own police department. Even the National Gallery of Art has its own law enforcement unit.

The U.S. Capitol Police employs more than 1,200 officers to provide police services for the grounds, buildings, and area immediately surrounding the Capitol complex. The U.S. Mint has a police department that provides police and patrol services for U.S. Mint facilities, including safeguarding the nation's coinage and gold bullion reserves. The Bureau of Engraving and Printing has a police department providing police services for its facilities, including those where currency, stamps, securities,

U.S. Capitol building.

TABLE 2.3 Major Federal Law Enforcement Agencies
Department of Justice
Federal Bureau of Investigation
Drug Enforcement Administration
U.S. Marshals Service
Bureau of Alcohol, Tobacco, Firearms, and Explosives
Department of the Treasury
Internal Revenue Service—Criminal Investigation Division
Executive Office for Asset Forfeiture
Executive Office for Terrorist Financing and Financial Crime
Office of Foreign Assets Control
Financial Crimes Enforcement Network
Department of Homeland Security (See Chapter 15)
Department of the Interior
National Park Service
Fish and Wildlife Service
U.S. Park Police
Bureau of Indian Affairs
Bureau of Land Management
Bureau of Reclamation
Department of Defense
Army Criminal Investigation Division
Naval Criminal Investigative Service
Air Force Office of Special Investigations
U.S. Postal Service
Postal Inspections Service
Department of Agriculture
U.S. Forest Service
Department of Commerce
Bureau of Export Enforcement
National Marine Fisheries Administration
Department of Labor
Office of Labor Racketeering
Department of State
Diplomatic Security Service
Other Federal Law Enforcement Agencies
Amtrak Police
Bureau of Engraving and Printing Police
U.S. Capitol Police
U.S. Mint Police
U.S. Supreme Court Police
Library of Congress Police
National Gallery of Art Police
Veterans Health Administration

SOURCE: Reaves, Brian A. *Federal Law Enforcement Officers, 2004.* Washington, D.C.: Bureau of Justice Statistics, 2006.

© AP Photo/Laurent Cipriani

Interpol, the International Criminal Police Organization, is a worldwide organization established for the development of cooperation among nations regarding common police problems.

and other official U.S. documents are made. The National Railroad Passenger Corporation, better known as Amtrak, has officers who provide police response, patrol, and investigative services for the railroad.

LO5 Explain International Police

Interpol, the International Criminal Police Organization, is a worldwide organization established for the development of cooperation among nations regarding common police problems. Interpol was founded in 1923, and the United States became a member in 1938. The mission of Interpol is to track and provide information that may help other law enforcement agencies apprehend criminal fugitives, thwart criminal schemes, exchange experience and technology, and analyze major trends of international criminal activity. Interpol attempts to achieve its mission by serving as a clearinghouse and depository of intelligence information on wanted criminals. Interpol's main function is informational; it is neither an investigative nor an enforcement agency. Police officials of any member country may initiate a request for assistance on a case that extends beyond their country's jurisdiction. Interpol headquarters are in France, and its U.S. representative is the U.S. Treasury Department.

 Log onto www.cengagebrain.com for additional study tools including videos, flash cards, games, self-quizzing, review exercises, web exercises, learning checks, and more.

WHY CHOOSE?

Every 4LTR Press solution comes complete with a visually engaging textbook in addition to an interactive eBook. Go to CourseMate for **POLICE2** to begin using the eBook. Access at **www.cengagebrain.com**

Complete the Speak Up survey in CourseMate at
www.cengagebrain.com

f Follow us at
www.facebook.com/4ltrpress

3

Organizing the Police Department

LO1 Define the Major Managerial Concepts of Organizing a Police Department

Some of you reading this text want to become members of a police or other law enforcement department, and some of you are just interested in what the police do and how they do it. Reading this chapter will give you a good insight into how a police department actually works.

This chapter deals with organizing a police department. Although it uses the term "police department," this is used as a generic term and includes other law enforcement agencies such as federal, state, and county law enforcement agencies, including sheriff's offices. In any organization, someone must do the work the organization is charged with doing, someone must supervise those doing the work, and someone must command the operation. Certain commonly accepted rules of management must be followed to accomplish the goals of the organization.

Organizing the Department's Managerial Concepts

Before discussing the organization of a police department, some managerial concepts common to most organizations should be understood. These concepts include division of labor; managerial definitions; leadership; organizational model and structure; chain of command (hierarchy of authority); span of control; delegation of responsibility and authority; unity of command; and rules, regulations, and discipline.

Division of Labor

All of the varied tasks and duties performed by an organization must be divided among its members in accordance with some logical plan. In police departments, the tasks of the organization are divided according to personnel, area, time, and function or purpose. Work assignments must be designed so that similar (homogeneous) tasks, functions, and activities are given to a particular group for accomplishment. In a police department, patrol functions are separate from detective functions, which are separate from internal investigative functions. Geographic and

organization
A deliberate arrangement of people doing specific jobs, following particular procedures to accomplish a set of goals determined by some authority.

bureaucracy
An organizational model marked by hierarchy, promotion on professional merit and skill, the development of a career service, reliance on and use of rules and regulations, and impersonality of relationships among career professionals in the bureaucracy and with their clientele.

management
The process of running an organization so that the organization can accomplish its goals.

PODSCORB
Acronym for the basic functions of management: planning, organizing, directing, staffing, coordinating, reporting, and budgeting.

Log onto www.cengagebrain.com to practice your vocabulary with flash cards and more.

time distinctions are also established, with certain officers working certain times and areas. The best way to think of the division of labor in an organization is to ask the question, "Who is going to do what, when, and where?"

The division of labor should be reflected in an organizational chart, a pictorial representation of reporting relationships in an organization (see Figure 3.1 on the following pages). A good organizational chart is a snapshot of the organization. Workers can see exactly where they stand in the organization (what functions they perform, to whom they report, and who reports to them).

Managerial Definitions

To understand the contents of this chapter, readers should know several managerial concepts.

Organization Nicholas Henry of Georgia Southern University, in the ninth edition of his classic text *Public Administration and Public Affairs*, gives us two definitions of *organization*: "a highly rationalized and impersonal integration of a large number of specialists cooperating to achieve some announced specific objective," and "a system of consciously coordinated personal activities or forces of two or more persons." (Henry 58) In 2006, Patrick O'Hara, in "Why Law Enforcement Organizations Fail: Mapping the Organizational Fault Lines in Policing," gives us a simpler, but no less useful, definition:

Organizations consist of a deliberate arrangement of people doing specific jobs, following particular procedures in order to accomplish a set of goals determined by some authority. (O'Hara 23–26)

Bureaucracy Max Weber, who many call "the father of sociology," gave us the classic features of the **bureaucracy**:

ELEMENTS OF A BUREAUCRACY

- Hierarchy
- Promotion based on professional merit and skill
- The development of a career service
- Reliance on and use of rules and regulations
- Impersonality of relationships among career professionals in the bureaucracy and with their clientele

Nicholas Henry further explains the principles of bureaucracy as he tells us that the closed model of organizations goes by many names, including bureaucratic, hierarchical, formal, rational, and mechanistic, and reports that *bureaucratic* theory or bureaucracy is one of the most common permutations, schools, or theories that has thrived. He says that the closed model of organizations has several characteristics, including those in Figure 3.2.

Surely, as you will find in this chapter, modern police organizations can be considered bureaucracies.

Management What is management? Who are managers? **Management** is the process of running an organization so that the organization can accomplish its goals. The traditional principles of management have been described using the acronym **PODSCORB**, which stands for:

Planning

Organizing

Directing

Staffing

COordinating

Reporting

Budgeting

Traditionally, managers and supervisors

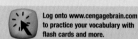

CLOSED MODELS OF ORGANIZATIONS

Routine tasks occur in stable conditions

Task specialization or division of labor is central

The proper ways to do a job are emphasized

Conflict within the organization is adjudicated from the top

One's formal job description is emphasized

Responsibility and loyalty are to the subunit to which one is assigned

Structure is hierarchical (like a pyramid)

One takes orders from above and transmits orders below, but not horizontally

Interaction is directed toward obedience, command, and clear superior–subordinate relationships

Loyalty and obedience to one's superior and the organization are emphasized, sometimes at the expense of performance

Personal status in the organization is determined largely by one's formal office and rank

FIGURE 3.2

Data Source: Nicholas Henry, *Public Administration and Public Affairs*, 9th ed. (Upper Saddle River, N.J.: Pearson Education, Inc., 2004), pp. 45–60.

FIGURE 3.1

Organizational Chart of Two Police Departments: (a) Large Department—Madison, Wisconsin; (b) Small Department—Hanson, Massachusetts

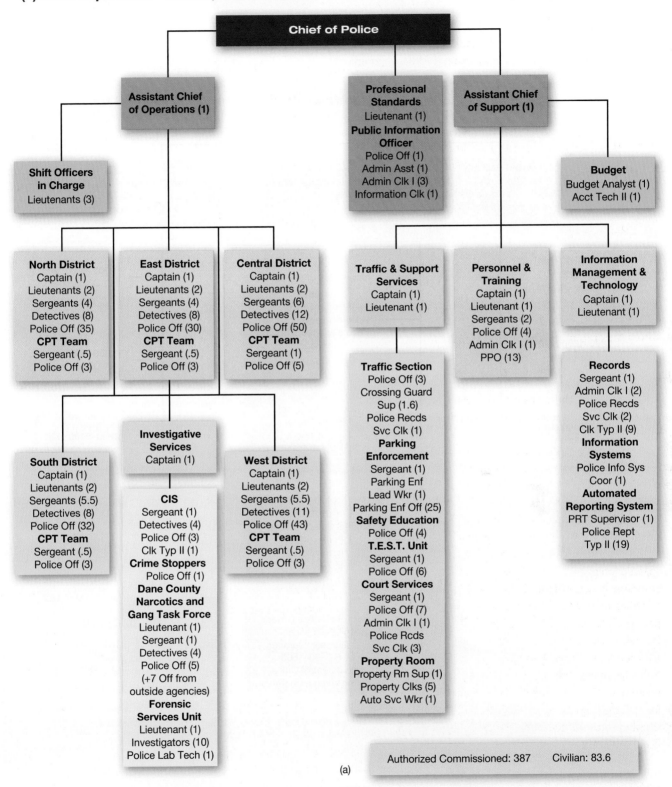

Chief of Police

Assistant Chief of Operations (1)

Professional Standards
Lieutenant (1)
Public Information Officer
Police Off (1)
Admin Asst (1)
Admin Clk I (3)
Information Clk (1)

Assistant Chief of Support (1)

Shift Officers in Charge
Lieutenants (3)

Budget
Budget Analyst (1)
Acct Tech II (1)

North District
Captain (1)
Lieutenants (2)
Sergeants (4)
Detectives (8)
Police Off (35)
CPT Team
Sergeant (.5)
Police Off (3)

East District
Captain (1)
Lieutenants (2)
Sergeants (4)
Detectives (8)
Police Off (30)
CPT Team
Sergeant (.5)
Police Off (3)

Central District
Captain (1)
Lieutenants (2)
Sergeants (6)
Detectives (12)
Police Off (50)
CPT Team
Sergeant (1)
Police Off (5)

Traffic & Support Services
Captain (1)
Lieutenant (1)

Personnel & Training
Captain (1)
Lieutenant (1)
Sergeants (2)
Police Off (4)
Admin Clk I (1)
PPO (13)

Information Management & Technology
Captain (1)
Lieutenant (1)

South District
Captain (1)
Lieutenants (2)
Sergeants (5.5)
Detectives (8)
Police Off (32)
CPT Team
Sergeant (.5)
Police Off (3)

Investigative Services
Captain (1)

CIS
Sergeant (1)
Detectives (4)
Police Off (3)
Clk Typ II (1)
Crime Stoppers
Police Off (1)
Dane County Narcotics and Gang Task Force
Lieutenant (1)
Sergeant (1)
Detectives (4)
Police Off (5)
(+7 Off from outside agencies)
Forensic Services Unit
Lieutenant (1)
Investigators (10)
Police Lab Tech (1)

West District
Captain (1)
Lieutenants (2)
Sergeants (5.5)
Detectives (11)
Police Off (43)
CPT Team
Sergeant (.5)
Police Off (3)

Traffic Section
Police Off (3)
Crossing Guard Sup (1.6)
Police Recds Svc Clk (1)
Parking Enforcement
Sergeant (1)
Parking Enf Lead Wkr (1)
Parking Enf Off (25)
Safety Education
Police Off (4)
T.E.S.T. Unit
Sergeant (1)
Police Off (6)
Court Services
Sergeant (1)
Police Off (7)
Admin Clk I (1)
Police Rcds Svc Clk (3)
Property Room
Property Rm Sup (1)
Property Clks (5)
Auto Svc Wkr (1)

Records
Sergeant (1)
Admin Clk I (2)
Police Recds Svc Clk (2)
Clk Typ II (9)
Information Systems
Police Info Sys Coor (1)
Automated Reporting System
PRT Supervisor (1)
Police Rept Typ II (19)

Authorized Commissioned: 387   Civilian: 83.6

(a)

SOURCE: Courtesy of the City of Madison Police Department, Madison, Wisconsin.

FIGURE 3.1 Continued

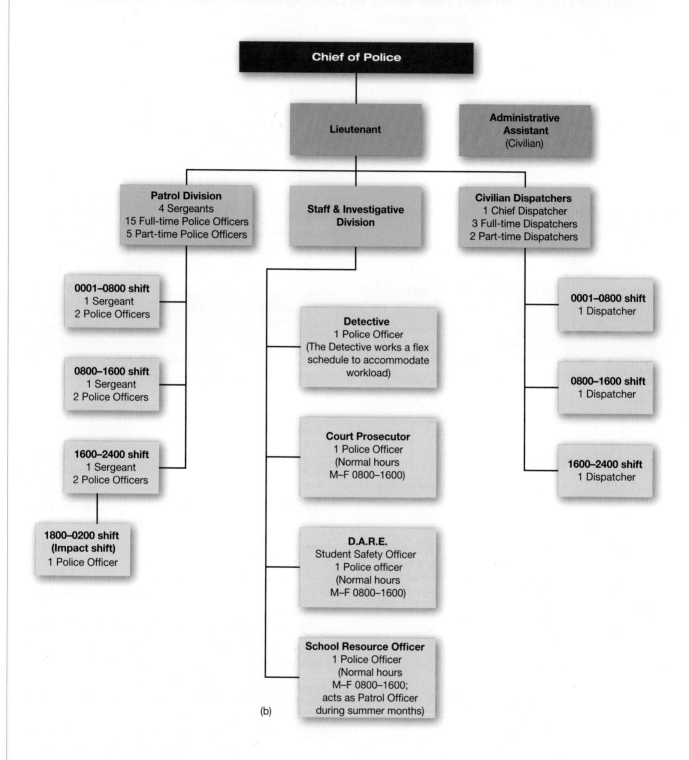

(b)

SOURCE: Courtesy of the Town of Hanson Police Department, Hanson, Massachusetts.

are the people tasked with the duty of managing—getting the functions of the organization accomplished through the members of the organization.

Managers/Supervisors or Leaders?

Leadership is an essential element in any organization. Are managers and supervisors leaders? Are the words *manage* and *supervise* analogous to the word *lead*? Think of some of the supervisors or bosses you have worked for. Did they merely tell you what to do and how to do it, and then discipline you if you did it poorly? Or did they motivate you to see the value of the work you were performing and how you fit into the broader mission of the organization, and inspire you to perform your job to the very best of your ability?

Consider and think about these descriptions of leadership.

- Scholar William Arthur Ward wrote, "Leadership is based on inspiration, not domination; on cooperation, not intimidation."

- Chinese philosopher Lao Tzu wrote, "A good leader inspires people to have confidence in the leader; a great leader inspires people to have confidence in themselves."

- Entrepreneur and author John C. Maxwell wrote, "A leader is one who knows the way, goes the way, and shows the way."

- Former Chairman of the U.S. Joint Chiefs of Staff and U.S. Secretary of State Colin Powell described the absence or failure of leadership: "The day soldiers stop bringing you their problems is the day you have stopped leading them. They have either lost confidence that you can help them or concluded that you do not care. Either case is a failure of leadership."

- Even former professional football player Joe Namath, the winning quarterback of Super Bowl III, gave us an example of leadership: "To be a leader, you have to make people want to follow you, and nobody wants to follow someone who doesn't know where he is going."

Leadership is essential in police management. Leaders, by teaching and setting examples, develop new leaders. Many law enforcement agencies are providing leadership training for their supervisors and managers, and this training is creating better agencies and better delivery of services to the communities they serve.

Traditional Organizational Model and Structure

The U.S. police are a civil, as opposed to a military, organization. Despite this, our police departments are **quasi-military organizations** (organizations similar to the military). Like the military, the police are organized along structures of authority and reporting relationships; they wear military-style, highly recognizable uniforms; they use military-style rank designations; they carry weapons; and they are authorized by law to use force. Also like the military, police officers are trained to respond to orders immediately.

Despite similarities, however, the police are far different from the military. They are not trained as warriors to fight foreign enemies but instead are trained to maintain order, serve and protect the public, and enforce the criminal law. Most important, the power of the police is limited by state laws and the Bill of Rights.

Todd Wuestewald and Brigitte Steinheider tell us that police administration gravitated toward a military orientation during a period of intensive reform early in the twentieth century. They write that a paramilitary model of policing evolved in response to the widespread corruption and political interference that threatened the credibility of U.S. policing. In an effort to instill discipline,

leadership
An influential relationship among leaders and followers who intend real changes that reflect their mutual purposes.

quasi-military organization
An organization similar to the military along structures of strict authority and reporting relations.

Log onto www.cengagebrain.com to practice your vocabulary with flash cards and more.

© Stephanie Sinclair/VII/Corbis

True leadership is not based on intimidation. Washington, D.C. police chief Cathy L. Lanier converses with a police officer on patrol.

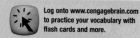
police leaders utilized authoritarian hierarchy as a tool against both political cooptation and low-level corruption. The scientific management principles of Frederick Taylor were applied to professionalize the police, and this management philosophy persists. This control-oriented supervision did succeed in bringing a degree of professionalism. (Wuestewald and Steinheider, "Shared Leadership" 48–55)

Chain of Command (Hierarchy of Authority)

The managerial concept of **chain of command** (also called hierarchy of authority) involves the superior–subordinate or supervisor–worker relationships throughout the department, wherein each individual is supervised by one immediate supervisor or boss. Thus, the chain of command as pictured in the organizational chart shows workers which supervisor they report to; the chain of command also shows supervisors to whom they are accountable and for whom they are responsible. All members of the organization should follow the chain of command. For example, a patrol officer should report to his or her immediate sergeant, not to the captain. A captain should send his or her orders through the chain of command to the lieutenant, who disseminates the directions to the sergeant, who disseminates the information

A new trooper recruit salutes commanding officers during graduation ceremonies.

AP Photo/Al Goldis

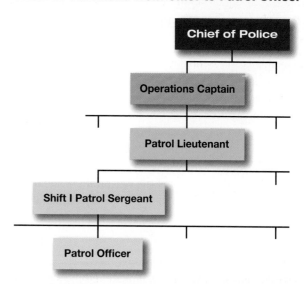

FIGURE 3.3

Chain of Command from Chief to Patrol Officer

- Chief of Police
- Operations Captain
- Patrol Lieutenant
- Shift I Patrol Sergeant
- Patrol Officer

SOURCE: Sheehan, Robert and Cordner, Gary W. Adapted from *Introduction to Police Administration*, 2nd ed., p. 189. Matthew Bender & Company, Inc., 1998. Reprinted by permission of the authors.

to the patrol officers (see Figure 3.3). Chain of command may be violated, however, when an emergency exists or speed is necessary.

Span of Control

The number of officers or subordinates that a superior can supervise effectively is called the **span of control**. Although no one can say exactly how many officers a sergeant can supervise or how many sergeants a lieutenant can supervise, most police management experts say the chain of command should be one supervisor for every 6 to 10 officers of a lower rank. It is best to keep the span of control as limited as possible so that the supervisor can more effectively supervise and control. The number of workers a supervisor can effectively supervise is affected by many factors, including distance, time, knowledge, personality, and the complexity of the work to be performed.

Delegation of Responsibility and Authority

Another important managerial concept in police organizations is delegation of responsibility and authority. Tasks, duties, and responsibilities are assigned to subordinates, along with the power or authority to control, command, make decisions, or otherwise act in order to complete the tasks that have been delegated or assigned to them.

Unity of Command

The concept of **unity of command** means that each individual in an organization is directly accountable to only one supervisor. The concept is important, because no one person can effectively serve two supervisors at one time. Unity of command may be violated in emergency situations.

Rules, Regulations, and Discipline

Most police organizations have a complex system of rules and regulations designed to control and direct the actions of officers. Most departments have operations manuals or rules and procedures designed to show officers what they must do in most situations they encounter. Rule books are often complex and detailed. In some major police departments, the police rule book is one-foot thick.

Police departments have disciplinary standards that are similar to, but less stringent than, the military's. Violation of department standards in dress, appearance, and conduct can lead to sanctions against officers such as reprimands, fines, or even dismissal from the department.

LO2 Discuss Alternative Organizations, Models, and Structures for Organizing a Police Department

In the face of continued corruption scandals, police administrators have tended to maintain an almost phobic preoccupation with accountability and conformity. But according to Wuestewald and Steinheider, these control-oriented approaches fail to recognize that police work is, and always has been, highly discretionary. The basic paradox of police hierarchy, they write, is that discretionary authority tends to be greater at the bottom of the police organization, where officers apply laws, policies, and regulations to situations that do not fit neatly into the rule book. Further, these discretionary choices are made in the field, far removed from the direct scrutiny of managers and supervisors. Many have lamented the apparent disjuncture between historically autocratic police management approaches and the requirements of community policing. (Wuestewald and Steinheider, "Shared Leadership" 48–55)

For many years, the corporate world has been moving toward more democratic processes such as shared leadership and participative management models in workplaces as companies try to improve their competitiveness by tapping the knowledge, talents, and creativity of their employees. In this process, organizational hierarchies have tended to flatten as autonomous work teams have replaced managerial levels. Scientific management theories have been replaced by more participative approaches such as employee empowerment, job involvement, and shared leadership. These methods of participative management have greatly improved organizations in terms of productivity, quality, and worker satisfaction. However, these power-sharing methods have found little acceptance in police organizations' administration.

Shared leadership is known by many names: participative management, employee empowerment, job involvement, participative decision making, dispersed leadership, total quality management (TQM), quality circles (QC), and others. These basic concepts involve any power-sharing arrangement in which workplace influence is shared among individuals who are otherwise hierarchical unequals. Such arrangements may involve various employee involvement schemes resulting in codetermination of work conditions, problem solving, and decision making.

Shared leadership attained renewed interest in the 1980s and 1990s in response to the success Japanese industry seemed to be having with empowerment strategies such as TQM and QC. Research in both the public and private sectors has revealed that participative leadership has

unity of command
A managerial concept that specifies that each individual in an organization is directly accountable to only one supervisor.

shared leadership
Power-sharing arrangement in which workplace influence is shared among individuals who are otherwise hierarchical unequals.

Log onto www.cengagebrain.com to practice your vocabulary with flash cards and more.

© Spencer Grant/Photo Researchers

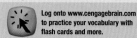
resulted in many improvements in job satisfaction, productivity, organizational citizenship behavior, labor–management relations, and overall organizational performance. The following is a recent example of a shared leadership program in policing.

In 2006, Todd Wuestewald, chief of the Broken Arrow, Oklahoma, Police Department (BAPD), a 164-person, full-time department that provides a full spectrum of police services to a metropolitan community of 91,000 in northeastern Oklahoma, and Brigitte Steinheider, director of organizational dynamics at the University of Oklahoma, reported on a program designed to incorporate frontline personnel into the important decision-making processes of the BAPD. Since 2003, the BAPD has had participative management in the form of a steering committee, called the Leadership Team, that is composed of 12 members of the BAPD who represent the police union, management, and most of the divisions, units, ranks, and functions in the department. The Leadership Team is an independent body with authority to make binding decisions on a wide range of policy issues, working conditions, and departmental strategies. The chief's office is not represented on the team, and all decisions are made democratically. The chief retains control of the team's agenda, but once an issue is referred to the team, its decisions are final and binding on all concerned. The team was trained by experts in organizational dynamics in order to facilitate team interactions and communication. An independent evaluation of the effects of the Leadership Team on departmental functioning, using quantitative and qualitative comparisons of the department before and after the establishment of the team, revealed a dramatic improvement in employee relations in such areas as discipline, promotions, hiring, recognition, rewards, and incentives, as well as employee organizational commitment, pride, morale, motivation, productivity, leadership development, and the acceptance of community policing methods. The productivity of the BAPD also improved, with increases in arrests of all types, traffic citations, field interview reports, and crime clearance rates.

LO3 Describe Methods of Organizing a Police Department by Personnel

A police department faces the same organizational challenges as any other organization, and a major challenge is personnel. The civil service system plays a large role in police hiring. This section will describe that role, along with sworn versus nonsworn personnel, rank structure, and other personnel issues.

The Civil Service System

The **civil service system** is a method of hiring and managing government employees that is designed to eliminate political influence, favoritism, nepotism, and bias. Civil service rules govern the hiring, promoting, and terminating of most government employees. The **Pendleton Act** created a civil service system for federal employees in 1883, following the assassination of President James Garfield, who was killed in 1881 by someone who had been rejected for appointment to a federal office. Eventually, many state and local governments adopted their own civil service systems.

Civil service regulations regarding hiring, promoting, and firing helped to remove the police from the partisan control of corrupt city political machines. Today, a vast majority of all government employees at the federal, state, and local levels are covered by the civil service system. Civil service has reduced political interference and paved

New police applicants fill out employment forms at the Police Recruitment Open House in Miami, Florida. Most police departments, particularly larger departments, are governed by civil service regulations.

© Jeff Greenberg/Photo Edit

the way for merit employment, a system in which personal ability is stressed above all other considerations. However, some civil service systems seem to guarantee life tenure in the organization and provide an atmosphere of absolute employee protection instead of stressing the merit that the system was initially designed to emphasize.

Most police departments, particularly larger departments, are governed by civil service regulations. Some complain that the civil service system creates many problems for police administrations because a chief or commissioner cannot appoint or promote at will but must follow the civil service rules and appoint and promote according to civil service lists. Additionally, it is often difficult to demote or terminate employees under the civil service system. Although many criticize civil service rules, it must be remembered that they help to reduce political influence and to eliminate the autocratic power of a supervisor to hire, fire, or transfer employees on a whim.

Sworn and Nonsworn (Civilian) Personnel

People who work for police departments fall under two major classifications: sworn members of the department, or police officers, and nonsworn members of the department, or civilians.

Sworn Members Sworn members are those people in the police organization we usually think of as police officers, troopers, or deputy sheriffs. They are given traditional police powers by state and local laws, including penal or criminal laws and criminal procedure laws. Upon appointment, sworn members take an oath to abide by the U.S. Constitution and those sections of state and local law applicable to the exercise of police power.

The best example of police power is the power to arrest. Police officers need only to have probable cause (not definite proof) to make arrests for any crimes or offenses committed in their presence or not. Probable cause is a series of facts that would indicate to a "reasonable person" that a crime is being committed or was committed, and that a certain person is committing or did commit it. A good example of facts leading to probable cause follows:

1. At 3:00 AM, screams from a female are heard in an alley.

2. An officer sees a man running from the alley.

3. Upon the officer's command, the man refuses to halt and rushes past the officer.

This gives the officer probable cause to stop the man, even though there is not yet "proof" of a crime. If it later turns out that no crime was committed, the officer has done nothing wrong, because he or she acted under probable cause.

Citizens, in contrast, cannot use probable cause, and the crime must have actually happened. (Actually, this leaves citizens open for false arrest lawsuits.) Additionally, citizens can only arrest for offenses actually committed in their presence, unless that offense was a felony.

In addition to the power of arrest, the police officer has the power to temporarily stop and question people in public places, to stop vehicles and conduct inspections, and to search for weapons and other contraband. The police officer also has significantly more power to use physical force, including deadly physical force, than does the citizen.

Nonsworn (Civilian) Members Nonsworn (civilian) members of police departments are not given traditional police powers and can exercise only the very limited arrest power given to ordinary citizens. Thus, they are assigned to nonenforcement duties in the department. They serve in many different areas of a police organization and in many roles. When we think of nonsworn members,

Sworn members take an oath to abide by the U.S. Constitution and those sections of state and local law applicable to the exercise of police power.

© Sarah Simonis/Star Ledger/Corbis

we usually think of typists, 911 operators, and police radio dispatchers. However, nonsworn members serve in many other capacities as well, including clerical, technical, administrative, and managerial jobs. Their rank structure is generally not as vertical as that of sworn officers.

Rank Structure

Sworn members generally have a highly organized rank structure (chain of command). The lowest sworn rank in the police organization is usually the police officer (or in sheriff's offices, the deputy sheriff), although many organizations have lower-ranked sworn officers, such as cadets or trainees, who generally perform duties similar to nonsworn members or assist sworn members in performing nonenforcement duties. Many cadets or trainees aspire to an eventual sworn position or are in training for one. In most organizations, those in training at the police academy are known as recruits or cadets and generally have the same legal authority as regular officers, except that they are generally not assigned to enforcement duties while still in training.

To say the police officer is the lowest rank in a police department may sound demeaning to the rank. However, it refers only to the relative rank in the organizational chart, not to the police officer's power or to the quality and importance of the service performed.

The following sections describe the various ranks in the police organization using generic terms. Most departments use the titles police officer, detective, sergeant, lieutenant, and captain. However, some organizations, such as state police departments and county sheriff's offices, use different terms to describe their members. In a state police force, the rank of trooper is almost identical to the rank of police officer. In a sheriff's office, the rank of deputy sheriff is synonymous with the rank of police officer.

The police officer/trooper/deputy sheriff is the most important person in the police organization. He or she is the person who is actually working on the streets attempting to maintain order and enforce the law. A police agency is only as good as the quality of the men and women it employs.

Police Officer Police officers serve as the workers in the police organization. The average police officer is assigned to patrol duties. Police officers perform the basic duties for which the organization exists. They are under the control of supervisors, generally known as ranking officers or superior officers. Ranking officers

are generally sergeants, lieutenants, and captains. At the highest level in most police organizations are chiefs or commissioners. In some state police organizations, military ranks such as major or colonel are used. In federal law enforcement organizations, nonmilitary terms are used to reflect rank structure, such as agent, supervisor, manager, administrator, and director.

Corporal or Master Patrol Officer Many police departments have established the corporal or master patrol officer rank as an intermediate rank between the police officers and the first-line supervisor, the sergeant. Often this intermediate rank is given to an officer as a reward for exemplary service or for additional services performed, such as training or technical functions.

Detective/Investigator Some police officers in a department are designated as detectives, investigators, or inspectors. (The various names for ranks may be confusing—investigators in the San Francisco Police Department are called inspectors, whereas in the NYPD and many others, the rank of inspector is that of a senior manager.) In either case, their role is to investigate past crimes. Detectives exercise no supervisory role over police officers except at a crime scene (the location where a serious crime occurred and where possible evidence may be present), where they are in charge and make most major decisions. In many departments, the assigned, case, or primary detective or investigator is the senior ranking officer at crime scenes and even outranks uniformed supervisors.

The role of the detective is generally considered more prestigious than that of the police officer. Detectives generally receive a higher salary and do not wear uniforms. They are usually designated detectives by appointment, generally for meritorious work, rather than through the typical

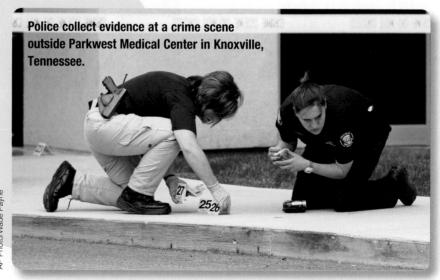

Police collect evidence at a crime scene outside Parkwest Medical Center in Knoxville, Tennessee.

civil service promotional examination. Often detectives do not possess civil service tenure and can be demoted back to the police officer rank without the strict civil service restrictions applicable to the other ranks in a police organization.

Sergeant The first supervisor in the police chain of command is the sergeant. The sergeant is the first-line or frontline supervisor and, many say, the most important figure in the police supervisory and command hierarchy. To most police officers, the sergeant is the boss. The

sergeant has two main responsibilities in police operations. First, the sergeant is the immediate supervisor of a number of officers assigned to his or her supervision. This group of officers is generally known as a **squad**. (Generally, 6 to 10 officers make up a squad, and several squads may work on a particular tour of duty.) The sergeant is responsible for the activities and conduct of members of his or her squad. In addition, the sergeant is responsible for decisions made at the scene of a police action until he or she is relieved by a higher-ranking officer.

Because the sergeant is responsible for getting the job done through the actions of other people, he or she must possess personal qualities such as intelligence, integrity, and dedication. The sergeant also draws on numerous organizational, motivational, and communication skills.

Lieutenant Just above sergeant in the chain of command is the lieutenant. Whereas the sergeant is generally in charge of a squad of officers, the lieutenant is in charge of the entire platoon. The **platoon** consists of all of the people working on a particular tour (shift or watch). The lieutenant is in charge of employees and all police operations occurring on a particular tour.

Recall that the terms *squad*, *tour*, *shift*, *platoon*, and *watch* are used in this textbook as generic terms, and many departments use different terms to identify these same concepts.

Captain Next in the chain of command above the lieutenant is the captain. The captain is ultimately responsible for all personnel and all activities in a particular area, or for a particular unit, on a 24-hour-a-day basis. The captain must depend on the lieutenant and sergeants under his or her command to communicate his or her orders to the officers and to exercise discipline and control over the officers.

Ranks above Captain Many larger municipal agencies have a hierarchy of ranks above the rank of captain. Inspectors generally have administrative control over several precincts or geographic areas, whereas assistant

chiefs or chiefs have administrative control of major units, such as personnel, patrol, or detectives.

Chief of Police/ Police Commissioner The head of the police agency is usually termed the *chief of police* or the *police commissioner*. Chiefs of police and police commissioners are generally appointed by the top official of a government (mayor, county executive, or governor) for a definite term of office. Generally, commissioners and chiefs do not have civil service tenure and may be replaced at any time.

Other Personnel

Police departments are increasingly using nonsworn employees and civilians to perform tasks in the police department. This effort can both increase efficiency in the use of human resources and cut costs. Police

New York City Police Commissioner Raymond W. Kelly speaks after a news conference in May, 2010.

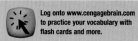
auxiliaries also help some departments operate more efficiently.

Civilianization

The process of removing sworn officers from noncritical or nonenforcement tasks and replacing them with civilians or nonsworn employees is called **civilianization**. Civilians with special training and qualifications have been hired to replace officers who did nonenforcement jobs (traffic control, issuing parking tickets, taking past crime reports, and so on). Additionally, civilians with clerical skills have been hired to replace officers who were assigned to desk jobs. Approximately one-quarter of all local police department employees are civilians.

The replacement of sworn officers by civilians in nonenforcement jobs is highly cost effective for police departments because civilian employees generally earn much less than sworn officers. This strategy also enables a department to have more sworn personnel available for patrol and other enforcement duties.

Police Reserves/Auxiliaries

Personnel shortcomings in police departments may be perennial or seasonal, depending on the jurisdiction. Some resort communities face an influx of vacationers and tourists during a particular season, which can more than double the normal size of the population. In response to this annual influx, some communities employ "summertime cops."

The term **reserve officer** can be confusing. In many jurisdictions, reserve officers are part-time employees who serve when needed and are compensated. In other jurisdictions, reserves are not compensated. The key element regarding the reserve officer is that he or she is a non-regular but sworn member of the department who has regular police powers. Other volunteer officers, sometimes referred to as auxiliaries, do not have full police power. Perhaps the best definition of a reserve officer has been provided by the International Association of Chiefs of Police (IACP):

The term "reserve police officer" usually is applied to a non-regular, sworn member of a police department who has regular police powers while

functioning as a department's representative, and who is required to participate in a department's activities on a regular basis. A reserve officer may or may not be compensated for his or her services, depending on each department's policy.

Reserve officers augment the regular force in police departments throughout the nation. Whether paid or not, they have full police powers. Many provide law enforcement services, including patrol, traffic control, assistance at natural and civil disasters, crime prevention, dispatch operations, and numerous other functions. It has been estimated that there are currently about 400,000 reserve officers in the United States. (Hedlund and Burke 12)

In some cities, auxiliary officers are unpaid volunteers. Although they wear police-type uniforms and carry batons, these auxiliaries are citizens with no police powers, and they do not carry firearms. They usually patrol their own communities, acting as a deterrent force and providing the police with extra eyes and ears.

Some Personnel Issues

Like all organizations with employees, police departments have a distinct set of personnel issues, including lateral transfers and police unions.

Lateral Transfers

Lateral transfers, or lateral movement, in police departments can be defined as the ability and opportunity to transfer from one police department to another. Some states allow lateral transfers from one department to another department and from out-of-state departments. Some states allow only in-state lateral transfers, and some states do not allow lateral transfers at all.

Some factors that must be considered in lateral transfers are differences in policing philosophy between the department the officer transferred from and the new department, how well the officer will fit with the image of the new department, and the degree to which the transferring officer must change in order to comply with the policies and procedures of the new department. Also, the new officer must be fully trained in the laws, procedures, and technology of the new department. (Blakely 92–96)

The major problem with lateral transfers is that many police pension systems are tied into the local government, and investments put into that fund cannot be transferred to other funds. Thus, lateral transfers in those cases can cause officers to lose all or some of their investments.

> ... the reserve officer ... is a non-regular but sworn member of the department who has regular police powers.

To remedy this situation, the President's Commission on Law Enforcement and Administration of Justice in 1967 recommended developing a national police retirement system that would permit the transfer of personnel without the loss of benefits. A few experiments with portable police pensions have been tried. (President's Commission on Law Enforcement and Administration of Justice 112)

Police Unions

Unions exist in order to harness the individual power of each worker into one group, the union, which can then speak with one voice for all the members. Unions in the private sector have been on the decline, but public-sector unionism is growing, particularly among police. Police unions have become increasingly political, endorsing and actively campaigning for candidates at the local, state, and federal levels. Although national umbrella police organizations tend to advocate adversarial tactics and rely on formal, legal redress of grievances, police unions are predominantly local organizations that bargain and communicate with the local police department and the mayor's or chief executive's office. Local unions often join into federations on a state or federal level to lobby state and federal legislative bodies.

Police unionism has a long and colorful history. Police employee organizations first arose as fraternal associations to provide fellowship for officers, as well as welfare benefits (death benefits and insurance policies) to protect police families. In some cities, labor unions began to organize the police for the purpose of collective bargaining, and by 1919, 37 locals had been chartered by the American Federation of Labor (AFL). The Boston Police Strike of 1919, as we saw in Chapter 1, was triggered by the refusal of the city of Boston to recognize the AFL-affiliated union. In response to the strike, Calvin Coolidge, then the governor of Massachusetts, fired all of the striking officers—almost the entire police department. Because of the Boston strike, the police union movement stalled until the 1960s, when it reemerged. During the 1960s, Patrolman's Benevolent Associations (PBAs) in major cities, using their rank and file officers, increased their lobbying, which ultimately weakened and reversed the political pressure against union recognition, leading to a major victory scored by New York City's PBA in 1964. Since then, the PBAs and the FOP have transformed from pressure groups into labor unions.

The ultimate bargaining tool of the union has traditionally been the strike. Members of many organizations, such as telephone companies, department stores, factories, and so on, strike to win labor concessions from their employers. Should police officers be allowed to strike? Many feel that police officers are special employees and should not have the right to strike. In fact, most states have laws that specifically prohibit strikes by public employees. Despite such laws, there have been strikes by police employees. In 1970, members of the New York Police Department staged a wildcat strike, for which all officers were fined two days' pay for each day they participated in the strike. Police strikes have also been staged in Baltimore, San Francisco, and New Orleans.

New Orleans police officers went out on strike twice in February 1979. The first walkout lasted for 30 hours and was designed to gain recognition of the union, bring the city to the bargaining table, and force agreement on selected economic demands. It was successful. The strike emboldened officers to seek additional concessions and to use the approaching Mardi Gras holiday as a bargaining chip. This second walkout was also intended to include ranking officers in the bargaining unit and to compel the city to enter into a collective bargaining agreement with the union. This strike, which forced the cancellation of Mardi Gras festivities, lasted 16 days and was unsuccessful. (Bopp 201–207)

W. J. Bopp writes that states lacking collective bargaining agreements for public employees are creating a climate in which strikes flourish. Even in cities that voluntarily negotiate with their police employees in the absence of enabling legislation, confusion and misunderstandings are likely to occur. Trouble is also likely to result when hostility, bitterness, distrust, and cynicism become dominant characteristics of the relationships between police labor and management. (Bopp 201–207)

© Rick Friedman/Corbis

To avoid the penalties involved in a formal police strike, police union members occasionally engage in informal job actions to protest working conditions or other grievances felt by the officers. These job actions include the **blue flu** (in which officers call in on sick report) and a refusal to perform certain job functions, such as writing traffic summonses.

Photo of police officer © Lisa F. Young/www. Shutterstock.com. Photo of thermometer and hot water bottle © iStockphoto/Nickilford. Photo illustration by Spitting Images for Cengage Learning.

LO4 Explain Methods of Organizing a Police Department by Area

Police departments must be organized by personnel functions and by the geographic area they serve. Each officer and group of officers must be responsible for a particular well-defined area. Geographic areas may be beats or posts, precincts, stations, or districts. Different organizations have very different words to describe these geographic groupings, so note that our terminology here is generic rather than specific. Figure 3.4 shows a map of the geographic breakdown of a precinct into beats or sectors.

Beats

The **beat** is the smallest geographic area that a single patrol unit—one or two people in a car or on foot—can patrol effectively. A beat may be a foot beat, patrol car beat, mounted beat, motorcycle or scooter beat, or even bicycle beat. Obviously, patrol car beats can be much larger than foot beats.

The beat officer ideally should know everyone living or doing business on his or her beat, as well as conditions and problems on the beat that require police assistance or concern. For this reason, a beat should be as geographically limited as possible, without being so small that it is nonproductive or boring to the officer.

Precincts/Districts/Stations

A **precinct/district/station** is generally the entire collection of beats in a given geographic area. In a small department, generally only one precinct serves as the administrative headquarters for the entire department.

The building that serves as the administrative headquarters of a precinct is generally called a precinct house or station house. The station house usually contains detention cells for the temporary detention of prisoners awaiting a court appearance after an arrest, locker rooms in which officers can dress and store their equipment, administrative offices, meeting rooms, and clerical offices.

Often in large urban departments, particularly in the Northeast, the *desk* serves as the centerpiece of the precinct/station/district. The desk is usually an elevated platform near the entrance of the station house, where all major police business is carried on. Prisoners are booked at the desk, and officers are assigned to duty from it. A ranking officer, generally a sergeant or lieutenant, is assigned as the desk officer and supervises all activities in the station house. The desk officer is usually in charge of the police blotter, a record in chronological order of all police activities occurring in the precinct each day. The blotter traditionally was a large bound

FIGURE 3.4

Map Dividing Precincts into Beats

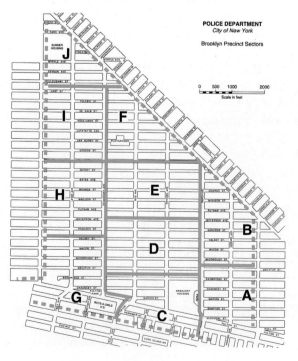

book in which all entries were handwritten by the desk officer. Although some departments still maintain the classic handwritten blotter, that term is now used more generically as the written record of all activity in a precinct, now that the blotter can include typed and computerized reports.

LO5 Describe Methods of Organizing a Police Department by Time

In addition to being organized by personnel and by area, a police department must organize its use of time. The following discussion will describe the tour system, including the common three-tour system, tour conditions, and steady (fixed) tours. Again, remember that different organizations have different words to describe these groupings of schedules, so our terminology here is generic rather than specific.

The Three-Tour System

Common sense dictates that police officers, like other workers, can work only a certain number of hours and days before fatigue sets in and they lose their effectiveness. Tradition and civil service rules have established the police officer's working day as 8 hours. The traditional police organization separates each day or 24-hour period into three tours (also called shifts, platoons, or watches): a midnight or night tour, which generally falls between the hours of 12:00 midnight and 8:00 AM; a day tour, which generally falls between the hours of 8:00 AM and 4:00 PM; and an evening tour, which generally falls between the hours of 4:00 PM and 12:00 midnight. Shifts, tours, or watches do not necessarily have to fall between these exact hours; they can be between any hours, as long as all 24 hours of the day are covered. Some departments have shifts that last longer than 8 hours, and they use the overlapping time as training time. Also, some departments use variations of the three-tour system, including two 12-hour tours a day or four 10-hour tours a week. An example of a department using 12-hour tours is the Nassau County, New York, Police Department, which uses a 7:00 AM to 7:00 PM and a 7:00 PM to 7:00 AM tour system. This department and others like it that use 12-hour tours thus have only two platoons as opposed to the traditional three-platoon system.

Using the traditional three-tour system, it takes three officers to cover each day, one on the night tour, one on the day tour, and one on the evening tour. When days off, vacation time, and sick time are factored into the three-tour system, approximately five officers are required to cover each beat 24 hours a day, 7 days a week, 365 days a year.

Historically, police officers have been allocated evenly during the three tours of duty each day, with equal

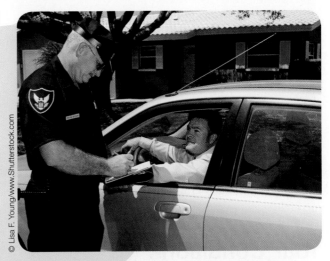

A police officer writes a traffic citation on a day tour.

Police officers question suspects on an evening tour.

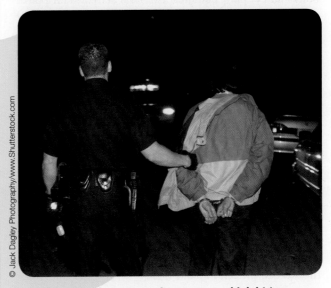

A police officer escorts a prisoner on a midnight tour.

numbers of officers assigned to each of the tours. However, beginning in the 1960s, academic studies of police discovered that crime and other police problems do not fit neatly into the three-tour system. The studies indicated that the majority of crime and police problems in the United States occur during the late evening and early morning hours. Many police departments thus began to change their methods of allocating police personnel. Most now assign their personnel according to the demand for police services, putting more officers on the street during those hours when crime and calls for police officers are highest.

Tour Conditions

Each of the three shifts in the three-tour system has its own characteristics, as any police officer will tell you.

The midnight tour is sometimes called the overnight or the graveyard shift. Most people are sleeping during this time, although in some large cities a good deal of commerce and business occurs. The most common problems for police officers during this tour are disorderly and intoxicated people at home and on the street, domestic violence, disorderly tavern patrons, commercial burglaries, prostitution, and drug sales. In addition to handling these specific problems, the police provide their normal duties, such as routine patrol, responding to emergency calls, aiding the sick and injured, and solving disputes.

The day tour occurs during the normal business hours in the United States. Stores and offices are open, highway and construction crews are working, and children are in school and at play. The most common activities for police officers during this tour are facilitating traffic flow and ensuring the safety of those traveling to and from work by enforcing parking and moving violations, ensuring the safety of children walking to and from school and entering and leaving school buses, preventing robberies and other property thefts in commercial areas, and providing other normal police services.

The evening tour is generally the busiest for the police. The work day and school day are over, the sun goes down, and the hours of darkness are here. During the evening hours, normal adherence to acceptable ways of behavior often gives way to alcohol and drug abuse, fights, and disputes. The most common activities of the evening tour are facilitating traffic for the homeward-bound commuter; dealing with bar fights, violence at home, and violence on the streets; preventing and dealing with street and commercial robberies; and providing routine police services.

Because the largest amount of police activity occurs on this tour, the majority of officers are assigned to it.

Steady (Fixed) Tours

Traditionally, some police departments have assigned their officers to rotating tours of duty: one or several weeks or months (or other periods) of night tours, one or several weeks or months (or other periods) of day tours, and one or several weeks or months (or other periods) of evening tours. Officers' days off are rotated to accommodate the three-tour system. This practice has caused problems for police officers in both their on-duty and off-duty lives. The strain of working different shifts repeatedly has a negative effect on eating, living, sleeping, and socializing, thus creating tremendous levels of stress.

There has been a move in recent years, therefore, to place officers on steady, or fixed, tours of duty, much like those of most other workers in the United States. Today, officers in many jurisdictions are assigned to steady night tours, day tours, or evening tours based on seniority or the officer's own choice. Police administrators hope that these steady tours will make officers' on-duty and off-duty lives more normal, thus eliminating the many problems created by shift work.

LO6 Discuss Methods of Organizing a Police Department by Function or Purpose

The best way to organize a police department in this way is to place similar police functions into similar units. Thus, all members of the department performing general patrol duties are placed into a patrol division, and all officers performing detective duties are placed into a detective division. Again, remember that different organizations have very different words to describe similar functions or units, so note that our terminology here is generic rather than specific.

Line and Staff (Support) Functions

The simplest grouping of units or divisions in a department differentiates between line functions and staff (support) functions. Line functions are those tasks that directly facilitate the accomplishment of organizational goals, whereas staff (support) functions are those tasks that supplement the line units in their task performance.

One of the organizational goals of a police department is maintaining order. The patrol officers who actually patrol the streets to preserve order are grouped under a patrol unit or patrol division. Another organizational goal of a police department is to investigate past crime. The detectives charged with investigating past crimes are grouped together under a detective unit or detective division. Patrol and detective units directly facilitate the accomplishment of the organizational goals of a police department; thus, they perform line functions.

Staff (support) functions are those functions of the police department that are not directly related to the organizational goals of the department but nevertheless are necessary to ensure the smooth running of the department. Investigating candidates for police officers and performing clerical work are examples of staff (support) functions.

Police Department Units

The late Robert Sheehan and Gary W. Cordner provide an excellent and comprehensive description of the basic tasks of a police department. (Sheehan and Cordner 113–162) They describe 30 tasks or duties the police must perform to have an effective police department. They state that in very large police departments, separate units may be established to perform each task. In smaller departments, the tasks may be grouped together in various ways to be performed by certain units or people. Sheehan and Cordner divide the 30 tasks into three subsystems that are similar to the previously mentioned division of line and staff functions. Their three task subsystems are operations, administration, and auxiliary services. See Table 3.1.

Operational Units Operations are activities performed in direct assistance to the public. These are the duties most of us think about when we think of police departments, including crime fighting, crime detection, and providing other services. Operational units include patrol, traffic, criminal investigations, vice, organized crime, juvenile services, community services, crime prevention, and community relations.

The *patrol* unit performs the basic mission of the police department: maintaining order, enforcing the law, responding to calls for assistance, and providing services to citizens. Patrol officers, who are usually on auto or foot patrol, are the backbone of the police service: They are the most important people in police service.

The *traffic* unit performs traffic control at key intersections and in other heavily traveled areas, enforces the traffic laws, and investigates traffic accidents. The *criminal investigations* unit investigates past crimes reported to the police in an effort to identify and apprehend the perpetrators of those crimes. The *vice* unit enforces laws related to illegal gambling, prostitution, controlled substances and other illegal drugs, pornography, and illegal liquor sales. The *organized crime* unit investigates and apprehends members of criminal syndicates who profit from continuing criminal enterprises such as the vice crimes just mentioned, extortion, loan sharking, and numerous other crimes. The *juvenile services* unit provides a multitude of services to juveniles, including advice and referral to appropriate social agencies designed to assist youth, particularly youthful offenders. This unit also investigates cases of child abuse and neglect.

The *community services* unit provides a multitude of services to the community, including dispute resolution, crime victim assistance, counseling, and other routine and emergency services. It also coordinates relationships between the police and the community, including numerous partnership programs. The police *crime prevention* unit attempts to organize and educate the public on methods people can take on their own and with the police to make themselves at less risk to crime. Some techniques include target hardening, neighborhood watch programs, and operation identification programs. The *community relations* unit attempts to improve relationships between the police and the public so that positive police–community partnerships can develop to decrease crime and improve the quality of life in U.S. neighborhoods.

TABLE 3.1 Organizing a Police Department by Function or Purpose

Operations	Administration	Auxiliary Services
Patrol	Personnel	Records
Traffic	Training	Communications
Criminal investigations	Planning and analysis	Property
Vice	Budget and finance	Laboratory
Organized crime	Legal assistance	Detention
Juvenile services	Public information	Identification
Community services	Clerical/secretarial	Alcohol testing
Crime prevention	Inspections	Facilities
Community relations	Internal affairs	Equipment
	Intelligence	Supply
		Maintenance

SOURCE: Used with permission from Robert Sheehan and Gary W. Cordner, *Introduction to Police Administration*, 2nd ed., pp. 114–115.

Administrative Units Administration in a police department is defined as those activities performed not in direct assistance to the public but for the benefit of the organization as a whole, usually from 9:00 AM to 5:00 PM, five days a week. Administrative units include personnel, training, planning and analysis, budget and finance, legal assistance, public information, clerical/secretarial, inspections, internal affairs, and intelligence.

The *personnel* unit performs the duties generally associated with corporate personnel departments, including recruiting and selecting candidates for police positions and assigning, transferring, promoting, and terminating police personnel. The *training* unit provides entry-level training to newly hired recruits and in-service training for veteran officers. The *planning and analysis* unit conducts crime analyses to determine when and where crimes occur so that they can be prevented. This unit also conducts operational and administrative analysis to improve police operations and the delivery of police services. The *budget and finance* unit of the police department is involved in the administration of department finances and budgetary matters, including payroll, purchasing, budgeting, billing, accounting, and auditing. The *legal assistance* unit provides legal advice to members of the department, including patrol officers. The *public information* unit informs the public, through the news media, about police activities, including crime and arrests. This unit also informs the public about actions they can take to reduce their chances of becoming crime victims. The *clerical/secretarial* unit prepares the necessary reports and documents required to maintain police record keeping. The *inspections* unit conducts internal quality control inspections to ensure that the department's policies, procedures, and rules and regulations are being followed. The *internal affairs* unit investigates corruption and misconduct by officers. Finally, the *intelligence* unit conducts analyses of radical, terrorist, and organized crime groups operating in a police department's jurisdiction.

Auxiliary Services Units Auxiliary services are defined as activities that benefit other units within the police department, but on a more regular and frequent basis than do administrative services. Auxiliary services functions are usually available to assist the police officer 24 hours a day. Auxiliary services units include records, communications, property, laboratory, detention, identification, alcohol testing, facilities, equipment, supply, and maintenance.

The *records* unit of a police department maintains department records, including records of crimes and arrests, statistics and patterns regarding criminal activity, and records of traffic accidents. The *communications* unit answers incoming calls to the department's 911 telephone lines and assigns police units to respond to emergencies and other requests for police services. The *property* unit inventories and stores all property coming into the custody of the police, including evidence, recovered property, and towed and recovered vehicles. The *laboratory* unit examines and classifies seized evidence, including drugs, weapons, and evidence found at crime scenes (for example, fingerprints, fibers, and stains). The *detention* unit provides temporary detention for prisoners awaiting their appearance in court. The *identification* unit fingerprints and photographs criminals, classifies prints, and maintains identification files. The *alcohol testing* unit administers driving-while-intoxicated tests for court prosecution.

The *facilities* unit of a police department maintains buildings designed for police use, such as station houses, offices, and detention facilities. The *equipment* unit maintains the numerous types of equipment necessary for the department's effective operation. The supplies necessary for the proper operation of the department are purchased by the *supply* unit. Finally, the *maintenance* unit keeps all facilities and equipment serviceable.

Table 3.2 shows the breakdown, by rank and assignment, of a police department. By reading the top line of the chart and following it down to the bottom line ("Total"), one can easily see that there are a total of 165 employees in this department, with 82 police officers, 19 ranking officers (1 chief, 2 captains, 6 lieutenants, and 10 sergeants), 5 civilians, 2 coordinators, and 57 crossing guards.

A police 911 dispatcher assigns police units to respond to emergencies and other requests for services.

© David R. Smith/www.Shutterstock.com

	Chief	Captain	Lieutenant	Sergeant	Police Officer	Civilian	Coordinators	Crossing Guards	Total
Office of the Chief	1					1			2
Operations Division		1				½			1 ½
Patrol Bureau									
8–4			1	3	21				25
4–Midnight			1	3	23				27
Midnight–8			1	3	15				19
Detective Bureau									
8–4			1		4				5
4–Midnight					1				1
6–2					1				1
Juvenile Bureau									
8–4			1		2				3
6–2					1				1
Traffic Bureau									
8–4				1	3		2	57	63
4–Midnight					3				3
Midnight–8					2				2
Prosecutions Unit					2				2
Fingerprint and Photography Unit					None full time				
Administration and Services Division		1	1			½			2 ½
Planning and Records Bureau					1	2			3
Payroll, Billing, and Budget Unit					1				1
Community Services and Training Unit					2				2
Custodial Services						1			1
Total	1	2	6	10	82	5	2	57	165

SOURCE: Sheehan, Robert and Cordner, Gary W. *Introduction to Police Administration*, 2nd ed., p. 18, Matthew Bender & Company, Inc., 1998. Reprinted by permission of the authors.

By reading the details under "Police Officers" from the top line down, one can see that 59 of the officers are assigned to the patrol bureau (21 to 8:00 AM to 4:00 PM tours, 23 to 4:00 PM to midnight tours, and 15 to midnight to 8:00 AM tours); 6 to the detective bureau; 3 to the juvenile bureau; 8 to the traffic bureau; 2 to the prosecutions unit; 1 to the planning and records bureau; 1 to the payroll, billing, and budget unit; and 2 to the community services and training unit.

 Log onto www.cengagebrain.com for additional study tools including videos, flash cards, games, self-quizzing, review exercises, web exercises, learning checks, and more.

4

Becoming a Police Officer

After studying this chapter, the student should be able to:

LO1 Find information on jobs in law enforcement

LO2 Explain the standards in the police selection process

LO3 Discuss the recruitment process

LO4 Define and explain the job analysis

LO5 Explain the police selection process

LO6 Explain the police training process, the probationary period, and in-service training

LO1 Find Information on Jobs in Law Enforcement

Where do you find information about available jobs in policing or criminal justice in general? Many traditional sources have been used for years, including media advertising, as many police departments today are recruiting through radio, television, and newspapers. Additionally, the Internet provides a wealth of information regarding police employment.

Job Hunt
- ☐ papers
- ☐ human resources/personnel offices
- ☐ agency websites
- ☐ law enforcement websites
- ☐ discoverpolicing.org
- ☐ officers I see on the street
- ☐ career fairs
- ☐ high school / college placement offices

© Kevin Renes/www.Shutterstock.com

Most police departments have their own websites with employment information and a wealth of other information provided to the public. These websites can even allow potential officers to get an idea of the department's organizational culture to help determine whether they feel they would fit in. Most departments also provide information about their requirements and the hiring process. Many address frequently asked questions, give advice on training for the physical agility portion of the test, and provide contact information for further clarification.

Word-of-mouth advertising by family members and friends is a common way people receive information about jobs in policing and criminal justice. Many police departments view their current officers as effective recruiters with an accurate perception of the job and what it entails.

An added bonus for college students is the intern program that is required in many criminal justice programs. Students work for a local government agency for a semester while earning college credit.

LO2 Explain the Standards in the Police Selection Process

Each police department sets standards, or necessary qualifications, that it requires in selecting its prospective police officers. In recent years, these standards have changed to allow a greater number of females and minorities to become police officers, but the standards are still more stringent than those in most other professions. The police standards cover physical, age, and education requirements, as well as criminal record restrictions.

Physical Requirements

Over the years, we have come to realize that brains are more important than brawn in police work. Also, the former physical requirements discriminated against women and minorities. Today, however, physical requirements are still stringent, and departments are under pressure to demonstrate that the physical requirements are job-related and not arbitrary.

Height and Weight Requirements
Courts typically do not support minimum height and weight requirements

© Robert Asento/www.Shutterstock.com

but do support the need for maximum weight standards or a weight-to-height proportion ratio.

Vision Requirements It has long been thought that a police officer should have relatively good vision because of the potential for officers to lose their glasses during an altercation with a suspect or have their glasses get fogged up or spotted with rain. Most agencies require vision that is correctable to 20/20, but the popularity of contact lenses and the increased utilization and success of vision correction surgery make this less of a concern for applicants today than it was even five years ago.

Smoking

Though over the years many police departments have prohibited smoking in public because of concerns for a professional appearance, health and monetary considerations have now become issues for law enforcement agencies as well. In an effort to respond to

© Tkemot/www.Shutterstock.com

rising medical costs for personnel and to keep officers healthy and productive for a longer time, many departments have implemented no-smoking policies. Courts have traditionally upheld that public safety employers have a legitimate interest in the health and fitness of their employees.

Age Requirements

Until recently, most police departments required that an officer be between the ages of 21 and 29 at the time of appointment. Anyone over the age of 29 was considered too old to begin employment, though exceptions were sometimes made for those with previous military or police experience.

Most departments do not have an official upper age limit. Their concerns in hiring revolve around pensions and health issues and the related medical costs. Some departments will hire officers retiring after 20 years with another department, and it is not unusual to see officers enjoy two lengthy police careers in two different departments. Actually, many law enforcement agencies have come to value the more mature and experienced candidate.

Education Requirements

Among local law enforcement agencies, as reported by the Bureau of Justice Statistics

(BJS) in 2010, 82 percent of local departments required a high school diploma, 16 percent had some type of college requirement, and only 1 percent required a four-year college degree in 2007. The minimum high school diploma requirement may not necessarily reflect actual selection practices because many departments favor applicants who meet more than the minimum standards, and value education for their officers. According to the BJS local police report, 32 percent of departments offer educational incentive pay, and 37 percent provide **tuition reimbursement** to their officers. (Reaves, *Local Police Departments*)

Considerable debate has arisen over the desirability of college education for police officers. Many experts believe that all police officers should have a college degree. The belief is that educated officers will be better equipped to serve in today's dynamic and challenging environment, promote the department's professional image and reputation, and minimize costs and negative publicity resulting from disciplinary issues. These officers will be comfortable in the community policing atmosphere, which encourages critical thinking, problem solving, and communication skills.

Over the years, police officers have gone from being minimally trained and poorly equipped to being highly trained in the latest technology, and the public expects police officers to be professional, educated, and up to date.

A recent concern for law enforcement agencies is the ability to have a high-quality applicant pool from which to select their candidates. Administrators feel that the higher the education requirement, the smaller their applicant pool will be. There is also a concern for possibly discriminating against minorities when a higher education requirement is imposed.

This issue is unlikely to go away. Overall, society, police administrators, and police officers see the value in having an educated police force. At times, the real-world problems and practical matters of recruitment and selection might interfere with the desired goal of more education. The demands placed on officers as our society rapidly changes will necessitate educational requirements being constantly reassessed by departments and state Peace Officer Standards and Training

commissions (POSTs). More and better incentives and requirements may need to be put in place to speed the realization of the goal for a fully college-educated police force.

© Mincemeat/Shutterstock

Prior Drug Use

Departments have continually faced the problem of a candidate's prior drug use. Should a candidate be disqualified because of prior drug use? Is experimentation with marijuana enough to dismiss a candidate? What about cocaine? How many prior uses of drugs are acceptable?

Recently, many departments around the country have liberalized their policies regarding drug use because of a smaller applicant pool as well as societal changes. According to John Firman, the research director for the International Association of Chiefs of Police (IACP), the most common restriction is 10 years free from using hard drugs and 5 years free from using marijuana. (Krause) Applicants are usually given an opportunity to explain their drug use, and the circumstances, how many times, and when it was used are examined by the hiring agency. Agencies prefer to look at the totality of the process rather than a single criterion, taking into consideration the individual and the organization's reputation as well as community expectations and desires. Drug restrictions vary widely from agency to agency and will require research by interested applicants for whom this is an issue. A policy or action that is too liberal can raise issues of liability for agencies. Most departments also have random drug testing, and officers can be fired and stripped of their state certificate if found to be using drugs.

Criminal Record Restrictions

People wishing to become police officers must respect the rules of our society and adhere to these rules. However, many police departments recognize that people may make mistakes, especially when young, that might

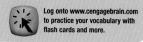
result in an arrest. A Justice Department survey discovered that 100 percent of all police departments conduct criminal record checks for all applicants and 99 percent conduct background investigations. (Reaves, *Local Police* Departments) Most departments will reject a candidate with a felony conviction, but a misdemeanor conviction does not necessarily prohibit a person from employment. Along with the issue of criminal records is undetected criminal activity, which is explored during the background investigation, polygraph exams, and interviews.

LO3 Discuss the Recruitment Process

In recent years, the **recruitment process** to attract adequate numbers of qualified police candidates has become increasingly challenging. The U.S. war on terror means that many potential police officer recruits are serving their country overseas. Other possible explanations cited in recent years for the recruitment challenges agencies face include the following:

- The strong economy (at times) luring candidates into the private sector
- Increased education requirements
- High attrition because of retiring baby boomers
- The deployment of qualified candidates in Iraq and Afghanistan
- The booming homeland security industry after 9/11 luring officers and candidates away from law enforcement

More than 80 percent of the nation's 17,000 law enforcement agencies are facing vacancies they're unable to fill. The recent downturn in the economy may in some way help recruitment efforts (Pomfret, 2006), although resulting budget cuts are also contributing to jobs remaining unfilled.

Successful police recruiters recruit in high schools and colleges, among other places. In an effort to attract minorities, many departments recruit at predominantly minority colleges in their region. Recruiters also often attend church gatherings, career exhibitions, and trade shows geared toward women, as well as men's and women's athletic events to reach others who may not have considered a law enforcement career.

Despite some of the recent recruiting challenges faced by departments, in the long term, law enforcement

is a good career choice for many people. It is an opportunity to serve the public and offers a steady income despite the ups and downs of the economy over 20 years. Individuals who choose to progress up the ranks have an opportunity to make a good salary and, ultimately, receive an excellent pension. In positions of leadership, they will also have an opportunity to shape law enforcement policies into the future.

Recruiters will have to tap into the desires of *Generation Next*—the label given to the current generation of 18- to 25-year-olds. At first glance, it might seem that this generation, who grew up with interactive technology and spends much of its time on the Internet, sending text messages and using social networking sites, might be vastly different from previous generations entering the workforce. In fact, they value many of the same things their predecessors did, including family, work, and public service. By tapping into their strengths, which include multitasking, problem solving, and group work, law enforcement can benefit from their technical abilities as well as their ability to think outside the box.

Recruiters can take advantage of this generation's desire for public service and meaningful work by making agency and career opportunities less traditional and more in keeping with the changing society and by promoting career paths, meaningful group projects, social outlets, flexibility, and activities consistent with heroism. Agencies that learn to be flexible will better meet crime-fighting challenges, and if they're adept at recruiting and retaining this Generation Next, they will thrive. (Harrison, 2007)

In recent years, law enforcement agencies around the country have found themselves in the unusual position of having to compete among themselves as well as with the private sector to fill vacancies. This has led to departments reexamining their employment requirements as well as employing new and smarter recruitment techniques. These techniques include using signing bonuses to obtain new

STRENGTHS of Generation Next

- Interactive Technology
- Multitasking
- Problem Solving
- Group Work
- See Outside the Box

BENEFITS OF A LAW ENFORCEMENT CAREER
- MEANINGFUL WORK
- CAREER PATHS
- FLEXIBILITY
- OPPORTUNITY FOR HEROISM
- ABILITY TO MAKE A DIFFERENCE

Photo © iStockphoto/Vladimir Kolobov. Photo illustration by Spitting Images for Cengage Learning.

recruits and increasing salaries to keep officers and reduce turnover. Agencies are conducting more targeted advertising as well as making recruiting trips across the country, targeting lateral transfers, and emphasizing the benefits and quality of life in their jurisdictions.

Recently, agencies have expressed an interest in attracting and building relationships with potential candidates years before the candidates may be eligible to be police officers. With increased "tracking" and "majors" being selected in high schools around the country, some public service advocates feel they need to reach students before they make some of these decisions. The hope is that by presenting the benefits and rewards of public service, they may attract students who might otherwise not have considered a law enforcement career. Many departments are also expanding or returning to their explorer and cadet programs in an effort to promote loyalty to their department in talented potential applicants. The **police cadet** position is generally a nonsworn, paid, part-time position for young adults 18 years of age and older who are interested in a law enforcement career.

The recruiting issue is currently being discussed by police leaders and within the membership of IACP and other police organizations, and recruiters are being encouraged to think outside the box in their efforts to reach qualified candidates. This may mean improving benefits and incentives such as salary, signing bonuses, uniform allowances, training dollars, educational incentives, overtime opportunities, take-home vehicles, and so forth. They can also make their process more user-friendly and convenient to the applicant by continually accepting applications, explaining the testing process on their websites, and offering help throughout various stages of the process. Others examine why recruits are attracted to law enforcement careers and build on that. (Taylor et al.)

This recruitment challenge is leading departments to "work smarter" in various ways, including **civilianization**, which involves using civilian personnel to fill nonhazardous positions in an effort to put more sworn officers on the street. This will increase the availability of jobs for individuals seeking public service positions in law enforcement but not as police officers. Civilianization is also seen as a way to assist departments in increasing staffing to help combat

police cadet
A nonsworn law enforcement position for young adults age 18 and over. Generally, these positions are part-time, paid, education-oriented positions in police departments, and the targeted candidates are college students interested in moving into a law enforcement career.

civilianization
Replacing sworn positions with civilian employees. Some positions that are often civilianized include call takers, dispatchers, front desk personnel, crime analysts, crime prevention specialists, accident investigators, crime scene technicians, public information officers, and training personnel.

Log onto www.cengagebrain.com to practice your vocabulary with flash cards and more.

Running away from your current job?
Call APD Recruiting 343-5020

OFFICER

AP Photo/Albuquerque Police Department

Agencies often use creative recruiting efforts when competing for police candidates. This billboard was inspired by the bride-to-be who skipped town days before her planned wedding in Georgia and later showed up in Albuquerque claiming she had been abducted.

job analysis
Identifies the important tasks that must be performed by police officers, and then identifies the knowledge, skills, and abilities necessary to perform those tasks.

knowledge, skills, and abilities (KSAs)
Talents or attributes necessary to do a particular job.

job-related
Concept that job requirements must be necessary for the performance of the job a person is applying for.

selection process
The steps or tests an individual must progress through before being hired as a police officer.

emotional intelligence
The ability to interpret, understand, and manage one's own and others' emotions. This encompasses the competencies valued in law enforcement such as self-awareness, self-control, conflict management, and leadership.

 Log onto www.cengagebrain.com to practice your vocabulary with flash cards and more.

the temporary vacancies caused by police officers who have been called up for military duty or to contend with hiring freezes due to budget issues.

LO4 Define and Explain the Job Analysis

Before the selection process for new members can actually begin, a police department must know what type of person it is interested in hiring. To determine this, the department must first perform a **job analysis** to identify the important tasks that must be performed by police officers and then identify the knowledge, skills, and abilities necessary to perform those tasks.

In the past, women and members of minority groups were often rejected from police departments because they didn't meet certain standards, such as height, weight, and strength requirements. A good job analysis can avoid that situation by measuring what current police officers in a department actually do. From this study, the department then can establish the standards and qualifications necessary for new officers to perform the needed duties.

If a competent job analysis is performed, the **knowledge, skills, and abilities (KSAs)** necessary for performance in that department are judged to be **job-related**. If a certain qualification is deemed to be job-related, that requirement can withstand review by the courts, and the specific test measuring for that knowledge or those skills or abilities is nondiscriminatory. Candidates are not expected to know how to do police work, but they must have the KSAs to learn how to perform the duties of the profession. For example, KSAs include the abilities to read, write, reason, memorize facts, and communicate with others, and physical abilities such as agility and endurance. The fact that a job analysis and the entrance examination based on it successfully pass the court's examination of job relatedness shows that a police department carefully constructed its entrance examinations based on the duties actually performed by police officers.

LO5 Explain the Police Selection Process

The police **selection process** is lengthy, difficult, and competitive. It involves a series of examinations, interviews, and investigative steps designed to select the best candidate to appoint to a police department from the many who apply. Practitioners relate that in many agencies, only 1 out of 100 applicants makes it into the employment ranks. This process can be intimidating to young applicants. The number of steps and all the rules and expectations can make them apprehensive. Reading texts like this can help to educate and prepare candidates about what to expect.

WHAT WE'RE LOOKING FOR:

▸ **Personality consistent with community expectations**

▸ **Maturity level / life experience**

▸ **Emotional intelligence**

▸ **Ability to communicate**

▸ **Ethical standards / integrity**

Photo © iStockphoto/jodie coston. Figure © 2013 Cengage Learning.

According to the Bureau of Justice Statistics, municipal police agencies use the screening procedures found in the chart shown in Figure 4.1. (Reaves, *Local Police Departments*)

In perusing police department websites, it is clear that this protocol is widespread among all types of law enforcement agencies. Typically a candidate has to pass each step before going on to the next step in the process and must pass all steps to become a police officer. The order of the steps in the selection process varies by department, depending on its philosophy and financial and personnel resources. However, it is fairly universal that the written and physical agility test will come at the beginning of the screening process and the psychological and medical evaluations will be the last screening procedures, after a conditional offer of employment has been made to the applicant.

FIGURE 4.1

Screening methods used in the selection of new officer recruits in local police departments across the nation.

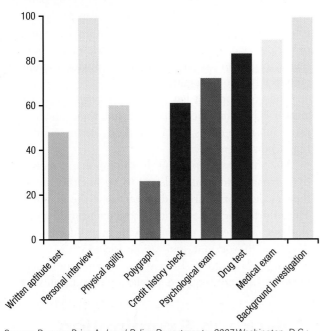

Source: Reaves, Brian A. *Local Police Departments, 2007.* Washington, D.C.: Bureau of Justice Statistics, 2010.

A crucial element of the police selection process is that each step is court defensible and has validity to the job performance of a police officer. Under the U.S. Equal Employment Opportunity Commission (EEOC) guidelines, **adverse impact**, or a different rate of selection, occurs when the selection rate for any gender, race, or ethnic group is less than 80 percent of the selection rate for the group with the highest selection rate. If adverse impact is noted and the test or selection criteria cannot be shown to be valid, the EEOC would classify the test as impermissible discrimination, which could result in legal problems for the police agency.

In addition to sworn or uniformed members of law enforcement agencies, nonsworn or civilian members of many departments—for example, 911 operators, community service officers, crime scene technicians, and so on—often receive preemployment screening similar to that of police officers.

Characteristics of Good Police Officers

What are the "right" characteristics police administrators should look for when selecting future police officers? Efforts have been made to determine the specific criteria that predict future police performance, but the results have been inconclusive in light of the shifting demands placed

on police officers in our rapidly changing society and the changing demographics of the officers themselves.

It is hard to define and measure—and consequently defend in court—personal characteristics such as judgment and decision-making abilities. To assist in this area and to further embrace the community policing philosophy, some agencies are systematically seeking input from the community about what types of police officers citizens are looking for in their community. This is a radical change in the selection process and, if it continues and spreads, could significantly affect that process. It would also have the potential to enhance the relationship between the community and the police. (Cordner, Scarborough, and Sheehan, 2007, p. 159)

The Department of Justice Office of Community Oriented Policing Services (COPS) published a report in 2006 presenting the findings from the Hiring in the Spirit of Service project. This federally funded project involved the community in the recruiting and hiring of service-oriented law enforcement personnel. Five agencies of various sizes and locations and facing various challenges were chosen to participate: the police departments of Sacramento, California; Burlington, Vermont; and Detroit, Michigan; and the sheriff's offices of Hillsborough County, Florida, and King County, Washington.

These agencies employed advisory committees to participate in activities and provide feedback regarding the recruiting and hiring process. They also used focus groups to engage community support and vision. The objectives of the Hiring in the Spirit of Service strategy included developing an agency image, revising the screening process, and incorporating hiring practices that coincided with the new trends in police service. It was a common finding across all sites that including the community in the recruitment and hiring process was not easy, nor was identifying service-oriented traits that all stakeholders could agree upon. (Scrivner, 2006)

Written Entrance Examination

With large numbers of individuals needing to be screened in this first step of the selection process, written tests are generally used to minimize the time and cost to the agency. These tests are often conducted on a regular basis so that there is a list of candidates from which to choose when an opening occurs. The tests may be held at schools, community buildings, and military bases for the applicants' convenience. Sometimes these tests are contracted out to private enterprise, with the cost to be borne by the applicant.

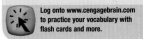

Because large numbers of applicants are screened out at this stage, the exams are often subject to litigation.

A written exam can be fair and unbiased when developed from a job analysis that incorporates the expertise of law enforcement practitioners in an effort to determine the KSAs required for the police position. Fairness is the degree to which all ethnic and gender groups are evaluated consistently. (Legel 66–69)

Many departments use tests specifically developed for the police selection process. Most of these new tests are administered through the use of computer simulations or assessment centers.

Physical Agility Test

Police departments are interested in candidates who are physically fit. During the past 20 years, **physical agility testing** has been criticized for discriminating against some candidates, particularly women and physically small members of certain minority groups. Some argue that the tests relate to aspects of the police job that are rarely performed. Others argue that, although these aspects of the police job

Physical agility testing is a crucial element of the selection process and is designed to ensure that candidates will be able to meet the physical demands of the academy and the job.

are not routinely and frequently performed, they are critically important. Not possessing the strength, endurance, or flexibility needed for the job could result in injury or death to the officer or a citizen. It also might increase the likelihood of an officer having to resort to deadly force.

Sometimes candidates don't adequately prepare for the exam but nevertheless assume they can pass it. Other candidates simply have a problem with a particular area of the physical agility test. Rather than lose an otherwise quality candidate, departments often provide training or guidance before the agility test.

The question that law enforcement agencies need to answer is how fit officers must be, and then they have to prove job relatedness to the standards, or the courts will find against them.

Most officers keep themselves in top shape, motivated by personal pride and a desire to be healthy, minimize their chance for injury, and better serve the community. This effort is facilitated by departments providing on-site workout facilities or contracts with fitness facilities, on-duty time to work out, and various incentives to maintain certain levels of fitness. In most cases, civilian or nonsworn personnel are not required to take a physical agility test.

Polygraph Examination

The **polygraph**, often called a lie detector test, is a mechanical device designed to ascertain whether a person is telling the truth. It was first used by the Berkeley, California, police department in 1921. The polygraph records any changes in such body measurements as pulse, blood pressure, breathing rate, and galvanic skin response. The effectiveness of the polygraph is based on the belief that a person is under stress when telling a lie. Therefore, if a person lies, the machine will record that stress in the body measurements.

The use of the polygraph was severely limited by the Employee Polygraph Protection Act (EPPA), signed into law in June 1988. The EPPA prohibits random polygraph testing by private-sector employers and the use of the polygraph for preemployment screening. However, the law exempts the U.S. government or any state or local government from its provisions and restrictions.

Some departments have switched from the polygraph to the voice stress analyzer because they find it to be easier to administer and less intrusive to the candidate. It operates under the similar theory that stress will be registered in an individual's voice.

© Photo by Mario Tama/Getty Images

Oral Interview

Oral boards can be used to examine a candidate's characteristics that might otherwise be difficult to assess, including poise, presence, and communication skills. The oral interview in the police selection process can be conducted by a board of ranking officers, a psychologist, the police chief, or an investigator. There often are multiple oral boards or interviews conducted by numerous representatives of the department. Stakeholders in the process may include representatives of other city, county, or state departments, such as personnel or community development, that may also actively participate on the board.

The oral interview may merely discuss the candidate's application and background or may be used to test the candidate's ability to deal with stressful situations. The candidate's demeanor while under pressure can be assessed. The oral board is a more structured and court-defensible process than an unstructured one-on-one oral interview. Generally, the oral board will consist of three to six members who develop specific, standardized questions. All candidates are asked the same questions and rated on their responses.

Background Investigation

In an effective **background investigation**, a candidate's past life, past employment, school records, medical records, relationships with neighbors and others, and military record are placed under a microscope. The investigator looks for evidence of incidents that might point to unfavorable traits or habits that could affect the individual's ability to be a good police officer. Such factors include poor work habits, dishonesty, use of alcohol or drugs, or a tendency to violence. Thorough background investigations by a hiring agency are critical to avoid hiring the wrong person for the job. Investigators are looking for officially documented incidents as well as unreported or undetected questionable activity and deception. Though the process may vary between agencies, a good, solid investigation will include the following:

- **Background interview.** The investigator advises the applicant about the process and meets the candidate for an initial impression.

- **Background investigation form.** Applicants are given a detailed form to fill out regarding their entire lives, including residences, schools, jobs, driving record, military experience, and criminal activity—detected and undetected.

- **Release of information form (waiver).** This form is signed by the applicant and notarized, allowing individuals to share information with the investigator.

- **Photos and fingerprints.** These are used for identification purposes and criminal records checks.

- **Educational records.** These are used to verify completion and degree and determine attendance and disciplinary issues.

- **Employment records.** These are used to verify or examine jobs, titles, absenteeism, job performance, honesty, initiative, and work relationships.

- **Credit check.** This check verifies past behavior of fulfilling obligations as well as determining the risk of being susceptible to graft. The credit check is also helpful for investigating the possibility of addictions.

- **Criminal history.** Every law enforcement agency that has jurisdiction over areas in which the candidate lived, went to school, or worked is contacted.

- **Driving record.** The applicant's record of accidents and traffic infractions is reviewed.

- **Military history.** This is used to determine any discipline issues while in the military, as well as the discharge type.

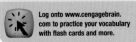

> **background investigation**
> The complete and thorough investigation of an applicant's past life, including education, employment, military service, driving record, criminal history, relationships, and character. This includes verification of all statements made by the applicant on the background form and the evaluation of detected and undetected behavior to make a determination if the candidate is the type of person suited to a career in law enforcement.

Log onto www.cengagebrain.com to practice your vocabulary with flash cards and more.

Oral interviews are an important step in the hiring process.

© Spencer Grant/Photo Edit

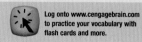
Psychological Appraisal

The preemployment psychological evaluation is an invaluable tool in the selection process and aids in assessing an individual's current level of functioning as a potential police officer. The psychological appraisal can assist in identifying individuals who may not adjust well to the law enforcement profession. This evaluation is typically done after a conditional offer of employment and evaluates many factors, including personality disorders that might affect an individual's functioning in a law enforcement agency and/or interacting with the public. This evaluation also considers issues such as substance abuse, self-management skills (anger management, team functioning abilities, impact of prior experiences and traumas), and intellectual abilities. (Holzman and Kirschner 85–87)

Medical Examination

Police departments generally want candidates who are in excellent health, without medical problems that could affect their ability to perform the police job. There are long-range and short-range reasons for using medical examinations in the police selection process. The short-range purpose is to ensure that candidates can do the police job. The long-range purpose is to ensure that candidates are not prone to injuries that may lead to early retirement and an economic loss to the department. Individuals who are unfit tend to have less energy and might not be able to work the sometimes-demanding hours and assignments required of a police officer. Drug testing is also part of the medical exam because departments want to ensure that candidates are drug-free.

LO6 Explain the Police Training Process, the Probationary Period, and In-Service Training

Once an individual has been chosen to be a member of a police department, he or she begins months of intensive training. Recruit training and in-service training programs vary from department to department, and, in reality, police training never ends. Veteran police officers continue their education and training in many areas to keep up with the latest trends in fighting crime as well as changing laws and procedures. Police officers also receive

© Joel Gordon

Education and training for police officers do not end after the academy. New officers rely on more experienced officers during the field training process and for mentoring once they are on their own on the streets.

training in preparation for serving in specialized units or managerial positions.

Recruit Training

Recruit training is the initial training a police officer receives. It teaches officers state laws and educates them in the goals, objectives, and procedures of their state and later their individual department. It provides them with the knowledge, skills, and abilities to do the job. Recruit training starts with the police academy, moves on to field training, and ends with the completion of the probationary period.

The Police Academy

The recruit **police academy** provides most of the average police officer's formal career training. It is often the beginning of the socialization process for the new officer. This will be discussed in a later chapter.

Most big cities in the United States have their own police academies. Although only 3 percent of departments operate their own academies, approximately 90 percent of the agencies serving populations greater than 250,000 do so. (Reaves, *State and Local Law Enforcement Training Academies*) Localities without their own academies often use a nearby state or regional police academy. Many academies are also based at colleges, community colleges, or technical schools or universities. Academies may be residential in nature, where the students go home only on weekends, or commuter facilities, where the students commute on a daily basis from their homes. The instructors may be full-time academy instructors or police officers on loan from their agencies to the academy for a predetermined amount of time.

During the last four decades, there has been a dramatic increase in the quality and quantity of police training, and departments are paying more attention to curriculum, training methods, and the development of training facilities. Perhaps the improvement in police training can be traced to the 1967 recommendation by the President's Commission on Law Enforcement and Administration of Justice that police departments provide "an absolute minimum of 400 hours of classroom work spread over a four- to six-month period so that it can be combined with carefully selected and supervised field training." The commission also recommended in-service training at least once a year, along with incentives for officers to continue their education. (President's Commission 112–113) The number of hours devoted to recruit training since then has increased dramatically.

Officers receive training in the use of Tasers while in the police academy.

AP Photo/The Crescent-News, Karen Sierer

Field Training

Field training is on-the-job training for recently graduated recruits from the police academy. The training is provided by specially selected patrol officers and is designed to supplement the theory taught at the police academy with the reality of the street. The length of field training can vary greatly among departments.

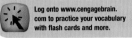

field training
An on-the-job training program that occurs after the police academy under the direction of an FTO.

field training officer (FTO)
An experienced officer who mentors and trains a new police officer.

Log onto www.cengagebrain. com to practice your vocabulary with flash cards and more.

The San Jose, California, police department created a field training program as early as 1972. The San Jose program consists of two phases of training: 16 weeks of regular police academy classroom training and 14 weeks of field training. During the field training phase, a recruit is assigned to three different **field training officers (FTOs)**. Recruits receive daily evaluation reports by their FTOs and weekly evaluation reports by the FTOs' supervisor. Many departments around the country use the San Jose program or a variation of it. However, in 1996 at a conference on field training held in Boulder, Colorado, the issue of reexamining the San Jose program was raised because trainers felt it hadn't kept up with changing times. Police chiefs were looking for ways to implement community policing into their agencies and felt the FTO program was a logical time to do so. After a study funded by the COPS office and conducted by the Police Executive Research Forum (PERF) and the Reno Police Department, the Police Training Officer (PTO) program, also known as the "Reno model," was born.

The objectives of the PTO program are to provide learning opportunities for the officer that meet or exceed the needs of both the police agency and the community, and the program was designed so that it could be modified to fit individual organizations. The program uses an adult learning and problem-based learning model that teaches transferable skills to the recruit. The Reno model is designed to produce graduates capable of providing customer-centered, responsible, community-focused police services. The Reno model is intended to be used as a variation of the San Jose model or in addition to it and would not benefit all departments; thus the San Jose model is still an important one in the field training process. (Hoover 10–17) The PTO program is growing in popularity because chiefs believe its emphasis on problem solving, self-directed learning, and lifelong learning will better prepare officers to adjust to the changing needs and demands of law enforcement in the future. (Pitts, Glensor, and Peak, 2007)

Firearms Training

In the 1960s, most police firearms training in the United States consisted of firing at bull's-eye targets. Later, training became more sophisticated, using more realistic silhouette targets shaped like armed adversaries. The FBI's Practical Pistol Course began to modernize firearms training; the course required qualification from different distances and different positions, such as standing, kneeling, and prone positions. As firearms training progressed, shoot/don't shoot training was introduced using **Hogan's Alley** courses. Today, many agencies have replaced Hogan's Alley programs with computer-controlled visual simulations. These simulations allow the officer to shoot at a target, and a laser indicates where the shot went. Some of these computer simulations allow the officer to interact verbally in the scenario, and the situation can be altered accordingly. These simulations can use local schools, businesses, and streets in the scenarios, allow for more than one officer to participate, and even shoot rubber bullets back at the officers. These simulations provide enlightening and realistic training for officers new to the position as well as for those that have been working the street for some time.

In-Service, Management, and Specialized Training

Police training generally does not end at the recruit level. In many departments, **in-service training** is used to regularly update the skills and knowledge base of veteran officers. Because laws and developments in policing are constantly changing, officers need to be kept up to date. Many states have chosen to mandate a required number of in-service training hours for officers to maintain their state certification. Primarily, this was done as a way to ensure departments were keeping their officers updated on the latest laws and procedures and to ensure some degree of uniformity from jurisdiction to jurisdiction.

Police officers receive training in the use of their firearms as well as in their less-than-lethal tools during the academy and throughout their career.

© Sundlof-Edco/Alamy

Police training does not end at the recruit level. It is used to update the skills and knowledge base of veteran officers throughout their law enforcement careers.

In addition to in-service training, many departments use management training programs to teach supervisory and management skills to newly promoted supervisors and managers. Many departments also offer specialized training programs for officers assigned to new duties. Recently, many of these training opportunities have been offered online. Training units can be developed that can be worked around an officer's schedule. They can be anywhere from 10-minute training segments to use during or after roll call or several hours long for a more in-depth discussion of a topic. This facilitates the ability of the officer to obtain desired training while minimizing the time away from work.

Probationary Period

A **probationary period** is the period of time that a department has to evaluate a new officer's ability to perform his or her job effectively. Generally, a probationary officer can be dismissed at will without proof of specific violations of law or department regulations. Once officers are off probation, civil service rules often make it very difficult to dismiss them. Probationary periods can last anywhere from 6 months to 3 years. Today, the average probationary period ranges from 12 to 18 months. It has lengthened in recent years because of the increased length of time devoted to academy training and field training. Agencies want to have enough time to evaluate officers' performance while they are performing on the street on their own.

probationary period
The period in the early part of an officer's career in which the officer can be dismissed if not performing to the department's standards.

Log onto www.cengagebrain. com to practice your vocabulary with flash cards and more.

 Log onto www.cengagebrain.com for additional resources including videos, flash cards, games, self-quizzing, review exercises, web exercises, learning checks, and more.

PART 2 POLICE

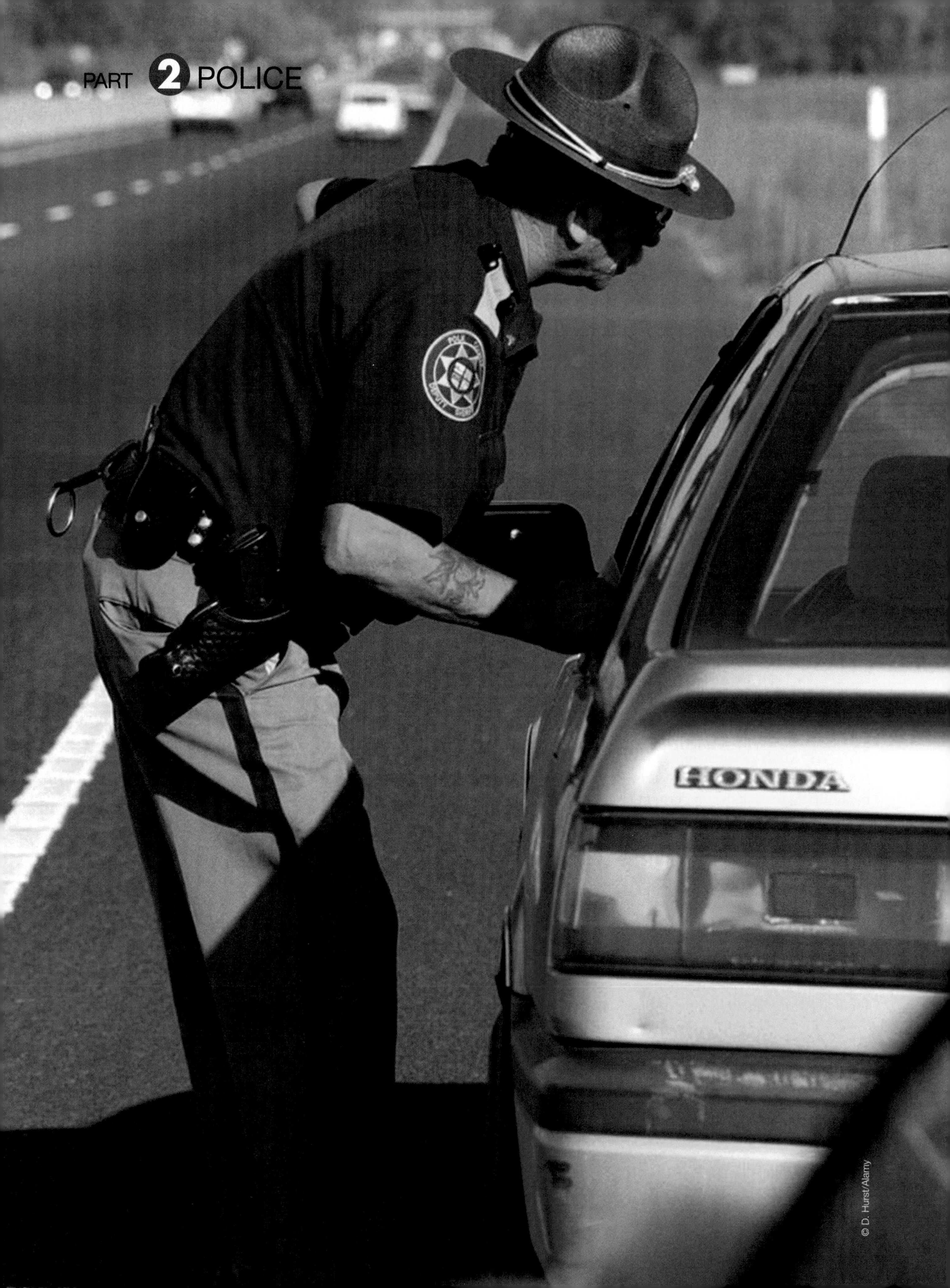

5

The Police Role and Police Discretion

After studying this chapter, the student should be able to:

LO1 Define the police role and the ambiguity of the police role

LO2 Discuss the goals and objectives of policing

LO3 Explain police operational styles

LO4 Discuss police discretion

LO5 Discuss police discretion and police shootings and the use of deadly force

LO1 Define the Police Role and the Ambiguity of the Police Role

The role of the police and the exercise of police discretion are among the most important issues in policing.

What is the **police role**? Who are the police in the United States? What do they do? How do they do what they do? What should they do? These are very difficult questions to answer. The scholar Herman Goldstein warns, "Anyone attempting to construct a workable definition of the police role will typically come away with old images shattered and a newfound appreciation for the intricacies of police work." (Goldstein, *Policing a Free Society* p. 21)

Two major views of the role of the police exist:

- The police are crime-fighters concerned with law enforcement (crime-fighting).
- The police are order maintainers concerned with keeping the peace and providing social services to the community (**order maintenance**).

> **police role**
> The concept of "what do the police do."
>
> **order maintenance**
> Major view of the role of the police that emphasizes keeping the peace and providing social services.

Log onto www.cengagebrain.com to practice your vocabulary with flash cards and more.

© Valentina Cavallini/www.Shutterstock.com

Crime-Fighting Role

Movies and television shows about the police emphasize the police **crime-fighting role**. If we believe these stories, the police engage daily in numerous gunfights, car chases, and acts of violence, and they arrest numerous people every day. Fictional books about police work also emphasize the crime-fighting role. Even the news media emphasize this role; television news shows and newspaper headlines dramatize exciting arrests and actions by the police.

The police themselves also emphasize their role as crime-fighters and deemphasize their jobs as peacekeepers and social service providers. As George L. Kirkham, a former professor turned police officer, states,

> The police have historically overemphasized their role as crime fighters and played down their more common work as keepers of the peace and providers of social services, simply because our society proffers rewards for the former (crime fighting) but cares little for the latter (peace-keeping and providing services). The public accords considerable recognition and esteem to the patrol officer who becomes involved in a shoot-out with an armed robber or who chases and apprehends a rapist, and therefore so do the officer's peers and superiors. (Kirkham and Wollan 336)

At first glance, there appears to be some truth to the belief that police are primarily crime-fighters. Statistics for the latest reporting year reveal that the U.S. police made more than 13.7 million arrests for all criminal infractions, excluding traffic violations. (FBI, *Uniform Crime Reports*, 2010)

An analysis of the arrests, however, shows a different perspective. About 2.31 million of the arrests were for the FBI's Index or Part I crimes. Of these arrests, about 582,000 were for violent crimes (murder, forcible rape, robbery, and aggravated assault), and about 1.73 million of the arrests were for property crimes (burglary, larceny/theft, motor vehicle theft, and arson). The following accounted for the other 11.38 million arrests:

- Driving under the influence (DUI) or driving while intoxicated (DWI)—about 1.4 million arrests.
- Drug abuse violations—about 1.7 million arrests.
- Misdemeanor assaults—about 1.3 million arrests.
- Liquor law violations, drunkenness, disorderly conduct, vagrancy, and loitering—about 1.97 million arrests.
- A large variety of lesser offenses, excluding traffic offenses (see Table 5.1).

From the analyses of the arrests made by police, we can see that the vast majority of the arrests are not serious Index crimes but, rather, what we might call crimes of disorder or actions that annoy citizens and negatively affect their quality of life (for example, offenses involving drugs and alcohol). Even the vast majority of the crime-fighting the police do is related to order maintenance rather than serious crime.

Furthermore, the 2007 report *Contacts between Police and the Public, 2005*, revealed that approximately 43.5 million citizens had contacts with the police during the previous reporting year. Most of the contacts involved motor vehicle or traffic-related issues. Only about 1.6 percent of all contacts involved the use of or threat of force by the police. (Durose, Smith, and Langan 1)

Order Maintenance Role

If police are not primarily crime-fighters, then what are they? In an effort to determine the proper role of the police, researchers have conducted numerous studies to determine what it is that police do and why people call on their services. Researchers have reported that the ordinary work routines of police officers include relatively little law enforcement and comprise a large variety of other activities that have come to be known as peacekeeping and order maintenance.

Ambiguity of the Police Role

The police role is extremely diverse, **ambiguous**, and dynamic. Egon Bittner has stated that from its earliest origins, police work has been a "tainted" occupation: "The taint

Deputy sheriffs making an arrest.

© iStockphoto/WH1600

TABLE 5.1 Arrests in the United States, by Crime Committed, 2009

Total*	**13,687,241**
Part 1 Crimes	
Murder and non-negligent manslaughter	12,481
Forcible rape	21,407
Robbery	126,725
Aggravated assault	421,215
Burglary	299,351
Larceny-theft	1,334,933
Motor vehicle theft	81,797
Arson	12,204
Violent crime arrests**	581,765
Property crime arrests***	1,728,285
Other assaults	1,319,458
Forgery and counterfeiting	85,844
Fraud	210,255
Embezzlement	17,920
Stolen property: buying, receiving, possessing	105,303
Vandalism	270,439
Weapons: carrying, possessing, etc.	166,334
Prostitution and commercialized vice	71,355
Sex offenses (except forcible rape and prostitution)	77,326
Drug abuse violations	1,663,582
Gambling	10,360
Offenses against the family and children	114,564
Driving under the influence	1,440,409
Liquor laws	570,333
Drunkenness	594,300
Disorderly conduct	655,322
Vagrancy	33,388
All other offenses	3,764,672
Suspicion	1,975
Curfew and loitering law violations	112,593
Runaways	93,434

* Does not include suspicion. Because of rounding, the figures may not add to total.

** Murder, forcible rape, robbery, and aggravated assault.

*** Burglary, larceny-theft, motor vehicle theft, and arson.

SOURCE: Federal Bureau of Investigation. *Uniform Crime Reports, 2009* March 8, 2010, p. 8. http://www.fbi.com.

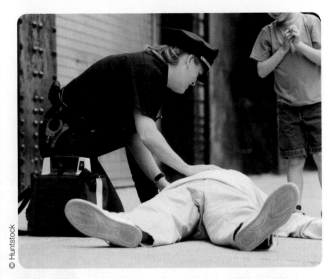

Police officer administering first aid to a fallen man.

that attaches to police work refers to the fact that policemen are viewed as the fire it takes to fight fire, that in the natural course of their duties they inflict harm, albeit deserved, and that their very existence attests that the nobler aspirations of mankind do not contain the means necessary to insure survival." (Bittner 8)

Carl B. Klockars, in *Idea of Police*, broadly defines the basic function of the police as dealing with all those problems that may require the use of coercive force. He emphasizes that democratic societies give the police the right to use morally dangerous, dirty, and illegal means to achieve good ends because in most cases, noble institutions do not contain the means to ensure their own survival. (Klockars)

We must remember that England's Sir Robert Peel, who arranged for the organization of the first paid, full-time, uniformed police department, conceived of the police role as a conspicuous community-oriented patrol designed more for prevention and deterrence than for enforcement. Peel designed the police to be an alternative to the repression of crime and disorder that could have been achieved through military might and severe legal sanctions.

One way of defining the police role may be to say that it is whatever the community expects the police to be. However, we must remember that most communities consist of many diverse groups with different goals and interests. One group in the community may expect the police to do something entirely different from what another group expects them to do. For example, older people in a community or store owners may want the police to hassle teenagers hanging out on the street, yet the teenagers, for their part, may feel that if the police do hassle them, the officers are being abusive. Parents in a community may want the police to search and arrest drug dealers and drug users, yet not want the police to search their own children.

In these and many other ways, the police are often in a no-win situation.

Robert Sheehan and Gary W. Cordner, using the work of previous scholars, offer the following synopsis of the police role:

1. The core of the police role involves law enforcement and the use of coercive force.

2. The primary skill of policing involves effectively handling problem situations while avoiding the use of force.

3. Skillful police officers avoid the use of force primarily through effective, creative communication. (Sheehan and Cordner 62)

In summing up the police role, we might agree with Joseph J. Senna and Larry J. Siegel, who say that

the police role has become that of a social handywoman or handyman called to handle social problems that citizens wish would simply go away. (Siegel and Senna, 2005)

The Police Role in the Aftermath of 9/11

The ambiguous role of the police has been further complicated by the September 11, 2001, terrorist attacks against the United States. Since 9/11, many have seen the police as the frontline of homeland defense against further terrorist attacks, and many police departments and officers are viewing themselves similarly. Police departments have responded by forming specialized, military-like antiterrorist units that appear in public as a strong deterrent force against would-be

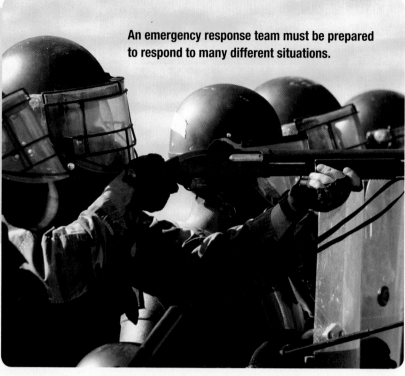

An emergency response team must be prepared to respond to many different situations.

terrorists. This has concentrated attention on the law enforcement role of the police.

The order maintenance role and social service role of the police have also been reemphasized because the police are the first responders to all emergencies and unusual occurrences in the nation. They are tasked with the many duties this entails, including crowd control, emergency medical response and treatment, and maintenance of public order in often catastrophic conditions.

LO2 Discuss the Goals and Objectives of Policing

Much research has gone into determining the proper goals and objectives of a police department. This topic can be discussed more easily by thinking in terms of primary and secondary goals and objectives.

Primary Goals and Objectives

The two primary goals and objectives of police departments, according to Sheehan and Cordner, are maintaining order and protecting life and property. (Sheehan and Cordner 16–21) These are among the most basic roles of government, and government hires the police to perform these services. To achieve these goals, the police perform a myriad of duties.

Siegel and Senna say that the police role has become that of a social handywoman or handyman.

PRIMARY GOALS

1. Maintaining order
2. Protecting life and property

Secondary Goals and Objectives

Sheehan and Cordner also list six secondary goals and objectives (Sheehan and Cordner 16–21) toward which police resources and activities are used to meet the two primary objectives:

SECONDARY GOALS

1. Preventing crime
2. Arresting and prosecuting offenders
3. Recovering stolen and missing property
4. Assisting the sick and injured
5. Enforcing noncriminal regulations
6. Delivering services not available elsewhere in the community

The police attempt to prevent crime by trying to create a sense of **omnipresence** (the police are always there) through routine patrol, responding to calls by citizens to deal with problems that may cause crime, and establishing and participating in police–citizen partnerships designed to prevent crime. Arresting offenders and assisting prosecutors in bringing charges against defendants is one of the primary methods used by the police to maintain order and protect life and property.

When people find property on the street, they often bring it to a police officer or to a police station. The police then attempt to find the owner. If that is not possible, they store the property in case the rightful owner comes in to claim it. When people lose property, they generally go to the nearest police station in the hopes that someone has turned it in. Besides all of their other duties, then, the police serve as society's foremost lost and found department.

Because they are available 24/7 and because they are highly mobile, the police generally are the closest government agency for any problem. In many jurisdictions, the police are called to emergency cases of sickness and injury to assess the situation before an ambulance is dispatched, or they are called to assist ambulance, paramedical, or other emergency response personnel.

In the absence of other regulatory personnel or during the times these personnel are not available, the police enforce numerous noncriminal regulations, including traffic and parking regulations, liquor law regulations, and many others. The police are generally the only government officials available every day, around the clock. When government offices close, the police become roving representatives of the government who assist people with problems no one else is available to handle. When the lights go off in an apartment building, people call the police. When a water main breaks, people call the police. When your neighbor's dog barks all night and keeps you awake, who do you generally call? The police, because let's face it, who else can you call at 3:00 in the morning? The police respond and take whatever action they can to ameliorate problems and to deal with emergencies. They direct traffic, evacuate residents, and decide who to call for assistance.

PRIMARY GOALS
✓ Maintaining order
✓ Protecting life and property

omnipresence
A concept that suggests that the police are always present or always seem to be present.

police operational styles
Styles adopted by police officers as a way of thinking about the role of the police and law in society.

Log onto www.cengagebrain.com to practice your vocabulary with flash cards and more.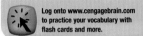

An officer responds to a call by neighbors about children left at home alone. Protecting life is one of the primary goals of police departments.

© Joel Gordon

LO3 Explain Police Operational Styles

People who research the police write about **police operational styles**—styles adopted by police officers as a way of thinking about the role of the police and law in society and how they should perform their jobs.

The concept of operational styles is useful in analyzing the police role and police behavior. However, no officer conforms solely to one of these styles to the exclusion of the others. Many officers show characteristics of several of these styles. Siegel and Senna tell us that several studies have attempted to define and classify police operational styles into behavioral clusters. These classifications or typologies attempt to categorize officers by groups, each of which has a unique approach to police work. They report that the purpose of these classifications is to demonstrate that the police are not a cohesive, homogeneous group, but rather individuals with differing approaches to their work. (Siegel and Senna 211) Siegel and Senna present four basic styles of policing or typologies.

Siegel and Senna's Styles

Crime fighters. Investigate serious crimes and apprehend criminals.

Social agents. Perform a wide range of activities without regard for their connection to law enforcement.

Law enforcers. Enforce the law "by the book."

Watchmen. Maintain public order.

John J. Broderick, in his *Police in a Time of Change*, also presents four distinct police operational styles: (Broderick)

Broderick's Styles

Enforcers. Their major role is maintaining order on their beat, keeping society safe, and protecting society by arresting criminals.

Idealists. Similar to enforcers, yet they place a higher value on individual rights and the adherence to due process as required by the U.S. Constitution.

Realists. Relatively low emphasis on both social

order and individual rights; they concentrate their efforts on the concept of police loyalty and the mutual support of their fellow officers.

Optimists. Place a relatively high value on individual rights and see their job as people oriented, rather than crime oriented.

In his seminal work *Varieties of Police Behavior: The Management of Law and Order in Eight Communities*, Wilson describes three distinct styles of policing that a police department can deploy in maintaining order and responding to less serious violations of law: the watchman style, the legalistic style, and the service style. (Within each style, the police treat serious felonies similarly.) (Wilson) He found that the political culture of a city, which reflects the socioeconomic characteristics of the city and its organization of government, exerts a major influence on the style of policing exercised by the police.

Wilson's Styles

Watchman style. Primarily concerned with order maintenance—maintaining order and controlling illegal and disruptive behavior. Officers in a watchman-style department exercise a great deal of discretion and ignore many minor violations, especially those involving juveniles and traffic. Officers use persuasion and threats, or even "hassle" or "rough up" disruptive people, instead of making formal arrests. This style, Wilson says, is generally found in working-class communities with partisan mayor–city council forms of government.

Legalistic style. Enforce the letter of the law strictly by issuing many citations and making many misdemeanor arrests. Officers proceed vigorously against illegal enterprises. This style of enforcement, Wilson says, occurs in reform administrations' government styles. Furthermore, this style often occurs in the aftermath of a scandal in a watchman type of department that results in the hiring of a "reform" police chief.

Service style. Emphasis on serving the needs of the community. The officers see themselves more as helpers than as soldiers in a war against crime. The service style, Wilson says, is generally found in more affluent suburban areas.

Jim Brackett of Nashua, New Hampshire, a United Nations police officer who patrols in the town of Kosovska Mitrovica, gives a lollipop to a young child.

LO4 Discuss Police Discretion

The use of discretion is one of the major challenges facing U.S. police today. The following sections will discuss the meaning of police discretion, how and why it is exercised, what factors influence discretion, and how it can be controlled.

What Is Discretion?

Discretion means the availability of a choice of options or actions one can take in a situation. We all exercise discretion many times every day in our lives. At a restaurant, we have discretion in selecting a steak dinner or a fish dinner. At the video store, we have discretion in picking a mystery or a comedy to view. Discretion involves making a judgment and a decision. It involves selecting one option from a group of options.

The criminal justice system involves a tremendous amount of discretion. A judge exercises discretion in sentencing. He or she can sentence a defendant to a prison term or to probation. A judge can release a defendant on bail or order the defendant incarcerated until trial. Prosecutors exercise discretion: they can reduce charges against a defendant or drop the charges entirely. Parole boards exercise discretion: they can parole a person from prison or order him or her to serve the complete sentence. The entire criminal justice system is based on the concept of discretion.

Why is there so much discretion in the U.S. system of criminal justice? In our system, we tend to treat people as individuals. One person who commits a robbery is not the same as another person who commits a robbery. Our system also takes into account why the person committed the crime and how he or she committed it. Were there any mitigating or aggravating circumstances? The U.S. system is thus interested in the spirit of the law, in addition to the letter of the law.

When a judge, a prosecutor, or a parole board member exercises discretion, each generally has sufficient time and data necessary to make a careful, reasoned decision. The judge can read the presentence report prepared by the probation department or consult with the probation department staff member preparing the report. The judge can also consult with the district attorney or the defense attorney. The prosecutor and the parole board member also have sufficient data and time in which to decide what action to take in a case.

However, most crucial decisions made in the criminal justice system do not take place as described in the previous paragraph. The most important decisions do not take place within an ornately decorated courtroom or a wood-paneled conference room. Rather, they take place on the streets. They take place at any time of the day or night, and generally without the opportunity for the decision makers to consult with others or to carefully consider all the facts. Indeed, these split-second decisions are often based on little information. Rather, they take place at the very lowest level in the criminal justice system, on the streets. Nevertheless, the police officer, generally the first decision maker in the U.S. criminal justice system, is often the most important.

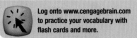

How Is Discretion Exercised?

The police exercise discretion to perform the following crucial actions:

- To arrest
- To stop, question, or frisk
- To use physical force
- To use deadly force
- To write traffic summonses
- To use certain enforcement tactics (harassment, moving loiterers, warnings, and so on)
- To take a report on a crime
- To investigate a crime

Why Is Discretion Exercised?

Discretion is an extremely necessary part of police work. Sheehan and Cordner tell us that the police exercise discretion for seven reasons:

A judge exercises discretion in sentencing.

© Guy Call/Corbis RF/Jupiter Images

A police officer exercises discretion when making a traffic stop.

1. If the police attempted to enforce all the laws all the time, they would be in the station house or court all the time and would not be on the street maintaining order and protecting life and property.

2. Because of political realities, legislators pass some laws that they do not intend to have strictly enforced all the time.

3. Lawmakers pass some laws that are vague and ill-defined, making it necessary for the police to interpret these laws and decide when to apply them.

4. Most violations of the law are minor (for example, traffic violations) and do not require full enforcement.

5. The complete enforcement of all the laws all the time would alienate the public from the police and the entire criminal justice system.

6. The full enforcement of all the laws would overwhelm the courts, jails, and prisons.

7. The police have so many duties to perform and such limited resources that good judgment must be exercised in when, where, and how they enforce the law. (Sheehan and Cordner 52–53)

What Factors Influence Discretion?

We know that officers practice discretion, and we know that discretion is necessary. Are there factors that cause the police to exercise discretion in a certain way? Scholars have been studying this issue for quite a while.

Herbert Jacob wrote that four major factors influence police officers in determining the exercise of discretion:

1. *Characteristics of the crime.* A serious crime leaves the police less freedom or ability to ignore it or exercise discretion regarding it.

2. *Relationship between the alleged criminal and the victim.* Generally, the police tend to avoid making arrests when a perpetrator and a victim have a close relationship. In recent years, however, many departments have limited discretion in domestic violence or family assault cases and have adopted pro-arrest policies.

3. *Relationship between police and the criminal or victim.* Generally, a respectful, mannerly complainant is taken more seriously and treated better by the police than an antagonistic one. In the same way, a violator who acts respectfully to the police is also less likely to be arrested than an antagonistic one.

4. *Department policies.* The preferences of the police chief and city administration, as expressed in department policy, generally influence the actions of the officer. (Jacob 27)

Research has identified other specific factors that could possibly influence police discretion to arrest, including the subject's offense, attitude, race, socioeconomic status, or gender; the officer's race; and police peer-group pressure.

Studies of police discretion have shown that the most significant factor in the decision to arrest is the seriousness of the offense committed. This factor is supplemented by other information, such as the offender's current mental state, the offender's past criminal record (when known to the arresting officer), whether weapons were involved, the availability of the complainant, and the relative danger to the officer involved. (Siegel, Sullivan, and Greene 132–142)

How Can Discretion Be Controlled?

In recent years, much attention has been given to the need to prepare police for the appropriate use of discretion. Most experts believe that discretion itself is not bad, and that the real problem is uncontrolled or unregulated discretion. These experts feel that discretion cannot and should not be abolished but believe that police departments should attempt to control or regulate it.

Most researchers believe that discretion should be narrowed to the point where all officers in the same agency deal with similar issues in similar ways. They feel there should be limits on discretion that reflect the objectives, priorities, and operating philosophy of the department, and they further believe that these limits should be sufficiently specific to enable an officer to make judgments in a wide variety of unpredictable circumstances in a proper, unbiased manner that will achieve a reasonable degree of uniformity in handling similar incidents in the community.

Police officers must be sensitive and tactful when dealing with victims of domestic violence.

One approach to managing police behavior involves requiring obedience to a formal set of policies or guidelines that can ensure the just administration of the law. Many police departments established written policies regarding the use of deadly force as far back as the early 1970s, even before the U.S. Supreme Court decision in *Tennessee v. Garner*, which will be discussed later in this chapter. These policies dramatically reduced the number of shootings of civilians by the police and reduced the number of officers shot by civilians. Since the 1980s, many departments have established formal procedures for dealing with emotionally disturbed persons, police pursuits, and other critical issues discussed in this text.

One way of controlling discretion, particularly improper application of discretion, is the establishment of employee early warning systems. These automated systems detect significant events in an officer's statistics, such as a high number of use of force incidents, vehicle pursuits, sick days, involvement in significant events, or low numbers of arrests or citizen contacts. These systems provide a warning to managers and supervisors, who can then investigate any irregular patterns.

Another method of controlling policing discretion is the use of police internal control mechanisms, such as

continual review of officers' actions by police supervisors, managers, and internal affairs and citizen review investigators. Other external methods of controlling policing discretion include local legislatures, independent citizen review boards, and the courts, through their process of judicial review.

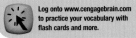

Most importantly, however, Wilson tells us that controlling discretion involves more than just establishing policies and ensuring that they are obeyed. Managing discretion involves an effort by management to instill a proper value system in officers. According to Wilson, controlling discretion "depends only partly on sanctions and inducements; it also requires instilling in them a shared outlook or ethos that provides for them a common definition of the situations they are likely to encounter and that to the outsider gives to the organization its distinctive character or 'feel.'" (Wilson 33)

LO5 Discuss Police Discretion and Police Shootings and the Use of Deadly Force

Police shootings or the use of **deadly force** by the police might be the ultimate use of discretion. Sometimes, officers are forced into making a split-second decision about whether to use deadly force. If they hesitate, they run the risk of being killed or seriously injured themselves, or allowing an innocent citizen to be killed or seriously injured. If their split-second decision is later found to be wrong and it is determined that they misused their discretion, they face public and legal criticism and perhaps arrest itself. They are also criticized by the press and the community. Worse still is that they may have to live with this mistaken decision for the rest of their lives. Clearly, being a police officer and using necessary discretion is not an easy job.

Police Use of Force

In 2007, the Bureau of Justice Statistics, in its *Contacts between Police and the Public, 2005*, which reported on 43.5 million contacts between police and citizens, noted that only about 1.6 percent of all of the contacts involved the police use or threat of force. About 14.8 percent of those who experienced force were injured as a result of the police action. About 86.9 percent of the persons who experienced the threat or use of force felt that the police had acted improperly, and about 16.8 percent of the persons involved in a police force incident reported that they

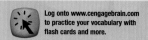
had done something to provoke the officer to use force, such as threatening the officer or resisting arrest. (Durose, Smith, and Langan 8–9)

However, statistics clearly indicate that police officers do not overuse force. In a report covering research in six law enforcement agencies, it was disclosed that officers used some physical force in about 17 percent of the adult custody arrests they made, and that suspects used some physical force in about 12 percent of their arrests. The researchers also found that the officers' use of force was low—weapons were used in only 2.1 percent of all arrests (the weapon most often used was pepper spray). (Garner and Maxwell 1)

Number of Citizens Shot by the Police

Historically, the shooting of a citizen by the police has been a major problem facing the police. Police shootings have had a serious negative impact on police–community relations. Numerous incidents of civil unrest have followed police shootings of civilians.

According to a National Institute of Justice report, during the three years from 2003 to 2005, police justifiably killed an average of 365 persons a year, 96 percent by firearms. Three-quarters of the justifiable homicides by officers involved arrests for violent crimes. In 80 percent of these cases, the deceased reportedly used a weapon to threaten or assault the arresting officers, and in 17 percent of the cases, the decedent grabbed, hit, or fought with the

A police officer fires pepper spray at demonstrators during a rally. A research study found that weapons were used in only 2.1 percent of all arrests, and the weapon most often used was pepper spray.

arresting officers. Ninety-seven percent of the decedents were male, and 30 percent were black. (Mumola 1–2) In 2006, police justifiably killed 376 individuals. (FBI, *Uniform Crime Reports*, 2007)

Do Police Discriminate with Their Trigger Fingers?

Numerous studies have been conducted to determine if there is, in fact, racial discrimination in the police use of deadly force. If one considers only total numbers, the overwhelming difference between the percentage of African Americans shot and the percentage of whites shot could lead one to conclude that discrimination does indeed exist. However, this percentage is similar to that of African Americans (40 percent) arrested by police for violent crime. It was also reported that the rate at which African Americans were fatally shot by the police declined from 1976 to 1998, whereas the rate for whites killed has remained steady. (Brown and Langan 1)

There is another side, however, to the analysis of race and police shootings. Some studies indicate that people who engage in violent crime or who engage the police in violent confrontations are much more likely to be the victims of police shootings.

Departure from the "Fleeing Felon" Rule

Before the great amount of attention given to police shootings in the wake of the civil disorders of the 1960s, most U.S. police departments operated under the common-law **fleeing felon doctrine**, which held that law enforcement officers could, if necessary, use deadly force to apprehend any fleeing felony suspect. This doctrine evolved from the common-law tradition of medieval England, when all felonies were capital offenses (liable for the death penalty).

Because there was very little official law enforcement in those days, and because very few escaping felons were apprehended, the law allowed a person who had committed a felony to be killed while fleeing the scene.

The fleeing felon rule, like most of England's common law, came to the United States. Today, however, there is little need for the fleeing felon rule in the United States because we have sufficient armed police and modern communications systems to aid in the apprehension of fleeing felons. Also, the legality and morality of the fleeing felon rule comes into question because of the U.S. legal concept of presumption of innocence. Most U.S. states, however, maintained the fleeing felon rule well into the 1960s and 1970s. In 1985, the fleeing felon rule was declared unconstitutional by the

Photo by Keith Bedford/Bloomberg via Getty Images

U.S. Supreme Court in the landmark case *Tennessee v. Garner*. (*Tennessee v. Garner* 1985)

Before the *Garner* case, and subsequent to the urban riots of the 1960s, many states replaced the fleeing felon rule with new state laws, internal rules of police departments, and court decisions. During the 1970s, many police departments developed an alternative to the fleeing felon doctrine based in part on recommendations by the American Law Institute and the Police Foundation. This rule used the **defense of life standard**, which allows a police officer to use deadly force against people who were using deadly force against him or her or another person, as well as in certain violent felony situations. The replacement of the common-law fleeing felon rule by the defense of life standard changed the incidence of police shootings.

Realizing how important this issue is and the need for guidance for officers, 95 percent of all local police departments and 97 percent of all sheriff's offices have a written policy on the use of deadly force. (Hickman and Reaves, *Local Police Departments, 2003* p. iv; Hickman and Reaves, *Sheriff's Offices, 2003* p. iv)

Less-than-Lethal Force

In 2005, the U.S. Government Accountability Office, in a report to the U.S. Congress, reported that the growing popularity of **less-than-lethal weapons** (LTLW) by police officers in the United States virtually ensured their increased use in the law enforcement community. (U.S. Government Accountability Office, 1)

In the mid-nineteenth century, police officers in New York and Boston relied on less-than-lethal weapons, mostly wooden clubs. By the late 1800s, police departments began issuing firearms in response to better-armed criminals. Today, many law enforcement agencies are again stressing the use of less-than-lethal weapons, but they are using devices that are decidedly more high-tech than their nineteenth-century counterparts. (Bulman, "Police Use of Force" p. 4)

In 2006, the Department of Justice reported that 97 percent of all local departments and 89 percent of

> Some studies indicate that people who engage in violent crime or who engage the police in violent confrontations are much more likely to be the victims of police shootings.

© CLKTTR37/www.Shutterstock.com

all sheriff's departments had a policy regarding nonlethal force, and almost all departments authorized the use of one or more nonlethal weapons. (Reaves, *Local Police Departments, 2007* p. 17; Hickman and Reaves, *Sheriff's Offices, 2003* p. iv)

- 97 percent of local police departments and 96 percent of sheriff's offices authorized the use of chemical sprays.

- 93 percent of local police departments and 92 percent of sheriff's offices authorized the use of batons of some type.

- 60 percent of local police departments and 30 percent of sheriff's offices authorized electronic devices (stun guns or Tasers) of some type.

- 13 percent of local police departments and 11 percent of sheriff's offices authorized choke holds, carotid holds, or neck restraints.

Departments have turned to some of these less-than-lethal weapons in an effort to give officers options other than deadly force when faced with a combative subject. Various forms of chemical sprays have been in the police arsenal for years. Controlled electronic devices (CEDs) have also given officers an alternative to deadly force by allowing a subject to be temporarily subdued without a gun. There have been several deaths in Taser or stun-gun situations, though none have been blamed on the Taser itself. Most of the time, drugs were found to be the primary cause of

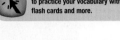

Tennessee v. Garner
U.S. Supreme Court case that ended the use of the fleeing felon rule.

defense of life standard
Doctrine allowing police officers to use deadly force against individuals using deadly force against an officer or others.

less-than-lethal weapons
Innovative alternatives to traditional firearms, such as batons, bodily force techniques, chemical irritant sprays, and Tasers or stun guns.

Log onto www.cengagebrain.com to practice your vocabulary with flash cards and more.

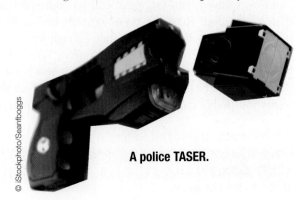

© iStockphoto/Seanfboggs

A police TASER.

A police officer knocking a suspect off his feet using a new weapon. The weapon's effect is causing the fence behind him to appear distorted.

© Pascal Goetgheluck/Photo Researchers, Inc.

death. Supporters of these weapons believe that the use of the Taser or stun gun has saved many lives.

Choke holds, carotid holds, and neck restraints became a source of controversy after some deaths were associated with their use. Many departments have removed this option from their policies. Some also consider the use of K-9s to be a less-than-lethal force, but there is a concern by some that they are utilized in a biased manner. Twenty-nine percent of local departments use dogs for law enforcement purposes; the bigger the department, the more likely it is to use dogs, with 94 percent of departments that serve over 100,000 people using dogs. Fifty-five percent of sheriff's offices use canines. (Hickman and Reaves, *Local Police Departments*, 2003 p. iv; Hickman and Reaves, *Sheriff's Offices*, 2003 p. iv)

Many less-than-lethal weapons, including the baton, oleoresin capsicum (OC), and the Taser or stun gun, are not control and restraint techniques; for example, a person sprayed with OC must still be controlled and then handcuffed. However, these weapons are useful in temporarily distracting a subject long enough for control and handcuffing to be achieved. Stun guns or Tasers shoot two barbs that are attached to wires that reach up to 35 feet. The barbs deliver a five-second electrical jolt that seizes the body's major muscle groups and temporarily

incapacitates the person, allowing the police to approach a dangerous suspect more closely.

In June 2008, the National Institute of Justice released their interim report, *Study of Deaths Following Electro Muscular Disruption*, which concluded that:

> Although exposure to CED [Controlled Electronic Devices] is not risk free, there is no conclusive medical evidence within the state of current research that indicates a high risk of serious injury or death from the direct effects of CED exposure. Field experience with CED use indicates that exposure is safe in the vast majority of cases. Therefore, law enforcement need not refrain from deploying CEDs, provided the devices are used in accordance with accepted national guidelines. (National Institute of Justice 3)

In response to the NIJ report, Philip Bulman concluded that although both pepper spray and CEDs cause pain, they reduce injuries; and according to current medical research, death or serious harm associated with their use is rare. In that sense, both are safe and similarly effective at reducing injury to suspects and officers alike. (Bulman, "Police Use of Force" pp. 5, 8)

 Log onto www.cengagebrain.com for additional resources including videos, flash cards, games, self-quizzing, review exercises, web exercises, learning checks, and more.

USE THE TOOLS.

- Rip out the Review Cards in the back of your book to study.

Or Visit CourseMate for:

- Full, interactive eBook (search, highlight, take notes)
- Review Flashcards (Print or Online) to master key terms
- Test yourself with Auto-Graded Quizzes
- Bring concepts to life with Games, Videos, and Animations!

Go to CourseMate for **POLICE2** to begin using these tools. Access at **www.cengagebrain.com**.

Complete the Speak Up survey in CourseMate at www.cengagebrain.com

f Follow us at **www.facebook.com/4ltrpress**

6

Police Culture, Personality, and Police Stress

After studying this chapter, the student should be able to:

LO1 Define the police culture or subculture and the police personality

LO2 Explain police stress

LO3 Discuss police suicide

LO4 Discuss police danger

LO1 Define the Police Culture or Subculture and the Police Personality

On September 11, 2001, police officers throughout New York City, many responding while off-duty, raced through the streets to respond to a 911 call reporting that a plane had crashed into New York City's World Trade Center. The rest is history. Many rushed into the building to help citizens get out. Thirty-seven Port Authority of New York/New Jersey police officers, 23 New York City police officers, and 3 New York court officers lost their lives in their valiant efforts to protect and serve. In the 1995 bombing of the Federal Building in Oklahoma City, officers rushed courageously into the building to help others get out. In fact, every day, in cities and towns all over the United States, law enforcement officers put their own safety and lives at risk in order to protect and serve. Are these brave officers displaying the traits of the police culture?

Many experts and researchers studying the police write about such concepts as a distinct police culture or subculture and a distinct police personality. Are the police different from most other people? Much research indicates that they are.

Numerous academic studies have indicated that the nature of policing and the experiences officers go through on the job cause them to band together into their own subculture, which many researchers call the police culture or police subculture. For example, if someone who was not a police officer walked into a bar at 1:00 AM and overheard a group of men and women engaged in an animated conversation using such words as *collars, mopes, skells, perps, vics, edps,* and *shoeflies,* he or she would have great difficulty understanding. However, to the off-duty police officers having a few drinks and talking about their previous tours of duty, each word has a precise meaning.

The word *culture* refers to patterns of human activity or a society's way of life. It includes informal codes or rules of manners, dress, language, behavior, rituals, and systems of belief. The key components of culture consist of values, norms, and institutions. Values comprise ideas about what in life seems important, and they tend to guide the

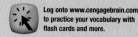
rest of the culture. Norms consist of expectations of how people will behave in various situations, and each culture has methods (sanctions) for enforcing its norms. Institutions are the structures of a society within which values and norms are transmitted.

Large societies often have subcultures, or groups of people with distinct sets of values, attitudes, behaviors, and beliefs that differentiate them from a larger culture of which they are a part. Sometimes subcultures can be defined by religious, occupational, or other factors. Many researchers point to a separate police culture or subculture. This does not mean that the police, in most important respects, do not share the dominant values of the larger culture. Rather, the **police culture** or **police subculture** is a combination of shared norms, values, goals, career patterns, lifestyles, and occupational structures that is somewhat different from the combination held by the rest of society. The police subculture, like most subcultures, is characterized by clannishness, secrecy, and isolation from those not in the group. Police officers work with other police officers during their tours of duty. Many socialize together after work and on days off, often to the exclusion of others—even old friends and family. When socializing, off-duty officers tend to talk about their jobs.

Working strange shifts of duty, especially 4-to-12s (4:00 PM to 12:00 midnight) and midnights (12:00 midnight to 8:00 AM), and working weekends and holidays makes it difficult for the police officer to socialize with the

© Linda Forst

Due to challenging work schedules, police officers often socialize more frequently with other officers than with the average citizen. Though this might increase isolation, in some cases it can be beneficial for stress reduction by providing a healthy opportunity to exercise.

average person, who works a 9-to-5 job Monday through Friday. Many police officers find it difficult to sleep after a tense, busy evening tour. If officers want to socialize or relax after work, instead of going home to a house whose inhabitants have to get up at 6:00 AM to go to regular jobs, many tend to socialize with their comrades from the job. When officers work weekends, their days off fall during the average person's workweek, so again, many tend to socialize with other officers. Police spouses tend to socialize with other police spouses, and police families tend to socialize with other police families. After a while, the police world is the only world for many officers.

CULTURE

- ▸ shared norms
- ▸ shared values
- ▸ shared goals
- ▸ shared career patterns
- ▸ shared lifestyle
- ▸ shared occupational patterns

Photo © R.Gino Santa Maria/www.Shutterstock.com. Figure © 2013 Cengage Learning.

Photo © Mediaonela/dreamstime. Figure © 2013 Cengage Learning.

POLICE CULTURE

- ▸ honor
- ▸ loyalty
- ▸ individuality

Michael K. Brown, in *Working the Street*, tells us that police officers create their own culture to deal with the recurring anxiety and emotional stress that are endemic to policing. Brown believes that the police subculture is based on three major principles: honor, loyalty, and individuality. (Brown 82)

Honor is given to officers who engage in risk-taking behavior. An example of risk-taking behavior is being the first one in the door to challenge an armed adversary, when taking cover and waiting for backup would be the more prudent course of action.

Loyalty is a major part of the police subculture, and police loyalty is extremely intense. The word *backup* occurs often in police officer conversations. Backup involves assisting other officers in emergency situations and coming to their aid when they are challenged, criticized, or even charged with wrongdoing. Brown explains the importance of backup by pointing out that the violence that police must deal with and the strong bonding that occurs among police officers "places the highest value upon the obligation to back up and support a fellow officer." (Brown 82)

The ideal officer, according to the police subculture, takes risks (honor), is first on the scene to aid a fellow police officer (loyalty), and is able to handle any situation by doing it her or his own way (individuality).

The idea of danger permeates the police subculture. George L. Kirkham, a college professor who became a police officer to better

© Tom Nulens

understand his police students, discusses the police mistrust of civilians and reliance upon their own peer-group support to survive on the streets: "As someone who had always regarded policemen as a 'paranoid lot,' I discovered in the daily round of violence which became part of my life that chronic suspiciousness is something that a good cop cultivates in the interest of going home to his family each evening." (Kirkham 81) (See Table 6.1.)

TABLE 6.1 Traits of the Police Culture/Subculture

- Clannishness
- Isolation from the public
- Secrecy
- Honor
- Loyalty
- Individuality

The Blue Wall of Silence

Studies of the police culture indicate that police officers protect one another from outsiders, often even refusing to aid police superiors or other law enforcement officials in investigating wrongdoing by other officers. Many believe that this part of the police culture or subculture produces a protective barrier known as the **blue wall of silence**. Writing about the police subculture and the blue wall of silence, Bittner says, "Policing is a dangerous occupation and the availability of unquestioned support and loyalty is not something officers could readily do without." (Bittner 63)

Robert Sheehan and Gary W. Cordner write about how this aspect of the police subculture can destroy the reputation and integrity of a police department: "The influence of dominant police subcultural role expectations can have a devastating effect on a police department. Actually, the existence of such unofficially established,

blue wall of silence
A figurative protective barrier erected by the police in which officers protect one another from outsiders, often even refusing to aid police superiors or other law enforcement officials in investigating wrongdoing of other officers.

 Log onto www.cengagebrain.com to practice your vocabulary with flash cards and more.

Photo © iStockphoto/xyno. Photo illustration by Spitting Images for Cengage Learning.

THE BLUE WALL OF SILENCE:

POLICE OFFICERS PROTECT ONE ANOTHER FROM OUTSIDERS.

negative, institutionalized role expectations is the primary reason that so many police departments are held in such low esteem by the public." (Sheehan and Cordner 286)

An example of the police subculture's blue wall of silence is William Westley's classic study of the Gary, Indiana, police department, in which he found a police culture that had its own customs, law, and morality. Westley says these values produce the **blue curtain**—a situation in which police officers trust only other police officers and do not aid in the investigation of wrongdoing by other officers. Westley calls the blue curtain a barrier that isolates police officers from the rest of society. (Westley)

The Police Personality

The police culture or subculture leads to what scholars call the **police personality**, or the traits common to most police officers. Scholars have reported that this personality is thought to include such traits as authoritarianism, suspicion, hostility, insecurity, conservatism, and cynicism. (Skolnick) (See Table 6.2.)

What Is the Police Personality?

Jerome Skolnick coined the term "working personality of police officers." Skolnick stated that the police officer's working personality is shaped by constant exposure to danger and the need to use force and authority to reduce and control threatening situations. He wrote,

> The policeman's role contains two principal variables, danger and authority, which should be interpreted in the light of a "constant" pressure to appear efficient. The element of danger seems to make the

policeman especially attentive to signs indicating a potential for violence and lawbreaking. As a result the policeman is generally a "suspicious person." Furthermore, the character of the policeman's work makes him less desirable as a friend since norms of friendship implicate others in his work. Accordingly the element of danger isolates the policeman socially from that segment of the citizenry whom he regards as symbolically dangerous and also from the conventional citizenry with whom he identifies. (Skolnick)

Regarding the requirements of the police profession and the police personality, Michael Pittaro wrote,

> Police officers are continuously challenged with a number of internal and external stressors, most of which can wreak havoc on the officer's physical and emotional well-being over time. Police work is essentially a dangerous profession in which danger looms in virtually every call for help. The profession requires someone with distinctive personality traits to be both law enforcer and social worker, which is not as simple as one would think. (Pittaro 4)

Are They Born Like That, or Is It the Job?

Two opposing viewpoints exist on the development of the police personality. One says that police departments recruit people who by nature possess those traits that we see in the police personality. The second point of view holds that officers develop those traits through their socialization and experiences in the police department.

Are these police cadets born with police personalities, or do they acquire them through training and on-the-job experiences?

TABLE 6.2 Traits of the Police Personality
• Authoritarianism
• Suspicion
• Hostility
• Insecurity
• Conservatism
• Cynicism

Edward Thibault, Lawrence M. Lynch, and R. Bruce McBride tell us that most studies have found that the police working personality derives from the socialization process in the police academy, field training, and patrol experience. (Thibault, Lynch, and McBride) John Van Maanen also asserts that the police personality is developed through the process of learning and doing police work. In a study of one urban police department, he found that the typical police recruit is a sincere individual who becomes a police officer for the job security, the salary, the belief that the job will be interesting, and the desire to enter an occupation that can benefit society. (Van Maanen 81) He found that at the academy, highly idealistic recruits are taught to have a strong sense of camaraderie with follow rookies. The recruits begin to admire the exploits of the veteran officers who are their teachers. From their instructors, the recruits learn when to do police work by the book and when to ignore department rules and rely on personal discretion.

Van Maanen says that the learning process continues when the recruits are assigned to street duty and trained by field training officers. The recruits listen to the folklore, myths, and legends about veteran officers and start to understand police work in the way that older officers desire them to. By adopting the sentiments and behavior of the older officers, the new recruits avoid ostracism and censure by their supervisors and colleagues.

In sum, the weight of existing evidence generally points to the existence of a unique police personality that develops from the police socialization process.

Police Cynicism

Police cynicism involves an attitude that there is no hope for the world and a view of humanity at its worst. This is produced by the police officer's constant contact with offenders and what he or she perceives as miscarriages of justice, such as lenient court decisions and plea bargaining.

Arthur Niederhoffer, a former NYPD lieutenant and professor at John Jay College of Criminal Justice, described police cynicism as follows:

> Cynicism is an emotional plank deeply entrenched in the ethos of the police world and it serves equally well for attack or defense. For many reasons police are particularly vulnerable to cynicism. When they succumb, they lose faith in people, society, and eventually in themselves. In their Hobbesian view, the world becomes a jungle in which crime, corruption, and brutality are normal features of terrain. (Niederhoffer 41–42)

The *Dirty Harry* Problem

Police officers are often confronted with situations in which they feel forced to take certain illegal actions to achieve a greater good. Indeed, one of the greatest and oldest ethical questions people have ever faced is, do the good ends ever justify the bad means? (Klockars, "Dirty Harry" pp. 33–47)

Carl B. Klockars has dubbed this moral dilemma of police officers the **Dirty Harry** problem, from the 1971 film *Dirty Harry* starring Clint Eastwood as Detective Harry Callahan. In the film, a young girl has been kidnapped by a psychopathic killer named Scorpio, who demands $200,000 in ransom. Scorpio has buried the girl with just enough oxygen to survive a few hours. Harry eventually finds Scorpio, shoots him, and tortures him to find out where the girl is. Finally, Scorpio tells him and Harry finds her, but she has already died from lack of oxygen.

Let's change the plot of the movie and say that Harry's actions resulted in his finding the girl and saving her life. This would be a great Hollywood ending, but think about it: Harry had a good end in mind (finding the girl before she died), but what about the means (torturing Scorpio and not giving him his constitutional rights before interrogation)?

Harry was wrong, right? He violated police procedure. He violated the precepts of the Fifth Amendment to the U.S. Constitution, which he had sworn an oath to obey. He committed crimes, the most obvious of which is assault.

Again, Harry was wrong, right? If Harry had used proper police procedure, had not violated the law, had not violated the Constitution of the United States, and had advised Scorpio of his right to an attorney, and if Scorpio had availed himself of one, there is no doubt the attorney

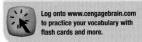

Actor Clint Eastwood on the set of "Dirty Harry."

© Sunset Boulevard/Corbis

would have told Scorpio to remain silent, and the little girl would have died.

Thus, is it more morally wrong (1) to torture Scorpio, thereby violating the police oath of office and legal obligations but finding the girl and saving her life, or (2) to act in accordance with the rules of the system and not make every effort, illegal or not, to force Scorpio to talk and thus permit the girl to die?

Sure, this is only Hollywood. You would never be faced with this dilemma as a police officer, would you? As Klockars writes,

> In real, everyday policing, situations in which innocent victims are buried with just enough oxygen to keep them alive are, thankfully, very rare. But the core scene in *Dirty Harry* should only be understood as an especially dramatic example of a far more common problem: real, everyday, routine situations in which police officers know they can only achieve good ends by employing dirty means. Each time a police officer considers deceiving a suspect into confessing by telling him that his fingerprints were found at the scene or that a conspirator has already confessed, each time a police officer considers adding some untrue details to his account of probable cause to legitimate a crucial stop or search . . . that police officer faces a Dirty Harry Problem. (Klockars, "Dirty Harry" pp. 33–47)

We can sympathize with Harry Callahan, and surely we can sympathize with the plight of the little girl about to die. However, despite Hollywood portrayals, police officers must operate within the boundaries of the law, because the law is what the people, through their representatives, want to be governed by. The police cannot make their own laws. Harry Callahan, although he attempted to save the life of the child, was wrong. In our system of law, we cannot use unlawful means to achieve worthy goals. Police work is a tough business. Tough choices must be made. As Klockars says,

> Dirty Harry Problems are an inevitable part of policing. They will not go away. The reason they won't is that policing is a moral occupation which constantly places its practitioners in situations in which unquestionable good ends can only be achieved by employing morally, legally, or politically dirty means to their achievements. The effects of Dirty Harry Problems on real police officers are often devastating. They can lead officers to lose their sense of

AP Photo/Bay Area News Group, Dan Rosenstrauch

Law enforcement officers find cover behind a car in Oakland, California, March 21, 2009, while responding to the second officer-involved shooting of the day. Shooting incidents are highly stressful to all concerned.

moral proportion, fail to care, turn cynical, or allow their too passionate caring to lead them to employ dirty means too readily or too crudely. They make policing the most morally corrosive occupation. (Klockars, "Dirty Harry" pp. 33–47)

Can the *Dirty Harry* (or *Dirty Harriet*) problem lead to a serious ethical problem facing our police? Certainly. Police officers must be always alert to the fact that bad means never justify good ends. The police swear allegiance to their oath of office and the U.S. Constitution and their state constitution. Although it may be tempting to try, police cannot solve all the problems of this world, and they certainly cannot solve them by violating their oath of office and their dedication to the Constitution of our land.

LO2 Explain Police Stress

Police officers are often faced with stressful situations during a routine tour of duty. The dispatcher may assign them to respond to a "gun run." (A gun run is a dispatcher's order to patrol units to respond to a certain location because of a report over 911 that a person has a gun in his or her possession. These calls receive immediate police response.) Citizens stop them to report a crime or dangerous condition. Officers find an open door to a factory and search for a possible burglar. They wait in a stakeout for an armed felon to appear. Police officers are always ready to react. Their bodies' response to these stressful situations is good in that it prepares them for any emergency, but the stress response takes its toll on officers' physical and mental states.

What Is Stress?

Stress is the body's reaction to internal or external stimuli that upset the body's normal state. A stimulus that causes stress (stressor) can be physical, mental, or emotional. The term *stress* is used to refer to both the body's reaction and the stimuli that caused it.

The body's reaction to highly stressful situations is known as the **flight-or-fight response**. Under stressful circumstances, large quantities of adrenaline, a hormone produced by the adrenal glands, are released into the bloodstream. This stimulates the liver to provide the body with stored carbohydrates for extra energy. It also results in quickened heartbeat and respiration, as well as increased blood pressure and muscle tension. The body is getting prepared for extraordinary physical exertion, which is good. However, if the need for this extraordinary exertion does not materialize, the frustrated readiness may cause headache, upset stomach, irritability, and a host of other symptoms.

Some experts say that stress alone probably does not cause illness, but that it contributes to circumstances in which diseases may take hold and flourish. Because stress weakens and disturbs the body's defense mechanisms, it may play a role in the development of hypertension, ulcers, cardiovascular disease, and as research indicates, probably cancer. (See Table 6.3.)

Nature of Stress in Policing

Although most people have stress in their careers or lives, studies have found evidence of particularly high rates of stress in certain professions. Some have called

policing the most stressful of all professions. The American Institute of Stress ranked police work among the top 10 stress-producing jobs in the United States. ("Stress on the Job," *Newsweek* p. 43)

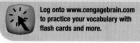
Some studies indicate that police officers have higher rates of divorce, suicide, and other manifestations of stress than do members of other professions. (Terry 67–70) One writer said, "It would be difficult to find an occupation that is subject to more consistent and persistent tension, strain, confrontations and nerve wracking than that of the uniformed patrolman." (Milanovich 20)

Researchers have identified four general categories of stress with which police officers are confronted: external, organizational, personal, and operational. (McGuire 27)

External Stress External stress results from real threats and dangers, such as responding to gun runs and other dangerous assignments and taking part in auto pursuits.

Consider the external stress faced by members of the New Orleans Police Department in the aftermath of Hurricane Katrina. Many of them were flooded out of their

Flight-or-fight response.

AP Photo/The Wilson Daily Times, Grant Roberson

TABLE 6.3 Mental and Physical Problems Associated with Stress
Cardiovascular problems:
• Heart attacks
• Coronary artery disease
• Hypertension
• Stroke
Gastrointestinal problems:
• Ulcers
Genitourinary problems:
• Failure to menstruate
• Impotence
• Incontinence
Immunology problems:
• Reduced resistance to infection
• Tumors
Psychiatric problems:
• Posttraumatic stress syndrome
• Neuroses
• Transient situational disturbances

SOURCE: Adapted from Geffner, Edwin S., ed., *The Internist's Compendium of Patient Information.* New York: McGraw-Hill, 1987, Sec. 30.

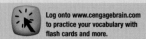
own homes and separated from their friends and loved ones, and they had to face constant attacks by armed assailants looking to loot and plunder the little that was left in New Orleans.

A reporter riding with the police addressed the stress that officers experience:

> The world inside the patrol car is a world of its own, two officers who are slaves to the dispatcher on the crackling radio who can send them speeding into adrenaline overdrive racing to catch a suspect with a gun and then can order "slow it down" after enough cars are already at a crime scene. The result is an emotional up and down in just six blocks. (Mitchell B1, B2)

Police officers also experience stress because they believe that the criminal justice system does not seem to help them. In 2008, a Nashville, Tennessee, police commander reflected on the recent arrest of a man who pulled a box cutter on an undercover decoy officer. Since 1982, the 60-year-old man had been arrested 416 times for an array of offenses. The commander, Andy Garrett, stated, "The biggest frustrating thing is the amount of resources I have to commit on this one person that has an extensive criminal history where I could be proactive in another area." ("Police Arrest Same Man 416 Times")

Organizational Stress Organizational stress results from elements inherent in the quasi-military character of the police service, such as constant adjustment to changing tours of duty, odd working hours, working on holidays, and the strict discipline imposed on officers. Organizational stress also results from workplace conditions, the lack of choice in work activities, and workplace bias.

Personal Stress Personal stress results from the interpersonal characteristics of belonging to the police organization, such as difficulties in getting along with other officers.

Responding to emergency calls can cause stress, regardless of whether the emergency still exists upon arrival.

Fatigue can affect officers' stress.

Operational Stress Operational stress results from the daily need to confront the tragedies of urban life: dealing with derelicts, criminals, the mentally disturbed, and the drug-addicted; engaging in dangerous activity to protect a public that often appears to be unappreciative of the police; and being constantly aware of the possibility of being legally liable for actions performed while on duty.

Factors Causing Stress in Policing

According to researchers, many factors lead to stress in police work, including poor training, substandard equipment, poor pay, lack of opportunity, role conflict, exposure to brutality, fears about job competence and safety, and lack of job satisfaction. Researchers also say that the pressure of being on duty 24 hours a day leads to stress and that the police learn to cope with that stress by becoming emotionally detached from their work and the people they are paid to serve.

Fatigue can also lead to officers' stress. Working long hours and overtime produces fatigue and consequently stress in officers. Bryan Vila, a professor of criminal justice and author of the book *Tired Cops: The Importance of Managing Police Fatigue*, stated, "Many police officers in the United States can't do their jobs safely or live healthy lives because of long and erratic work hours, insufficient sleep, and what appears to be very high levels of sleep disorders among experienced cops." (Vila, *Tired Cops: The Importance of Managing Police Fatigue* 51–92)

Suicide by Cop Compounding the stress problems of police officers is the phenomenon known as **suicide by cop**, in which a person wishing to die deliberately places an officer in a life-threatening situation, thus resulting in the officer using deadly force against that person.

In 2006, for example, in St. Charles, Missouri, a man pointed what police believed to be a real gun at them, and they fatally shot him. It was later discovered that the man's gun was a pellet gun and that the man had earlier had a discussion with his brother about provoking the police to kill him. He also had a history of alcohol abuse and had tried to commit suicide previously. (Weich)

Perhaps the classic case of suicide by cop occurred on a Long Island, New York, expressway when a 19-year-old man, despondent over a gambling debt, drove recklessly, causing the police to pull him over. He then pulled a "very real-looking gun" (actually, a $1.79 toy revolver) on them. Police fatally shot him. Inside the youth's auto were goodbye cards for his friends and a chilling suicide note addressed "To the officer Who Shot Me," in which he apologized for getting the police involved. (Buffa and Massarella 3)

Police officers involved in these cases are devastated. According to David Klinger, a former police officer and now a professor at the University of Missouri at St. Louis, "Police find out after the fact that they did not need to shoot to protect themselves. It angers them that they hurt or killed someone." Klinger also said that even though police officers are trained to use deadly force, actually using it on someone, especially someone who has a death wish, can be life-altering for the officers involved. "Police officers generally can develop a bit of a thick skin about dealing with individuals who have killed themselves, but when you are the instrument of that death, it can take quite a toll."

In addition to being left with feelings of guilt and of being tricked into using deadly force, police often have

> The suicide by cop phenomenon became widely reported in 1996 by a Canadian police officer, Richard B. Parent, in a landmark report on victim-precipitated homicide.

these feelings compounded by media accounts that depict the deceased as the victim. In the St. Charles case mentioned earlier, the daughter of the man who had caused the police to shoot him questioned the officers' use of force because he had not fired at them. She said that the police should have wounded him instead. However, St. Charles Police Chief Tim Swope determined that the officers' actions were justified. He said, "These officers have families; they want to go home at the end of the day. It's unfortunate that they had to do this, but that's part of the job." St. Charles County Sheriff Tom Neer agreed, saying, "We are trained to eliminate the threat. I know it sounds cold, but we aren't trained to wound people because wounded people kill others." (Weich)

The suicide by cop phenomenon became widely reported in 1996 by a Canadian police officer, Richard B. Parent, in a landmark report on victim-precipitated homicide. Parent, who interviewed cops after they had been involved in such incidents, said many quit the police department, got divorced, and abused drugs or alcohol after the killings. (Parent)

An analysis of 437 deputy-involved shootings occurring in the Los Angeles County Sheriff's Department disclosed that suicide by cop incidents accounted for 11 percent of the shootings and 13 percent of all deputy-involved justifiable homicides. The victims in these cases enacted elaborate schemes, including doing something to draw officers to the scene; disobeying commands to put down the weapon; continuing to threaten officers and other individuals; and escalating the encounter to the point where police felt that they had to use deadly force to protect themselves, their partners, and civilians. The study also indicated that most of the subjects in these cases were male and had a history of domestic violence, suicide attempts, and alcohol and drug abuse. Police officers involved in these incidents experienced emotions ranging from shock and remorse to shame, anger, and powerlessness. The report concluded that

An unidentified male suspect appears to be holding a pistol in his hand as he falls to the ground while exchanging shots with law enforcement officials. In the phenomenon known as "suicide by cop," a person wishing to die deliberately places an officer in a life-threatening situation, causing the officer to use deadly force against that person.

suicide by cop constitutes an actual form of suicide. (Huston and Anglin)

Effects of Stress on Police Officers

Too much stress negatively affects a person's health. Police officers encounter stress because they must always be ready for danger, day in and day out. In addition, the working hours of police officers and the resultant living conditions have further negative effects on their health.

A National Institute of Justice report lists the following consequences of job-related stress commonly reported by police officers: ("On-the-Job Stress in Policing" 18–24)

* Cynicism and suspiciousness
* Emotional detachment from various aspects of daily life
* Reduced efficiency
* Absenteeism and early retirement
* Excessive aggressiveness (which may result in an increase in citizen complaints)
* Alcoholism and other substance abuse problems
* Marital or other family problems (for example, extramarital affairs, divorce, or domestic violence)
* Posttraumatic stress disorder
* Heart attacks, ulcers, weight gain, and other health problems
* Suicide

In an extremely important 2004 article, Chad L. Cross, a research scientist, and Larry Ashley, an internationally recognized expert on combat trauma and addictions, both of whom are also faculty members at the University of Nevada, Las Vegas, write that studies have estimated that nearly 25 percent of law enforcement officers are alcohol-dependent as a result of on-the-job stress, and indicate that this estimate probably falls well below the true number because of incomplete reporting. (Cross and Ashley 24–32)

Cross and Ashley assert that the unique subculture of the law enforcement profession often makes alcohol use appear to be an accepted practice to promote camaraderie and social interaction among officers. However, they add that what starts as an occasional socializing activity, later can become a dangerous addiction as alcohol use evolves into a coping mechanism to camouflage the stress and trauma experienced by officers on a daily basis. When the effects of the alcohol wear off, the stress or trauma that led to the drinking episode still exists.

Other studies indicate that police officers are 300 percent more likely to suffer from alcoholism than the average citizen (Hibberd 26) and that policing ranks at the top of professions in rates of workers' heart disease, hypertension, and diabetes. ("Dispatches" 25)

Stress and Police Families

Police work not only affects officers, it also affects their families, loved ones, and friends: "Police work . . . affects, shapes, and at times, scars the individuals and families involved." Studies of stress in the immediate families of police officers reveal that between 10 and 20 percent of all police wives are dissatisfied with their husbands' job and would like to see their husbands leave the police department. (Rafky 65) In addition, rotation shift work interferes with planning and celebrating holidays and important family events such as birthdays and anniversaries. Rotating shifts also makes it difficult for a spouse to pursue another career.

Ellen Scrivner, the former director of the Psychological Services Division of the Prince George's County, Maryland, police department and now on the faculty of John Jay College of Criminal Justice in New York City as well as the president of the Psychologists in Public Service Division of the American Psychological Association, identified a number of job-related issues that contribute to dysfunction in police families: (Scrivner, "Helping Families" p. 6)

* *Family disruption due to rotating shifts.* Problems caused by rotating shifts include providing child care, unavailability on holidays and at other family events, and physical problems caused by overtime and shift work, which cause irritability and increased tension.

Stress can affect officers in many ways.

© Frances Twitty

Police stress also affects families, loved ones, and friends.

© Tony Kurdzuk/Star Ledger/Corbis

Police Departments Dealing with Stress

A 1981 report by the U.S. Commission on Civil Rights emphasized the need to provide stress management programs and services for police. The commission noted that most police departments lack such programs, despite the recent emphasis on viewing stress as "an important underlying factor in police misconduct incidents." The commission also recommended the following: "Police officials should institute comprehensive stress management programs that include identification of officers with stress problems, counseling, periodic screening and training on stress management." (U.S. Commission on Civil Rights) Since then, many police departments around the nation have developed stress programs for their officers.

Following the terrorist attacks of September 11, 2001, the NYPD ordered all 55,000 of its employees to attend mental health counseling to deal with the stress brought about by this event. (Jones A1) A similar program of mental health counseling was implemented to help Oklahoma City rescue workers in 1995 following the terrorist attack in that city. (Law Enforcement News 1)

Today, there are numerous training programs and support groups for police officers and their families. Many of these programs have a presence on the Web. However, it has been reported that some officers avoid using employee assistance programs (EAPs) because they feel that such programs do not provide enough confidentiality, that program staff do not understand law enforcement, and that stigma is attached to using an EAP.

Stressing the importance of police administrators in dealing with the problems of police stress, Pittaro writes,

> Police occupational stress is widespread and particularly troublesome, yet it can be eliminated, or at the very minimum, controlled as long as police administrators admit that a problem exists and commit to making changes within the organization. Avoiding stress is unlikely, but learning to cope with the internal and external stressors commonly associated with police occupational stress will minimize the potentially damaging effects of chronic stress. To be truly effective, change must begin within the organization since this appears to be the catalyst to police occupational stress. The dangerousness of the profession is something beyond the organization's control; however, police administrators can begin by creating an organization-wide culture that is committed to reduce stress within the organization. Education and awareness are two key elements that must be factored into any strategic plan in that officers need to understand and recognize the symptoms commonly associated with stress and

- *Unpredictable work environment.* The constantly changing work setting of the police officer leads to crisis and emergency responses, as well as fear of death or injury and of being the target of internal investigations.

- *Job-related personal changes and family relationships.* An officer is forced to see much human tragedy and is always personally affected. Changes in the officer's personality and attitudes, in turn, affect the family.

- *Community expectations and demands.* The public seems to hold police officers to a higher standard of behavior in comparison to that of other workers. People often expect their police officer neighbors to take care of neighborhood problems and be available for emergencies.

- *Intrusion into family life.* The police officer may have to bring parts of his or her job home. For example, police officers generally carry weapons, which they must secure in a safe place at home. Officers also must be available 24 hours a day.

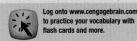

Counseling can help police officers to deal with stress.

© Brad Killer

the coping skills necessary to combat stress. (Pittaro 12)

LO3 Discuss Police Suicide

Closely associated with the problem of stress in policing is the problem of **police suicide**, which seems to worsen over the years. Despite all the programs existing to deal with officer problems that may result in suicide, the toll continues to mount. Studies indicate that the suicide rate among police officers is much higher than that of the general population, and that the rate of police suicides has doubled in recent decades.

The suicide rate for police officers is three times that of the general population, and three times as many officers kill themselves than are killed by criminals in the line of duty. Other studies show that police officers are six times more likely to kill themselves than average members of the public—60 for every 100,000 police officers each year, compared with 10 for every 100,000 members of the general public. This figure more than triples for police officers who retire. Officers who are disabled are 45 times more likely to commit suicide than the average person. (Kissinger)

In 2006, based on data from the Centers for Disease Control and Prevention, Robert Douglas of the National P.O.L.I.C.E. Suicide Foundation estimated that police officers commit suicide at a rate of 300 to 400 a year. (Kelly and Martin 93–95) In a 2007 article, Michele Perin wrote that the National P.O.L.I.C.E. Suicide Foundation calculates that an officer kills himself or herself every 17 hours and that 97 percent of officers use their own service weapon in committing suicide. The foundation further reports that many elements of law enforcement contribute to stress reactions with the potential to lead to suicide, including shift work, pending retirement, unsupportive management, and physical ailments. (Perin 8–16)

John M. Violanti, a professor in the Criminal Justice Department of the Rochester Institute of Technology in Rochester, New York, and a member of the Department of Social and Preventive Medicine, University of New York at Buffalo, works on the problem of police suicide. Violanti, who also served 23 years with the New York State Police, notes that the police culture and the reluctance of police officers to ask for help complicates the problem of police suicide. His research revealed that the police are at higher risk for committing suicide for a variety of reasons, including access to firearms, continuous exposure to human misery, shift work, social strain and marital difficulties, drinking problems, physical illness, impending retirement, and lack of control over their jobs and personal lives. Violanti's work indicates that police commit suicide at a rate of up to 53 percent higher than other city workers. (Violanti 1)

Traditionally, no matter what their problems, police officers refrain from asking for help. There are various reasons for this reluctance. The primary reason, however, is that officers do not wish to appear weak or vulnerable in front of their peers. Individuals who perceive themselves as problem solvers often have great difficulty admitting that they have problems of their own. As a result, some officers who feel they can no longer tolerate psychological pain choose to solve the problem themselves through suicide rather than asking others for help.

LO4 Discuss Police Danger

How often are police officers killed or injured in the line of duty? What are the specific threats to the police regarding personal safety? No one would disagree with the statement that police work is dangerous. Unfortunately, its dangers are increasing. Each year many officers are injured or killed in the line of duty. The chances of contracting life-threatening diseases, such as AIDS, are increasing as more of the general population is affected. This section puts these dangers into perspective.

Police officers perform necessary and often dangerous tasks. They deal constantly with what may be the most dangerous species on this planet—the human being—and often do so in the most stressful and dangerous situations. They regularly respond to people shooting at each other, stabbing each other, and beating each other. In a typical tour of duty, officers can deal with the full range of human emotions. They respond to calls where they may meet armed adversaries during robberies in progress or hostage situations. Most frequently, officers respond to "unknown problems" or "unknown disturbances" types of calls, where someone is calling for help but the officers are unable to gather further information and really don't know what they're walking into. The dangerous conditions facing U.S. police officers are compounded by the irrationality produced by alcohol and drugs. The urban drug business since the 1980s has been characterized by an emphasis on tremendous inflows of cash and instant gratification. The proliferation of young, urban, uneducated, and unemployable males who are armed with a plethora of weapons (including military-like automatic assault weapons) makes officers more and more fearful for their safety.

Also, the risk of exposure to dangerous chemicals in police work is always present. Deputies and police officers are always subject to the possibility of contamination from a variety of toxic chemicals, such as lye, iodine, and lithium, when they must enter methamphetamine (meth) labs to place offenders under arrest or while processing those under arrest who are contaminated themselves.

Police officers perform necessary and often dangerous tasks.

© Lilac Mountain/www.Shutterstock.com

Relatives grieve over the casket of a police officer who was killed while interviewing people on the street near an open-air drug market in East Baltimore.

© AP Photo/Roberto Borea

Officers Killed in the Line of Duty

The FBI (which maintains records of law enforcement officers murdered, accidentally killed, and injured in the line of duty each year) reported that 128 state and local law enforcement officers were either feloniously slain or accidentally killed in the line of duty during the latest reporting year, 2010. (FBI, *Law Enforcement Officers Feloniously Killed—2010*)

Fifty-six officers were feloniously slain in the line of duty in 2010. Of these officers, 15 were killed during ambushes; eight were investigating suspicious persons or circumstances; seven were killed during traffic pursuits or stops; six interrupted robberies in progress or were pursuing robbery suspects; and six were responding to disturbance calls (four of them being domestic disturbances). Three of the officers interrupted burglaries in progress or were pursuing burglary suspects; three died during tactical situations; two were conducting investigations; one was killed while handling or transporting a prisoner; one was killed during a drug-related conflict; and four officers were killed while attempting to make arrests for other situations. Of the 56 officers murdered in 2010, 55 were slain with firearms. Of these, 38 were slain with handguns, 15 with rifles, and two with shotguns. The only officer who was not a victim of firearms was killed with a vehicle.

Of the 56 victim officers, 38 were wearing body armor at the time of their deaths. In some of these cases, the bullets entered the officers' bodies in areas not covered by the body armor, and in other cases, the bullets penetrated the armor.

Accidents killed 72 law enforcement officers in 2010. This is an increase of 24 officers accidentally killed in

2009. (FBI, *Law Enforcement Officers Feloniously Killed—2010*)

One federal law enforcement officer was killed in the line of duty in 2009. He was assigned to the Department of Homeland Security. (FBI, *Federal Law Enforcement Officers Killed and Injured—2009*)

The 1970s were the deadliest decade for American law enforcement, with an average of 228 officers killed in the line of duty each year, compared to the average of 190 in the 1980s, 160 in the 1990s, and an average of 160 in each year from 2000 to 2009.

When one looks at the number of police officer–citizen contacts each year—about 43.5 million, according to the Bureau of Justice Statistics (Durose, Smith, and Langan 1)—and the dangerous situations officers often find themselves in, the police have relatively low murder rates. What accounts for these relatively low rates despite the constant possibility of violence with which officers are faced? There are several explanations.

First of all, people who would not think twice about shooting a fellow citizen might hesitate in shooting a police officer, knowing that society places a special value on the lives of those they depend on for maintaining law and order on the streets. People also know that the criminal justice system reacts in a harsher way to a "cop killer" than to an ordinary killer.

Also contributing to the relatively low number of officer killings is the fact that professional criminals, including organized crime members and drug dealers, know that killing a police officer is "very bad for business." Such a killing will result in tremendous disruption of their business while the police hunt for, and prosecute, the killer.

Another reason is police officers' awareness of the dangers they face every day and the resultant physical and mental precautions they take to deal with such dangers. The discussion of the police personality earlier in this chapter characterized it as suspicious, loyal, and cynical. Most experts believe that the police personality is caused by the dangers of police work. However, it's possible that the negative aspects of the police personality keep officers relatively safe. Advances in medical

© Justasc/www.Shutterstock.com

San Diego officers salute during a memorial service for a fallen comrade.

science, and improved training and equipment, have also helped to save the lives of police officers. Officers are now trained not to blindly rush into situations but to obtain as much information as possible (aided by improved records systems) while en route and upon arrival. Obtaining cover and waiting for backup are also stressed.

Another possible explanation for the decrease in officer murders is the increased use of body armor. The latest statistics released in 2006 indicate that most departments today require their field officers to wear protective body armor—75 percent of local police departments, compared with 30 percent in 1990, and 76 percent of sheriff's offices, compared with 30 percent in 1990. (Reaves, *Local Police Departments, 2007* p. 19; Hickman and Reaves, *Sheriff's Offices, 2003* p. iv) Recall, however, that the majority of officers murdered by people with firearms were wearing body armor at the time of their deaths. Some of the slain officers wearing body armor died from torso wounds caused by bullets entering despite the armor. This reinforces the fact that body armor is not "bullet proof."

Officers Assaulted in the Line of Duty

As we have seen, police officers have relatively low murder rates, but how often are officers injured by criminal assaults in the line of duty? In 2009, over 57,368 assaults were committed against state and local police officers. About 26.2 percent of the officers assaulted were injured. The assaults most commonly involved personal weapons such as hands, feet, and fists (27.6 percent). Firearms were used against officers in 8.8 percent of assaults and knives or cutting instruments in 13.3 percent of the assaults. Other types of dangerous weapons were used in 23.5 percent of assaults. The rate of officer assaults in 2009 was 10.3 assaults per 100 officers. (FBI, *Law Enforcement Officers Assaulted—2009*)

About 32.6 percent of the assaults occurred while officers were responding to disturbance calls (family fights, bar fights, etc.); 15.4 percent while attempting other arrests; and 12.7 percent while handling, transporting, or otherwise having custody of prisoners. The other assaults occurred while the officers were performing other duties.

In 2009, 1,807 federal law enforcement officers were the subjects of assaults in the line of duty and 181 of these assaults resulted in injuries; 1,203 of the assaulted officers were from the Department of Homeland Security; 493 from the Department of the Interior; 83 from the Department of Justice; six from the U.S. Postal Inspection Service; 19 from the U.S. Capitol Police; and three from the Department of the Treasury. In addition, 1,304 of the federal officers assaulted were performing patrol or guard duties when assaulted; 351 were attempting arrests or trying to serve summonses; 51 were maintaining custody of prisoners; 13 were on protection duty, and 10 were on desk duty when assaulted.

For the five-year period of 2005 through 2009, there were 7,959 federal officers assaulted, four of whom were killed. Three of the officers who were slain during the five-year time frame were employed by the Department of Homeland Security. One was murdered in 2005, one in 2008, and the third in 2009. The fourth officer, who was slain in the line of duty in 2008, was employed by the U.S. Department of Justice, Federal Bureau of Investigation. (FBI, *Federal Law Enforcement Officers Killed and Injured—2009*)

> In 2009, 1,807 federal law enforcement officers were the subjects of assaults in the line of duty and 181 of these assaults resulted in injuries. . . .

Police and AIDS

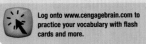
Since the 1980s, human immunodeficiency virus (HIV), acquired immune deficiency syndrome (AIDS), and hepatitis B and C have become sources of great concern to U.S. police officers, as well as to everyone else. **AIDS**, a deadly disease, is transmitted mainly through sexual contact and the exchange of body fluids. Although AIDS was formerly associated mainly with male homosexuals, intravenous drug users, and prostitutes, it is now known that anyone could be subject to infection by this disease.

The impact of HIV/AIDS is readily apparent. According to the Centers for Disease Control and Prevention (CDC), the estimated cumulative number of AIDS diagnoses in the United States for the latest reporting year was 984,155, with 9,101 of those being children younger than 13. The estimated cumulative number of deaths from AIDS in the United States was 550,394, including 4,865 children younger than 13. In 2005, in the United States alone, 433,760 people were living with AIDS and the estimated deaths from AIDS totaled 17,011. (Centers for Disease Control and Prevention)

Police officers frequently come into contact with all types of people—including those having infectious diseases—and officers often have contact with blood and other body fluids. Therefore, officers are at special risk for catching communicable diseases. They must take precautionary measures during searches and other contacts with possible carriers of infectious diseases, as well as at crime scenes, where blood and other body fluids may be present.

Despite these serious medical risks, police officers are not permitted to refuse to handle incidents involving persons infected with the AIDS virus or with other infectious diseases. Failing to perform certain duties—such as rendering first aid, assisting, or even arresting a person—would be a dereliction of duty, as well as discrimination against a class of people.

Log onto www.cengagebrain.com for additional resources including videos, flash cards, games, self-quizzing, review exercises, web exercises, learning checks, and more.

© Joel Gordon

7

Minorities in Policing

After studying this chapter, the student should be able to:

LO1 Describe the history and problems of minorities in policing and how it impacted their ability to obtain jobs and promotions in law enforcement

LO2 Discuss the provisions of the U.S. legal system that enabled minorities to overcome job discrimination

LO3 Discuss the issue of white male backlash

LO4 Introduce the academic studies reviewing the performance of minorities in police work

LO5 Describe the status of the various minority groups in law enforcement today

LO6 Examine some of the current and emerging challenges faced by minorities in law enforcement in current times

LO1 Describe the History and Problems of Minorities in Policing and How It Impacted Their Ability to Obtain Jobs and Promotions in Law Enforcement

The United States has a long history of **job discrimination** against women and minorities. Discrimination is the unequal treatment of persons in personnel decisions (hiring, promotion, and firing) on the basis of their race, religion, national origin, gender, or sexual orientation. Only in the past several decades have women and minorities been able to share the American dream of equal employment.

Discrimination against Women

In 1910, Los Angeles appointed the nation's first "officially designated" policewoman, Alice Stebbins Wells, a social worker in the city. Wells and other women who followed (until after the Great Depression) embodied the concept of policewoman-as-social-worker and tended to be educated, upper-middle-class social workers as opposed to male officers, who were largely working-class immigrant men.

After World War II, there was an emergence of middle-class female careerists, "depression babies," many of whom

> **job discrimination**
> Unequal treatment of persons in personnel decisions on the basis of their race, religion, national origin, gender, or sexual orientation.

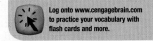
Log onto www.cengagebrain.com to practice your vocabulary with flash cards and more.

were not college educated and did not want to be social workers. Their police duties expanded, but they were frustrated with their limited roles and opportunities. They were thus a bridge generation from the early pioneers to today's female police officer. (Schulz, *From Social Worker to Crimefighter* pp. 115–116)

In 1968, the Indianapolis Police Department assigned Betty Blankenship and Elizabeth Coffal to patrol. They were the first females to wear a uniform and a gun belt and to drive a marked patrol car responding to calls for service on an equal basis with men. Today, female officers are much like their male colleagues, entering law enforcement, in part, with working-class concerns, including salary, benefits, and opportunities as crimefighters to enforce the law, keep the peace, and provide public safety functions. (Schulz, *From Social Worker to Crimefighter* pp. 131–137)

Women have faced an enormous uphill struggle to earn the right to wear the uniform and perform the same basic police duties that men have performed for years. Why were women excluded from performing regular police work? Until the 1970s, it was presumed that women, because of their gender and typical size, were not capable of performing the same type of patrol duty as men. Other social forces also contributed to the discrimination against women: If women could do the police job, the macho image of the job would be challenged.

Until the 1970s, women constituted only a very small percentage of U.S. police officers. The early female officers were restricted to issuing parking tickets or performing routine clerical tasks. As mentioned earlier, in the early days of female policing, women were normally used in only three actual police-related jobs: vice, juvenile work, and guarding female prisoners. In the late 1960s and early 1970s, however, the role of women in U.S. police departments began to change. To some degree, this was facilitated by the 1964 Civil Rights Act, which barred discrimination on the basis of sex. The change can also be attributed to the women's rights movement and efforts by female officers themselves to gain the right to perform patrol duty and achieve equality with male officers. (Walker and Katz 47) Even as late as the mid-1970s, however, female officers in some jurisdictions experienced different sets of rules, as their administrators and coworkers fluctuated between

> Until the 1970s, it was presumed that women, because of their gender and typical size, were not capable of performing the same type of patrol duty as men.

endorsing their full equality and wanting to "protect" them.

Discrimination against African Americans

In 1867, after receiving numerous complaints from the *New Orleans Tribune*, Governor Wells appointed Charles Courcelle, a "newly enfranchised" citizen, to the board of police commissioners in New Orleans. Three days later the paper reported that Dusseau Picot and Emile Farrar, both African Americans, had been appointed to the police department. These two pioneers seem to be the first documented African American police officers in the nation. Within 10 years, numerous other cities began appointing blacks to police departments, and just after the turn

Female and minority officers are more visible in law enforcement today.

© A. Ramey/Photo Edit

of the twentieth century, significant appointments began taking place in St. Louis, Dayton, Berkeley, and Atlanta. (Dulaney 10–15)

Even in the North, however, African Americans faced discrimination in assignments and promotions. Black police officers felt their issues were not addressed by their administrations and took matters into their own hands. Though not identified as such at the time, an early form of **double marginality** (which will be discussed shortly) led the black officers to socialize with each other and teach each other how to successfully deal with the discrimination and dual system of law enforcement. It also led to increased camaraderie and organization within their group.

LO2 Discuss the Provisions of the U.S. Legal System that Enabled Minorities to Overcome Job Discrimination

Despite pronouncements by national commissions, minorities were forced to take their cases to the U.S. courts in an attempt to achieve equality with white men in U.S. police departments. The primary instrument governing employment equality, as well as all equality, in U.S. society is the **Fourteenth Amendment** to the U.S. Constitution. This amendment, passed in 1868, guarantees "equal protection of the law" to all citizens of the United States.

More than the Fourteenth Amendment was needed, however, to end job discrimination in policing. In addition to the Fourteenth Amendment, the path to equality had as milestones the **Civil Rights Act of 1964**, Title VII of the same law, the **Equal Employment Opportunity Act of 1972 (EEOA)**, the Civil Rights Act of 1991, federal court cases on discrimination, and government-mandated affirmative action programs.

Federal Courts and Job Discrimination

Job discrimination may take several forms. The most obvious, of course, is where there is a clear and explicit policy of discrimination—for example, separate job titles, recruitment efforts, standards, pay, and procedures for female or minority employees. The second, and probably most prevalent, form of job discrimination is **de facto discrimination**. De facto discrimination is discrimination that is the indirect result of policies or practices that are not intended to discriminate but do, in fact, discriminate. For example, if a certain examination results in almost all women failing that test and almost all men passing it, the particular examination is said to have an adverse impact on women. Adverse impact can be seen as a form of de facto discrimination.

Job Relatedness

The first important job discrimination case was *Griggs v. Duke Power Company* in 1971, which declared that the practices of the Duke Power Company were unconstitutional because they required that all of its employees have a high school diploma and pass a standard intelligence test before being hired. (*Griggs v. Duke Power Company*) The court ruled that these requirements were discriminatory unless they could be shown to measure the attributes needed to perform a specific job. The decision in *Griggs v. Duke Power Company* established the concept that job requirements must be job-related—they must be necessary for the performance of the job a person is applying for.

How did all these regulations apply to police departments? Candidates who formerly were denied acceptance into police departments because they could not meet certain standards (height and weight) or could not pass certain tests (strength) began to argue that these standards were not job-related—that is, the standards did not measure skills and qualifications needed to perform police work.

The requirement that officers not be less than a certain height (height

© DRGill/Shutterstock

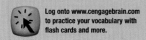
requirement) was probably the strongest example of discrimination against women candidates. With very few exceptions, police departments lost court cases involving the height requirement, including *Mieth v. Dothard* (1976) and *Vanguard Justice Society v. Hughes* (1979). (Gaines, Worrall, Southerland, and Angell 367)

Previous forms of physical ability testing were also challenged and found discriminatory by the courts. Newer tests, known as physical agility tests, were developed to reduce adverse impact. These newer physical agility tests require much less physical strength than the former tests and rely more on physical fitness.

Affirmative Action Programs

The most controversial method of ending job discrimination is the concept of **affirmative action**. In 1965, in Executive Order 11246, President Lyndon B. Johnson required all federal contractors and subcontractors to develop affirmative action programs. Subsequent orders have amended and expanded the original executive order. In essence, the concept of affirmative action means that employers must take active steps to ensure equal employment opportunity and to redress past discrimination. It is an "active effort" to improve the employment or educational opportunities of members of minority groups. This differs from equal opportunity, which ensures that no discrimination takes place and that everyone has the same opportunity to obtain a job or promotion.

The major concept behind affirmative action, and possibly the most disturbing concept to many, is the establishment of **quotas**. To implement affirmative action plans, departments incorporate goals and objectives involving numbers and timetables to correct past underrepresentation. These plans do not necessarily involve rigid quotas, just hiring and promotion goals to strive for. Some feel that affirmative action plans and quotas lead to **reverse discrimination**.

The Path to Equality: Court Cases

1980
Guardians Association of NYC Police Department v. Civil Service Commission of NY

1979
United States v. State of New York

1979
Vanguard Justice Society v. Hughes

1976
Mieth v. Dothard

1973
Vulcan Society v. Civil Service Commission

1971
Griggs v. Duke Power Company

Photo © iStockphoto/Hsing-Wen Hsu. Photo illustration by Spitting Images for Cengage Learning.

L○3 Discuss the Issue of White Male Backlash

As more police jobs and promotions begin to go to minorities, fewer white males receive these jobs and promotions. White males are passed over on entrance and promotion examinations by minorities, some of whom receive lower test scores. This results in turmoil and angry white males voicing anger and resentment, and counterlawsuits follow.

Though the EEOC prohibits all discrimination and consequently does not use the theory of "reverse discrimination," majority individuals often label the preferential treatment received by minority groups as reverse discrimination. (Swanson, Territo, and Taylor 293) They argue that selecting police officers based on their race or gender actually violates the 1964 Civil Rights Act and is discriminatory. Critics also argue that selecting officers who have scored lower on civil service tests lowers the personnel standards of a police department and will result in poorer performance by the department.

Even in law enforcement, with the loyalty that generally exists and where officers depend on each other when responding to calls, tensions can arise between various groups in the workplace.

LO4 Introduce the Academic Studies Reviewing the Performance of Minorities in Police Work

Much of the discrimination against women in police departments was based on a fear that they could not do police work effectively because of their gender and size. Much of the discrimination against minorities was based on the fear that they would not be accepted by nonminority citizens. The academic studies and anecdotal evidence presented in this section show that minorities do indeed make effective police officers.

Women are entering all aspects of law enforcement. Here a Lieutenant is congratulated by her son after becoming the first female to join the Memphis Police Department motor squad.

Two important academic studies—one by the Police Foundation and the other by the Law Enforcement Assistance Administration (LEAA)—found that women are just as effective on patrol as comparable men.

The study by the Police Foundation (Bloch and Anderson 5–6) found that women exhibit extremely satisfactory work performance. The women in the study were found to respond to similar types of calls as men, and their arrests were as likely as the men's arrests to result in convictions. The report also found that women are more likely than their male colleagues to receive support from the community, and are less likely to be charged with improper conduct.

The LEAA study was titled *Women on Patrol: A Pilot Study of Police Performance in New York City*. It involved the observation of 3,625 hours of female police officer patrol in New York and included 2,400 police–citizen encounters. The report concluded that female officers are perceived by citizens as being more competent, pleasant, and respectful than male officers. This study also found that women perform better when serving with other female officers and that when serving with male partners, women seem to be intimidated by their partners and are less likely to be assertive and self-sufficient. (Sichel, Friedman, Quint, and Smith xi–xiii)

In an analysis of the existing research on female police officers, Merry Morash and Jack Greene found that the traditional male belief that female officers cannot be effective on patrol is not supported by existing research. Morash and Greene concluded that in fact, evidence exists showing that women make highly successful police officers. (Morash and Greene 230–255)

And most recently, the International Association of Chiefs of Police (IACP) conducted a study of 800 police departments in 1998. The researchers found that law enforcement administrators felt overwhelmingly that women possess exceptional skills in the area of verbal and written communications as well as outstanding interpersonal skills. (International Association of Chiefs of Police, "Future of Women")

In contrast to the situation for women, there have been no studies regarding the ability of African Americans to do police work. Anecdotal evidence, however, suggests that they perform as well as any other group. There have been some inquiries regarding the attitudinal beliefs of African American officers as well as examinations of the early career experiences of current black police administrators; these seem to indicate that African American officers and white police officers have very different attitudes. They also reveal that black officers are more supportive of innovation and change within the policing occupation and are generally more supportive than are white officers of community policing. (Walker and Katz 47)

Many in the police field feel that interracial working relations within law enforcement have improved during the past decade, albeit gradually, making the workplace more congenial. (Thompson 81–154)

LO5 Describe the Status of the Various Minority Groups in Law Enforcement Today

As this chapter has shown, during the past three decades, U.S. police departments have attempted to better reflect the communities they serve. Police administrators have intensified the recruitment of minorities to have more balanced police departments. They've also directed their efforts toward the retention of these officers. Many departments have links on their websites for the targeted population that provide additional information and outreach as well as mentoring services.

Female Representation

A 2010 Bureau of Justice Statistics (BJS) publication reports that 11.9 percent of all full-time sworn officers in local law enforcement in 2007 were women, up from 11.3 percent in 2003 and 7.6 percent in 1987. Numbers ranged from 17.9 percent in departments serving populations of 1 million or more to approximately 7.5 percent in departments serving fewer than 10,000. (Reaves, *Local Police Departments, 2007*)

More women are now attaining the length of service and breadth of experience typically associated with command positions.

It is not uncommon to see women working the street in uniform today.

© Jeff Greenberg/Alamy

Academic studies and anecdotal evidence show that minorities do make effective police officers.

© Dennis MacDonald/Alamy

Consequently, recent years have seen a significant increase in the numbers of women in administrative positions and serving as chiefs and sheriffs. The numbers of female police chiefs and sheriffs doubled from 1994 to 2004, compared to the previous 10 years. (Schulz, *Breaking the Brass Ceiling* 29) Women have been or are currently executives in all sizes of municipal agencies and sheriff's departments, and in state police, campus police, transit police, and federal agencies.

African American Representation

In the 1970s and 1980s, African Americans began to be appointed as police commissioners or chiefs in some of the nation's biggest city police departments, and by 2004, many police departments had African Americans in their command staff or serving as chiefs of police.

According to a Bureau of Justice Statistics Report, in 2007, approximately a quarter of full-time local law enforcement officers were members of a racial or ethnic minority, an increase from 14.6 percent in 1987. African American officers represented 11.9 percent of all law enforcement officers, up from 9.3 percent in 1987. Their representation is highest in agencies serving more than 250,000 people and in departments serving over 1 million residents they comprised 11.9 percent of officers. (Reaves)

Strides are being made, however, and police departments are becoming more representative of the people they serve.

Hispanic Representation

The number of Hispanic American officers has increased significantly in the last two decades, as has their percentage in the general population. According to the Department of Justice, Hispanic or Latino officers accounted for 10.3 percent of police officers nationwide in 2007. This was an increase over the year 2003, when 9.1 percent of officers nationwide were Hispanic. In 1987 only 4.5 percent of officers across the nation were Hispanic. The highest percentage of Hispanic officers was in departments serving populations of greater than 1 million, in which they represented 22.9 percent of the officers. (Reaves)

These officers are extremely valuable to law enforcement agencies. The diversity of the department is a plus, the officers' ability to relate to the Hispanic community is an asset, and they can help bridge the language and cultural barriers.

Nevertheless, Hispanic officers' assimilation has not been without controversy. They have been involved in discrimination issues and affirmative action plans. Several organizations have arisen to serve as support groups for Hispanic officers and to facilitate communication between those officers around the country.

An ongoing major challenge is reaching out to these communities to educate them about what the police in the United States are like and what they do, and to encourage immigrants to pursue law enforcement as an occupation to help make their communities safer and serve their community.

Asian Representation

Though their numbers have increased slightly during the last few years, Asian Americans are poorly represented in police departments across the country. According to the latest statistics, these minorities—including Asians,

The recruitment of Asian American officers is a challenge faced by law enforcement.

> Strides are being made, however, and police departments are becoming more representative of the people they serve.

Pacific Islanders, and Native Americans—constituted 2.7 percent of local police officers in 2007. This compares with 2.8 percent in 2003 and 0.8 percent in 1987. (Reaves) The biggest challenge concerning Asian Americans in law enforcement appears to be recruitment. Despite dramatic increases in the Asian population across the nation, most departments have few if any Asian officers. According to police administrators, Asians are just not applying for the jobs. It seems to be a cultural issue: Asian parents are not encouraging their children to seek this type of employment. In some homelands, police officers are looked upon as corrupt, brutal, or uneducated. Police departments are thus making efforts to overcome these cultural barriers.

Muslim Representation

A small but increasingly visible group that has experienced discrimination is Muslim officers. Since September 11, 2001, this group has received increased attention from the media, the public, and their coworkers. Recently, cases have arisen in which Muslim officers have claimed they've been discriminated against. These claims usually involve grooming issues, including the wearing of untrimmed beards by male public safety personnel and the wearing of head coverings by Muslim females. These conventions are an important part of Muslim religious and cultural traditions. However, departments usually back their own policies, claiming it's a safety and discipline issue. It is believed to be most important for the community and the citizens who encounter police officers that they have a uniform appearance.

Gay and Lesbian Representation

Another group with a challenging history in law enforcement is gay officers. Police departments have had a history of discriminating against job applicants because of their sexual orientation. Until the beginning of the focus on equal employment opportunity, many police departments discriminated against homosexuals in employment decisions, and the International Association of Chiefs of Police (IACP) maintained a policy of opposing the employment of gay officers. In 1969, however, the IACP rescinded its policy of opposing the employment of gay officers.

© Colin Anderson/Blend Images/Jupiter Images

CHALLENGES
facing women today

- Women's perception of the job
- Recruitment
- Acceptance by coworkers
- Workplace harassment
- Dating and relationships
- Pregnancy
- Family issues

Photo © iofoto/www.Shutterstock.com. Figure © 2013 Cengage Learning.

CHALLENGES
facing African Americans and other minorities

- Recruitment
- Acceptance by coworkers
- Workplace harassment
- Competition from the private sector
- Tokenism
- Job assignments
- Friendly fire incidents

Photo © David Hiller/Jupiter Images. Figure © 2013 Cengage Learning.

The percentage of gay and lesbian officers is a difficult number to determine. Many departments do not ask about sexual orientation, and, because of a fear of making their sexual orientation known to their coworkers, many police officers hide the fact that they are gay or lesbian. Police work has traditionally been thought of as a "macho" occupation, and thus the perception has been that gay male officers don't fit the mold.

Today, some cities are recruiting openly gay officers in an attempt to bridge a perceived gap with their gay community. They also hope to improve the environment within law enforcement agencies for gays which will further enhance the relationship between the police and the gay community.

LO6 Examine Some of the Current and Emerging Challenges Faced by Minorities in Law Enforcement in Current Times

As we have just discussed, minorities have made great strides in the law enforcement field. Some minorities are represented within the rank and file of law enforcement agencies in numbers increasingly representative of their presence in their communities.

This increase in numbers together with the passing of time has allowed minorities to acquire the needed time in rank. This has resulted in a larger pool of competent minority candidates for higher-ranking positions. Consequently, more women and minorities now occupy high-ranking positions within law enforcement agencies, up to and including the rank of police chief or sheriff. This gives these individuals increased opportunities to impact the policies and procedures of their departments and have input in the decision-making process in all kinds of situations within their departments and their communities. It also provides them opportunities to serve as mentors and role models to others.

Problems for Women

Women in law enforcement have progressed tremendously during the last three decades, but challenges remain. These include recruiting and hiring (including the physical agility part of the testing process), acceptance of women, workplace harassment, and dating, pregnancy, and family issues. The IACP believes the recruitment of women is an important issue for law enforcement today. Thus the IACP is involved in investigating the climate in law enforcement regarding women and has actively educated departments on recruiting and retaining female officers. Departments are also addressing these challenges on their own.

Problems for African Americans

As with female officers, recruitment of qualified African American candidates is the first challenge to be faced, and it is as formidable as ever. In recent years, however, there has been less of a problem with African Americans seeing themselves as police officers and even police executives because they have significant role models.

Another issue that arises with African American police officers more than with other officers is the issue of friendly fire shooting incidents. These officers are often in the undercover or off-duty capacity and intervening in a situation with their weapons. As they are taking action or detaining a suspect with the aid of their weapons, they are often mistaken for an offender by responding on-duty uniformed personnel.

An ongoing challenge for African American officers is the perception of tokenism by themselves, their coworkers, and the public. In their efforts to promote diversity and enhance recruiting, departments will often use African Americans in recruiting literature or at recruiting events, where it's hoped their visibility will help other African Americans see themselves in the job and wearing the uniform. Unfortunately, this can lead to the perception that black officers are getting particular assignments because they are African American. This may seem like tokenism.

> Minority groups continue to face stereotypes that people, both other officers and community members, hold but don't vocalize.

Problems for Other Minorities

Other minority groups seem to face the same problems. Because their rise in law enforcement is relatively more recent than that of African Americans and women, other minorities face the challenge of getting more representation in the command structure of police departments.

Minority groups continue to face stereotypes that people, both other officers and community members, hold but don't vocalize. Realizing that minorities may be closely scrutinized, minority officers know they are under the microscope and that any error they make may be generalized to their minority group. They usually have to work longer and harder to get ahead, but they are generally devoted to their chosen profession and serve as great role models for the community.

Police officers today are a reflection of the community they serve.

© Frances Roberts/Alamy

Log onto www.cengagebrain.com for additional resources including videos, flash cards, games, self-quizzing, review exercises, web exercises, learning checks, and more.

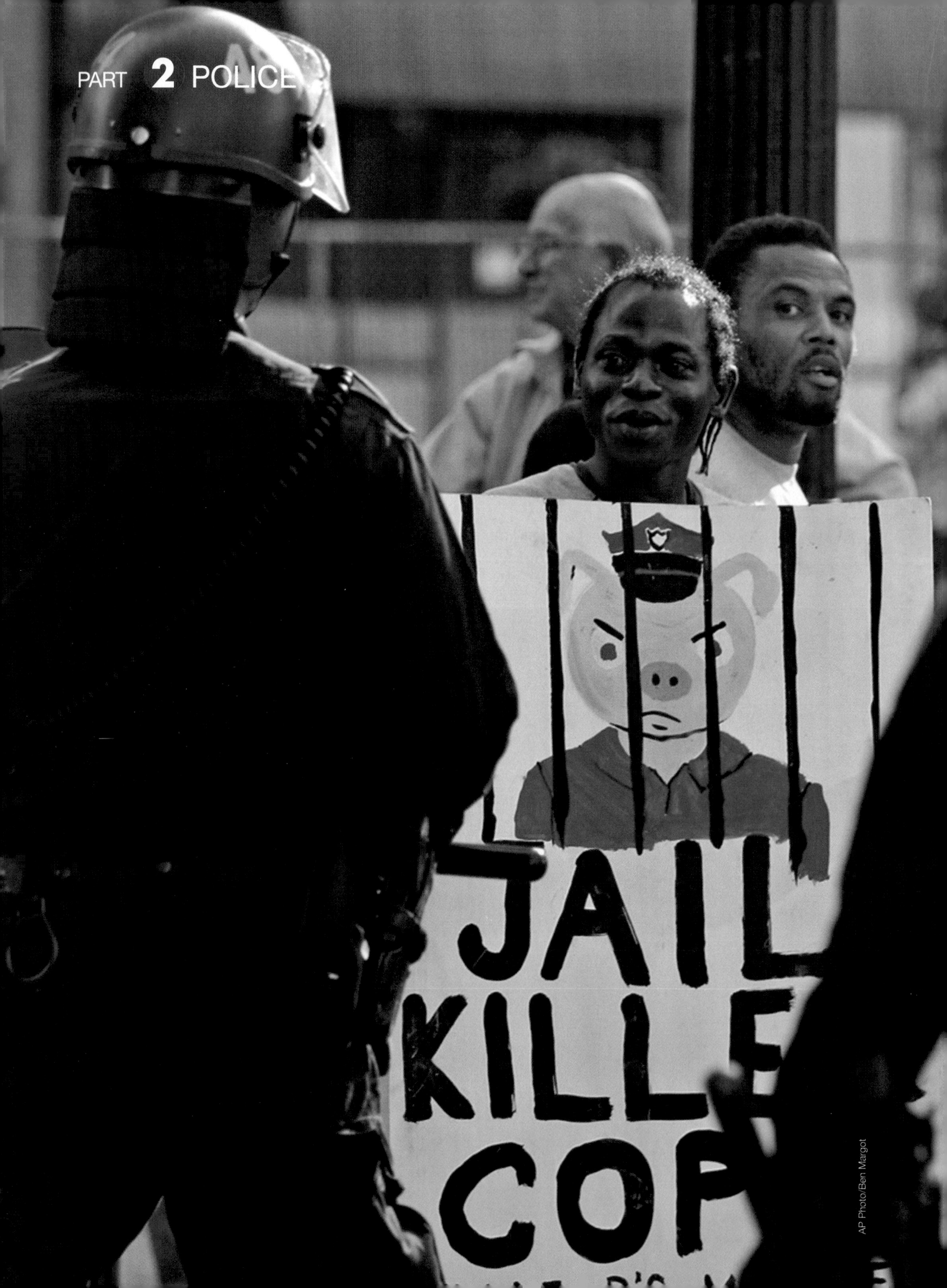

AP Photo/Ben Margot

8

Police Ethics and Police Deviance

After studying this chapter, the student should be able to:

LO1 Define and describe ethics

LO2 Discuss the various ways police actions are reviewed

LO3 Identify the various definitions, types, and extent of police corruption and explore the reasons for police corruption

LO4 Describe other forms of police misconduct including drug-related corruption, police deception, sex-related corruption, and domestic violence

LO5 Define and discuss biased-based policing

LO6 Discuss the definition, types, and extent of police brutality

LO7 Explore various responses to police corruption

LO8 Discuss the issue of liability and the effects of lawsuits on police officers and police agencies

LO1 Define and Describe Ethics

What is ethics? **Ethics** is defined as the study of what constitutes good or bad conduct. The term is often used interchangeably with *morals*, which is understandable because the terms have similar root meanings pertaining to behavioral practices or character. Applied ethics is concerned with the study of what constitutes right and wrong behavior in certain situations. (Pollock 10) Basic ethics consists of the rather broad moral principles that govern all conduct, whereas applied ethics focuses these broad principles upon specific applications. For example, a basic ethical tenet assumes that lying is wrong; applied ethics would examine under what conditions such a wrong would occur.

Aristotle defined virtue as what he called the Golden Mean or *Nicomachean ethics*. This philosophy suggests that life circumstances trigger a natural range of responses that include a mean between excessive and defective responses. A person's "character traits" are his or her habitual ways of responding, and the individuals who are the most admirable are those who find the norm between the two extremes regularly. The virtues cited by Aristotle more than 2,000 years ago include courage, self-control, generosity, high-mindedness, gentleness, truthfulness, and modesty. (Perez and Moore 49) These traits are still looked upon as evidence of good character.

Over the past few decades, there has been a growing interest in ethics in the academic and law enforcement literature, including textbooks, studies, journal articles, and media articles. Many departments and law enforcement organizations are promoting in-service training in the area of ethics. The International Association of Chiefs of Police

ethics
The study of what constitutes good or bad conduct.

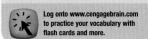
Log onto www.cengagebrain.com to practice your vocabulary with flash cards and more.

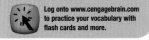
(IACP) offers courses in ethics, including "Ethical Standards in Police Service, Force Management, and Integrity Issues" and "Value-Centered Leadership: A Workshop on Ethics and Quality Leadership." The IACP and the Office of Community Oriented Policing Services (COPS) have made a resource called the "Ethics Toolkit" available on their websites for increasing awareness of law enforcement ethics. These organizations recognize that trust is a vital element of community policing and that ethical people inspire trust but unethical people do not. They further realize that ethics training will help departments recognize their full potential.

It is important for police officers to study ethics for many reasons. Police officers use a lot of discretion, and one of their duties is the enforcement of the law. At the same time, it is their duty to protect the constitutional safeguards that are the basis of our legal system, due process, and equal protection. Lastly, they are public servants and their behavior involves the public trust. (Pollock 5) Education and training that address the issue of ethical decision making will aid officers in the decision-making process. As mentioned, the IACP and police departments across the nation have recognized this importance, and ethics training takes place in academies and is also a part of in-service training.

How do we measure police ethical standards? What standards have been established to determine how police officers should act? Joycelyn Pollock, in her excellent book *Ethical Dilemmas and Decisions in Criminal Justice*, identifies some of these standards:

Organizational value systems or codes of ethics designed to educate and guide the behavior of those who work within the organization

An oath of office, which can be considered a shorthand version of the value system or code of ethics

The Law Enforcement Code of Ethics, as promulgated by the International Association of Chiefs of Police (IACP). (Pollock 195)

Other standards governing police ethics are the U.S. Constitution and the Bill of Rights, case law as determined by appellate courts and the U.S. Supreme Court, and federal and state criminal laws and codes of criminal procedure.

Perhaps it is the police subculture, or perhaps the individual actions of officers or groups of officers that create police deviance. Whatever the reason, deviance certainly occurs in policing. However, remember, as most

BEHAVIORAL GUIDELINES

▶ U.S. Constitution and Bill of Rights

▶ Appellate courts and U.S. Supreme Court

▶ Federal and state criminal laws

Photo © Jean Schweitzer/www.Shutterstock.com. Figure © 2013 Cengage Learning.

officers know, that most of our nation's police officers are highly ethical. Evidence also exists that the U.S. public believes to a great extent that our police are good, ethical, and do the right thing.

Police officers face ethical dilemmas every day. They make difficult decisions on a daily basis using discretion. Officers have to weigh many variables and sometimes contemplate accomplishing the most good for the greatest number of people. Whenever they do this, they are open to questioning and criticism. If they considered the wrong factors (race, ability to gain influence, payoffs) in making these decisions, they could be on the slippery slope to **corruption**. The slippery slope concept suggests that when people begin to deviate, they do so in small ways. But once they have deviated, they begin to slide down a slope that leads to greater and more pronounced types of deviance. Therefore, there is no such thing as "minor" unethical behavior. (Perez and Moore 146)

LO2 Discuss the Various Ways Police Actions Are Reviewed

Police are constantly under review by government agencies, including federal, state, and local agencies; the courts; academics; the media; and the general public. Numerous national commissions have looked into the operations of the police. In addition to the national commissions, numerous state and local commissions, panels, and hearings have looked into the behavior and operations of the police. The most notable was the Knapp Commission to Investigate Allegations of Police

National Commissions over see ing the Police

1931	National Commission on Law Observance and Enforcement (Wickersham Commission)
1967	President's Commission on Law Enforcement and Administration of Justice
1968	National Advisory Commission on Civil Disorders
1973	National Advisory Commission on Criminal Justice Standards and Goals
1982	Commission on Accreditation for Law Enforcement Agencies

themselves, or to other legal authorities. Officers' high visibility often puts them under the microscope.

LO3 Identify the Various Definitions, Types, and Extent of Police Corruption and Explore the Reasons for Police Corruption

Police corruption has many definitions, but we can find enough commonalities to define corruption for our purposes as follows: A police officer is corrupt when he or she is acting in his or her official capacity and receives a benefit or something of value (other than his or her paycheck) for doing something or for refraining from doing something.

Is giving an officer a free cup of coffee or a sandwich an act of corruption? It can be difficult to distinguish between genuine gifts (such as Christmas gifts) and gratuities, bribes, and corruption. At times, accepting any kind of gift is the beginning of the slippery slope syndrome, where it becomes easier to accept other, larger gratuities in the future and eventually bribes.

Knapp Commission
Commission created in 1970 to investigate allegations of widespread, organized corruption in the New York City Police Department.

judicial review
Process by which the actions of the police in areas such as arrests, search and seizure, and custodial interrogation are reviewed by the court system to ensure their constitutionality.

 Log onto www.cengagebrain.com to practice your vocabulary with flash cards and more.

Corruption in New York City, commonly known as the **Knapp Commission**. (Knapp Commission)

The police are also under constant review by the U.S. judicial system through the process of **judicial review**. Judicial review is the process by which the actions of the police in such areas as arrests, search and seizure, and custodial interrogation are reviewed by the U.S. court system at various levels to ensure the constitutionality of those actions. Judicial review has resulted in such landmark Supreme Court cases as *Mapp v. Ohio* (1961) and *Miranda v. Arizona* (1966). In addition, the police are reviewed daily by the media: newspapers, magazines, radio, and television. Finally, they are under constant review by citizens, many of whom do not hesitate to report what they consider to be deviant conduct to the media, to the police

Reasons for Police Corruption

When we consider the enormous authority given to our police officers, the tremendous discretion they are allowed to exercise, and the existence of the police personality and police cynicism, it is easy to see that police work is fertile ground for the growth of corruption. Add to this environment the constant contact police have with criminals and

Corruption has been the subject of many movies and books.

TOWER
- SERPICO
- PRINCE OF THE CITY
- BUDDY BOYS
- L.A. CONFIDENTIAL
- TRAINING DAY
- DARK BLUE

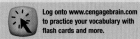

Log onto www.cengagebrain.com to practice your vocabulary with flash cards and more.

unsavory people, the moral dilemma they face when given the responsibility of enforcing unenforceable laws regarding services people actually want (illegal drugs, gambling, alcohol, and prostitution), and the enormous amount of money that can be made by corrupt officers. Based on all these factors, it is little wonder that corruption emerges in police departments.

Samuel Walker and Charles Katz cite several possible theories of corruption:

* **Individual officer explanations:** Blame is placed on the "rotten apple" in the department.

* **Social structural explanations:** Certain social structures in America tend to encourage and sustain corruption, including criminal law, cultural conflict, and local politics.

* **Neighborhood explanations:** Neighborhoods with social disorganization have higher levels of poverty, lower levels of social control, and higher levels of corruption.

* **The nature of police work:** Officers work alone and with little supervision and with constant exposure to wrongdoing. This can lead to the feeling that "everyone is doing it."

* **The police organization:** Corruption flourishes in departments in which the organizational culture tolerates it.

* **The police subculture:** The emphasis on loyalty and group solidarity can lead to lying and cover-ups. (Walker and Katz 455–460)

Any or all of these issues can be at work in influencing the existence and extent of corruption in police agencies. But some view the police subculture and the values associated with that subculture as particularly problematic in regard to the corruption issue. The informal code of policing seems to contradict the formal codes as presented by the IACP. (Pollock 203)

The code of silence—often referred to as the "blue curtain" or "blue veil," which is the tendency of law enforcement personnel to not share information with others—can make it difficult to get at the truth. The belief that others outside the police profession couldn't possibly

understand the challenges officers face is absorbed early in the training and socialization process and is reinforced with time on the job.

Types and Forms of Corruption

Corruption is not limited to the present day. Lawrence W. Sherman reports, "For as long as there have been police, there has been police corruption." (Sherman, *Police Corruption* p. 1) Goldstein says, "Corruption is endemic to policing. The very nature of the police function is bound to subject officers to tempting offers." (Goldstein, *Police Corruption* p. 218)

When the Knapp Commission reported on the police corruption in New York City in the early 1970s, it distinguished between two primary types of corrupt police officers. **Grass-eaters** are more passive and will accept what is offered to them. **Meat-eaters** are more aggressive and search out opportunities to exploit for financial gain. Most officers who accept bribes are grass-eaters. (Knapp Commission 4)

Walker and Katz describe four general types of police corruption: taking gratuities, taking bribes, theft or burglary, and internal corruption. (Walker and Katz 452–454) **Gratuities** are small tips or discounts on goods purchased. Pollock defines gratuities as items of value received by someone because of his or her role or job rather than because of a personal relationship. (Pollock 235) Whether to define the acceptance of gratuities as corruption has been and continues to be hotly debated by both police professionals and the community. The concern of those who feel it is corruption is that it may be the beginning of

Grass-eaters are a more passive type of corrupt officer.

© Image Copyright R. Fassbind, 2009. Used Under License from Shutterstock.com

Meat-eaters tend to search out opportunities for corruption.

that slippery slope and may make it easier for officers to justify participating in more serious acts of wrongdoing.

Police corruption also may involve taking **bribes**— the payment of money or other consideration to police officers with the intent of subverting the aims of the criminal justice system. This is a far more serious form of corruption and often involves payment for nonenforcement of laws or ordinances.

Theft or burglary—the taking of money or property by the police while performing their duties—is another form of police corruption, according to Walker and Katz. The police have access to numerous premises, including warehouses and stores, while investigating burglaries, open doors, or alarms. They also have access to homes while on official business. This is especially true of and tempting at narcotics investigations. There are often huge amounts of cash or drugs lying around, and often no one, not even the suspects, knows exactly how much is there. Until an official cash count or drug inventory is done (which can take hours), exact amounts of contraband are unknown. A corrupt police officer thus has plenty of opportunity to take property from others.

Walker and Katz's final type of police corruption is internal corruption, in which officers pay members of their departments for special assignments or promotions.

Sherman discusses three general levels of police corruption based on the pervasiveness of the corruption, the source of the bribes, and the organization of the corruption (Sherman, *Police Corruption* p. 7) The first is the "**rotten apples** and rotten pockets" theory of police corruption, which holds that only one officer or a very small group of officers in a department or precinct is corrupt. The second level of corruption that Sherman found might exist in a police department is pervasive, unorganized corruption, where most of the officers are corrupt but are not actively working with one another on an organized or planned basis. Sherman's third level of corruption is pervasive, organized corruption, where almost all members of a department or precinct are working together in systematic and organized corruption.

Noble Cause Corruption

Noble cause corruption refers to situations where a police officer bends the rules to attain the "right" result. This is also often referred to as the *Dirty Harry* syndrome. In the extreme situation, an officer might justify violating a suspect's rights to save someone's life. More commonly, the rights violation would be justified in the officer's mind by the ultimate good of putting the bad guy in jail where he belongs. These behaviors involve police officers misusing their legal authority, but they are not doing so for personal gain. They rationalize the behavior to get the bad guys behind bars and consider it a noble cause type of corruption. (Perez and Moore 134)

Effects of Police Corruption

For the past few decades, police misconduct has made headlines far too often. This gives a black eye to the

bribe
Payment of money or other contribution to a police officer with the intent of subverting the aim of the criminal justice system.

"rotten apple" theory
Theory of corruption in which it is believed that individual officers within the agency are bad, rather than the organization as a whole being bad.

noble cause corruption
Stems from ends-oriented policing and involves police officers bending the rules to achieve the "right" goal of putting a criminal in jail.

Log onto www.cengagebrain.com to practice your vocabulary with flash cards and more.

There is an ongoing debate as to whether accepting a free cup of coffee is a form of corruption.

officers who have never, and would never, consider any type of misconduct as well as to agencies with similar standards. Police misconduct also affects the reputations of police officers and police agencies in general. Misconduct committed by an officer affects that officer, the department that the officer works for, the community he or she serves, and every police department and police officer in America. (Palmiotto 39–40) It also affects the police–community relationship in general and can and will undermine the public's trust in the police.

LO4 Describe Other Forms of Police Misconduct Including Drug-Related Corruption, Police Deception, Sex-Related Corruption, and Domestic Violence

Police corruption and police brutality are the most serious forms of police deviance. Police brutality will be discussed later in the chapter. Other types of police deviance also exist. Chief among them are drug-related corruption, sleeping on duty, police deception, sexual violence, and domestic violence.

A narcotics officer in Providence, R.I. is arraigned on charges that he aided a cocaine ring.

Drug-Related Corruption

Drug-related corruption is similar to other types of corruption, but it is an added concern to modern law enforcement agencies because of the frequency with which these incidents can occur. Drug users and dealers make good targets for corrupt officers because they are less likely to report being victimized. There is also an opportunity to make a lot of money simply by looking the other way.

Sleeping on Duty

Fatigue is an issue for all involved in police work, and, consequently, sleeping on duty intentionally or unintentionally is an important concern. With officers working the night shift and the rest of the world functioning on a day-shift schedule, conflicts arise. Officers attend court and meetings during the day when they should be sleeping. Their sleep is also interrupted by phones, delivery personnel, repair people, children, and family responsibilities. Because of the nature of police work and the

Sleeping on duty, whether intentional or accidental, is a safety issue.

© AP Photo/Paul Sancya

Police officers, a prosecutor and a judge appear at their arraignment in Detroit for allegedly allowing the police and a key witness to give false testimony.

lack of activity and supervision during the early morning hours, it can be easy for an officer to find a "hiding place" and attempt to sleep for a while. This is clearly inattention to duty and is hazardous for the officer and his or her coworkers.

Police Deception

Another form of police misconduct is **police deception**, which includes perjury while testifying in court, attempts to circumvent rules regarding searches and seizures of evidence, and falsifying police reports.

Deception is a serious issue. Police administrators will tell you that honesty is the most crucial trait of a police applicant and police officer. Deception in the hiring process will disqualify applicants, no questions asked, and deception by police officers will result in termination. With officers routinely swearing to the truth in everything they do and write, deception cannot be tolerated. Yet, as administrators will tell you, deception can be difficult to prove, as it is often one person's word against another's. When deception is discovered in any aspect of the job, it can taint any case the officer has ever been involved in. A U.S. Supreme Court decision, *Brady v. Maryland*, requires prosecutors to notify defense attorneys whenever a cop involved in their case has a record of knowingly lying in an official capacity. (*Brady v. Maryland*) These cops have become known as "Brady cops" and can be liabilities to their agencies.

Sex-Related Corruption

Police sexual violence incorporates many behaviors and involves situations in which officers use their author-

ity to extort sex from female citizens or conduct some type of invasion of privacy of those female citizens. (Pollock 236–237) These are very serious offenses against the public trust. Most police officers detest this behavior of the few who perpetrate it. The community is also shocked to think an officer would use his position of trust to violate some of the most vulnerable citizens.

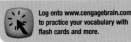

Police administrators need to be aware of this type of violation and vigilant in looking for warning signs. Often, behavior can signal a potential problem; if that behavior is handled quickly and effectively, administrators might be able to avert a bigger problem or give the organization documentation of behavior for a discipline case.

Examples of warning signs might include a male officer pulling over female drivers, spending a lot of time outside bars at closing time, spending an inordinate amount of time at any place women tend to congregate, or conducting follow-ups that he wouldn't conduct for the average citizen. Most of these activities can be explained away in the context of performing good police service, but together they could be a pattern of behavior worth watching. Law enforcement agencies also need to communicate to all personnel a zero tolerance for this type of violation. A well-written policy outlining the process for reporting, documenting, and investigating these incidents will further strengthen an agency's position.

Domestic Violence in Police Families

Some studies indicate that domestic violence may be more prevalent in police families than in the general population. (National Center for Women and Policing) Such violence has traditionally been a hidden problem because victims are hesitant to report it. Domestic violence is only beginning to be addressed, and it is an uphill battle. If the victim is a spouse of a police officer, then the offender has friends and supporters in the department who may not believe the allegations; the offender has a gun; and the offender knows the legal system and knows where the shelters are.

The International Association of Chiefs of Police (IACP) has developed a model policy regarding police-involved domestic violence, and some departments are building on that policy and becoming proactive. The IACP policy stresses that zero tolerance toward domestic

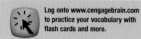
violence should be established in agencies through the education and training of all personnel as well as the development of clear and comprehensive policies and procedures. The 1996 federal law (18 U.S.C. 925) widely referred to as the Lautenberg Act, which prohibits anyone convicted of a misdemeanor from owning or using a firearm, further complicates the law enforcement issue.

A tragic domestic violence case occurred in Tacoma, Washington. On April 26, 2003, David Brame, the Tacoma chief of police, fatally shot his wife and then himself in front of their children in a parking lot in a neighboring community. This came several days after allegations of abuse and impending divorce had become public, despite his wife's efforts to minimize his anger and embarrassment by filing the divorce papers in a neighboring county. Brame's wife, Crystal, had filed these divorce papers and moved out of the home with the children in February,

Domestic violence can be a problem in police families.

© Janine Wiedel Photolibrary/Alamy

alleging that her husband was abusive and possessive. Brame was assistant chief and a 20-year veteran of the department when he was named chief in December 2001, and there were allegations that the city manager knew of the rumors of abuse and an acquaintance rape issue in Brame's past but did not investigate them thoroughly before appointing Brame chief. The state of Washington concluded an investigation of the incident in November 2003 and found no grounds for criminal charges but significant evidence of mismanagement within the city of Tacoma. Relatives of Crystal Brame filed a $75 million wrongful-death civil suit, with the belief that the city's inaction or inappropriate actions ultimately led to Crystal's death. (Ko) The family settled the suit, with the city of Tacoma paying the family $12 million in addition to establishing a city–county domestic violence center named after Crystal and implementing new policies and procedures regarding police officer–involved domestic violence.

LO5 Define and Discuss Biased-Based Policing

Biased-based policing has emerged as an important issue in communities in the last two decades. But, in reality, the government has faced this problem since *Plessy v. Ferguson* (1896) and *Brown v. Board of Education of Topeka* (1954). Providing equal protection and equal opportunity is a critical issue to the American people. The behavior that has led to the coining of the phrase *biased-based policing* has existed for years. When the behavior increased in frequency and severity in the 1980s and 1990s in an attempt to fight the rising crime rate and escalating drug problem, the community began to notice and speak out. The issue of whether this practice of stopping individuals based on their race or ethnicity was proper police procedure or ethical police behavior was raised.

Racial profiling, the term commonly used for bias-based policing, is generally defined as any police-initiated activity that relies on a person's race or ethnic background rather than on the person's behavior as a basis for identifying that individual as being involved in criminal activity. Police may not use race or ethnicity to decide whom to stop or search, but they may use it to determine whether an individual matches a specific description of a suspect. (U.S. Department of Justice, *Resource Guide* 10)

The validity of stops may be questioned when police are investigating a crime committed by a group of

individuals who may share ethnic or racial characteristics. Some criminal enterprises are composed of persons with similar ethnic or racial or national origins, but using this characteristic as a determining factor could be interpreted as racial profiling. (U.S. Department of Justice, *Resource Guide*)

During the 1990s, racial profiling became a hot topic in the media. New terms were coined, such as "driving while black" (DWB). Media attention brought the topic up for discussion in communities. Recently, the Department of Justice found that nationwide, among all traffic stops, though all races were stopped at similar rates by police, blacks (9.5 percent) and Hispanics (8.8 percent) were more likely to be searched during their stops than whites (3.6 percent). (Durose, Smith, and Langan 1)

Most recently, the issue of biased-based policing has often involved individuals of Muslim descent. In the aftermath of 9/11, the community as well as the police began to report an increased awareness of the activities of people who appear to be of Middle Eastern descent.

Regardless of whether racial profiling occurs, the mere perception of its existence can result in problems in the community. Realizing this, many states have instituted legislation requiring the gathering of data and the implementation of racial profiling policies. In fact, most police academies in the country address racially biased policing as part of their basic training program, and according to the Department of Justice's Survey of Local Police Departments, 67 percent of departments have written policies about racial profiling by officers. (Reaves, *Local Police Departments, 2007*)

Police officers have a lot of discretion in their jobs, and this is particularly evident in traffic stops. First, officers decide whether or not to stop a car; then, they decide how to handle the stop—that is, whether to remove occupants from the vehicle, call for a drug dog, ask for a consent search, and so on. Citizens have questioned how officers make these discretionary decisions, and some allege that these decisions are based on race or ethnicity. Many members of minority groups feel they are being stopped for petty traffic violations, such as failure to use a turn signal or an equipment violation, just so that officers can use the opportunity to question occupants or search vehicles.

More data are needed to better determine if there is a specific problem in various cities and states across the country. In response to the community outcry, most states have implemented some type of data collection system.

Collecting these data will either help the community see there is no problem with the activities of their police or help the police and community understand the scope of the problems. This data collection will also send a message to all concerned that racial profiling is unacceptable. Analyzing the data and initiating an early warning system can also help identify the officers or squads who may be prone to inappropriate stops. The data should be looked at as part of a big picture, however. Characteristics of a particular jurisdiction can skew the data—major highways, large shopping centers, and large employers can affect the amount of nonresidential population traveling to or through a jurisdiction. Some agencies may not be pleased with the analysis of their data, but others will be reassured.

If analysis of these data reveals a problem, it can be addressed. New procedures, training, or counseling can be employed to make changes. Some departments are reassured when they find there is not a bias-based policing problem, and the data can help them counter allegations of unfair treatment. A community that trusts its police department is more likely to work with the department in making the community safe, and this is a good thing for all concerned.

Agencies are training their officers in the area of racial profiling and ensuring that data regarding stops are collected and analyzed to determine if there is a problem.

LO6 Discuss the Definition, Types, and Extent of Police Brutality

Use of force is a necessary part of police work. Officers are allowed to use the level of force necessary to counter a suspect's resistance and get the suspect to comply with a lawful order. Use of force can range from a loud, commanding voice to deadly force. The use of force must be reasonable and it must be appropriate. When officers exceed this necessary level of force to achieve compliance, they are using excessive force. Police brutality is more severe and represents a significant disparity between the level of compliance by the citizen and the level of police force used (Caldero and Crank 194) When an officer uses physical violence against citizens, it is a significant occurrence. When it is excessive, not warranted, and qualifies as brutality, it is further along the slippery slope of corruption. Further, police brutality involves significant risk, including injury or death to the suspect, officer, or other officers, as well as the risk of citizen retaliation.

internal affairs division
The unit of a police agency that is charged with investigating police corruption or misconduct.

integrity test
Proactive investigation of corruption in which investigators provide opportunities for officers to commit illegal acts.

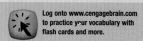
Log onto www.cengagebrain.com to practice your vocabulary with flash cards and more.

RESPONSES TO CORRUPTION

▶ **investigation**

▶ **discipline**

▶ **termination**

▶ **decertification**

Photo © Patrick Hermans/www.Shutterstock.com. Figure © 2013 Cengage Learning.

LO7 Explore Various Responses to Police Corruption

Investigations

The most important step in eliminating or reducing police corruption is to admit that corruption exists. The need for candor, Goldstein argues, is paramount. Police officials have traditionally attempted to ignore the problem and deny that it exists. (Goldstein, *Police Corruption* pp. 6–8) However, many police departments have established **internal affairs divisions** as their major

> The ideal way for police agencies to handle the deviance and corruption issue is through prevention.

department resource to combat corruption. Internal affairs divisions or units are the police who police the police department. Though it can vary by department, depending on the organizational climate in the agency, sometimes internal affairs investigators are not very popular with other members of the department because many officers see them as spies who only want to get other officers in trouble.

In understanding both the negative connotations of the "internal affairs" title and the need for systematic preventive initiatives regarding corruption, many departments have implemented "professional standards" units, "compliance" units, or "integrity" units. These divisions within the police department investigate allegations of wrongdoing, but are also actively involved in developing and implementing policies and procedures to minimize the chances of corruption occurring. These units conduct audits and inspections to ensure that safeguards are in place and procedures are being adhered to. Good record keeping is essential to preventing corruption, or, if it occurs, helpful in the investigative process.

Internal affairs divisions can attack corruption in two ways: reactively and proactively. In a reactive investigation, the investigator waits for a complaint of corruption from the public and then investigates that specific complaint using traditional investigative techniques. In a proactive investigation into police corruption, investigators provide opportunities for officers to commit illegal acts, such as by leaving valuable property at a scene to see if officers follow normal procedures regarding found property. Proactive investigations are often called **integrity tests**.

Police corruption can also be investigated by local district attorneys, state and federal prosecutors, and special investigative bodies.

In addition, the FBI has jurisdiction to investigate police corruption, and these investigations have had a major effect on several police departments, including the Philadelphia and the New Orleans departments.

Discipline and Termination

When corruption has been discovered in an agency, discipline is in order. This will start with any individuals directly involved and move up the chain to "clean house." Typically, anyone who could have or should have known there was a problem (and perhaps chose to look the other way and ignore it, or was simply an ineffective leader) will be terminated. This usually will include the chief. At times, this can be problematic. Officers, like everyone else, are entitled to due process. With civil service protections and union representation, what can appear to administrators to be a clear violation worthy of discipline or termination (especially in the case of noncriminal misconduct) can be ultimately overturned by arbitrators, civil service boards, or courts. Departments can be in a state of limbo as these cases work through their various appeals.

Decertification is also an option for law enforcement agencies. This is an administrative action coordinated through the state police standards organization that will determine if cause exists to strip an officer of his or her state certification to be a police officer.

Preventive Administrative Actions

The ideal way for police agencies to handle the deviance and corruption issue is through prevention. The hiring and screening process is the first step in preventing police corruption and misconduct. By screening out of the process those applicants who might be prone to violence, have a quick temper, hold inappropriate attitudes, show a

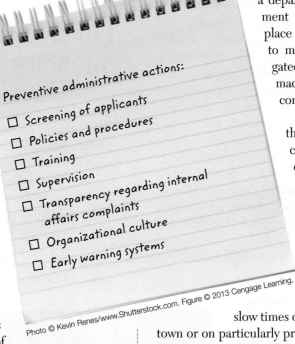

Preventive administrative actions:

☐ Screening of applicants

☐ Policies and procedures

☐ Training

☐ Supervision

☐ Transparency regarding internal affairs complaints

☐ Organizational culture

☐ Early warning systems

Photo © Kevin Renes/www.Shutterstock.com. Figure © 2013 Cengage Learning.

tendency to be "badge heavy," or already have committed criminal acts, many problems can be avoided.

Another administrative tool to prevent corruption and misconduct is a good policy and procedure manual that lets officers, supervisors, administrators, and the public know what behavior is allowed and what is not acceptable.

In addition to being knowledgeable about the department's policies and procedures, citizens should also be informed about the procedure for making a complaint against a department employee. The department should have a procedure in place to govern these complaints to make sure they all are investigated and that a determination is made regarding the validity of the complaint.

Training is a follow-up to the development of good policies. Ongoing training is necessary because laws and policies change. Supervisors can ensure that officers receive the updated training and understand how to put these new policies into practice. Additionally, adequate supervision can help prevent misconduct during slow times of the shift or in certain areas of town or on particularly problematic types of calls.

The organizational culture can help prevent corruption and misconduct. If a department takes a proactive stance toward promoting integrity throughout the entire agency, the environment will not be conducive toward the development of corruption or deviance. If officers know where the chief stands and the chief models ethical behavior, officers will know which behavior will not be tolerated. This, together with rewarding good officer behavior, including that of officers who report wrongdoing by others, will help establish an ethical climate in the agency.

Computerized early warning systems have made it easier in the last few years to identify officers who might have a problem. These are generally now referred to as early intervention systems. Early warning systems typically use computer programs that flag officers who may be prone to problems when interacting with the public.

When a department incorporates all these preventive methods, works to promote integrity, and, consequently, works with the community to solve problems and reduce crime, an improved environment for all will result.

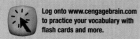
Citizen Oversight

Citizen oversight (also referred to as civilian review, citizen complaint boards, or external review) is a method designed to allow for independent citizen review of complaints filed against the police through a board or committee that independently reviews allegations, monitors the complaint process, examines procedures, and makes recommendations regarding procedures and the quality of the investigations in the department. Citizen oversight has generally been implemented when the community is unhappy with its police department and believes that citizens have not had adequate input into how the department is operated. When the community feels that internal affairs is not doing its job, citizen's rights groups demand some type of citizen oversight to ensure that complaints against the police are adequately investigated.

There are four basic models of oversight systems:

- Citizens investigate allegations of misconduct and make recommendations to the head of the agency.

- Officers conduct the investigations and develop findings that the citizens then review, recommending to the head of the agency to approve or reject the findings.

- Officers investigate misconduct and render recommendations, but citizens can appeal the findings to citizens who make recommendations to the head of the agency.

- An auditor investigates the process the department uses to investigate misconduct and reports on the fairness and thoroughness of the process to the community. (Siegel and Senna 160)

In general, citizens are in favor of the citizen review process. Police can be somewhat resistant regarding the use of civilian review boards, but often come to see their value when they realize the effect the process can have on the community's perception of their department. However, most departments like to have the final say in the discipline, policies, and training they implement.

Despite the valid arguments on both sides of the issue of citizen oversights, processes involving citizens are widely used.

LO8 Discuss the Issue of Liability and the Effects of Lawsuits on Police Officers and Police Agencies

Misconduct by police officers can lead to civil and criminal liability, and police officers may be held legally liable—that is arrested, sued, and prosecuted for their conduct. This concept of police legal liability comes in many different forms. Police **civil liability** means that a police officer may be sued in civil court, using such civil law concepts as negligence and torts, for improper behavior. Civil liability, using lawsuits and the resultant monetary judgments, is a relatively new approach to correcting improper actions by the police. Officers may also be sued under the provisions of a state civil rights law for violation of a person's civil rights.

Officers often testify in civil lawsuits including wrongful death lawsuits.

AP Photo/Cherie Diez, Pool

As for **criminal liability**, many states have provisions in their penal codes that make certain actions by police officers or other public servants a crime. Police officers, like everyone else, are subject to being charged with violations of the state penal law, such as murder, assault, or larceny.

Police officers are also subject to administrative liability: They are liable for the rules and regulations established by their department to govern the conduct of its officers. Officers charged with violations of their department's internal rules and regulations may be subject to discipline in the form of fines, demotions, and even dismissal from the department.

In recent years, an increasing number of lawsuits against police officers have been brought to federal courts on civil rights grounds. These federal suits are known as 1983 suits because they are based on Section 1983 of Title 42 of the U.S. Code (Civil Action for Deprivation of Civil Rights): The violation of these regulations may lead to such disciplinary actions as fines, demotions, or dismissal.

Reasons for Suing Police Officers

In *Civil Liabilities in American Policing: A Text for Law Enforcement Personnel*, Rolando del Carmen includes chapters on the following types of liabilities affecting law enforcement personnel: liability for nondeadly and deadly use of force; liability for false arrest and false imprisonment; liability for searches and seizures; liability for negligence, specific instances of negligence in police work; liability for jail management; liabilities of police supervisors for what their subordinates do; and liabilities of police supervisors for what they do to their subordinates. (del Carmen, *Civil Liabilities in American Policing* pp. 2–3)

In his text *Critical Issues in Police Civil Liability*, Victor Kappeler addresses the issue of negligence and discusses areas of concern to law enforcement officers. These areas of potential liability include negligent operation of emergency vehicles; negligent failure to protect; negligent failure to arrest; negligent failure to render assistance; negligent selection, hiring, and retention; negligent police supervision and direction; negligent entrustment and assignment; and negligent failure to discipline and investigate. Some of these issues are of more concern to law enforcement administrators, but many should be of concern to the street officer as well. (Kappeler 26)

Effects of Lawsuits on Police Departments and Officers

The use of civil lawsuits against the police has been increasing at a rapid rate and is having a dramatic effect on the treasuries of some counties and cities. Advocates of police civil damage lawsuits see these lawsuits as a vehicle for stimulating police reform. They assume that the dollar cost of police misconduct will force other city officials to intervene and force improvements in the police department through discipline, policy change, or training.

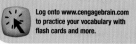

criminal liability
Being subject to punishment for a crime.

Log onto www.cengagebrain.com to practice your vocabulary with flash cards and more.

Increased media attention, coupled with some high judgments and out-of-court settlements, has encouraged individuals and lawyers to go after the most visible arm of the criminal justice system—the police. There is the perception that the government has "deep pockets" and the ability to pay these judgments and settlements. However, the cost to taxpayers for civil suits is extremely high when one factors in the cost of liability insurance, litigation, out-of-court settlements, and punitive damage awards. It is unfortunate, but because of the high costs, many governments pay minimal out-of-court settlements to get rid of the case and avoid the costs of litigation. This angers the police officers involved, who feel they did nothing wrong and that the government should always defend them and stand up for what is right rather than just look for the least expensive way to resolve the situation. Police also fear that settlements encourage frivolous lawsuits.

Officers and administrators thus need to be aware of the issue of civil liability and the police. Sometimes the threat of civil suits and large penalties proves to be an effective deterrent to excessive force, but unrealistic fears of civil liability have a number of negative effects, including morale problems, alienation from the public, and, sometimes, misunderstandings. Some officers may develop a reluctance to take action that should be part

Police chiefs will have to face the media when allegations of wrongdoing surface within their departments.

© Allen Fredrickson/Reuters/Corbis

© Albany Times Union/The Image Works

Testifying in civil lawsuits can be stressful and police administrators must be cognizant of the emotional toll on officers.

of their job because of the fear of being sued. This could result in an ineffective police agency, with many officers doing just enough to get by and stay out of trouble. However, the increase in litigation does have a positive side in that it allows for proper redress of police wrongdoing and promotes better police training and more responsible police practices; it also sets the standard for police behavior. (Kappeler 11)

The Emotional Toll

The emotional toll that internal affairs investigations can cause is a subject often ignored by academics. Although it is important for many reasons to receive, document, and track complaints against the police, people have all sorts of reasons for complaining about police officers. Many mistakenly hope to get out of whatever charges they face, from traffic tickets to arrests. Often the person charged is not the person who makes the complaint. Instead, he or she tells someone about it, and that third party may decide to make an issue of it. These complaints can generate a lot of media attention. The media love to report on "bad cops," sometimes without all the facts being in.

> Sometimes fellow officers may unintentionally distance themselves from an accused officer. . . .

The public reads about the complaint in the paper or hears about it on the news, and the statement is often made that "Officer Smith would not comment," which the public may view negatively. The press does not usually mention that most of the time, department policy, and sometimes state law, prevents an officer from discussing an ongoing investigation. This results in the citizen complainant getting to tell his or her story, often repeatedly, with that account not being disputed by the police until the conclusion of the investigation. Unfortunately, this process can take weeks or months, depending on how involved the investigation is, by which time the public or the press no longer cares about the case.

This has a dramatic impact on the psychological well-being of the officers involved, as well as on that of their families, who see their names trashed in the papers and on the news. Sometimes fellow officers may unintentionally distance themselves from an accused officer, wanting to avoid any negative publicity or association. Command staff and supervisors may also avoid contact with the officer in hopes of not contaminating the investigation, and the involved officer is often placed on administrative leave. This leads to the officer feeling abandoned and alone, with no one to talk to about the incident. Departments often don't consider the isolation and lack of support the officer may experience because their most pressing concern becomes distancing the department and its policies from the officer's behavior, if necessary. Police administrators and officers thus need to remind themselves that police officers go into law enforcement to serve the public and do the right thing. If by being wrongly accused or by making a mistake they are now vilified, the effects can be devastating. The worst-case scenario is the officer who commits suicide as his or her world crumbles; lesser problems include turning to alcohol, experiencing marital problems, or having extreme cynicism for the remainder of his or her career. Police administrators need to be cognizant of the emotional toll of internal investigations and have some procedures in place to help minimize those effects.

 Log onto www.cengagebrain.com for additional resources including videos, flash cards, games, self-quizzing, review exercises, web exercises, learning checks, and more.

THE IN-CROWD

Share your 4LTR Press story on Facebook at
www.facebook.com/4ltrpress for a chance to win.

To learn more about the
In-Crowd opportunity 'like'
us on Facebook.

9

Patrol Operations

After studying this chapter, the student should be able to:

LO1 Understand the traditional methods of doing police work and examine their effectiveness

LO2 Discuss the activities involved in the patrol function

LO3 Describe the findings of the Kansas City patrol study

LO4 Examine the issue of rapid response to citizens' 911 calls

LO5 Discuss some of the innovative ways of performing the patrol function

LO6 Describe some of the innovative ways of responding to 911 calls and crime problems in the community

LO7 Examine new methods of resource allocation

LO8 Discuss new tactical approaches to patrol operations

LO9 Describe new efforts to combat the drunk driving problem and efforts targeting aggressive driving

LO10 Discuss special operations, including SWAT teams, emergency service units, and K-9 units

LO1 Understand the Traditional Methods of Doing Police Work and Examine Their Effectiveness

The three cornerstones of traditional police work are (1) random routine patrol, (2) rapid response to calls by citizens to 911, and (3) retroactive investigation of past crimes by detectives. (Cordner, Scarborough, and Sheehan, 2007, 383)

The average U.S. police officer arrives at work at the beginning of his or her shift and receives the keys and the patrol car from the officer who used it on the previous tour. The officer then drives around a designated geographic area (**random routine patrol**). When the officer receives a call from the police dispatcher, he or she responds to the call and performs whatever police work is required—making an arrest, administering first aid, breaking up a fight, taking a crime report, and so on (**rapid response to citizens' calls to 911**). If the call involves a crime, the officer conducts a preliminary investigation and often refers the case to a detective, who conducts a follow-up investigation of the crime (**retroactive investigation of past crimes by detectives**). As soon as the officer is finished handling the call, he or she resumes patrol and is ready to respond to another call.

random routine patrol
Officers driving around a designated geographic area.

rapid response to citizens' calls to 911
Officers being dispatched to calls immediately, regardless of the type of call.

retroactive investigation of past crimes by detectives
The follow-up investigation of crimes by detectives that occurs after a crime has been reported.

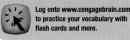
Log onto www.cengagebrain.com to practice your vocabulary with flash cards and more.

123

LO2 Discuss the Activities Involved in the Patrol Function

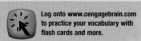
When we think of the police, our first image is that of a man or woman in uniform driving a police car, at rapid speeds with lights and siren, to the scene of a crime or an accident. We also may think of the uniformed officer on foot patrol ("walking a beat") in a downtown business area moving a drunk and disorderly citizen away from a group of shoppers. (**Foot patrol** is a method of deploying police officers that gives them responsibility for all policing activity by requiring them to walk around a defined geographic area.) We may think of a police officer on horseback or on a motorcycle. All these officers have one thing in common: they are patrol officers.

Since the time of Sir Robert Peel (the promoter of the first organized, paid, uniformed police force in London in 1829), patrol has been the most important and visible part of police work to the public. Peel's major innovation and contribution to society was the idea of a continuous police presence throughout a community that is organized and delivered by means of regular patrol over a fixed beat by uniformed officers. Patrol is the essence of policing.

Activities of the Patrol Officer

Patrol is known as the foundation of the police department. Patrol officers are the uniformed officers who respond to calls for service, emergencies, and all sorts of disturbances that occur. They are the most visible arm of the criminal justice system as well as the gatekeepers to that system.

The patrol function has changed little since 1829 and has three main goals:

- The deterrence of crime
- The maintenance of a feeling of public security
- Twenty-four-hour availability for service to the public

Traditionally, the primary services provided by the patrol function include activities that involve both enforcing the law and serving the public.

ACTIVITIES OF A PATROL OFFICER:

- ▶ Enforcing laws
- ▶ Deterring crime
- ▶ Maintaining order
- ▶ Keeping the peace
- ▶ Enforcing traffic laws
- ▶ Keeping traffic flowing
- ▶ Investigating accidents
- ▶ Conducting preliminary investigations
- ▶ Responding to calls for assistance
- ▶ Assisting vulnerable populations

LO3 Describe the Findings of the Kansas City Patrol Study

Random routine patrol, otherwise known as preventive patrol, involves a police officer driving around and within a community when he or she is not on an assignment from the radio dispatcher or a supervisor. Tradition has held that random routine patrol creates a sense of omnipresence and deters crime because a criminal will not chance committing a crime if a police officer might be just around the corner. Random routine patrol was believed to enable police officers to catch criminals in the act of committing their crimes. Just how effective is random routine patrol? The **Kansas City patrol study** was the first attempt to actually test the effectiveness of random routine patrol.

The Kansas City Study in Brief

During 1972 and 1973, the Kansas City (Missouri) Police Department, under the leadership of Police Chief Clarence Kelly (who later became the director of the FBI) and with the

KANSAS CITY PATROL STUDY

5 Beats	control group	no change in behavior of officers
5 Beats	reactive	all preventive patrolling eliminated
5 Beats	proactive	provided 2-3x the level of normal patrol activity

Photo © Jim Lopes/www.Shutterstock.com. Figure © 2013 Cengage Learning.

support of the Police Foundation, conducted an experiment to test the effects of routine preventive patrol. This yearlong experiment has been both influential and controversial.

Fifteen patrol beats in Kansas City's South Patrol Division were used for the study. Five of these beats were assigned to a control group, with no changes in normal patrol staffing or tactics. Five other beats were chosen as reactive beats, and all preventive patrolling was eliminated. Outside patrol units handled calls in the reactive beats, and units left the beats once they had handled the calls. The final five beats in the experiment were proactive beats, in which two to three times the usual level of preventive patrolling was provided. If random routine patrol is an effective way of policing our communities, we should expect to see changes in the reactive and proactive beats.

When the Kansas City study was finished, the researchers concluded, "Decreasing or increasing routine preventive patrol within the range tested in [the] experiment had no effect on crime, citizen fear of crime, community attitudes toward the police on the delivery of police service, police response time, or traffic accidents." (Kelling, Pate, Dieckman, and Brown 16) In effect, the study demonstrated that adding or taking away police patrols from an area does not make any difference within the community. Indeed, at the end of the experiment, no one in the community had any idea that an experiment regarding policing had been conducted in the community.

The conclusions of the Kansas City study shocked many people and differed from all the assumptions we had always made regarding police patrol. It had been commonly believed that putting more officers on patrol would cause a decrease in crime, and taking away police would cause an increase in crime.

Gary W. Cordner, Kathryn E. Scarborough, and Robert Sheehan describe the value of the Kansas City study by saying that although the study did not result in the elimination of preventive or random routine patrol, it

set the stage for further experimentation with alternative patrol strategies and tactics. Because of the study, police executives realized that they could try alternative patrol tactics without fearing that reduced random routine patrol would result in calamity. (Cordner, Scarborough, and Sheehan, 2007, 386) It paved the way for using some, if not all, of the time that had previously been used in preventive patrol in the pursuit of more innovative and creative methods of addressing the crime problem.

LO4 Examine the Issue of Rapid Response to Citizens' 911 Calls

Rapid response to citizens' calls to 911 has traditionally been thought of as a way in which the police could catch criminals while they are in the act of committing their crimes or as they are escaping from their crimes. The ideal scenario is this: A citizen observes a person committing a crime and immediately calls 911. The police respond in seconds and arrest the perpetrator. This sounds great, but it rarely works that way.

In 1967, the President's Commission on Law Enforcement and Administration of Justice, in its *Task Force Report: Science and Technology*, found that quick response to a citizen's report of a crime to 911 made an arrest more likely. However, the commission emphasized that only extremely quick response times were likely to result in arrest.

In 1973, the National Advisory Commission on Criminal Justice Standards and Goals observed, "When the (response) time is cut to 2 minutes, it can have a dramatic effect on crime." (National Advisory Commission on Criminal Justice Standards and Goals 194)

In time, further studies of rapid response to citizens' calls to 911 were carried out. These studies took into account the complexity of response time, which consists of three basic components:

1. The time between when the crime occurs and the moment the victim or a witness calls the police

2. The time required for the police to process the call

3. Travel time from the time the patrol car receives the call from the dispatcher until it arrives at the scene

Studies found that victims, for varied reasons, often delay calling the police after a crime or other incident has occurred. The discovery that citizens often wait several minutes before calling the police puts response time in a different light and suggests that rapid response may not be as significant as was once thought. (Kansas City Police Department, 1978; Spelman and Brown, 1981) Studies also found that in cases in which citizens returned home

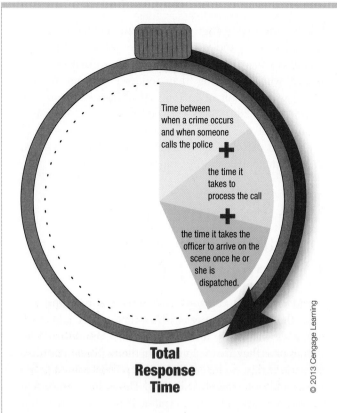

Time between when a crime occurs and when someone calls the police

+

the time it takes to process the call

+

the time it takes the officer to arrive on the scene once he or she is dispatched.

Total Response Time

© 2013 Cengage Learning

and "discovered" crimes as opposed to seeing crime occur, the response time was irrelevant.

We will always need some type of rapid police response to citizens' calls to 911 in violent and emergency situations. However, as the academic studies have indicated, alternative strategies to rapid response to citizens' calls to 911 are needed to make better use of police officers.

Academic Studies of the Police Patrol Function

Patrol Activity Studies To determine what police actually do, researchers have conducted patrol activity studies.

The collection of data regarding the actual activity of patrol officers during each hour of their tours is probably the best answer to the question, "What do police officers do?" This information includes activities the police are directed to perform by the 911 dispatcher, as well as the officers' self-initiated activities. These data can usually be retrieved from officers' activity reports and observations by researchers riding with police patrol officers. (Cordner, 1989, 60–71) Data on what occurs when an officer encounters a citizen—either when the officer is on assignment from the dispatcher or is on self-initiated activities—can best be retrieved from researcher observations.

Observations on the Studies Over the years academic studies have been conducted examining the patrol function. Most experts today agree that the bulk of police patrol work is devoted to what has been described as random routine patrol, administrative

matters, order maintenance, and service-related functions. Cordner, Scarborough, and Sheehan state that, although the studies performed a valuable function by challenging the crime-fighting image of police work, by the late 1970s many police chiefs and scholars carried the studies too far and began to downplay and deemphasize the crime-related and law enforcement aspects of police work. (Cordner, Scarborough, and Sheehan, 2007, 31) James Q. Wilson noted that he would "prefer the police to act and talk as if they were able to control crime."

Cordner, Scarborough, and Sheehan sum up all the studies on "what do cops do" as follows:

Taking all of these studies into consideration, we think a middle of the road position is advisable. It is obvious now that police work is not so completely dominated by crime fighting as its public image and media misrepresentations would suggest. However, it is equally clear that crime-related matters occupy an appreciable portion of the police workload. The available research conclusively demonstrates that those who have been arguing that police work has little or nothing to do with crime know little or nothing about police work. (Cordner, Scarborough, and Sheehan, 2007, 32)

Additionally, because departments today have the data to analyze specifically how their officers are spending their time, they can staff their patrol forces accordingly.

From the Foot Beat to the Patrol Car

Patrol allocation models give the police answers as to where and when to assign officers. Over the years, however, different methods of deploying police officers have been used. The two major deployments are motorized patrol and foot patrol.

By the late 1930s and 1940s, police management experts stressed the importance of motorized patrol as a

Foot patrol has always been a part of the police patrol function.

© AP Photo/Michael Conroy

There is an ongoing debate about deploying one officer or two in patrol cars.

means of increasing efficiency, and the number of cities using motorized patrol grew.

By the 1960s, the efficiency of the remaining foot patrols was being challenged. Foot patrols were considered geographically restrictive and wasteful of personnel. In addition, foot officers, who at the time had no portable radios (these did not become available until the 1970s), were not efficient in terms of covering large areas or being available to be signaled and sent on assignments. Thus, to management experts, foot patrols were not as efficient as the readily available radio cars.

The change from foot to motor patrol revolutionized U.S. policing. It fulfilled the expectations of the management experts by enabling police departments to provide more efficient patrol coverage—that is, covering more areas more frequently and responding more quickly to calls for service. However, one major, unforeseen consequence of the shift to motorized patrol continues to haunt us. Motorized patrol tends to isolate police officers from the community as they quickly drive through the streets to respond to calls for service, and the personal contact with the officer on the foot beat is lost.

One-Officer versus Two-Officer Patrol Cars

There has been an ongoing debate about having one officer or two in patrol cars. Typically, the larger urban departments in such cities as New York City, Chicago, Washington, D.C., and Los Angeles have deployed two-officer cars. Most suburban and rural departments prefer one-officer cars, which allows them to better deploy their limited number of officers. Since many calls for service do not necessitate two officers, smaller departments believe they get more coverage this way. The theory is that if an officer goes to a dangerous call or encounters a dangerous situation, he or she will automatically have a backup dispatched or can call for backup from a neighboring beat or zone. Having one officer in a car allows departments to

maximize their resources and have the ability to respond to more calls for less money. This is especially important with the recently declining budgets and the difficulty in recruiting officers and filling vacancies. Some agencies compromise by using primarily one-officer cars supplemented by two-officer cars in high-crime areas or during peak hours.

Many officers state that police departments are compromising officer safety in an effort to save money. However, it can be difficult to ascertain the deterrent effect that seeing two officers together might have on someone who was considering assaulting an officer or trying to escape.

On the other hand, it is thought that when officers work in pairs, they might become distracted and not be as observant as they would be on their own. They can also become overly confident and have a false sense of security about their abilities as a team.

Felonious attacks on officers have increased in recent years. Police unions and state and local officials in some parts of the country are thus advocating reexamining the issue of two-officer cars.

Return to Foot Patrol

In the mid-1980s, in an attempt to get the police closer to the public and to avoid the problems resulting from the alienation of radio car officers from the community, an emphasis on foot patrol began to return in many cities.

Citizens want and like foot patrol officers. Why does this more expensive form of policing seem more effective than traditional radio car patrol? It's not necessarily the implementation of foot patrol itself but, rather, the relationship that develops between the officer and the community because of the officer's increased accessibility. Through relationships with community members, the officer will feel a part of the community and work to address the true underlying issues affecting the community, and citizens will feel an improved sense of safety when they feel they can trust their police officers.

LO5 Discuss Some of the Innovative Ways of Performing the Patrol Function

evidence-based policing
Using available scientific research on policing to implement crime-fighting strategies and department policies.

directed patrol
Officers patrol specific locations at specific times to address a specific crime problem.

 Log onto www.cengagebrain.com to practice your vocabulary with flash cards and more.

The studies that have been done and the resulting challenging of long-term beliefs regarding policing in general and patrol in particular have caused law enforcement to examine traditional ways of doing things. If random patrol produces no real benefit, how can that time be better spent? Is there another type of patrol activity that might prove more productive? If responding immediately and in emergency mode is not necessarily beneficial, how can the police organize their response so that it is appropriate to the call for service and reduces the potential danger to the officer and the public? Can police departments couple the two issues and come up with blocks of time to spend in other ways in an effort to address crime problems?

In the overall realization that the crime problem is not entirely under the control of law enforcement, the importance of involving the community in the crime-fighting effort has become clear. Much of the police role involves order maintenance and service activities. Developing a partnership and a working relationship with the community can help address these issues and make the law enforcement mission successful. This is the driving force behind community policing, which will be more thoroughly discussed in Chapter 12.

Evidence-Based Policing

The revelation that some experimentation could be conducted and could possibly challenge long-held beliefs led some researchers to stress that using scientific research could provide great information for improving police response to and tactics in various situations. To the extent that relevant scientific research can be conducted without endangering the community or raising ethical issues, it could provide an excellent scientific basis for future activities and programs. Noted criminologist Lawrence W. Sherman proposed this concept in 1998 and calls it **evidence-based policing** ("evidence" in this case refers to scientific evidence, not criminal evidence). Sherman defines it as "the use of the best available research on the outcomes of police work to implement guidelines and evaluate agencies, units, and officers." To successfully

make use of evidence-based policing, departments will have to let go of the traditional wisdom that has become part of department history and be willing to deviate from "the way we've always done it." Sherman recommends that departments access the "best practices" from the literature and adapt them to their specific laws, policies, and communities. He then advocates monitoring and evaluating the project to determine if it is working and if it could be improved. Further, the sharing of the information with other agencies will continue to add to the knowledge available. (Sherman, 1998; Jensen 98–101) This philosophy can be used in most areas of patrol in which police are looking to improve effectiveness.

LO6 Describe Some of the Innovative Ways of Responding to 911 Calls and Crime Problems in the Community

The current popular alternatives to random routine patrol and rapid response to citizens' 911 calls are directed patrol, split-force patrol, and differential response to calls for service. These innovative approaches to policing are designed to make better use of officers' patrol time and department resources.

Directed Patrol Assignments		
Location	Days/Hours	Crime Information
North end of Mall parking lot	Mondays–Fridays/noon–2pm	unknown subjects breaking into parked vehicles, possibly using spark plugs to shatter windows, removing GPS devices

Directed Patrol

An alternative to random routine patrol is **directed patrol**, in which officers are given specific directions to follow when they are not responding to calls. The directed patrol assignments are given to officers before they begin their tour and are meant to replace uncommitted random patrol time with specific duties that police commanders believe will be effective. Directed patrol assignments can be based on crime analysis, specific problems, or complaints received from the community. In departments using the community policing philosophy, patrol officers are often given the freedom to determine where and when their patrol efforts should be directed based on crime analysis and their experiences.

Several studies present some evidence that target crimes were reduced by directed patrol. By basing directed patrol assignments on statistical studies, many of the inadequacies of random, unstructured patrol may be overcome. The data suggest that citizen satisfaction and crime control efforts increase when patrol is based on a systematic analysis of crime.

Split-Force Patrol

As we have just seen, directed patrol is designed so that officers can pay particular attention to specific crimes and disorders while they are not on assignment from the police dispatcher. One of the problems with directed patrol, however, is that calls for service often interrupt the performance of directed patrol assignments. **Split-force patrol** offers a solution to this problem. One portion of the patrol force is designated to handle all calls dispatched to patrol units. The remaining portion of the officers working that tour are given directed patrol assignments, with the assurance that except for serious emergencies, they will not be interrupted.

SHIFT ASSIGNMENTS			
Shift 1500–2300			Date: 03/11
ZONE	OFFICER	ID	SPECIAL INSTRUCTIONS
1 A 31	Smith	026	1700–1800 patrol beach area
1 A 32	Fredricks	189	
1 A 33	Wilson	221	2000–2200 hospital parking lot ref car thefts
1 B 34	Duke/Jones	045/301	training unit/can jump calls
1 A 35	Washington	126	2200–2300 high visibility patrol Bud's Bar area
1 A 36	Erickson	203	1600–1700 bike patrol in business district

Differential Response to Calls for Service and the 911 System

Differential response to calls for service is a policy that abandons the traditional practice of responding to all calls for service. In differential response, responses to citizens' calls to 911 for service are matched to the importance or severity of the calls. Reports of injuries, crimes, or emergencies in progress, as well as reports of serious past crimes, continue to receive an immediate response by sworn police. However, less serious calls are handled by alternative methods. Conditions for which delayed or alternative responses are appropriate include delayed burglaries, thefts, vandalisms, lost property, and insurance reports.

Differential response alternatives can replace sending a patrol unit to investigate a past crime. A patrol unit can be sent later, when there are fewer calls for service. The caller can be asked to come into the precinct headquarters to report the crime. The call can be transferred to a nonsworn member, who then takes the report over the phone. In some departments, the report can be made online. Finally, the dispatcher can make an appointment for a nonsworn member to respond to the caller's home to take a report. Differential response to calls for service is designed to reduce and better manage the workload of patrol officers by giving them more time to devote to directed patrol, investigations, or crime prevention programs.

In addition to the benefits to the departments, citizens are not unhappy with delayed response from police departments even when they must wait an hour or more for a police response. This is especially true when the citizen is aware there will be a delay and the rationale is explained. Many citizens find the new options, including online reporting, phone reporting, and referrals, more convenient for their busy schedules.

The 911 and 311 systems have evolved over the years to make police departments more effective and to assist their efforts to manage their resources. Traditionally, the 911 call has determined the police department's priorities. Calls to 911 have skyrocketed over the years because of the promotion and advertising regarding this number. Police departments strive to educate their citizens to use 911 only in true emergencies, and that is often the first question the call takers ask the callers. Unfortunately, when someone needs help but doesn't know whom to call, 911 is often the number that the person remembers. Recently, a movement has been undertaken to implement a 311 system to take some of the demand off the 911 lines and keep them open for true emergencies. A 311 system allows nonemergency calls to be redirected or referred to other referral agencies or government agencies, either by citizens directly calling 311 or by 911 operators quickly rerouting the appropriate calls to 311.

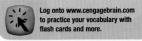

Reverse 911 allows police departments to disseminate emergency information to its residents within minutes.

Reverse 911

With the advancement in communications technology as well as the progression of mapping abilities, the use of reverse 911 systems has expanded. This allows police departments to call citizens in the entire jurisdiction or limit their call to a particular neighborhood where something is occurring. They can disseminate emergency information to residents within minutes. It is a valuable tool when there are in-progress events or a pursuit or manhunt in a certain neighborhood. The system can call the phone numbers of residents within minutes. Recently, the use of this type of program was expanded to include cell phone numbers when users voluntarily sign up. This was spurred by the Virginia Tech shootings, when it became apparent that such a notification system would have helped students know what was going on and respond appropriately. It has become widespread among colleges and cities, where residents sign up to receive text messages or calls about crime incidents occurring. This arrangement can allow the community to work with the police to solve crimes as well as to minimize injury and death to innocent bystanders. This increased awareness will allow the police to work more effectively and, ultimately, to better serve the public and improve the safety of their community.

LO7 Examine New Methods of Resource Allocation

Personnel

Personnel are the most expensive part of a police department's budget. In this day of shrinking budgets, agencies must allocate their personnel in the most efficient way possible and consider nontraditional ways of doing things. Most departments have reexamined their roles and tasks and are questioning whether certain jobs need to be done, how they might be done better—say, over the phone or online—and who should do them. Many departments have increased their use of civilians for nonhazardous jobs such as evidence technician, accident investigator, property technician, call taker, and front-desk attendant. This allows the sworn officers to be used for the more hazardous duties and puts more officers on the street in an effort to combat crime and keep residents safe.

Scheduling officers is also a big issue. Police departments don't want to have too many officers on duty at one time, with the result being that they are climbing all over each other to respond to calls, nor do departments want to be understaffed should a significant emergency arise. Unfortunately, law enforcement is a very unpredictable field. It can be extremely quiet and boring one minute, but in the second it takes for an alert tone to come over the radio, the day or night can become crazy. Scheduling is especially important if the department wants to conduct directed patrol activities to address certain crime problems.

Traditionally, departments used equal staffing for every shift. In other words, there were 10 officers on days, 10 officers on evenings, and 10 officers on midnights. Officers and administrators alike knew the workload wasn't spread equally, but it was difficult to quantify before computers. Now plenty of data are available; departments must simply know how to collect and analyze them. Departments can determine workload by types of call and areas of the city by the hour, which can help them design beats or zones so that the workload is more evenly divided among officers. Departments can also determine what kinds of calls happen at what hours of the day, how much time the particular calls take, and whether they are and can be handled by one officer, two officers, or perhaps even more.

With computers and the knowledge of what type of information they want to collect, departments can conduct their own studies on a yearly or quarterly basis and have exactly the information they need for their particular circumstances. In general, officers working the day and evening shifts have more of their time devoted to calls for service and little "free time" in which to conduct activity aimed at discovering suspicious activity or individuals. During the midnight shift, when most residents are asleep, there are far fewer calls for service received through dispatch and much more officer-initiated activity, as officers drive their beats looking for suspicious activity, checking on their businesses, and so forth. These officer-initiated activities also frequently involve arrests that can keep an officer tied up for several hours with paperwork and possibly transporting prisoners.

A city that correctly analyzes all these data will have a better working knowledge of how many officers are needed per shift and each day of the week. It is a very complicated issue, however, because this information and these needs must be tempered by proper or humane work schedules and contract or collective bargaining restrictions.

But in a 24/7 service such as law enforcement, there is no getting around the fact that all shifts must be appropriately staffed.

© Lana V. Erickson/www.Shutterstock.com

Vehicles

Most departments use fleet vehicles—that is, patrol vehicles that are used by different officers around the clock. This allows the jurisdiction to get the most use of its vehicles and have the fewest number of vehicles needed to patrol the streets. This is viewed as an efficient use of resources because all officers report to the same location for the start and end of their shifts. However, agencies that cover a bigger geographical area, such as sheriff's departments and state patrols, often find fleet vehicles impractical. Thus they issue officers their own vehicles, which the officers take home with them at the end of every shift. This allows officers to go in service from their homes and start responding to calls immediately. Officers also have all of their equipment already loaded and stowed in the vehicle. In addition, the vehicle loading and inspection time is greatly reduced for these officers, which maximizes their in-service time.

Some cities with a central shift change area have also looked at and implemented take-home vehicle plans. Although initially this program is significantly more expensive than fleet programs, the patrol vehicles last longer because they receive less of the wear and tear and abuse that comes from 24-hour usage. It is also believed that officers take better care of these vehicles when they are "theirs" and maintain them and drive them more carefully. Added incentives for cities to undertake programs like this are the ability to attract quality candidates with the lure of the extra benefit of a take-home vehicle and the increased police visibility when these vehicles are driven around town, to and from work, and parked in neighborhoods.

> In general, officers working the day and evening shifts have more of their time devoted to calls for service and little "free time" in which to conduct activity aimed at discovering suspicious activity or individuals.

The allocation of police vehicles is a significant part of the police budget, and consequently, how best to accomplish this task is a big decision. Motor vehicles are a major part of most police departments' operations, so many policies and procedures govern the usage and maintenance of the vehicles, regardless of which plan the department elects to follow.

LO8 Discuss New Tactical Approaches to Patrol Operations

Police departments use varying strategies to combat the crime problem. These include tactical operations, decoy vehicles, and various types of vehicles used for patrol.

Uniformed Tactical Operations

Uniformed tactical operations involve the use of traditional patrol operations in a more aggressive manner. The two basic kinds of uniformed tactical operations are aggressive patrol tactics and saturation patrol. Uniformed tactical units are officers who are relieved of routine patrol responsibilities, such as random routine patrol and handling calls for service, so that they can concentrate on proactive crime control.

Some bigger cities have large tactical units able to heavily patrol many areas of the city, but most departments have smaller tactical units that may be full-time units or may be assembled on a temporary basis in response to a particular crime problem. Typically, these units work flexible

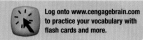

schedules and employ varying techniques depending on the particular problem they're addressing.

Aggressive Patrol

Uniformed tactical operations make use of aggressive patrol tactics: stopping numerous people and vehicles in an attempt to find evidence that they may have committed a crime or may be committing a crime. Patrol tactics using field interrogations can be very effective in reducing crime. However, such tactics often cause problems with the community because of their potential for abusing citizens' rights.

In growing numbers, police executives are convinced that effective policing can decrease crime, and even a growing cohort of criminologists is conceding that police work was responsible for the notable decline in crime throughout the 1990s and early 2000s. Nationwide, there are clear signs of departments reorganizing and implementing anticrime strategies, targeting problems, and attacking those problems.

The evidence seems to suggest that proactive, aggressive police strategies are effective in reducing crime, at least in target areas. However, many believe that these patrol tactics breed resentment in minority areas; citizens there often believe they are the target of police suspicion and reaction. This leads to a serious conflict for police administrators. Should they reduce crime rates by using effective yet aggressive police techniques and therefore risk poor relationships with lawful members of the community? It must be stated, however, that despite the credit paid to the police in reducing crime, many criminologists and other students of crime and criminal justice point to other possible reasons for crime reduction, including the aging of the criminal-prone population, increased prison and jail populations, increased commitment of community groups in addressing crime conditions, and other such factors.

Saturation Patrol

Another kind of uniformed tactical operation is **saturation patrol**, in which a larger number of uniformed officers than normal is assigned to a particular area to deal with a particular crime problem. The results of this type of strategy are mixed, according to studies involving saturation patrol that have been conducted over the years.

Recently, faced with an increasing violent crime rate in Washington, D.C., Chief Cathy Lanier has employed an aggressive saturation patrol operation called All Hands on Deck, which she developed in 2007. The

Tactical operations may be used by police departments to address specific crime problems.

goal is to increase police presence during concentrated time periods to deter crime and improve community relations. Administrative and desk officers are added to the patrol force for a total of 3,500 officers on the street on selected weekends. Results have been positive, particularly one weekend when the city had no shootings, which was a significant accomplishment. That weekend saturation patrol activity was the fifth one of the year, and violent crime dropped sharply over that weekend. Police made more than 400 arrests and seized $94,000 in cash and $52,000 worth of drugs. This was in fact fewer arrests than they'd made on other All Hands on Deck weekends, but was nevertheless noteworthy because of the lack of shootings and homicides that weekend. (Klein B1)

Police agencies continue to use saturation patrols in addressing problems such as narcotics, robberies, burglaries, auto thefts, and other crimes.

Decoy Vehicles

Though individuals have been used as decoys for years, typically by investigations units but sometimes by and with the assistance of patrol, another type of decoy operation has been used recently with success. It involves no danger to officers, and its primary goal is preventing crime violations rather than catching criminals. This decoy operation involves placing unoccupied marked police vehicles in strategic locations to give the impression of police omnipresence. This tactic has been used successfully to address less serious but demanding crime problems and traffic violations in the least resource-intensive way.

Sometimes police agencies park a marked vehicle on a roadside where there is a problem with speeding.

Drivers see the unit in the distance and slow down. Even if they see that the vehicle is unoccupied, it serves as a reminder that it could have been occupied and they could have gotten a ticket. It thus helps drivers become more aware of their driving habits and slows them down. This technique allows police agencies to address traffic problems without tying up an officer for extended periods.

This idea can be and has been expanded upon. When faced with numerous and persistent "smash and grabs" at exclusive women's clothing stores, the Boca Raton, Florida, police department had a problem. With no discernable pattern to the crimes, a limited number of midnight-shift officers, many square miles of territory, and a high number of women's clothing stores, the police department had to come up with a method to address this problem and assure the community that the police considered it a priority. They started parking unoccupied marked vehicles in front of some of the more vulnerable targets. Unfortunately, as is common with law enforcement efforts at crime prevention, it was difficult to measure success. However, businesses with police vehicles in the area were not broken into and store owners appreciated police efforts.

Although this strategy alone might not solve the crime, in these situations the police hope that with a surveillance effort put into effect at remaining stores the criminals might be displaced from the decoy stores to the establishments under surveillance, and an arrest could result. At the least, it would be a preventive technique for the businesses and might lead to displacement of the crime to another area or town. Unfortunately, as with "target hardening" prevention techniques, this is sometimes all the police can hope to accomplish.

Alternative Vehicle Deployment

Most police patrol today is performed by uniformed officers in radio-equipped patrol cars or on foot. Police also patrol on motorcycles, scooters, boats, planes, helicopters, horses, and bicycles. Some patrol in golf carts or all-terrain vehicles, or on in-line skates or Segways. Departments are willing to explore new ways of providing their services, especially when the method will assist them in being among the people, responding more quickly, and, in this time of escalating fuel costs, saving money on the cost of fuel.

A common method of transportation used by police officers in many different jurisdictions around the country is the **bike patrol**. It's hard to imagine that as recently as two decades ago, police officers were rarely seen on bicycles. Now there are bicycle "police packages" recommended for officers using bikes to patrol, and training programs are conducted around the country to teach new bike officers techniques for policing and ways to stay safe. Bike patrols are used for congested downtown areas, major sporting events and community gatherings, beach and park properties, and even residential areas. They are very adaptable and can be moved around town on bike racks on the back of patrol vehicles. They consume no fuel, emit no pollution, are quiet, and give the officers time to interact with the public. This method can even enhance the officer's fitness and health. Bike patrols thus seem an ideal solution in many situations.

bike patrol
Officers patrol an assigned area on bicycle rather than in a patrol car.

Log onto www.cengagebrain.com to practice your vocabulary with flash cards and more.

© Michael Rubin/www.Shutterstock.com

Police officers often ride bicycles when patrolling community events to maximize mobility in congested areas.

LO9 Describe New Efforts to Combat the Drunk Driving Problem and Efforts Targeting Aggressive Driving

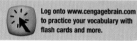

red light cameras
Automated cameras mounted on poles at intersections. The cameras are triggered when a vehicle enters the intersection after the light has turned red. The camera records the violation and the license plate number. A citation and the photos are sent to the owner of the vehicle along with instructions on how to pay the fine or contest the ticket.

police pursuits
The attempt by law enforcement to apprehend alleged criminals in a moving motor vehicle when the driver is trying to elude capture and increases speed or takes evasive action.

Though some may underestimate the importance of policing's role in regulating traffic, it always ranks high as an area of concern among the public. Being able to get where you need to go in a fluid manner as well as being confident that drivers are driving through your neighborhood responsibly are important. Feeling safe in your vehicle as you go about your daily life is part of what defines the concept of "quality of life." Controlling the movement of vehicular traffic and enforcing the traffic laws are thus other important activities the police engage in. Most law enforcement agencies have traffic units that are able to spend most of their time on traffic education and enforcement, but this is also seen as one of the primary tasks of patrol officers. Traffic incidents can place a significant demand on officers' time; consequently, departments are always exploring better ways to handle these incidents as well as prevent them from occurring. The International Association of Chiefs of Police (IACP) realizes the importance of this function as well as the importance of sharing information among police agencies and thus has a highway safety committee that works closely with the National Highway Traffic Safety Administration (NHTSA) and offers numerous publications.

Video Camera Traffic Enforcement

Taking traffic surveillance a step further, some agencies are employing the use of **red light cameras** and, on occasion, cameras coupled with electronic speed monitoring. Violators can receive citations, though generally the offenses do not go on their driving record. This is a controversial program. While public opinion surveys repeatedly indicate that 75 to 80 percent of the public support red light cameras, opponents are very vocal and have concerns about the constitutionality of these cameras, as they put the violator in the position of fighting accusations from a technological device. Opponents also view these cameras as nothing more than a cash cow for cities needing revenue rather than a true traffic safety strategy. Studies, however, seem to indicate that driver behavior changes when red light cameras are used.

Police Automobile Pursuits

The police practice of using high-powered police vehicles to chase speeding motorists, or **police pursuits**, has resulted in numerous accidents, injuries, and deaths to innocent civilians, police officers, and the pursued drivers.

Geoffrey Alpert and Patrick R. Anderson characterize the police high-speed automobile pursuit as the most deadly force available to the police. They define high-speed pursuits as "an active attempt by a law enforcement officer operating an emergency vehicle to apprehend alleged criminals in a moving motor vehicle, when the driver of the vehicle, in an attempt to avoid apprehension, significantly increases his or her speed or takes other evasive action."

A current debate questions whether the police should pursue fleeing vehicles, especially when such a pursuit could risk injuries to the police or innocent civilians. Certainly, no one wants officers or civilians injured. However, people on the other side of the debate say that if the police do not pursue fleeing drivers, they are sending a message to violators that they can get away with traffic violations by fleeing.

The Evolution of Pursuits Departments are examining their long-standing policy of actively pursuing anyone who fails to stop for a police officer. As mentioned earlier, these pursuits cause a lot

Traffic control is an important function of law enforcement agencies.

© Sylumagraphica/www.Shutterstock.com

of injury, death, damage, emotional pain, and economic costs. With today's technology, the offender can often be apprehended in safer ways.

The number of accidents and injuries resulting from police high-speed pursuits has led many U.S. police departments to establish formal **police pursuit policies** (policies regulating the circumstances and conditions under which the police should pursue or chase motorists driving at high speeds in a dangerous manner). Some departments are even telling their officers to discontinue a pursuit under certain circumstances.

In 2003, nearly all departments had pursuit policies; 60 percent of local police agencies had a restrictive pursuit policy (restrictions based on speed, type of offense, and so on), including agencies in major cities such as Los Angeles, Chicago, and Seattle; 25 percent of departments had a judgmental pursuit policy, leaving it to the officer's discretion; and 6 percent discouraged all vehicle pursuits. (Alpert and Anderson, 1986, 1–14)

Pursuit policies can also cause conflicts between neighboring towns or counties when their policies differ; one jurisdiction may initiate a pursuit that crosses into a jurisdiction where officers won't take up that pursuit. The agencies thus need to communicate their policies and plan how they will handle the conflicts that may arise.

In 2007, the U.S. Supreme Court ruled on the issue of reasonableness in using force to terminate a pursuit. The case, *Scott v. Harris*, involved a deputy pursuing Harris and ultimately ramming the back of his vehicle to get him to stop. (This case is discussed in Chapter 13.) The case made its way to the U.S. Supreme Court, and the Court issued an opinion holding that police officers may use potentially deadly force to end a high-speed chase of a suspect whose actions risk the safety of other drivers and pedestrians. (International Association of Chiefs of Police website, www.theiacp.org)Though this ruling would seem to strengthen law enforcement's position in pursuits, departments still prefer to avoid these kinds of situations if at all possible. Consequently, as mentioned earlier, the vast majority of departments have some restrictions in their pursuit policy.

Efforts against Drunk Drivers

During the 1990s, much attention was paid to the tremendous damage done on our highways by drunk drivers. Efforts by such groups as Mothers Against Drunk Driving (MADD) and Students Against Drunk Driving (SADD) caused the police to pay particular attention to this problem.

According to the NHTSA website, there were 11,773 fatalities in alcohol-related crashes in 2008, a decrease of 9.7 percent from 2007. (National Highway Traffic Safety Administration, 2008 *Traffic Safety Annual Assessment*) It can be difficult for patrol officers to deal effectively with the problem of drunk drivers because so much of the officers' time is occupied with other duties, but there are things they can do. To enforce the laws against DWI or DUI, the police have resorted to sobriety checkpoints. Officers conducting a roadblock may stop all traffic or may stop traffic after a set number, such as every fifth vehicle. After a vehicle is directed to the side of the road, the officer may request to see the driver's license, registration, and insurance card. The officer may also ask several questions to determine the driver's demeanor, and if the officer detects signs of inebriation, the motorist may be directed to move the vehicle to a secondary area and submit to a roadside sobriety test or Breathalyzer test. The failure to pass either test constitutes sufficient probable cause for arrest. Police are also using saturation patrol to combat the drunk driving problem. In this case, officers saturate a predesignated area with roving police officers to monitor traffic for signs of impaired driving. Officers also pay attention to speeding and seat belt violations.

Studies indicate that laws establishing administrative license revocation (ALR) have reduced alcohol-related crashes by almost 40 percent. (*Alcohol and Highway Safety 2001*) Police can continue to work with legislative bodies to implement these types of driver's license sanctions.

NHTSA supports all these efforts targeting impaired drivers. In an effort to assist departments in running saturation patrols and sobriety checkpoints, the NHTSA's website provides guidelines and covers issues that need to be addressed to successfully run checkpoints. In 2006, MADD expanded its previous efforts in the DUI battle. An integral strategy in this campaign is the push for states to enact laws requiring breath-test interlock devices in the vehicles of all those convicted of drunk driving, including first-time offenders. These devices prevent the car from starting if alcohol is detected on the driver's breath. (Mothers Against Drunk Driving, 2006)

police pursuit policies
Policies regulating the circumstances and conditions under which the police should pursue or chase motorists driving at high speeds in a dangerous manner.

Log onto www.cengagebrain.com to practice your vocabulary with flash cards and more.

© AP Photo/Sun Journal/Russ Dillingham

Police pursuits are a dangerous but necessary part of law enforcement.

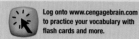
The Department of Justice (DOJ) has published a guide, available on the DOJ website, for law enforcement that addresses the drunk driving problem using the problem-oriented approach. The guide advocates that law enforcement personnel analyze their community's DUI problem: where and when people are drinking, who is doing the drinking, and what approach is best to address these specifics. It may be through legislation, enforcement, training, education, sanctions, environmental design, or a combination of some or all of these techniques. Law enforcement personnel should monitor and evaluate the effectiveness of these strategies and follow up appropriately. This is also an example of Sherman's evidence-based policing. The challenge will be isolating the effectiveness of the various strategies independently, if that is desired. However, the scientific method lends itself most effectively to determining what is successful. (*Drunk Driving*, 2006)

In following this advice, many states are trying some new tactics. A few states have begun to gather "last drink" data as a means of coming up with the names of lounges or bars that consistently serve that last drink to people who are obviously impaired. The information goes into a database, and states may pursue, against the biggest offenders, sanctions involving investigations or licensing. They may explore providing training to employees. The goal is to get the word out and prevent violations, thereby keeping the streets safe.

Fighting Aggressive Driving

In recent years, road rage has become a serious problem. People have been assaulted and even murdered in road rage incidents. Sometimes road rage takes the form of aggressive driving, and innocent people die because of the recklessness of aggressive drivers. Aggressive driving is not necessarily a specific offense but, rather, may be a combination of several violations, including speeding, tailgating, driving on the shoulder, and not signaling when changing lanes. NHTSA defines aggressive driving as "the commission of two or more moving violations that is likely to endanger other persons or property." (National Highway Traffic Safety Administration, 2011) Many states are targeting this aggressive driving in an effort to reduce crashes and make the roads safer.

LO10 Discuss Special Operations, Including SWAT Teams, Emergency Service Units, and K-9 Units

Two types of police work that have increased greatly in recent years are special weapons and tactical (SWAT) teams and emergency service units (ESUs). SWAT teams and ESUs address specific emergency and lifesaving situations that regular officers on routine patrol do not have the time or expertise to handle. K-9 units are a supplement to the patrol force that greatly enhances police response and efforts to keep citizens and officers safe.

SWAT Teams and Police Paramilitary Units

SWAT teams were created in many cities during the 1960s, generally in response to riots and similar disturbances. SWAT teams are commonly used around the country but sometimes have other names. Some believe that the name SWAT sounds a little too aggressive and militaristic, and some cities have chosen variations of the name for the same type of team, such as special response unit (SRU) or special response team (SRT).

Police paramilitary unit (PPU) is a term made popular by Peter Kraska and Victor Kappeler in the 1990s to refer to units within police departments that are organized in a more militaristic manner, with their primary function being to threaten or use force collectively and not necessarily as a last resort. This includes units that are or had

© Ron Brown

SWAT teams are used in many high-risk situations.

often been referred to as SWAT teams or special response units and are "distinguished by power and number of weapons." (Gaines and Kappeler, 243-247) These units are highly trained as use of force specialists.

These units have grown tremendously since the 1970s, when fewer than 10 percent of police departments had PPUs, to 89 percent having a unit in 1995. (Gaines and Kappeler 243–247) Their use over the years has also changed from handling the occasional dangerous situation call-outs to being involved on a more routine basis in such things as serving high-risk search warrants and arrest warrants. Kraska and Kappeler also found that 20 percent of the departments they surveyed use PPUs for patrolling urban areas on a somewhat regular basis.

No matter how the SWAT team or police paramilitary unit is formed, the most important consideration is training. The units must be constantly training and working together so that any action they take will be appropriate and court defensible. The bulk of these units were created in the 1980s and 1990s, and their effect on the organizational culture of departments is unknown. Kraska and Kappeler feel this interaction should be closely scrutinized.

Emergency Service Units

Police departments provide numerous emergency services, including emergency first aid to sick and injured citizens, rescues of people trapped in automobiles at accident scenes, rescues of those trapped in burning or collapsed buildings, and often rescues of people attempting to commit suicide by jumping from buildings and bridges. These duties involve specialized training and, often, sophisticated rescue equipment. The first aid and rescue services are often provided by patrol officers as part of their routine services. Many larger cities or counties, however, provide special patrol units whose primary responsibility is to respond to these emergencies. Often these emergency duties are merged into a department's SWAT operations or are provided by specialized emergency service units (ESUs) with sophisticated rescue and lifesaving equipment. Some of these services, especially search and rescue services, may be provided by the fire department. Some agencies have smaller versions of these units, and they often have names such as critical incident teams.

K-9 Units

Most departments today employ K-9 (canine) units. These talented dogs have been used for many years, but during the last few years, their role has expanded and the need for them has grown. Traditionally, K-9 units have supplemented the patrol function by responding to burglary calls

© AP Photo/Patrick Whittemore, pool

Most police departments have K-9 units, which are utilized in many different situations.

or open doors where a premises search is needed. These dogs can do it more safely and accurately than human officers, particularly when the area to be searched is large or difficult to reach, such as a crawl space. This aids in the effort to keep officers safe. The dogs have also been used for tracking when crimes have just occurred. They can help officers identify the direction of travel of a suspect or if the suspect got in a vehicle, and if so, where the vehicle was parked. Dogs have also been a big asset in the war on drugs, sniffing vehicles and packages and signaling if drugs are present. Since September 11, 2001, there has been an increase in the demand for dogs that sniff out bombs and explosives. These dogs are used routinely at airports, train stations, ferry terminals, ports, subways, highways, bridges, and tunnels.

The dogs are also a public relations asset and a great tool for bridging the gap between the community and the officers at special events. Departments that cannot justify having their own dog will often have an arrangement with other local agencies or the county or state to have a dog available when needed.

 Log onto www.cengagebrain.com for additional resources including videos, flash cards, games, self-quizzing, review exercises, web exercises, learning checks, and more.

10

Investigations

After studying this chapter, the student should be able to:

LO1 Discuss traditional detective operations

LO2 Describe the activities of a detective in a police agency

LO3 Introduce alternatives to retroactive investigation of past crimes by detectives

LO4 Discuss the importance of crime analysis and information management

LO5 Describe the proactive tactics being used by investigators

LO6 Describe undercover operations, including undercover drug operations

LO7 Define entrapment and show how it relates to police tactical and undercover operations

LO1 Discuss Traditional Detective Operations

Before the Rand study *The Criminal Investigation Process*, it was common for police departments to have policies and procedures in place that emphasized the retroactive investigation of past crimes by detectives. The investigation of almost all felonies and of some misdemeanors was the sole responsibility of the detective division of a police department. The patrol officer merely obtained information for a complaint or incident report and referred the case to the detectives for follow-up investigation. Theoretically, detectives would interview complainants and witnesses again, respond to the scene of the crime, and search for clues and leads that could solve the crime.

In 1975, the Rand Corporation think tank found that much of a detective's time is spent in nonproductive work—93 percent is spent on activities that do not lead directly to solving previously reported crimes—and that investigative expertise does little to solve cases. The Rand report said that half of all detectives could be replaced without negatively influencing crime clearance rates. (Greenwood and Petersilia, 1975)

Though the Rand finding regarding detectives' value in the investigative process was controversial, and the investigative process itself has not changed much in the years since the study, most researchers feel the detective's role is an important one. The key variable among departments is whether they utilize the more traditional model, with patrol officers doing little investigative work, or subscribe to the model advocated by the Rand study, where patrol officers take a great deal of the workload off of the

© Stephen Mulcahey/Alamy

detectives. Several studies indicate that as reported in the *National Survey of Police Practices Regarding the Criminal Investigations Process: Twenty-Five Years After Rand*, detectives "play critical roles in routine case resolutions and in post-arrest activities, and that many of their duties require highly specialized skills." (Womack 97) It is generally believed that the patrol officer–detective relationship and role in an investigation are complementary and symbiotic and do make for successful investigative outcomes. This chapter will explore some more efficient techniques that departments have developed to investigate past crimes.

> Our data consistently reveal that an investigator's time is largely consumed in reviewing reports, documenting files, and attempting to locate and interview victims on cases that experience shows will not be solved. For cases that are solved (i.e., a suspect is identified), an investigator spends more time in post-clearance processing than he does in identifying the perpetrator. (Greenwood and Petersilia)

LO2 Describe the Activities of a Detective in a Police Agency

Most of the activities of a police department involve police patrol operations. As we saw in earlier chapters, however, the police engage in numerous other activities. For example, detective operations and investigations are an important part of police work.

What Detectives Do

The detective division of a police department is charged with solving, or clearing, reported crimes. In traditional detective operations, detectives conduct a follow-up investigation of a past crime after a member of the patrol force has taken the initial report of the crime and conducted some sort of preliminary investigation.

The detective generally begins an investigation upon receipt of an incident report (complaint report) prepared by the officer who conducted the initial interview with the victim. The incident report contains identifying information regarding

the victim, details of the crime, identifying information regarding the perpetrator(s) or suspect(s), or a description of them, and identifying information regarding any property taken. As the detective begins the investigation, he or she maintains a file on the case, using follow-up reports for each stage of the investigation.

Detective units may be organized on a decentralized or a centralized basis. In a decentralized system, each precinct in a city has its own local detective squad, which investigates all crimes occurring in the precinct. Detectives or investigators in a decentralized squad are considered generalists.

In a centralized system, in contrast, all detectives operate out of one central office or headquarters and are each responsible for particular types of crime in the entire city. These detectives are considered specialists. Some departments separate centralized or specialty squads into crimes against persons squads and crimes against property squads. Other departments operate specialized squads or units for most serious crimes—for example, they may have a homicide squad, sex crime squad, robbery squad, burglary squad, forgery squad, auto theft squad, bias crimes squad (which investigates crimes that are motivated by bigotry or hatred of a person's race, ethnic origin, gender, or sexual orientation), and most recently, computer crimes squads. Some cities use both decentralized and centralized investigatory units. In smaller departments, detectives tend to be generalists. There may be one detective with expertise and special training in sex crimes, juvenile crimes, cybercrimes, and homicide crimes. Or, one or two detectives may receive all of this training and conduct all major investigations in their jurisdiction. In some cities, the police department may call for assistance from county or state law enforcement when confronted with a homicide or rash of sex crimes. It really doesn't matter which approach the jurisdiction

Detective units may be organized on a decentralized or centralized basis.

Photo of "All Felonies" detective courtesy John Kruse, Wenatchee Police Dept. Photo of "Burglary," Homicide" and "Auto Theft" detectives courtesy M.J. Rose Images. Photo of "All Felonies" desk plaque © Alaettin YILDIRIM/www.Shutterstock.com. Photo of remaining desk plaques © zimmytws/www.Shutterstock.com. Photo illustration by Spitting Images for Cengage Learning.

uses as long as the individuals who investigate the major crimes have the latest training available and have current information about the legal issues. It is also helpful for investigators to work closely with the prosecutor's office as early in the investigation as possible.

The Detective Mystique

Detectives work out of uniform, perform no patrol duties, and are sometimes paid at a higher rate than regular uniformed officers. The assignment to detective duties has in the past been a promotion that an officer attained through a promotional exam process. That has changed during the last couple of decades for several reasons, though in larger, big-city departments, it is still a promotion with higher pay. In most small and mid-sized departments, a detective is a plainclothes police officer. They are the same rank as a police officer, but through a competitive process have attained an assignment in the detective bureau or division. The important distinction between the detective as a plainclothes police officer versus as a promotional rank is that when the position is not a rank, it is a temporary assignment. If it doesn't work out or the department needs to downsize the detective division, the officer can be transferred back to the road without being demoted or violating the contract. There can be many reasons an assignment to the detective bureau might not last. Most prominently, new detectives may tire of the constant stress of conducting investigations and never feeling that they have finished their job. Most road officers start their shift with a clean slate, whereas at the start of each tour, detectives find themselves facing the cases and work that they'd left the day before. They tend to take their cases home with them and think about them at night and sometimes even dream about them. This doesn't create a problem for many or most detectives, who learn to cope in their own ways, but it makes some prefer to go back to the patrol division. When the positions are the same rank, this can be done with minimal embarrassment and a minimal impact to the officer's career or financial status.

Why would there be embarrassment? Even in police departments, not to mention in the general community, detectives generally enjoy much greater status and prestige than patrol officers do. Detectives have also historically been seen as the heroes of police work in novels, television shows, and the movies. Are real-life detectives as heroic, smart, individualistic, tough, hardworking, and mysterious as their fictional counterparts? Or is there a mystique attached to the detective position?

The **detective mystique** is the idea that detective work is as glamorous, exciting, and dangerous as it is depicted in the movies and on television. In reality, however, detectives spend most of their time filling out reports and reinterviewing victims on the telephone.

The reality of detective work usually has little in common with its media representations. Indeed, much of what detectives do consists of routine and simple chores, and the job is somewhat boring; further, it is debatable whether any special skills are required to be a detective. (Goldstein, *Policing* pp. 55–56)

Because of the Rand study and other studies, police administrators can now make some generalizations about detective operations. First, the single most important determinant of whether or not a crime is solved is not the quality of the work performed by the detectives but the information the responding officers obtain from the victim and witnesses at the scene. (Greenwood and Petersilia) Next, detectives are not very effective in solving crimes. Nationally, police are able to clear (solve) only 46.3 percent of all violent crimes (murder, forcible rape, robbery, aggravated assault) and only 16.5 percent of the property crimes (burglary, theft, and motor vehicle theft) reported to them. These figures are relatively consistent from year to year. The difference between the clearance rates for violent versus property crimes comes about because of the vigorous investigation put forth in the more serious cases and because violent crimes often have a victim or witness available to provide police with information. (FBI, *Uniform Crime Reports*, "Crime") Furthermore, because not all cases are reported to the police, the clearance rate is actually even lower. (Police cannot clear crimes not reported to them.) Finally, patrol officers, not detectives, are responsible for the vast majority of all arrests, which they generally make at the scene of the crime.

detective mystique
The idea that detective work is as glamorous, exciting, and dangerous as it is depicted in the movies and on television.

Log onto www.cengagebrain.com to practice your vocabulary with flash cards and more.

NBC/NBCU Photo Bank via AP Images

Detective work is portrayed as exciting and glamorous in the media.

LO3 Introduce Alternatives to Retroactive Investigation of Past Crimes by Detectives

Improved Investigation of Past Crimes

> **Managing Criminal Investigations (MCI)**
> Proposal recommended by the Rand study regarding a more effective way of investigating crimes, including allowing patrol officers to follow up on cases and using solvability factors to determine which cases to follow up.
>
> **solvability factors**
> Factors considered in determining whether or not a case should be assigned for follow-up investigation.
>
> Log onto www.cengagebrain.com to practice your vocabulary with flash cards and more.

The National Advisory Commission on Criminal Justice Standards and Goals has recommended the increased use of patrol officers in the criminal investigation process. The commission also recommended that every police agency direct patrol officers to conduct thorough preliminary investigations and that agencies establish written priorities to ensure that investigative efforts are spent in a manner that best achieves organizational goals. The commission further recommended that investigative specialists (detectives) be assigned only to very serious or complex preliminary investigations. (National Advisory Commission on Criminal Justice Standards and Goals) As a consequence of the Rand study and other studies, the

Law Enforcement Assistance Administration (LEAA) funded research that led to the publication and wide dissemination of a new proposal regarding methods that should be used to investigate past crimes. (Cawley, Miron, et al.)

Managing Criminal Investigations (MCI)

The proposal that resulted from the LEAA research, **Managing Criminal Investigations (MCI)**, offers a series of guidelines that recommend (1) expanding the role of patrol officers to include investigative responsibilities and (2) designing a new method to manage criminal investigations by including **solvability factors**, case screening, case enhancement, and police and prosecutor coordination. (Cawley, Miron, et al.) Under an MCI program, the responding patrol officer is responsible for a great deal of the follow-up activity that used to be assigned to detectives. These duties include locating and interviewing the victim and witnesses, detecting physical evidence, and preparing an initial investigative report that will serve as a guide for investigators. This report must contain proper documentation to indicate whether the case should be assigned for continued investigation or immediately suspended for lack of evidence. (Cawley, Miron, et al.) The other major innovation under MCI involves the use of a managerial system that classifies cases according to their solvability; detectives then work only on cases that have a chance of being solved. Though it can vary by department, the road supervisor will often make the decision about whether the case will be followed up by the road officer or by a detective or will be "inactivated" based on these solvability factors. Some solvability factors include the following:

Solvability Factors

1. Are there witnesses?
2. Is a suspect known?
3. Can a suspect be identified?
4. Is there a vehicle description?
5. Is there physical evidence?
6. Will the complainant cooperate in the investigation?
7. Can property be identified?

The MCI method of managing investigations is designed to put most of an investigator's time and effort only into very important cases and cases that actually can be solved. Research conducted by numerous police departments has demonstrated that scoring systems using

Detectives often reinterview victims and witnesses.

© Jeff Greenberg/Alamy

checklists and point scores successfully screen out cases with a low probability of being solved and identify promising cases. (Eck)

Sometimes the solvability factors may be disregarded, and because of officers' concern, political reasons, or public safety, a case will be investigated that does not meet the numerical criteria. Some cases are so important or serious that they demand a follow-up regardless of their potential solvability based on the solvability factors. The MCI approach gives investigators a more manageable caseload and an opportunity to be more organized and methodical in their efforts. The improved methods of investigation have also resulted in less waste and more efficiency in police detective operations and have allowed departments to use personnel in more proactive policing.

Mentoring and Training

Training for investigators or detectives has long been viewed as a way to improve their productivity. Specialized investigations require specialized training. This includes homicide investigation, sex crime investigation, juvenile crime and juvenile offenders, cybercrime,

white-collar crime, and even auto theft. Detectives or investigators are usually sent to specialized schools as soon as practical or perhaps even before they are appointed as investigators.

Informal **mentoring** programs have gone on for years as experienced detectives have taught new detectives what they know. Often detectives see potential in a patrol officer, and then mentor or work with that officer, even when he or she is still a patrol officer.

Some departments have also implemented formal mentoring programs. Typically, a mentor is a role model, teacher, motivator, coach, or advisor who invests time in facilitating another person's professional job growth. A mentor program allows a non-investigator to be paired with an experienced investigator to become familiar with the investigative process. Overall, mentoring improves the quality of investigations throughout the department and improves the skills of all personnel involved. (Colaprete, "The Case for Investigator Mentoring" 47–52)

LO4 Discuss the Importance of Crime Analysis and Information Management

Crime Analysis

Crime analysis has grown tremendously in the last two decades. Crime analysis is the process of analyzing the data collected in a police organization to determine exactly what the crime problem is and where, when, and possibly even why it is happening. Crime analysis goes hand in hand with community-oriented policing and problem-oriented policing. Analysis allows for the smarter use of information and, consequently, the smarter use of personnel and resources to address the true crime problem. Many departments employ full-time civilian crime analysts, but others have their investigators do the crime analysis as part of their investigative responsibility. The goal of crime analysis is to determine crime patterns and problems. (Reiner, Sweeney, et al.) It begins with collating the information that comes in to the police department. This includes the information from dispatch, the police reports, and intelligence information, as well as information gathered

Mentoring is an important part of developing skilled investigators.

© Gideon Mendel/Corbis

from parking citations, traffic citations, and field interviews. Crime analysis allows police to make links among incidents that have occurred and people and vehicles passing through town. This information can help the agency, and the beat officer in particular, know how to direct their efforts in directed patrol activities on particular shifts. It can also help shift supervisors know how to allocate their personnel and can help the appropriate division determine the best strategy to address a particular crime pattern, such as decoys, stings, or public notification and education. This results in "working smarter" with the resources at hand.

© Joel Gordon

Information sharing between departments strengthens investigative efforts.

Information Management

The key to police work, and investigations in particular, is information, and obtaining good information is critical. Whether it is information from complainants, victims, witnesses, the suspect, or all the various files of data that are kept, information can enhance and strengthen the investigation. In this computer age, we have a lot of information at our fingertips. Sometimes, it may seem that there is too much information, and we may experience information overload. Although this increased amount of information generally helps with solving crimes, it can also require many hours to go through the information and discern which data are valuable and pertinent to the case. The computer age also allows law enforcement agencies to share information with each other, which enhances investigations and assists with detecting patterns and similar modus operandis or method of operations (MOs).

Detectives can obtain information from a number of sources and share it in several ways. The Internet provides an opportunity for police personnel to research topics and share knowledge with other officers through internal e-mail lists, expert directories, professional organizations, and outside e-mail lists that pertain to certain areas of interest. Journals, trade magazines, and newspaper articles that may be available online can provide a wealth of information regarding what strategies are being used in other departments and can also alert investigators to crime trends in neighboring communities. (Colaprete, "Knowledge Management" 82–89) Information sharing has traditionally been done and continues to be done in person as well: Investigators hold monthly meetings with investigators from other agencies who work similar types of crime (such as sex crimes, auto thefts, and so forth) and compare and share information.

Whereas crime analysis addresses routine crime, intelligence analysis tends to emphasize organized crimes (usually involving narcotics, human smuggling, gambling, and terrorism). This intelligence can be obtained from many sources (as with crime analysis), evaluated for reliability and validity, and used in a proactive manner. (Cordner, Scarborough, and Sheehan 334)

When departments are better able to record, analyze, share, and disseminate information to the needed parties, more crimes can be solved, more offenders jailed, and more incidents prevented.

Multi-Agency Investigative Task Forces

In recent years, there has been an increase in the use of multi-agency **investigative task forces**. With the realization that criminals know no boundaries, and often intentionally cross jurisdictional lines to commit crimes, the importance of sharing information and working together has been increasingly recognized. With some areas of the country experiencing record-breaking crime rates and violence, agencies are willing to try new approaches to solve the crimes, including cooperative investigative efforts. Detectives gather information from their informants and use it to solve these cases, regardless of jurisdiction. It has also proved beneficial to have a prosecutor involved from the beginning, helping investigators build stronger cases to get and keep these offenders off the street. (Fooksman)

One of the largest multi-agency task forces was involved in the Washington, D.C., area sniper investigation in 2002. This manhunt and investigation, which led to the capture of two individuals, involved more than 20 local, 2 state, and at least 10 federal law enforcement agencies. The investigation spanned 23 days in October 2002 while

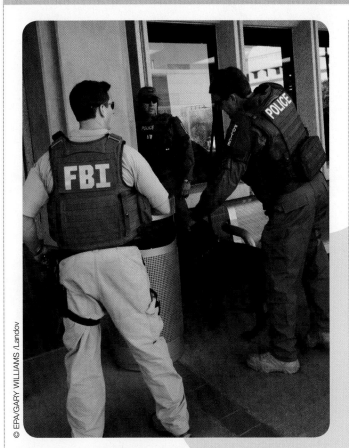

The use of multi-agency investigative task forces has increased in recent years.

the Virginia, Maryland, and D.C. areas were terrorized by snipers with high-powered rifles shooting at people indiscriminately. John Allen Muhammad and Lee Boyd Malvo were arrested at a rest area in Myersville, Maryland, but not before they'd shot 14 people, 10 of whom died. In 2004, Muhammad was sentenced to death (and executed in 2009), and Malvo (a teenager) was sentenced to life in prison. The Police Executive Research Forum (PERF) issued a report entitled *Managing a Multijurisdictional Case: Identifying Lessons Learned from the Sniper Investigation*, which identified the challenges faced by law enforcement personnel in this particular incident, including having to conduct criminal investigations simultaneously on each incident, trying to prevent more from occurring, and responding to the scenes as new ones occurred.

PERF identified information management and teamwork, or relationships, as being the most critical issues in a major investigation such as this. The difference between a quick apprehension and a prolonged, frustrating effort, said the report, lies in the development of an effective information management system. (Murphy and Wexler 113–118)

In today's extremely mobile society and with copycat crimes as well as individuals wanting their 15 minutes of fame, a well-thought-out plan for law enforcement can greatly enhance the likelihood of a quick resolution to a serious incident.

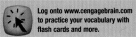
Repeat Offender Programs (ROPs)

U.S. criminologist Marvin Wolfgang discovered that only a few criminals are responsible for most of the predatory street crime in the United States. Most Americans do not commit street robberies; only a relatively small group of people do, but these people commit a tremendous amount of crime each year. Borrowing from Wolfgang's research, police started to focus their investigative resources on the career criminal using **repeat offender programs (ROPs)**. These programs can be conducted in two major ways. ("Mugged by Reality")

First, police can identify certain people to be the target of investigation. Once a career criminal is identified, the police can use surveillance techniques, follow the criminal, and wait to catch the person either in the act of committing a crime or immediately after the crime occurs. These target offender programs are labor intensive.

The second way police can operate the ROP is through case enhancement. Specialized career criminal detectives can be notified of the arrest of a robbery suspect by other officers and can then determine from the suspect's conviction or arrest rate whether or not the arrest merits enhancement. If the case is enhanced, an experienced detective assists the arresting officer in preparing the case for presentation in court and debriefs the suspect to obtain further information. A major tactic behind case enhancement is liaison with the district attorney's office to alert the prosecuting attorney to the importance of the case and to the suspect's past record. Such information helps ensure zealous efforts by the prosecutor.

Police may use surveillance to target a repeat offender.

Internet Registries

Some jurisdictions are enacting laws requiring the registration of various types of criminals. For years, sex offenders have been tracked in most states. This primarily serves as a public notification system that allows parents to know if there are any sex offenders living in their neighborhood, further allowing parents to take the proper precautions to keep their children safe, and notifies local law enforcement of individuals residing in their community who have a past in this particular type of crime. If a crime occurs, the officers have individuals they can contact, possibly increasing the chances of a successful investigation. Some states have added to the information they provide on the registry. Some jurisdictions post information on their websites regarding prostitution arrests, and recently, some states have created a similar registry for meth offenders. The U.S. Drug Enforcement Administration maintains a National Clandestine Laboratory Registry on its website, which allows the public to access information on labs in their state.

Global Positioning System (GPS) Technology

Surveillance of offenders is extremely labor intensive and costly. Today, technology has improved to a degree that allows law enforcement to track offenders without having to physically follow them 24 hours a day. Global positioning system (GPS) technology has allowed many states to implement programs that monitor offenders. This monitoring saves the state the cost of incarcerating the offender, and most states require the offender to pay for the costs of the device and its monitoring unless he or she is indigent. Though some states are using this technology to monitor paroled gang members, most are using it to monitor sex offenders.

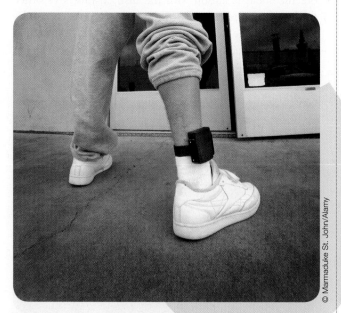

Some offenders may be required to wear GPS devices.

© Thinkstock Images

Closed-Circuit TV and the Internet

Surveillance cameras are everywhere today, and despite some challenges, most courts have upheld their use, stating that they are not a violation of individuals' rights because there is no expectation of privacy in most of the locations. Although these cameras have been touted as a crime prevention tool, they have also been critical in solving some major cases in the last few years. Many cities across the country, large and small, are allocating budget dollars to install surveillance cameras. Some dispute their value in crime-fighting and crime prevention and even their constitutionality. (Moran) However, it is hard to dispute the contribution they have made in some high-profile cases that might not have been solved had it not been for surveillance cameras installed by property owners.

When 11-year-old Carlie Brucia was reported missing in Sarasota, Florida, on February 1, 2004, police had few leads other than where she had been and that she was believed to have been heading home. Detectives obtained a surveillance video from a car wash located along Carlie's route home that showed Carlie walking along the rear of the car wash and a man approaching her and forcibly walking her out of view of the camera. This video was released to the media, and an AMBER Alert system was activated. Numerous phone calls identified the suspect, Joseph Smith, and he was subsequently arrested and convicted (Associated Press, "Man Guilty") of raping and murdering Carlie.

Law enforcement has recently started to present the surveillance tapes they acquire in their investigation of crimes to the Internet-savvy public by posting them on YouTube. Typically, they will do this when they have footage of the suspect but can't identify him or her. Sometimes, frustrated business owners or homeowners who have been victimized in less serious ways may post their own surveillance tapes on YouTube.

The use of YouTube in solving crimes has evolved to the point that individuals desiring their 15 minutes of fame have posted videos of fights and assaults on the site. These videos have then been used as evidence by law enforcement to prosecute the individuals committing the assaults. MySpace, Facebook, and Twitter have also had an increase in use by law enforcement agencies reaching out to the public, including soliciting their input regarding crime information and suspect identification.

a change of heart over the years or forgotten what he or she had said initially, thus allowing police to uncover new information.

Mike Evanoff, owner of Evie's Car Wash, testifies about this security video footage from his business, which was used in the trial of Joseph Smith. Smith was charged in the death of 11-year-old Carlie Brucia after he was identified in the security video footage approaching Brucia and taking her forcibly by the arm.

Cold-case detectives also use the passage of time in another way. They take advantage of the tremendous advances in forensic science, especially DNA testing. Much smaller samples are now necessary to get a more definitive match through DNA than even a few years ago. Cold-case detectives are thus able to solve many cases solely by reexamining the evidence.

Cold-case squads are providing great hope and comfort to families of victims of old, unsolved crimes and a sense of justice to the community when detectives are able to solve these long-dormant cases and hold the defendants accountable for their actions.

Cold-Case Squads

Advances in DNA technology have led to the increased use of cold-case squads to solve crimes. **Cold-case squads** reexamine old cases that have remained unsolved. They use the passage of time, coupled with a fresh set of eyes, to help solve cases that had been stagnant for years and often decades.

Over time, relationships change. People may no longer be married, may no longer be friends, or may no longer be intimidated by or afraid of the same people. Someone who was reluctant to talk because of fear or loyalty may decide years later to tell the truth. Individuals may have found religion or changed their lifestyles, and years later realized that what they did, witnessed, or knew about was bad and they want to set the record straight. Cold-case detectives reinterview all individuals involved and hope someone has had

K ♠ MISSING PERSON

Tiffany Sessions
20 Year Old White Female

The victim disappeared from UF in Gainesville on 2/9/89. At approximately 6pm she told her roommate she was going for a walk and never returned. She was last seen wearing red sweatpants, a long sleeved pullover sweatshirt with gray stripes and the word "Aspen" in green letters on front and blue or white low cut Reebok sneakers. She has a crescent shaped scar on left knuckle.

If You Have Any Info Regarding This Case
Call Heartland Crime Stoppers
1-800-226-TIPS

♥ K

Q ♦ UNSOLVED HOMICIDE

Jennifer Odom
12 Year Old White Female

On 2/19/93 the victim stepped off her school bus around 3pm and started walking the short 200 yards to her rural Pasco County, FL home. She never made it. Children on the bus reported they saw a faded blue pickup following her. On 2/25/93 her body was found in an abandoned orange grove in SE Hernando County. Approximately two years later her missing bookbag and clarinet case were found near a dirt road 12 miles west of where she was found. Her clothes, including a red sweater and Hooters sweatshirt have never been found.

If You Have Any Info Regarding This Case
Call Heartland Crime Stoppers
1-800-226-TIPS

♦ Q

Many jurisdictions use "cold case" playing cards to highlight unsolved murders and missing person cases to inmates and others with the goal of generating leads and solving the cases.

LO5 Describe the Proactive Tactics Being Used by Investigators

Decoy Operations

decoy operations
Operations in which officers dress as and play the role of potential victims in the hope of attracting and catching a criminal.

blending
Plainclothes officers' efforts to blend into an area in an attempt to catch a criminal.

sting operations
Undercover police operations in which police pose as criminals in order to arrest law violators.

Log onto www.cengagebrain.com to practice your vocabulary with flash cards and more.

One of the primary purposes of police patrol is to prevent crime by creating a sense of omnipresence; potential criminals are deterred from committing crime because of the presence or potential presence of the police. Omnipresence does not always work well, however. We have crime both on our streets and in areas where ordinary police patrols cannot see crime developing, such as the inside of a store or the hallway of a housing project. We have also seen that retroactive investigations of crimes, with the intent to identify and arrest perpetrators, are not very effective.

One proactive approach to apprehending criminals in the course of committing a crime is **decoy operations**. Decoy operations take several forms, among them blending and decoy. In **blending**, officers dressed in civilian clothes try to blend into an area and patrol it on foot or in unmarked police cars in an attempt to catch a criminal in the act of committing a crime. Officers may target areas where a significant amount of crime occurs, or they may follow particular people who appear to be potential victims or potential offenders. To blend, officers assume the roles and dress of ordinary citizens—construction workers, shoppers, joggers, bicyclists, physically disabled persons, and so on—so that the officers, without being recognized as officers, can be close enough to observe and intervene should a crime occur.

In decoy operations, officers dress as, and play the role of, potential victims—drunks, nurses, businesspeople, tourists, prostitutes, blind people, isolated subway riders, or defenseless elderly people. The officers wait to be the subject of a crime while a team of backup officers is ready to apprehend the violator in the act of committing the crime. Decoy operations are most effective in combating the crimes of robbery, purse snatching, and other larcenies from the person, as well as burglaries and thefts of and from automobiles.

Stakeout Operations

Many crimes occur indoors, where passing patrol officers cannot see their occurrence. A stakeout consists of a group of heavily armed officers who hide in an area of a store or building waiting for an impending holdup. If armed robbers enter the store and attempt a robbery, the officers yell, "Police!" from their hidden areas. If the perpetrators fail to drop their weapons, the officers open fire. Stakeouts are effective when the police receive a tip that a crime is going to occur in a commercial establishment or when the police discover or come upon a crime pattern. However, stakeouts are extremely expensive in terms of police personnel and are also controversial because they can be dangerous for all involved. The situations are always dynamic, and officers have to decide how far to let the incident progress. There are so many variables in a stakeout that even in the case of a previously nonviolent pattern of crimes, police can never know when violence may erupt, and law enforcement personnel don't want to risk standing by and having innocent people get hurt.

Sting Operations

Sting operations, which have become a major law enforcement technique in recent years, involve using various undercover methods to apprehend thieves and recover stolen property. For example, the police rent a storefront and put the word out on the street that they will buy any stolen property—no questions asked. The police set up hidden video and audio recorders that can be used to identify "customers," who are then located and placed under arrest several months later. The audio and video recorders provide excellent evidence in court.

Traditionally, sting operations involved setting up false storefronts to deal in stolen property, but over the years

Retired Police Chief Jim Murray regularly patrols the Internet in the persona of a 13-year-old girl and his work has resulted in many arrests of men making online solicitations for sex.

AP Photo/Mark Schiefelbein

the parameters of sting operations have expanded. They now often include corruption, prostitution, car theft, drug dealing, child pornography, child sexual abuse, and tobacco and alcohol sales to minors. Generally, a sting operation includes four elements:

Four Elements of a Sting Operation

- An opportunity or enticement to commit a crime
- A targeted likely offender or offender group
- An undercover or hidden police officer or surrogate, or some form of deception
- A "gotcha" climax when the operation ends with arrests ("Problem Oriented Guides for Police")

Studies of sting operations have found that they account for a large number of arrests and the recovery of a significant amount of stolen property. However, the studies have failed to demonstrate that the tactic leads to reductions in crime. (Klockars "The Modern Sting") Another major drawback to sting operations is that they can serve as inducements to burglary and theft because they create a market for stolen goods. Sting operations can also lead to questions regarding ethics. ("Problem Oriented Guides for Police")

Another kind of sting operation that has been widely discussed is the child predator sting aired on NBC. Law enforcement has been working with the media in operating some of these child pornography stings. Since 2004, *Dateline* on the NBC network has been airing "To Catch a Predator," in which a sting is set up in a rented home. When the operation began, *Dateline* staff members worked with an organization from Portland, Oregon, called Perverted Justice, whose volunteer members posed as young boys and girls in Internet chat rooms and waited to be contacted by adult men seeking sex with minors. The volunteers lured the men to the rented house, where they were confronted by a *Dateline* reporter on camera. In many situations, NBC did not notify local law enforcement. Citizens became outraged because these men were not arrested, and law enforcement had to explain that they need a certain standard of proof and an investigation has to be conducted. After seeing the popularity of the show, NBC formalized its relationship with Perverted Justice, compensated their members financially, and started working more closely with law enforcement, which resulted in police making more arrests after the confrontations. These operations are not without controversy, however, as roles and relationships have become blurred. (Fahri) The public seems hungry for this type of story and eager to put pedophiles behind bars. Legal outcomes and court challenges will help determine whether these types of arrangements and stings continue.

Civil Liability and Code Enforcement Teams

"Vacant apartments have become a maze of traps, meant to block out drug dealers' rivals and the police. Electrified wires have been stretched across window frames. Holes have been smashed in the walls and floors to provide easy escape routes. And hallway floors have been smeared with Vaseline to trip unwary intruders." (Sullivan 25–26) This is an example of the squalid and dangerous conditions that cities and their residents have had to deal with. Many have turned to **civil liability (or code) enforcement teams** in an to attempt to deal with local problems that have a negative effect on the quality of life in their communities. These cities use civil, as well as criminal, laws to force property owners and others in control of premises to correct illegal conditions. These cities have also established code enforcement teams, which consist of a number of agents from different municipal agencies working together using local ordinances and codes, as well as the criminal law, in an attempt to solve particular crime problems.

Nine out of 10 local law enforcement agencies perform drug enforcement functions.

© Geoff/www.Shutterstock.com

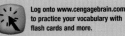
LO6 Describe Undercover Operations, Including Undercover Drug Operations

An **undercover investigation** may be defined as one in which an investigator assumes a different identity to obtain information or achieve another investigatory purpose. In an undercover investigation, the investigator can be doing many things, including merely observing or performing certain actions that are designed to get other people to do something or to react to or interact with the investigator in a certain way. The primary function of the investigator in these cases is to play a role without anyone realizing that he or she is playing a role. In policing, the primary purpose of the undercover operation most often is the collection of evidence of crimes.

Undercover Police Investigations

These investigations generally include undercover drug investigations; stings, including warrant stings and fencing stings that involve the buying and selling of stolen goods and other contraband; decoy operations targeted against the crimes of robbery, burglary, and assault; anti-prostitution operations; and operations involving the infiltration and arrest of people involved in organized crime, white-collar crime, and corruption. Undercover police officers have a dangerous yet often rewarding job. It can be rewarding as well as a relief when the undercover officer gets to arrest the offender at the end of the investigation. Offenders are often very surprised when they realize the role an undercover officer played in their arrest. However, undercover investigations can present some significant challenges to police officers and police organizations. Officers who infiltrate that lifestyle are living a lie. They spend their working hours in a role quite contrary to who they are. The difficulty involved in doing so will vary with the type of assignment and the length of the assignment.

Realizing the difficult challenges and conditions that undercover officers face, departments are implementing policies to minimize the chance of officers going astray and to protect them and the department.

Federal Undercover Investigations

These investigations generally include efforts to detect and arrest people involved in political corruption, insurance fraud, labor racketeering, and other types of organized conspiracy-type crimes.

Federal agencies, including the Drug Enforcement Administration (DEA), Customs, and the Bureau of Alcohol, Tobacco, Firearms, and Explosives (ATF), often form joint task force investigations with local, county, and state law enforcement agencies. Some of the agents work undercover and others work surveillance. This allows them to pool resources and expertise. Many major drug or arms smuggling operations have been broken up, arrests made, and millions of dollars' worth of property confiscated.

Undercover Drug Investigations

Most law enforcement agencies have devoted resources to drug enforcement. Nine out of 10 local law enforcement agencies perform drug enforcement functions. Although only 18 percent of all local departments operate a special unit for drug enforcement, with one or more full-time officers assigned, most departments serving populations of greater than 50,000 have a full-time drug enforcement unit. Nationally, approximately 12,300 local police officers are assigned full time to drug enforcement, for an average of six officers per department (Hickman and Reaves, "Local" p. 15) What do these officers do? What type of drug enforcement activities do they engage in?

Undercover drug operations can be very dangerous. Drug dealers are usually armed, the encounter may be a rip-off instead of an actual deal, and the dealers may be in a paranoid state or under the influence of narcotics at the time of the deal. Caution also needs to be taken to make sure that the deal is not being done between two law enforcement agencies. That has happened in the past, and most agencies now have procedures in place to check out that possibility before the deal goes down.

At least three general methods can be used in conducting undercover drug investigations. The first involves infiltrating criminal organizations that sell large amounts of drugs and then buying larger and larger amounts of drugs so that the buyer can reach as high as possible into the particular organization's hierarchy.

The next method that can be used to attack drug syndicates or drug locations is the process of staking out (a fixed surveillance) a particular location and making detailed observations of the conditions that indicate drug sales, such as the arrival and brief visit of numerous autos and people.

The third method is the undercover "buy-bust," an operation in which an undercover police officer purchases a quantity of drugs from a subject and then leaves the scene,

Youthful officers sometimes work undercover in high schools.

contacts the backup team, and identifies the seller. The backup team, in or out of uniform, responds to the location of the sale and arrests the seller, based on the description given by the undercover officer.

Sometimes, law enforcement may then conduct a reverse-sting operation. This is where after the buy-bust, an officer poses as the drug dealer and arrests the buyers that come to purchase drugs. This is usually done in areas that readily attract buyers. As soon as an exchange is made, the backup team makes the bust. This type of operation can often lead to accusations of entrapment, so officers must be thoroughly versed in their state laws and court rulings regarding entrapment.

LO7 Define Entrapment and Show How It Relates to Police Tactical and Undercover Operations

Often people believe that undercover operations by the police are entrapment. **Entrapment** is defined as inducing an individual to violate a criminal statute he or she had not contemplated violating, for the sole purpose of arrest and criminal prosecution. (Falcone 84) Entrapment is a defense to criminal responsibility that arises from improper acts committed against an accused by another person, usually an undercover agent. *Inducement* is the key word; when police encouragement plays upon the weaknesses of innocent persons and beguiles them into committing crimes they normally would not attempt, it can be deemed improper because it is entrapment and the evidence is barred under the exclusionary rule. Entrapment is an affirmative defense and is easily raised at trial. It is based on the principle that people should not be convicted of a crime that was instigated by the government, and it arises when "government officials 'plant the seeds' of criminal intent." (Hemmens, Worrall, and Thompson 147)

The police, by simply giving a person the opportunity to commit a crime, are not guilty of entrapment, however. For example, an undercover officer sitting on the sidewalk, apparently drunk, with a $10 bill sticking out of his or her pocket, is not forcing a person to take the money but giving a person the opportunity to take the money. A person who takes advantage of the apparent drunk and takes the money is committing a larceny. The entrapment defense is thus not applicable to this situation. However, when the police action is outrageous and forces an otherwise innocent person to commit a crime, the entrapment defense may apply.

The issue of entrapment is a contentious one, with the defendant's predisposition being evaluated against the government's activities. Although the defendant's predisposition is very subjective, the government's activities are more objective and easier to evaluate. The American Law Institute's Model Penal Code looks at the entrapment defense in this way: "If the government employed methods of persuasion or inducement which create a substantial risk that such an offense will be committed by persons other than those who are ready to commit it," then the defense is available despite the offender's predisposition (Hemmens, Worrall, and Thompson 148) The Supreme Court, however, has predominantly focused on the predisposition of the defendant and ruled that the entrapment defense does not apply. (*United States v. Russell*) Although in *Hampton v. United States* the Court held that it is the defendant's predisposition, rather than the government's conduct, that matters regarding the entrapment defense, justices did state in a concurring opinion that if government behavior "shocks the conscience," it could violate due process. (*Hampton v. United States*)

© AP Photo/Kim Johnson Flodin

In most tactical and undercover investigations, detectives need to be aware of the possibility of the issue of entrapment being raised as a defense.

11

Police and the Community

After studying this chapter, the student should be able to:

LO1 Illustrate the meaning of police–community relations and their importance to the safety and quality of life in a community

LO2 Define human relations, public relations, and community relations

LO3 Explore public attitudes regarding the police and efforts undertaken around the nation to improve public perceptions

LO4 Describe various minority populations and some of their issues regarding police interactions

LO5 Explore the challenges various populations—including the aging population, youth, crime victims, victims of domestic violence, the mentally ill, and the homeless—face when interacting with the police

LO6 Discuss some innovative community crime prevention programs that focus on crime reduction and improving the quality of life in communities

LO7 Describe the latest trends in the police–business relationship

LO1 Illustrate the Meaning of Police–Community Relations and Their Importance to the Safety and Quality of Life in a Community

The police are needed to handle emergencies, maintain order, regulate traffic, and promote a sense of security within a community. To accomplish all these functions, the police must be part of the community. They cannot be viewed as mercenaries or as an army of occupation. When the police see themselves as an occupying army or are seen that way by the community, urban unrest results. Therefore, the police can best serve the community when they are regarded, both by the residents and themselves, as part of the community.

The police and community need each other to help communities be as vibrant and safe as possible. Police–community relationships must be two-way partnerships. In a democratic society, the legitimacy of the police depends on broad and active public acceptance and support. Police chiefs or police commissioners have the responsibility and obligation to educate the public about the many causes of crime and the inability of the police acting alone to control crime.

The most important person in the police department, in terms of improving police–community relations, is the individual police officer. Patrol officers, traffic officers, and detectives are the individuals within the department who come into contact with the public on a regular basis. Thus most people receive their impression of a particular police department through the actions of the police officers they encounter.

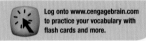
LO2 Define Human Relations, Public Relations, and Community Relations

Numerous textbooks and courses exist on police–community relations and police human relations. What do these terms mean? Are they interchangeable? Are community relations and human relations the same as police public relations? Steven M. Cox and Jack D. Fitzgerald perhaps best define these terms. They define police **human relations** as follows: "In the most general sense, the concept of human relations refers to everything we do with, for, and to each other as citizens and as human beings." (Cox and Fitzgerald) Human relations thus connotes treating others with respect and dignity and following the Golden Rule—acting toward others as you would want others to act toward you. Cox and Fitzgerald define **police public relations** as "a variety of activities with the express intent of creating a favorable image of themselves . . . sponsored and paid for by the organization." Then, using these two definitions, they define **police–community relations** as follows:

> Community relations are comprised of the combined effects of human and public relations. Police community relations then encompass the sum total of human and public relations, whether initiated by the police or other members of the community. . . . Police community relations may be either positive or negative, depending upon the quality of police interactions with other citizens (human relations) and

the collective images each holds of the other (which are derived from public as well as human relations). (Cox and Fitzgerald)

The **International Association of Chiefs of Police (IACP)** understands the importance of public relations and the interactions between the police and the community, and in recent years has issued several training keys on this topic.

LO3 Explore Public Attitudes Regarding the Police and Efforts Undertaken Around the Nation to Improve Public Perceptions

Although it's well known that the police have a difficult job, the role of the police has always been somewhat ambiguous. The perception of the police mission by police leaders as well as by community leaders has varied during the last few decades. With the adoption of the community policing philosophy (discussed in the next chapter), many law enforcement agencies have seen their roles expand to include activities that previously were not viewed as police functions.

Given the difficult job the police have, it is easier for them to perform their duties if they have the support of the public. The media often portray a police force that is not liked by the public. However, this is a false perception.

The public's opinion of the police has remained relatively constant over time, with most of the public giving favorable ratings to the police and supporting their performance.

Generally, however, the police feel that the public does not like them or support them. Perhaps one reason many officers believe the public does not like them is that officers, particularly in high-crime areas, spend a significant proportion of their time dealing with criminals and unsavory people. Further confusing perceptions, any conflicts or

> The International Association of Chiefs of Police (IACP) understands the importance of public relations and the interactions between the police and the community, and in recent years has issued several training keys on this topic.

Police officers spend a good part of the day reaching out to citizens in need.

negative issues that arise are played out repeatedly in the media and the community.

LO4 Describe Various Minority Populations and Some of Their Issues Regarding Police Interactions

One of the most significant problems facing the police during the past three decades has been the tension, and often outright hostility, between the police and minority group citizens. Most of this tension has focused on relationships between African Americans and the police. However, tension has existed between police and other minority groups. One of the best ways to improve relationships between the police and minority groups is to ensure that minority groups are adequately represented in a jurisdiction's police department.

Increasing cultural awareness and understanding of these minority populations, as well as opening the lines of communication with these communities, will also result in greater cooperation.

Multiculturalism

The 2000 U.S. Census reported that 11.1 percent of the total U.S. population is foreign born, accounting for 32.5 million people. Of these, 52 percent were born in Latin America, 26 percent in Asia, and 14 percent in Europe, with the remainder coming from other areas of the world, including Africa. Almost 18 percent of American households now report that they speak a language other than English at home. (U.S. Census) This has implications for police officers responding to calls involving these residents. Not only is there likely to be a communication problem, but there may also be a lack of trust and understanding of police, possibly resulting in fear.

The United States is very rapidly becoming even more diverse, and this diversity is no longer limited to border and southern states. The national percentage of non-Hispanic whites declined from 70 percent in 2000 to 67 percent in 2005. (William Frey, as quoted in Ohlemacher)

African Americans

African Americans currently make up 13 percent of the population, compared with 10 percent in 1950, but their percentage of the population is expected to remain relatively constant. In fact, the 2005 census found that blacks represent 12.8 percent of the population, and they have been surpassed by Hispanics as the country's largest minority group. (U.S. Census)

Despite the elimination of legal racism and the increased acceptance of minorities into mainstream society, the problems confronting African Americans have not disappeared. Racism and hatred still exist in our society. Often African Americans in the inner cities remain unemployed or underemployed. Many live below the poverty level and remain in a state of chronic anger or rage. This rage may well have led to the 1992 Los Angeles riots.

There continues to be a concern among individuals in the African American community about unfair treatment by law enforcement and the criminal justice system. The terms *racial profiling* and *driving while black* have become commonplace. Racial profiling or biased-based policing is a form of discrimination that singles out people of racial or ethnic groups based on the belief that these groups are more likely than others to commit certain

often been as tense as the relationships between the police and the African American community.

Asian Americans

According to the 2000 U.S. Census, of the 11 percent of the population born outside the United States, 26.4 percent were born in Asia. (U.S. Census) These Asian Americans include many distinct and separate cultures—from China, Japan, Korea, Vietnam, Laos, Cambodia, Thailand, and other countries of the Far East. Chinese Americans are among the most visible of the Asian American community, with Chinatowns in many large U.S. cities. Pockets of Koreans, Vietnamese, and Cambodians have also grown in certain areas of the country and become strong economic and cultural forces in certain cities and towns. Many police departments are strengthening their relationships with the Asian population by reaching out to the community and educating Asian Americans about the role of police in the United States.

Native Americans

In the 2000 Census, Native Americans numbered almost 2.4 million, or a little under 1 percent of the U.S. population. (U.S. Census) Native American nations, reservations, colonies, and communities with criminal jurisdiction have traditionally been policed in two ways: by federal officers from the Bureau of Indian Affairs (BIA) or by their own police departments, like any other governmental entity. American Indian tribes operate 171 law enforcement agencies and employ about 2,300 full-time, sworn officers. (*American Indians and Crime* 35)

types of crimes. This kind of policing is illegal. This issue was discussed in Chapter 8.

Hispanic Americans

The Hispanic community is composed of many different cultures. The Census Bureau uses the term *Hispanic* for people with ethnic backgrounds in Spanish-speaking countries. Hispanics can be of any race, and most in the United States are white. (Ohlemacher) (To differentiate between white Hispanics and Caucasians, the term *non-Hispanic whites* is often used.) Officers must understand and acknowledge this diversity. Hispanic Americans have suffered discrimination, and many are also handicapped by language and cultural barriers. Their relationships with the police have

Throughout the United States, there are more than 500 different tribal groups, all with distinct histories, cultures, and often separate languages. (*American Indians and Crime* 11) The various cultural beliefs filter the residents' perceptions of information they receive from governmental personnel or law enforcement. These beliefs also influence how Native Americans interact with others, including law enforcement, and may result in misunderstandings if officers aren't aware of these cultural differences.

Law enforcement is continuing to examine issues involving Native Americans and what efforts can be undertaken to address those issues.

Los Angeles police officers pray at the Islamic Center of Southern California.

Arab Americans and Muslims

Since September 11, 2001, there has been an increased awareness of the needs and issues of the Middle Eastern community. After it was revealed that the 9/11 terrorists had lived, worked, and gone to school in South Florida communities without arousing any suspicion, many residents became alarmed at the prospect of any individual of Middle Eastern descent living in their neighborhoods. The Muslim community has since raised concerns about the infringement of their civil rights and the suspicion that seems to have been generated within their communities.

Many Muslims have asked law enforcement for extra protection because they fear hate crimes being perpetrated because of their ethnicity. The Community Relations Service of the Department of Justice has written a guide to help law enforcement respond to this issue. (U.S. Department of Justice, Community Relations Service)

In addition, for the long term, increasing police recruiting efforts within these ethnic minorities will facilitate understanding. All these efforts should help members of the community of Middle Eastern descent feel less threatened and less ostracized.

Jews

Since September 11, 2001, there has been fear among the Jewish population of being considered a "soft" terrorism target. In cities with large Jewish populations, this fear is particularly dramatic. These fears and concerns for the safety of Jewish residents, synagogues, temples, schools, and group homes can cause a surge in demand for police protection. The American public was reminded of this attraction of soft targets with the shooting in the Jewish Federation of Greater Seattle offices in July 2006 in which a Muslim gunman killed one, injured five, and shattered the peace and tranquility of many. He told the dispatcher during the incident, "These are Jews and I'm tired of getting pushed around and our people getting pushed around by the situation in the Middle East," referring to the fighting between the Israelis and Hezbollah then occurring on the border with Lebanon. (Jacoby) To prevent copycat crimes and increased violence aimed at the Jewish population, demands for police protection increased in the Seattle area as well as around the country.

Women

Women make up approximately 50 percent of the U.S. population, so police officers have frequent interactions with women. Unfortunately, law enforcement often becomes involved with women when they are victims of crimes. In the last few years, however, officers' contact with women offenders has increased as, statistics indicate, there are more women being arrested for crimes. Although women are often victims of the same

Police officers frequently interact with women.

types of crimes as men, they also are more vulnerable to certain crimes that men usually don't have to be overly concerned about. Thus it can be difficult for men to understand what it is like to feel vulnerable and sometimes fear the other 50 percent of the population because under ordinary living conditions, men don't feel vulnerable or fearful of women. During the past three decades, however, the police have become much more sensitive to women in rape, sexual assault, and domestic violence cases.

Gays and Lesbians

In cities with large visibly gay populations, there have been numerous verbal and physical attacks on members of the gay community (sometimes called "gay bashing"). Police departments across the United States have created bias units to investigate crimes that are the result of racial, religious, ethnic, or sexual-orientation hatred. Earlier in the text, we discussed the efforts to recruit gay police

Law enforcement is often involved in the immigration issue.

officers. It is believed that all of these efforts will help to reduce these types of crimes and allow these minority populations to live free of fear as well as improve relationships between the police and the gay community.

New Immigrants

The rate of new immigrants, including many illegal immigrants, coming to this country has increased tremendously in the last decade, which has resulted in many challenges to law enforcement. Large cities and border states are not the only places confronting the immigrant issue anymore. Rather, there have also been dramatic increases in the immigrant populations in the South and Midwest, as immigrants have shown they will go wherever the jobs are. This has affected smaller towns in a dramatic way. There has also been some backlash in towns and cities around the country. Many states and communities have enacted immigration-related laws. Law enforcement has been thrown in the middle of this controversy because towns and cities want something done and the federal government is unresponsive. It thus falls to law enforcement personnel to enforce these local ordinances and state laws and also intervene in disturbances that arise over their implementation.

The immigration issue has created a lot of debate and turmoil in the law enforcement community and in local and state governments. Some jurisdictions instruct their officers to investigate immigration status on all calls; others allow officers to determine status only after someone has been arrested; and still others feel that local government should not get involved at all. This issue and how it is handled will continue to evolve.

LO5 Explore the Challenges Various Populations—Including the Aging Population, Youth, Crime Victims, Victims of Domestic Violence, the Mentally Ill, and the Homeless—Face When Interacting with the Police

As we have seen, the community the police serve is extremely diverse. Special populations offer unique challenges for police departments. Some of the groups with special needs are the physically challenged, the aging population, young people, crime victims, victims of domestic violence, the mentally ill, and the homeless.

The Physically Challenged

Depending on the definition of physically challenged, there are between 40 million and 70 million physically challenged people in the United States. According to the Census Bureau, among the 53 million adults with disabilities in the United States in 1997, 33 million had a severe disability and 10 million needed assistance in their daily lives. In 1997, almost 1 in 5 adults had some type of disability, and the likelihood of a disability increases with age. (U.S. Census) Those with disabilities include the deaf and hard of hearing; those who use wheelchairs, walkers, canes, and other mobility aids; the blind and

Police officers often encounter physically challenged individuals and must be sensitive to their needs.

visually impaired; diabetics; those with communication problems; the mentally ill; and the developmentally challenged.

The National Crime Victimization Survey is beginning to examine crimes against people with disabilities and indications are that, when adjusted for age variations, people with disabilities experience higher rates of violence than people without a disability. It is imperative that law enforcement ensure that this segment of the community will feel comfortable interacting with the police and reporting their victimization. (Rand and Harrell)

The Aging Population

America is getting older. Nationally, the median age—the age at which half the population is older and half is younger—increased from 35.3 in 2000 to 36.4 in 2005. (U.S. Census) By the year 2030, there will be 66 million older people in our society. Senior citizens experience particular problems that necessitate special attention from the police. Although seniors have the lowest criminal victimization rates of all age groups, they have a tremendous fear of crime, often refusing to leave their homes because of the fear of being a victim. Many senior citizens are infirm and require emergency services. Police often provide special programs and services for senior citizens.

Also of concern to older Americans is retaining their independence. An AARP (originally, the American Association of Retired Persons) study found that 85 percent of people over the age of 60 want to remain living independently as they age. Only one in eight lives with relatives. (Forst 7)

Although there are many innovative programs to assist the aging population, law enforcement leaders have realized that education and training must occur for officers to foster a good relationship with this segment of the population. As has been mentioned earlier, the patrol officer is the ambassador for the department. The way these officers treat older people will affect what the seniors think of the department.

It is important for officers to understand the physical, emotional, and social challenges that people face as they age. Officers can then adapt some of their procedures to minimize the affect that some older people's physical challenges (changes in vision, hearing, and mobility) have on their interactions with the police. (Forst 31)

Today, police departments have created numerous special programs to assist with the challenges faced by the aging population. One such program is **Triad**, a partnership between the police and senior citizens to address specific problems seniors encounter with safety and quality-of-life issues. Triad was started by the International Association of Chiefs of Police (IACP) in cooperation with AARP and the National Sheriffs' Association (NSA).

> **Triad**
> A joint partnership between the police and senior citizens to address specific problems seniors encounter with safety and quality-of-life issues.
>
> **Drug Abuse Resistance Education (DARE)**
> The most popular antidrug program, in which police officers teach students in schools about the dangers of drug use.
>
> Log onto www.cengagebrain.com to practice your vocabulary with flash cards and more.

NSA

TRIAD

IACP

AARP

Photo ©Gwoeii/www.Shutterstock.com. Figure © 2013 Cengage Learning.

Young People

Young people are a special target of police community relations programs because they are impressionable, and it is believed that if children learn something early enough in life, it will stay with them forever. The problem of crime and young people has been a concern for decades. During the 1980s and early 1990s, crime involving juveniles soared. To try to address this issue, the nation responded by implementing many different types of programs such as programs addressing family issues and living conditions, educational and school programs, and law enforcement–implemented programs. Among the factors studied were educational attainment, substance abuse, mentors and role models, and supervision. Police felt that if the American public cared about the crime problem, then programs targeting children and youth needed to be undertaken. Many departments also realized that by getting involved in young people's lives, they could have a positive impact and minimize the chances of the youth making bad choices.

Antidrug Programs for Young People

Currently, the most popular antidrug program aimed at children is **Drug Abuse Resistance Education (DARE)**. In DARE programs, police officers teach students, in their own classrooms, about the dangers of drug abuse. Although DARE has been popular, some believe that it is not an effective use of resources in combating drug use among young people. Studies on the DARE program and other antidrug programs are ongoing.

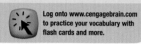
Other Programs for Young People

Some police programs for young people exist to address concerns other than drugs. In this section, we discuss some of the most popular programs.

The **Gang Resistance Education and Training (GREAT)** program is modeled after DARE but specifically addresses the issue of gangs.

Other programs include Youth Crime Watch of America, a youth-led movement to create a crime-free, drug-free, and violence-free environment in the schools and neighborhoods (Youth Crime Watch website), and anti-bullying programs, which are becoming more prevalent. In the wake of recent school violence, many schools and communities are addressing the issue of bullying in their schools by developing various educational and prevention programs. Community Emergency Response Team (CERT) training has also been made available to high school students in many schools throughout the country.

Officer Friendly and other programs designed to help children meet and talk to police officers are popular with schools and police administrators alike. The **Police Explorers** program is part of the Boy Scouts and is a popular program available around the nation.

Police trading cards are another popular youth program. These trading cards have the format of baseball cards and feature the photographs and personal information of officers in the local police department. The cards provide a good icebreaker for officers as well as youth to initiate conversations.

The school resource officer, a position designed to combat the increase in juvenile crime and improve relationships between schoolchildren and the police, has proven to be effective.

Police athletic programs or **Police Athletic Leagues (PALs)** have long been one of the most popular programs involving the police and youth and sports participation.

Crime Victims

"Victim issues and concerns are becoming an integral part of policing in the 21st century. We have to prioritize this in our law enforcement mission," according to Chief Frank Winters, Chairman of the IACP Victim Services Committee. (IACP, "What Do Victims Want?" p. 3)

There are as many as 31 million victims of violent or property crime in the United States annually. (IACP,

The DARE program is used throughout the United States.

TO RESIST DRUGS AND VIOLENCE.

© Ap Photo/Damian Dovarganes

"What Do Victims Want?" p. 96) Many efforts have been undertaken to assist victims of crime, including victims' rights laws, victim assistance programs, and crime compensation funds. Recently, law enforcement has realized that by working more closely with these victims, they can better serve the victims and enhance community support, and they can also help advance the law enforcement mission and goal of reducing and solving crime and reducing the fear of crime. (IACP, "What Do Victims Want?" p. 6)

Victims have traditionally been considered law enforcement clients because they receive law enforcement services. Recently, the criminal justice system has recognized that victims are powerful and resourceful stakeholders in the system and that by working more closely with them and incorporating their assistance, police can have a greater impact on crime and the perception of community safety. (National Center for Victims of Crime)

Victims of Domestic Violence

There has been increased demand on law enforcement to be responsive to the needs of domestic violence victims. (Kindschi-Gosselin 274) Family violence is one of the most frequent types of violence that police encounter, and though it is not necessarily considered the most dangerous police call (because of improved training and procedures), it is one filled with danger and emotional trauma for all concerned.

Despite the sometimes-harsh criticism directed toward women reluctant to leave abusive partners, an abusive relationship is a dangerous situation. A woman is most at risk of being murdered when she tries to break off an abusive relationship. (Kindschi-Gosselin 298, 364) Recently, in an attempt to reduce this risk, some states have begun to allow GPS monitoring of individuals who violate protection orders.

Traditionally, the criminal justice system took a hands-off approach toward domestic violence, treating it as a private affair that should be handled within the family, and police didn't make arrests even when the violence qualified as a felony. From 1981 to 1982 The Police Foundation conducted the **Minneapolis Domestic Violence Experiment**, which was designed to examine the deterrent effect of various methods of handling domestic violence, including mandatory arrest. The findings indicated that arrest prevented further domestic violence more effectively than did separation or mediation. One recommendation the authors made was that mandatory arrest should not be employed until more data were in. (Sherman and Berk) Despite these concerns, mandatory arrest laws were adopted around the country, fueled by women's rights groups and battered women's advocates.

The Mentally Ill

Police officers frequently encounter people with mental illness, a situation that poses a significant challenge for law enforcement. Approximately 10 to 15 percent of jail inmates have severe mental illness. In jurisdictions with populations greater than 100,000, approximately 7 percent of police contacts involve the mentally ill. (Cordner, "People" p. 1) The encounters involving people with mental illness can be some of the most dangerous that officers face. Often the calls come from family members who have tried to handle the situation themselves but found that they are unable to do so. This is often an ongoing problem; they have been able to handle it many times in the past and do not wish to involve the police if they don't have to. If, however, they start to fear for their safety or the safety of the mentally ill person, they will call the police.

The other way that officers encounter mentally ill persons is when these persons are causing some type of disruption in public and someone observes this odd or threatening behavior and calls the police. Sometimes officers encounter individuals acting strangely in public and believe they need to take some type of action. Often, the mentally ill person is in the process of committing a crime. Officers have several difficult decisions to make. Some of these decisions will depend on what mental health services and facilities are available. However, police officers are limited in what they can do with people who are acting strangely and, consequently, frequently use creative problem solving—a form of problem-oriented policing—when no other remedy seems available.

Though dealing with mental health issues is not a police job per se, it has become one because these individuals are in the community and get involved in disturbances, assaults, suicide attempts, or other criminal actions. Confrontations with a person who may be delusional often end with the individual, the officer, or a bystander being injured or killed. Police departments have thus worked hard to develop policies and procedures, and weapons or technology, to minimize the chances of this outcome. Society needs to have all sectors of the community that deal with these problems work together to develop proactive solutions.

The Homeless

Police departments are generally the only agency available 24 hours a day, 7 days a week. Therefore, the police are frequently called to deal with alcoholics, the mentally ill, and the homeless (street people). Large numbers of people live on the streets today. Many of these people are in drug or alcoholic stupors or frenzies, or they exhibit wild and chaotic behavior. The roots of the homeless problem include the policy in the 1960s and 1970s of releasing the institutionalized mentally ill, today's jail overcrowding, the

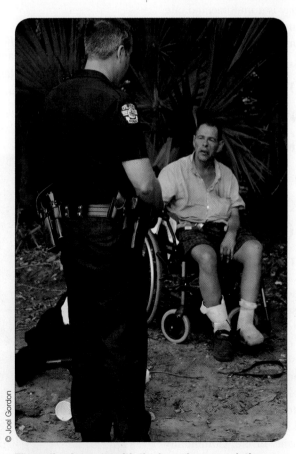

© Joel Gordon

The police interact with the homeless population on a daily basis.

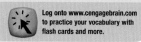

Neighborhood Watch
Crime prevention programs in which community members participate and engage in a wide range of specific crime prevention activities as well as community-oriented activities.

citizen patrols
A program that involves citizens patrolling on foot or in private cars and alerting the police to possible crimes or criminals in the area.

Operation Identification
Engraving identifying numbers onto property that is most likely to be stolen.

Log onto www.cengagebrain.com to practice your vocabulary with flash cards and more.

decriminalization of public intoxication, the breakdown of the traditional family, and the lack of affordable housing.

Community residents often call the police and insist they remove homeless people from the streets. Residents do not realize, do not understand, and perhaps do not care that the police have very few options for dealing with these needy members of the community. Today's homeless population, compared with the homeless before the 1990s, has caused special problems for the police. The public is fearful, or at least uncomfortable, in the presence of strangers loitering and asking for money, and this generates calls to the police. The police are also concerned about the high degree of victimization of the homeless and their inability to quickly report incidents to the police. Additionally, over the years the homeless population has grown to include more women and children. (Trojanowicz, Kappeler, et al. 248–249) The homeless issue today is a multifaceted one that requires many organizations working together to attempt to solve the underlying problems.

LO6 Discuss Some Innovative Community Crime Prevention Programs That Focus on Crime Reduction and Improving the Quality of Life in Communities

Citizens are worried about crime and have taken measures to isolate or protect themselves from it. However, the police have an obligation to help citizens protect themselves against crime. It is obvious that the police cannot solve the crime and disorder problems of the United States by themselves, but they cannot let citizens take the law into their own hands. To address these problems, the police must turn to the public for its support and active participation in programs to make the streets safer and improve the quality of life. Community crime prevention programs include **Neighborhood Watch**, National Night Out, **citizen patrols**, citizen volunteer programs, home security surveys and **Operation Identification**,

Photo © filipw/www.Shutterstock.com. Photo illustration by Spitting Images for Cengage Learning.

Operation Identification, Neighborhood Watch, and McGruff are all examples of widely recognized crime prevention programs.

© S. Meltzer/Photolink

© Jeff Greenberg/Alamy

Many police departments operate storefront locations in an effort to reach out to the community.

© AP Photo/Robert Button

police storefront station or mini-station, Crime Stoppers, mass media campaigns (including McGruff), chaplain programs, citizen police academies, and other police-sponsored programs including ride-alongs and Community Emergency Response Team (CERT).

Citizen involvement in crime prevention programs has increased greatly during the past three decades. The idea behind these various programs goes back to the early days of law enforcement in the United States when citizens were the eyes and ears of the community and worked with their neighbors to keep it safe. Community-based crime prevention programs require strong, committed leadership. The partnership between the citizens and the community empowers the citizens with an active role in crime prevention.

LO7 Describe the Latest Trends in the Police– Business Relationship

Businesses throughout the United States have become increasingly involved in assisting their local police departments in the last couple of decades. This assistance becomes more pronounced and necessary in times of tight budgets, when governments don't allow police to offer programs they may wish to provide, attend training they may find beneficial, or buy equipment that could

improve the effectiveness of the police department. Businesses may provide vehicles for DARE or crime prevention, buy advertising on marked vehicles, donate computers, donate printing for trading cards or brochures, donate food for police–community meetings, provide and outfit bikes for a bicycle unit, provide prizes for children in safety contests such as helmet safety or bike rodeos, fund police dogs or equipment for them, or provide bullet-proof vests. As with volunteer opportunities, the possibilities are endless. However, the problem with such donations is that, like with gratuities, they can lead to a "slippery slope." Departments and businesses thus have to be aware of how a donation might look to the public as well as how it is perceived within the department and the business community. Many cities and towns address this ethical issue for businesses (as well as individuals) that want to donate money or equipment to the police department by forming a private foundation to which businesses and individuals can donate. Overall, there is great potential in the business–police relationship. However, it is incumbent on government to scrutinize this relationship in terms of ethics, fairness, and public perception.

police storefront station or mini-station
A small satellite police station designed to serve a local part of the community and facilitate the community's access to police officers.

Crime Stoppers
A program where a cash reward is offered for information that results in the conviction of an offender.

citizen police academies
Academies provided by the police department for the citizens of a community to enhance their understanding of the workings of their police department.

Community Emergency Response Team (CERT)
A program in which civilians are trained in basic emergency response, first aid, and search and rescue.

 Log onto www.cengagebrain.com to practice your vocabulary with flash cards and more.

Boston Globe Staff Photo, Mark Wilson/Getty Images

A good working relationship between the police and business can benefit the entire community. This may even include selling advertising space on police vehicles to generate funds.

 Log onto www.cengagebrain.com for additional resources including videos, flash cards, games, self-quizzing, review exercises, web exercises, learning checks, and more.

12

Community Policing: The Debate Continues

After studying this chapter, the student should be able to:

LO1 Discuss the current thinking about corporate strategies for policing, including strategic policing, community policing, and problem-solving policing

LO2 Explore the philosophy and genesis of the current corporate strategies of community policing and problem-solving policing

LO3 Discuss the effect of community policing on current policing

LO4 Explain the process of implementing problem-solving policing

LO5 Describe some successful examples of problem-oriented policing

LO6 Examine the status of community policing today

LO7 Discuss how community policing strategies can be useful in the fight against terror

LO1 Discuss the Current Thinking about Corporate Strategies for Policing, Including Strategic Policing, Community Policing, and Problem-Solving Policing

For several decades, police chiefs and academics throughout the United States have discussed changes in the traditional methods of policing and have explored new ways of accomplishing the police mission. Many of these strategies have been discussed in this text. Since the mid-1980s, Harvard University's prestigious John F. Kennedy School of Government has held periodic meetings to discuss the current state of policing in the United States.

Harvard's Executive Sessions on Policing identified three corporate strategies for policing that are presently guiding U.S. policing: (1) strategic policing, (2) community policing, and (3) problem-solving policing. (Moore and Trojanowicz 2)

Strategic policing involves a continued reliance on traditional police operations, but with an increased emphasis on crimes that are not generally well controlled by traditional policing (for example, serial offenders, gangs, organized crime, drug distribution networks, and white-collar and computer criminals). It represents an advanced stage of traditional policing that uses innovative enforcement techniques including intelligence operations, electronic surveillance, and sophisticated forensic techniques. Much of this textbook, particularly the chapters on police operations and technology, deals with strategic policing issues.

strategic policing
Involves a continued reliance on traditional policing operations.

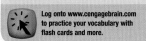
Log onto www.cengagebrain.com to practice your vocabulary with flash cards and more.

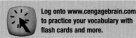
Community policing is an attempt to involve the community as an active partner with the police in addressing crime problems in the community. It involves a true, trusting partnership with the community and a willingness to accept and use input from the community.

Problem-solving policing emphasizes that many crimes are caused by underlying social problems and attempts to deal with those underlying problems rather than just responding to each criminal incident. Problem-solving or problem-oriented policing seeks to solve problems and have a positive outcome.

Community policing and problem-solving policing are very similar approaches to the crime and disorder problems in our communities. Most departments adopting a community policing program also follow many of the tenets of problem-solving policing. These two philosophies or strategies tend to go hand in hand.

fighting crime to the community as a whole and, through a partnership with the community, addresses the community's concerns and the underlying problems that lead to crime. The police and community thus work toward the ultimate goal of reducing the fear of crime as well as the crime rate. (Stevens 13)

Many believe that the modern stage of community policing began with the seminal 1982 *Atlantic Monthly* article by **James Q. Wilson and George L. Kelling**, "'Broken Windows: The Police and Neighborhood Safety." This has come to be known as the **broken windows model** of policing. Wilson and Kelling made several very critical points.

First, disorder in neighborhoods creates fear. Urban streets that are often occupied by homeless people, prostitutes, drug addicts, youth gangs, and the mentally disturbed, as well as regular citizens, are more likely than other areas to have high crime rates. Second, certain neighborhoods send out "signals" that encourage crime. A community in which housing has deteriorated, broken windows are left unrepaired, and disorderly behavior is ignored may actually promote crime. Honest and good citizens live in fear in these areas, and predatory criminals are attracted to these areas. Third, community policing is essential. If police are to reduce fear and combat crime in these areas, they must rely on the cooperation of citizens for support and assistance. Wilson and Kelling argued that community preservation, public safety, and order maintenance—not crime-fighting—should be the primary focus of police patrol. From this concept, many believe, the modern concept of community policing began.

LO2 Explore the Philosophy and Genesis of the Current Corporate Strategies of Community Policing and Problem-Solving Policing

Modern community policing, compared with the Police Community Relations (PCR) movement mentioned in Chapter 11, entails a substantial change in police thinking. It expands the responsibility for

© Alex James Bramwell/www.Shutterstock.com

Certain neighborhoods send out "signals" that encourage crime.

Robert C. Trojanowicz
Founded the National Center for Community Policing in East Lansing, Michigan.

Log onto www.cengagebrain.com to practice your vocabulary with flash cards and more.

LO3 Discuss the Effect of Community Policing on Current Policing

Community-oriented policing is an approach toward crime that addresses the underlying causes of crime and endeavors to apply long-term problem solving to the issues through improved police–community partnerships and communication. **Robert C. Trojanowicz** founded the National Center for Community Policing in East Lansing, Michigan, in 1983 and was its director until his death in 1994. Trojanowicz believed that community policing can play a vital role in reducing three important kinds of violence in the community: (1) individual violence, ranging from street crime to domestic abuse to drug-related violence; (2) civil unrest, which often includes gang violence and open confrontations among various segments of society, including the police; and (3) police brutality. (Trojanowicz 7–12)

Community policing is not a new concept. As we saw in Chapter 1, policing, from its early English roots, has always been community oriented. The concept of community policing goes as far back as London's Sir Robert Peel, when he began building his public police in 1829. In his original principles, he said, "The police are the public and the public are the police; the police being only members of the public who are paid to give full-time attention to duties which are incumbent on every citizen in the interests of community welfare and existence." (Weigand 70–71)

Photo © iStockphoto/Brian Powell. Photo illustration by Spitting Images for Cengage Learning.

Community policing seeks to replace our traditional methods of police patrol with a more holistic approach. Some scholars liken this approach to the medical model. Traditional law enforcement held the belief that the "experts" would save us, but over the years, law enforcement has moved to a holistic concept in which we are all partners in the health of our communities, just as we are partners in the health of our bodies in the medical model. Although there is a need for experts to save us in the emergency room or operating room, just as there is a need for police officers to make arrests, there is also a need for us to maintain our health and prevent certain illnesses and a need for us to prevent crimes from happening or to intervene before they reach the emergency or critical stage. In this approach, a community policing officer working in a particular neighborhood fills a role similar to that of a family physician, and the street officer responding to the emergency call is fulfilling the role of society's emergency room physician. The community policing officer thus acts as a problem solver and an ombudsman to other social service agencies that can assist in addressing the problem. (Bucqueroux)

Community policing mandates that the police work with the community, rather than against it, to be effective. The foot patrol experiments described earlier in the text are examples of the community policing model suggested by Wilson and Kelling in their broken windows approach to policing.

In *"Broken Windows" and Police Discretion*, Kelling notes that the community policing model expands and encourages the use of discretion among officers at all levels of the organization. The traditional method of telling officers what they can and can't do, as is commonly found in police manuals, will not greatly improve the quality of policing. He instead advocates teaching officers how to think about what they should do, do those things, and then review their actions with coworkers. With time, this procedure should lead to improved practices and the sharing of values, knowledge, and skills that will prove valuable in the performance of their job. (Kelling, *Broken Windows* pp. 1–5) Kelling supports "guideline development" in police agencies to facilitate the discretionary behavior

Some scholars liken the community policing approach to the medical model: We are all partners in the health of our communities, just as we are partners in the health of our bodies.

Community policing stresses developing relationships between the police and the community.

© AP Photo/Tim Shaffer

LO4 Explain the Process of Implementing Problem-Solving Policing

The idea of problem-solving policing can be attributed to **Herman Goldstein**, a law professor at the University of Wisconsin who spent a great deal of time in the trenches with different police departments. Goldstein first mentioned the problem-solving approach to policing in a 1979 article calling for a new kind of policing, which he termed problem-oriented policing. (Walker and Katz 335)

In traditional policing, most of what the police do is incident driven—they respond to incident after incident, dealing with each one and then responding to the next. In contrast, problem-solving policing, or problem-oriented policing, forces the police to focus on the problems that cause the incidents.

The problem-oriented policing strategy consists of four distinct parts: scanning, analysis, response, and assessment. Problem-oriented policing practitioners call this process by the acronym SARA.

To summarize, the SARA process is:

SCANNING: Identifying the neighborhood crime and disorder problems

ANALYSIS: Understanding the conditions that cause the problems to occur

RESPONSE: Developing and implementing solutions

ASSESSMENT: Determining the impact of the solutions

Herman Goldstein
First mentioned the concept of "problem-solving or problem-oriented policing" in 1979.

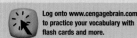
Log onto www.cengagebrain.com to practice your vocabulary with flash cards and more.

of police officers and enable them to better work with the public in enhancing the quality of life.

Community policing is also more easily facilitated with the technology available today. Departments are taking advantage of computers and the Internet to maximize their outreach to the community. Most departments today have a Web page. A presence on the Internet with a high-quality, interactive Web page can be a highly successful way to share the department's philosophy, beliefs, and practices with the community, as well as sharing information about the law enforcement personnel, facilitating a relationship, and encouraging a partnership. Sharing procedures, resources, and crime statistics in an open way can show the community the department's commitment to a partnership and to providing citizens with as much information as possible in an effort to meet their needs. Communication is further enhanced with links, e-mail, and the availability of reports online. Departments realize this is a crucial element to their outreach and are devoting dollars and personnel to this effort.

Photo by Robert Nickelsberg/Getty Images

The Baltimore Police Department is working on reducing its crime rate by analyzing when and where incidents are occurring and developing a proactive approach to the bigger crime problem.

Problem-oriented policing involves officers thinking, not just responding to yet another call for duty. It involves officers dealing with the underlying causes of incidents to prevent those incidents from happening again, and it encourages officers to use a wide use of resources (not just police resources) to engage in developing solutions. This process necessitates improving various skill sets, including communication (agreement to share thoughts and ideas with various groups), coordination (networking), cooperation (two or more parties agreeing to assist each other), and collaboration (a formal, sustained commitment to work together to accomplish a common mission). (Goldstein, *Problem-Oriented Policing*)

It is hoped that this problem analysis occurs within the department, using the latest research to develop appropriate procedures to successfully address problems in the community.

California Highway Patrol implemented a program to keep farm laborers safe.

LO5 Describe Some Successful Examples of Problem-Oriented Policing

The California Highway Patrol (CHP) implemented a program to keep the thousands of farm laborers who are hired to work the fields safe while being transported to work sites, as there had been a large number of collisions resulting in fatalities and injuries. The mandatory use of seat belts, stronger safety and inspection programs for the farm vehicles, increased staff within CHP to handle inspections, enforcement of these safety violations, and an increased public education effort had a significant impact on the safety of the workers while being transported. For the first time in eight years, there were no fatalities resulting from farm labor vehicle collisions, and the number of collisions involving farm labor vehicles dropped 73 percent. (PERF)

The Charlotte-Mecklenburg (North Carolina) Police Department used problem-oriented policing to address an increasing domestic violence rate. Analysis revealed that the average domestic violence victim had filed nine previous police reports, most involving the same suspect and some crossing district boundaries. In analyzing the situations, the officers determined it would be desirable to regard the victim and suspect as "hot spots," rather than as traditional fixed locations, and developed a detailed database allowing this to be done. Repeat calls for service were reduced by 98.9 percent at seven target locations.

In addition, domestic assaults decreased 7 percent in the district targeted while the rest of the city experienced a 29 percent increase. (PERF)

The Charlotte-Mecklenburg Police Department also used problem-oriented policing to address an increase in robbery victimization among the Hispanic population. Police found that most robberies occurred in parking lots near laundry facilities, that the residents were doing their socializing in the parking lots, and that they frequently had large sums of money because they didn't trust banks. Officers worked with the apartment complexes' management and improved the safety, access, and lighting. They shared information gathered with the robbery unit, arrested several suspects, and worked to build relationships with the Hispanic residents. Officers also partnered with the local banking industry to educate the residents and facilitate banking activities. These efforts produced a 72 percent decline in robbery rates in one apartment complex, and overall calls for service also declined. Police replicated the strategy in five other areas and produced an average decrease of 8 percent in robberies. In addition, residents reported increased trust in police and greater use of bank accounts. (PERF)

LO6 Examine the Status of Community Policing Today

Many of the programs and outreach efforts discussed in Chapter 11 are examples of community policing strategies. When departments use storefront substations, mini-stations, or kiosks, they are seeking to allow citizens to interact with them on a more frequent basis. The hope is that by decentralizing police operations and making officers and information more available, residents will become more involved with their police department and local government.

All the programs aimed at working with various populations to serve them better are examples of community policing. Most departments today use a multitude of programs to express and demonstrate their community policing philosophy.

Although most of the academic and professional writing about policing centers on our nation's big cities, many crime and disorder problems occur in small towns and mid-sized suburban departments as well. Community-oriented policing strategies have proven successful and are also widely used in these cities and towns. The true community policing philosophy is one that permeates the department and is put into action by all officers and personnel who have contact with the public. But, as the following examples will show, successful community policing initiatives can be undertaken in any size community.

The Wilson, North Carolina, Police Department targeted a four-block area plagued by violence and substandard living conditions. By surveying the community, the police department determined that gangs and drug activities were the residents' primary concerns and that the residents didn't trust the police. With the help of clergy from local churches (the strongest organized link to the community), the police department worked on improving communication and enhancing relationships with the community. They worked with property owners to clean up the area and, together with the clergy, concentrated efforts on youth truancy and drug violations. They also educated the community on the signs of gang recruitment. A follow-up survey indicated a 90 percent approval rating for the police coupled with a 38 percent reduction in calls for service. The department believes that police transparency is the greatest tool for collaboration and building trust within the community. (IACP website, *2009 Community*)

Like many cities, the city of Herndon, Virginia, was significantly impacted by the mortgage lending crash. The small community soon had more than 300 foreclosed homes. These abandoned homes were not maintained, resulting in a disordered appearance, and they were often vandalized and became locations for criminal activity. This situation resulted in a significant number of calls for service. Besides working with zoning, public works, realtors, bankers, and homeowners associations (HOAs) to design a program to reduce the number of illegal activities, the police department also addressed the care of these neglected properties by working with banks to secure the properties and with HOAs to maintain them. Calls for service in these vacant homes were successfully reduced by 65 percent in one year, and citizens' quality of life was improved. A town ordinance also was enacted that required banks to pay restitution for any services the town had to provide, thereby allowing the police department to recover some of its expenditures. (IACP website, *2009 Community*)

The Louisville, Kentucky, division of police was also recognized by the IACP for a community policing initiative developed to improve success on calls involving mental illness. After consulting with mental health professionals in the community, the Louisville police developed a 24-hour proactive, citywide crisis intervention team based on a program in place in Memphis, Tennessee, composed of specially trained crisis intervention team (CIT) officers. The primary objective of the program

The mortgage lending crash caused home foreclosures in many cities. Police in Herndon, Virginia worked with community organizations to address crime issues related to abandoned homes.

includes increased training for all officers in the area of mental health issues and a reduction in the use of force as well as an increase in options involving less-than-lethal force in the handling of these calls.

The program seems to be successful; in a three-month period, CIT officers responded to 503 calls. Of those, 401 of these individuals were hospitalized for evaluation or treatment, 11 were charged with offenses, and force was used in only three cases, and that force was "empty-hand control" only. The program continues to be closely monitored and evaluated by the CIT committee initially formed to implement the plan. (IACP website, *2009 Community*)

Resident Officer Programs: The Ultimate in Community Policing?

Numerous initiatives generally known as **resident officer programs** have sprung up around the nation since the early 1990s. Supporters of these programs believe they capture the essence of community policing: improved relationships between police and their neighbors, who team together to fight crime and address quality-of-life conditions that contribute to crime.

Elgin, Illinois's ROPE, which started in 1991 with three officers, grew to eight officers by 1997. One of the original locations closed after three years, in 1993, because of its success and a sustained decrease in crime. The ROPE officers, living in donated or subsidized homes or apartments, normally work an 8-hour day, but for all practical purposes, they are on 24-hour-a-day call, because residents can call them at all hours for assistance. The officers listen and work closely with the residents to creatively address the community's problems and challenges. They are also the liaison with government resources. Everyone understands that community policing is not a "quick fix," and the whole community thus engages in long-term problem solving to achieve mutually agreed-upon goals. The mission statement for ROPE is "By working and living in a distressed neighborhood, we will provide police service and be the stimulus that empowers the residents to problem-solve, improve their quality of life and independently take ownership of the neighborhood." (Elgin Police Department)

The city of Phoenix, Arizona, has a Police Officer Placement Solutions (POPS) program. According to the police department, the purpose of the POPS program is to enable the city to assist neighborhoods in recruiting officers to become residents in their community. The program is an element of an overall commitment between the city and its neighborhoods and is related to a community-based policing philosophy. The intended goal is to enhance the quality of life in the neighborhoods by making them safe enough for people to live in without fear of crime. The officers become familiar with the neighborhood and function as an avenue of communication as well as a deterrent to crime. The officers also benefit from financial incentives regarding rent and utilities and the opportunity to drive a marked take-home police vehicle. The officers are expected to be good neighbors and act as resources for the community, with police services and 911 calls being handled by on-duty personnel. This program was started in 1993 and is still going strong, with guidelines for participation and application procedures available on the department's website. (Phoenix Police Department)

In 1997, President Clinton joined the resident officer bandwagon when he announced a plan to give 50 percent discounts to 2,000 police officers so that they could buy federally foreclosed homes in 500 low-income neighborhoods nationwide. Participants must agree to live in the homes for at least three years. This program, called **Officer Next Door (OND)**, is part of the wide-ranging Urban Homestead Initiative designed to reduce crime and make low-income neighborhoods more attractive to homeowners. The OND is also part of the Good Neighbor Next Door program. Teachers, firefighters, and emergency medical technicians have been included in the program in recent years.

Many communities are adopting resident officer programs because of the belief that resident officers provide a high-profile presence that helps to prevent crime.

resident officer programs
Programs through which officers live in particular communities to strengthen relations between the police and the community.

Officer Next Door (OND) program
A plan initiated in 1997 that allows police officers to receive 50 percent discounts and low-cost loans to purchase homes in "distressed" areas nationwide. It is under the umbrella Good Neighbor Next Door program, which also includes teachers, firefighters, and emergency medical technicians.

 Log onto www.cengagebrain.com to practice your vocabulary with flash cards and more.

Photo © iStockphoto/Andy Dean. Photo of police cap © iStockphoto/Michelle Milliman. Photo illustration by Spitting Images for Cengage Learning.

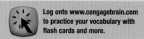
The Department of Housing and Urban Development (HUD) states that having these public safety personnel living in these communities makes American communities stronger, which helps to build a safer nation. The OND program helps make this goal a reality by encouraging public servants to become homeowners in these revitalization areas. (HUD website)

The Federal Government and Community Policing

In the 1992 presidential race, Bill Clinton championed the concept of community-oriented policing and promised to add 100,000 more police officers to the nation's streets. After the election, the federal government made tremendous contributions to community policing strategies throughout the nation. This section will discuss the 1994 Crime Bill and the Department of Justice's Office of Community Oriented Policing Services.

After much political debate, the Violent Crime Control and Law Enforcement Act (the **Crime Bill of 1994**) was signed into law by President Clinton in 1994. The provisions of this bill authorized the expenditure of nearly $8 billion over six years for grants to law enforcement agencies to reduce crime.

As the research and evaluation arm of the Department of Justice, the National Institute of Justice (NIJ) has mounted a broad agenda to study changes in policing. In the wake of the passage of the Crime Bill, Attorney General Janet Reno established the **Office of Community Oriented Policing Services (COPS)**. (Roth and Ryan 1) The COPS office was established to administer the grant money provided by the Crime Bill and to promote community-oriented policing.

"The Office of Community Oriented Policing Services is the component of the U.S. Department of Justice responsible for advancing the practice of community policing by the nation's state, local, territory, and tribal law enforcement agencies through information and grant resources." (COPS website)

COPS also supports the **Regional Community Policing Institutes (RCPIs)**, which consist of partnerships across a variety of police agencies, community groups, and organizations to create a delivery system for training police officers in community-oriented policing. Each of the more than 30 RCPIs develops innovative, region-specific curricula for community policing training as well as provides technical assistance opportunities for policing agencies and community members.

The RCPI network is facilitating the growth of community policing throughout the United States. The COPS program is also active in publishing articles, researching strategies, and conducting training (either through the RCPI or nationally) for law enforcement. Many of its publications can be downloaded from the COPS website.

The COPS office continues to respond to the changing needs of law enforcement and the American community. After 9/11, COPS reassessed some of law enforcement's processes and decided to address the information-sharing aspect of law enforcement. COPS thus funded a project of the IACP to determine ways to improve information sharing between federal, state, local,

Surrounded by law enforcement officers, President Clinton signs two crime bills. The Violent Crime Control and Law Enforcement Act (the Crime Bill) was signed into law by President Clinton in 1994.

© AP Photo/Ron Edmonds

SUPPORTING COPS
PROTECTING COMMUNITIES

and tribal law enforcement agencies. The result was a report entitled "Criminal Intelligence Sharing: A National Plan for Intelligence-Led Policing at the Local, State and Federal Levels." Among other things, the report recommended the creation of a Criminal Intelligence Coordinating Council (CICC) to help the Department of Homeland Security share criminal intelligence. (U.S. Department of Justice 2002) COPS members view community policing as a strong weapon in the fight against terror, so they will continue to address the issue.

The biggest study conducted so far that examined the COPS programs was led by Jihong "Solomon" Zhao and Quint Thurman, who found that the COPS programs were very effective. Over a seven-year period, they examined almost 6,000 cities that had been the recipients of grant funding through COPS. Zhao and Thurman found that COPS hiring and innovative grant programs were related to significant reductions in local crime rates, in both violent and nonviolent offenses, for cities with populations of greater than 10,000. (Zhao and Thurman 1) A report released in 2010 also indicates that problem-oriented policing is associated with reductions in crime and disorder. (Weisburd, Telep, Hinkle, and Eck)

Despite Zhao and Thurman's and Weisburd et al.'s research, other research on the effectiveness of community-oriented policing has yielded mixed results. Many experts are not overly enthusiastic about the idea of community policing. One of the problems faced in community policing is that of defining what is meant by *community*. In many community policing projects, the concept of community is defined in terms of the "administrative areas" traditionally used by police departments to allocate patrols, instead of in terms of the "ecological areas" defined by common norms, shared values, and interpersonal bonds. If the police are using administrative areas instead of ecological areas, they lose the ability to incorporate a community's norms and cultural values.

Some administrators are also uncomfortable with dividing a community up into "parcels" and possibly having those parcels competing against each other for funding, attention, and service. Though it is important for various sections of towns to have their say, it is also important for cities or towns to work on problems that affect the entire population communitywide rather than just leaving it for the neighborhood to work on them. Community members should be able to come together, discuss issues and challenges, and prioritize action plans to address those issues and challenges. (Lee)

In addition to this issue of community, Merry Morash and J. Kevin Ford, in their book *The Move to Community Policing: Making Change Happen*, cite other challenges that law enforcement agencies face when implementing community policing. For example, the move to community-oriented policing involves major changes in how traditional police organizations operate. They will need to take a customer-based approach and constantly learn about and improve their policing efforts. It's a transformational process that is complex and long term. (Morash and Ford 1–10)

A concern that has been raised by some law enforcement leaders is whether the activities that officers engage in under the umbrella of community policing (recreational roles, tutoring roles, social work roles) are the types of activities that law enforcement officers should be doing. Departments need to address that issue on a continuing basis.

Some law enforcement leaders question whether activities that officers engage in under the umbrella of community policing are in fact the role of the police officer whether it is speaking to teens about the dangers of texting and driving or reading to young children.

Another concern is the debate about community policing and reverting to the older, foot patrol model of close interactions with the community. As discussed earlier in the text, there is always a concern regarding corruption and unfair influence when officers get too involved or too close to community groups. Are the community policing strategies placing officers in an ambiguous position and perhaps enhancing relationships (and consequently, the influence of one group over another)? This also leads back to the earlier discussion about zero-tolerance policies and aggressive patrolling to clean up the streets, make community groups happy, and improve the quality of life. Can this desire to please and be successful lead to overly aggressive techniques and possibly cross the line to abuse? These concerns need to be continually considered and examined.

Some believe the empirical evidence for community policing's effectiveness in solving the crime problem is both limited and contradictory. (Schobel, Evans, and Daly 64–71) Other researchers admit there are a number of documented successes of community policing programs, but point out that there is also an indication that community policing may merely displace crime. Indeed, several studies indicate that there has been an increase in crime in the areas surrounding the community policing impact area. (Reichers and Roberg 110)

Recently the success of broken windows was challenged by Bernard Harcourt, a professor at the University of Chicago Law School. Harcourt and Jens Ludwig, an associate professor at Georgetown University, reanalyzed Northwestern University professor Wesley Skogan's *Disorder and Decline: Crime and the Spiral of Decay in American Neighborhoods*, originally presented in 1990. As Bratton and Kelling note, Skogan's original findings supported the link between disorder and serious crime, fortifying support for the broken windows theory. (Bratton and Kelling) Harcourt and Ludwig, however, argue that the "popular crime fighting strategy is, well, wrong," and it doesn't work in practice. (McManamy) Harcourt states that the targeted areas chosen for the initiative were also the areas most affected by the crack cocaine epidemic and that when the epidemic ebbed, so did the crime rate, which would have happened with or without the broken windows policing. He and Ludwig conclude, "In our opinion, focusing on minor misdemeanors is a diversion of valuable police funding and time from

> Can this desire to please and be successful lead to overly aggressive techniques and possibly cross the line to abuse?

what really seems to help—targeted police patrols against violence, gang activity and gun crimes in the highest-crime 'hot spots.'... it's not about being pro-cop or anti-cop. It's about using police officer time and limited resources intelligently." (McManamy) William J. Bratton and George L. Kelling, in turn, criticize Harcourt's analysis, charging that he had eliminated two areas from the study that showed strong relationships between disorder and crime. Bratton was the New York City police commissioner at the time and now heads the Los Angeles Police Department, where he has employed similar strategies: in three years, crime went down 26 percent and homicides decreased 25 percent. (Bratton and Kelling) Thus Bratton stands firmly behind the broken windows strategy, as do many law enforcement leaders who are employing it.

The biggest recent threat to community policing and, consequently, the biggest criticism of the initiatives that have been undertaken concern the current inability to keep police departments fully staffed and to keep the money flowing to these initiatives. Bratton spoke at a conference and declared that community policing had caused a downward trend in crime nationally in the 1990s, but added that crime is beginning to rebound because less money and attention have been devoted to community policing since September 11, 2001. Many of the resources previously devoted to community policing have been siphoned to prevent terrorism. He believes local jurisdictions as well as states and the federal government need to reexamine this issue. (Bratton and Kelling 1)

LO7 Discuss How Community Policing Strategies Can Be Useful in the Fight against Terror

Since September 11, 2001, some departments have made increased efforts to get back to essential police services. Budget dollars are at a premium and "extra" programs may be viewed as nonessential. Some feel that going back to more traditional law enforcement, with more militaristic tactics, is the only way to fight the war on terror.

One of the primary goals would be to prevent terrorist acts. Through partnerships with other agencies and the community, "hard" and "soft" targets can be identified, vulnerability assessed, and responses planned. Additionally, with established, positive, and trusting relationships, members of the community will be more likely to come forward with good intelligence information, thus allowing law enforcement to "connect the dots" before it is too late. (COPS website)

Many states and larger cities have thus created state and local **fusion centers** to share information and intelligence within their jurisdictions as well as with the federal government. The Office of Intelligence and Analysis of the Department of Homeland Security (DHS) provides assistance to these fusion centers, which can be tailored to the unique needs of the locality. Their goal is to facilitate the flow of classified and unclassified information, provide local awareness and access, and provide expertise, and there would be coordination with local law enforcement and other agencies. As of July 2009, there were 72 designated fusion centers around the country, with 36 field representatives deployed. (Department of Homeland Security website)

In the event of a catastrophic incident, community leaders—possibly already CERT-trained (as discussed in Chapter 11)—could be called to assist with responding. Previous relationships and knowledge of the neighborhood would facilitate this response. Police officers accustomed to making decisions and not having to rely on superiors would be an advantage in a crisis situation, where events are unfolding, communication is challenged, and innovative responses are needed. (Chapman and Scheider)

Police agencies are joining with federal law enforcement and state and county agencies to integrate responses to significant events and train personnel from all areas of life to recognize and share appropriate information on a timely basis. The assistant director of the FBI stated, "The FBI fully understands that our success in the fight against terrorism is directly related to the strength of our relationship with our state and local partners." (Louis F. Quijas, 13 December 2006, www.cops.usdoj.gov) To facilitate this success, the Department of Justice Office of Community Oriented Policing Services (COPS) and the Police Executive Research Forum (PERF) have produced a guide for

law enforcement entitled "Protecting Your Community from Terrorism: Strategies for Local Law Enforcement," which addresses partnerships to promote homeland security. As another way of recognizing efforts in this area, the International Association of Chiefs of Police (IACP) began giving community policing awards in the homeland security category in 2004.

Community policing is an excellent vehicle for addressing homeland security. The value of the partnership and the trusting relationship with the community will prove to be invaluable as the entire community—in the largest sense—contributes to keeping our homeland safe.

Community policing can be an important tool in preventing terrorist attacks like those of September 11, 2011.

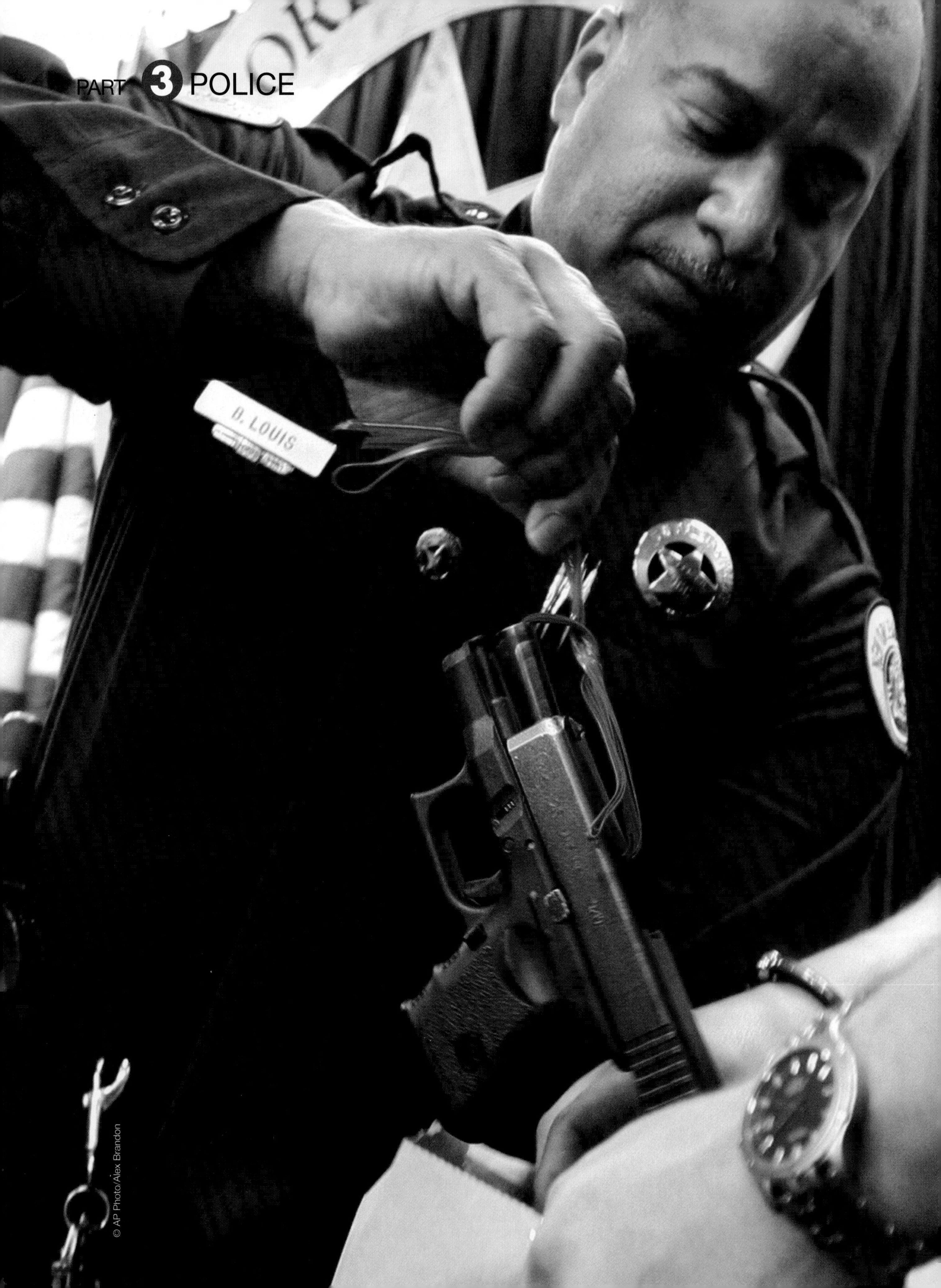
D. LOUIS

13

Police and the Law

LO1 Describe the Police and the United States Constitution

The United States is a nation governed by law. The primary law regulating life in the United States is the U.S. Constitution, including its many amendments.

It must be remembered that the U.S. Constitution is a continuing, dynamic document constantly being reviewed by the U.S. Supreme Court. Because this judicial review process of the Court is constantly reinterpreting the Constitution and constantly changing the rules that govern police behavior, all officers must constantly review their own organization's rules and directives with the realization that the law is always changing.

After studying this chapter, the student should be able to:

LO1 Describe the police and the United States Constitution

LO2 Discuss the police and arrest

LO3 Discuss the police and search and seizure

LO4 Describe the warrant requirement and the search warrant

LO5 Discuss the police and custodial interrogation

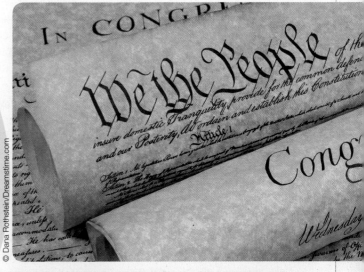

© Dana Rothstein/Dreamstime.com

The U.S. Constitution is the primary law regulating life in the United States.

judicial review
Process by which actions of the police in areas such as arrests, search and seizure, and interrogations are reviewed by the U.S. Court system at various levels to ensure the constitutionality of these actions.

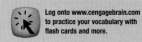
Log onto www.cengagebrain.com to practice your vocabulary with flash cards and more.

The Bill of Rights and the Fourteenth Amendment

The U.S. criminal justice system is based on the Bill of Rights, the first 10 amendments to the U.S. Constitution. Five of the first 10 amendments specifically address freedoms or rights that people possess when involved with the criminal justice system.

To understand the U.S. system of criminal justice, we must go back to the birth of the United States. The early colonists came to escape persecution by the English king and to seek freedom. The colonists, however, continued to be persecuted and to be denied freedom. Thus they rebelled, wrote the Declaration of Independence, fought for independence from England, and were able to defeat the British troops. As newly freed people, the former colonists wrote the U.S. Constitution to govern themselves. They then wrote the first 10 amendments to the Constitution, which form the basis of our criminal justice system—the rights and freedoms we possess that can be used against government tyranny.

The Fourteenth Amendment also affects the U.S. criminal justice system. The Supreme Court, over the years, has extended the Bill of Rights to the states through the due process clause of the Fourteenth Amendment, which protects all citizens of the United States from any state depriving them of life, liberty, or property except through the proper legal processes guaranteed by the U.S. Constitution. This section has been the vehicle through which much of the Bill of Rights has been interpreted to apply to state courts as well as federal courts. (See Table 13.1.)

The Role of the Supreme Court in Regulating the Police

The U.S. Supreme Court, through its policy of **judicial review**, has made a significant impact on the way the police do their job. As early as 1914, in *Weeks v. United States*, the Court influenced the police by regulating how they should conduct their searches and seizures. In 1936, in *Brown v. Mississippi*, the Court began to influence the

TABLE 13.1 U.S. Constitution: Amendments Governing the U.S. Criminal Justice System	
First Amendment	Congress shall make no law respecting an establishment of religion, or prohibiting the free exercise thereof; or abridging the freedom of speech, or of the press; or the right of the people peaceably to assemble, and to petition the government for a redress of grievances.
Fourth Amendment	The right of the people to be secure in their persons, houses, papers, and effects against unreasonable searches and seizures, shall not be violated, and no warrants shall issue, but upon probable cause, supported by oath or affirmation, and particularly describing the place to be searched, and the persons or things to be seized.
Fifth Amendment	No person shall be held to answer for a capital, or otherwise infamous crime, unless on a presentment or indictment of a grand jury, except in cases arising in the land or naval forces, or in the militia, when in actual service in time of war or public danger; nor shall any person be subject for the same offense to be twice put in jeopardy of life or limb; nor shall be compelled in any criminal case to be a witness, against himself, nor be deprived of life, liberty, or property, without due process of law; nor shall private property be taken for public use, without just compensation.
Sixth Amendment	In all criminal prosecutions, the accused shall enjoy the right to a speedy and public trial, by an impartial jury of the State and district wherein the crime shall have been committed, which district shall have been previously ascertained by law, and to be informed of the nature and cause of the accusation; to be confronted with the witnesses against him; to have compulsory process for obtaining witnesses in his favor, and to have the assistance of counsel for his defense.
Eighth Amendment	Excessive bail shall not be required, nor excessive fines imposed, nor cruel and unusual punishments inflicted.
Fourteenth Amendment (Section 1)	All persons born or naturalized in the United States and subject to the jurisdiction thereof, are citizens of the United States and of the State wherein they reside. No State shall make or enforce any law which shall abridge the privileges or immunities of citizens of the United States; nor shall any State deprive any person of life, liberty, or property, without due process of law; nor deny to any person within its jurisdiction the equal protection of the laws.

United States Supreme Court.

© Rena Schild/www.Shutterstock.com

police by ruling certain methods of police interrogation unconstitutional.

Most Supreme Court cases regarding criminal justice try to strike a balance between the rights of the individual and the rights of society. The Supreme Court thus has the difficult task of bringing balance between these two often-conflicting goals. There is an inherent inconsistency between protecting the rights of the individual and protecting the rights of society. To have unlimited individual rights risks limiting the rights of society to be safe from crime. To have unlimited rights of society to be safe from crime risks giving up individual rights.

In police matters, the Supreme Court hears cases on appeal from people who have been the subject of police actions, including arrest, search and seizure, and custodial interrogation. The justices then decide whether the police action violated the person's constitutional rights. In most cases, they do this by interpreting one of the amendments to the Constitution. Supreme Court decisions can bring about changes in police procedures. Certain significant cases, such as *Mapp v. Ohio* and *Miranda v. Arizona*, are known as landmark cases. The major method of the Supreme Court to ensure that the police do not violate people's constitutional rights is the use of the exclusionary rule.

The Exclusionary Rule

The **exclusionary rule** is not a part of the U.S. Constitution. Rather, it is an interpretation of the Fourteenth Amendment by the Supreme Court that holds that evidence seized in violation of the U.S. Constitution cannot be used in court against a defendant. Such evidence is suppressed (not allowed to be used in court).

The exclusionary rule evolved in U.S. law through a series of Supreme Court cases. Since at least 1914, the Supreme Court has been concerned with the use of illegal means by the police to seize evidence in violation of the Constitution, and then using that evidence to convict a defendant in court. Because the Bill of Rights, when written, applied only to agents of the federal government—not to those of local governments—the Court first applied the exclusionary rule only to federal courts and federal law enforcement officers. However, the Court continually warned state courts and law enforcement agencies that they must amend their procedures in order to comply with

exclusionary rule
An interpretation of the U.S. Constitution by the U.S. Supreme Court that holds that evidence seized in violation of the U.S. Constitution cannot be used in court against a defendant.

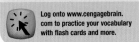 **Log onto www.cengagebrain. com to practice your vocabulary with flash cards and more.**

the U.S. Constitution, or they would risk the exclusionary rule being imposed on them as well. By 1961, the Supreme Court, noting that states had not amended their procedures to conform to the Constitution, had begun applying the exclusionary rule to state courts and law enforcement agencies as well as to federal ones. (See Table 13.2.) The following four landmark cases show how the exclusionary rule developed in this country.

Weeks v. United States

Weeks v. United States (1914) was the first case in which the exclusionary rule was used. It involved federal law enforcement personnel entering an arrested person's home and seizing evidence without a warrant. The evidence was used against him in court, and he was convicted based on it.

The exclusionary rule provided that any evidence seized in violation of the Fourth Amendment could not be used against a defendant in a criminal case. The exclusionary rule, as enunciated in the Weeks case, applied only to evidence seized in an unconstitutional search and seizure by a federal agent and used in a federal court. It did not apply to state courts.

The exclusionary rule also gave rise to another form of police misconduct that has been called the **silver platter doctrine**. Under the silver platter doctrine, federal prosecutors were allowed to use "tainted" evidence obtained by state police officers seized through unreasonable searches and seizures, provided that the evidence was obtained without federal participation and was turned over to federal officers. In Silverthorne Lumber Co. v. United States (1920), the Court, in its colorful language, compared the illegal search to be the "poisoned tree" and any evidence resulting from the illegal search as the "fruit of the poisoned tree."

Wolf v. Colorado

Another case that involved the exclusionary rule was Wolf v. Colorado in 1949. Mr. Wolf was suspected of being an illegal abortionist. A deputy sheriff seized his appointment book without a warrant and interrogated people whose names appeared in the book. Based on the evidence from these patients, Wolf was arrested, charged with committing illegal abortions, and convicted in court.

On appeal, the Supreme Court issued what could be seen as a rather strange decision: It ruled that although the Fourth Amendment did bar the admissibility of illegally seized evidence, the Court would not impose federal standards (the exclusionary rule) on state courts. Instead, the Court directed the states to create stronger state rules that would prevent illegally obtained evidence from being admitted into state courts.

© REUTERS/John Gress /Landov

A police officer executes a search warrant for marijuana at a Kalamazoo, Michigan home. Under the exclusionary rule, any evidence from this search would be inadmissible in court if the evidence was seized in violation of the U.S. Constitution.

Rochin v. California

In Rochin v. California (1952), another landmark case in the development of the exclusionary rule, the police entered Mr. Rochin's home without a warrant and, upon seeing him place what they believed to be narcotics into his mouth, forcefully attempted to extract the narcotics from him. Failing this, they brought Rochin to a hospital, where his stomach was pumped. The stomach pumping produced two capsules as evidence of illegal drugs. Rochin was convicted in court and sentenced to 60 days' imprisonment. The chief evidence against him was the two capsules. The Supreme Court overturned Rochin's conviction, considering the forcible seizure of evidence to be a violation of the Fourteenth Amendment's due process clause.

In the Rochin case, the Court did not make the exclusionary rule applicable in all state cases, but only in those cases of extremely serious police misconduct—misconduct that, in Justice Frankfurter's words, shocks

TABLE 13.2 Landmark U.S. Supreme Court Decisions: Exclusionary Rule in Police Search and Seizure Cases	
Weeks v. United States (1914)	Exclusionary rule applies to federal law enforcement agents
Rochin v. California (1952)	Exclusionary rule applies in shocking cases
Mapp v. Ohio (1961)	Exclusionary rule applies to all law enforcement agents

the conscience. The Court again urged the states to enact laws prohibiting the use of illegally seized evidence in state courts and threatened that if the states did not enact those laws, the Court might impose the exclusionary rule upon the states.

Mapp v. Ohio *Mapp v. Ohio* (1961) was the vehicle the Supreme Court used to apply the exclusionary rule to state courts. The case involved the warrantless entry of police into a woman's home to search for a man in connection with a bombing. While in her home, the police searched it and found "obscene materials," for which she was arrested and ultimately convicted in court.

LO2 Discuss the Police and Arrest

The police authority to **arrest** is restricted by the Fifth Amendment, which forbids depriving citizens of life, liberty, or property without due processes of law. An arrest is also controlled by the Fourth Amendment's restrictions on searches and seizures because an arrest is the ultimate

A police officer arrests a suspect for burglary. Arrests are governed by federal and state guidelines.

© Jeff Greenberg/Alamy

seizure—the seizure of one's body. A state's criminal procedure law defines an arrest and directs who can make an arrest, for what offenses, and when. Most states define an arrest as "the taking of a person into custody, in the manner authorized by law for the purpose of presenting that person before a magistrate to answer for the commission of a crime."

arrest
The initial taking into custody of a person by law enforcement authorities to answer for a criminal offense or violation of a code or ordinance.

Log onto www.cengagebrain.com to practice your vocabulary with flash cards and more.

Arrests can be made with or without a *warrant* (a writ, or formal written order, issued by a judicial officer that directs a law enforcement officer to perform a specified act and affords the officer protection from damage if he or she acts according to the order). In general, police officers can arrest a person (1) for any crime committed in the officers' presence, (2) for a felony not committed in the officers' presence if they have probable cause to believe that a felony has occurred and that the person they have arrested committed the felony, or (3) under the authority of an arrest warrant. As an example of the first circumstance, officers can arrest a man they observe committing a robbery with a gun. An example of an arrest in the second scenario is the following: an officer is called to a scene where there is a dead body and is told by witnesses that a woman in a black leather jacket was engaged in an altercation with the deceased and took out a gun and shot him. The officer searches the area around the crime scene and finds a woman in a black jacket hiding under a staircase. Upon searching the woman, the officer finds a gun. In the third scenario, the officer does not find the woman after the crime, but witnesses positively identify her. The officer can then go to court and obtain an arrest warrant for the woman and a search warrant to search her house for the gun.

However, if a routine arrest is to be made in a suspect's home, an arrest warrant is necessary, unless the suspect gives consent or an emergency exists. In *Payton v. New York* (1980), New York City police were attempting to arrest Payton based on probable cause for a murder. They attempted to gain entrance to Payton's apartment, but there was no response to their knocks. Officers then went into the apartment by breaking down the door. Upon entering the apartment, they observed in plain view a .30 caliber shell casing, which was later used as evidence of the murder. The Supreme Court ruled that this was a routine arrest and that the police had had ample time to gain a warrant before entry.

Probable Cause

Most of the arrests made by the average police officer do not involve a warrant because most crimes an officer becomes aware of on the street necessitate immediate

probable cause
Evidence that may lead a reasonable person to believe that a crime has been committed and that a certain person committed it.

reasonable suspicion
The standard of proof that is necessary for police officers to conduct stops and frisks.

search and seizure
Legal concept relating to the searching for and confiscation of evidence by the police.

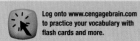
Log onto www.cengagebrain.com to practice your vocabulary with flash cards and more.

action and do not allow the officer the time necessary to go to court to obtain a warrant. Therefore, most of the arrests made by the police are based on the probable cause standard.

Probable cause can be defined as evidence that may lead a reasonable person to believe that a crime has been committed and that a certain person committed it. Probable cause is less than *beyond a reasonable doubt*, which is the standard used by a court to convict a person of a crime. On the other hand, probable cause is more than **reasonable suspicion**, which is a standard of proof that would lead a reasonable person (a police officer) to believe a certain condition or fact (that a crime is, will be, or has occurred) exists. This is the standard necessary for police officers to conduct stops and frisks.

The evidence needed to establish probable cause must be established prior to arrest. For example, if an officer sees a man walking down the block and then adjust his jacket to the extent that a gun can be seen protruding from his waistband, the officer has reasonable suspicion to stop and question the man. If the possession of the gun is illegal, the officer has probable cause to make an arrest. Because the arrest is legal, the search that produced the gun is legal; therefore, the gun can be entered into evidence. In contrast, if an officer stops all people walking down the street and searches them without sufficient justification, any arrest for possession of a gun would be illegal, and the gun would be suppressed in court.

Police Traffic Stops

"It was a routine traffic stop," was the statement many officers used to testify in court regarding summonses and arrests of drivers of automobiles. The routine traffic stop came to an end, however, in 1979, with the case of *Delaware v. Prouse*. In this case, the Supreme Court ruled that the police cannot make capricious car stops and that "random spot checks" of motorists are a violation of citizens' Fourth Amendment rights.

However, the Court stated that police may still stop automobiles based on reasonable suspicion that (1) a crime is being committed or (2) a traffic violation occurred. The Court also said that the police can establish roadblocks as long as (1) all citizens are subject to the stop or (2) a pattern is set, such as that every third car is stopped.

Police stopping a motorist. Not all routine traffic stops are routine!

© Anne Kitzman/www.Shutterstock.com

LO3 Discuss the Police and Search and Seizure

Search and seizure refers to law enforcement officers' search for and taking of persons and property as evidence of crime. In other words, searches and seizures are the means police use to obtain evidence that the courts can use to prove a defendant's guilt. Police searches are governed by the Fourth Amendment, which prohibits all unreasonable searches and seizures and requires that all warrants be based on probable cause and particularly describe the place to be searched and the persons or things to be seized.

The sanctity of one's home is very important in U.S. legal tradition, and it is commonly assumed that *a person's home is his or her castle.* The U.S. Supreme Court has consistently ruled that the police must use due process to enter someone's home. In *Payton v. New York* (1980), discussed earlier in this chapter, the Court ruled that the police need a warrant to enter a person's home to make a routine arrest, absent consent or emergency situations.

Canine Sniffs

The U.S. Supreme Court has consistently ruled that canine sniffs by a trained drug dog are not actual search and seizures controlled by the Fourth Amendment. In 1983, in *United States v. Place*, the U.S. Supreme Court ruled that exposure of luggage in a public place to a trained drug canine does not constitute a search within the meaning of the Fourth Amendment. The Court explained that the dog's alert to the presence of drugs creates probable cause for the issuance of a search warrant for drugs. It further explained that the dog's sniff is nonintrusive and reveals only the possible presence of contraband. Many cases have ruled that a dog's positive alert alone generally constitutes probable cause to search a vehicle under the motor vehicle exception to the search warrant requirement.

LO4 Describe the Warrant Requirement and the Search Warrant

In the United States, the general rule regarding search and seizure is that law enforcement officers must obtain a search warrant before they conduct any search and seizure. A **search warrant** is an order from a court, issued by a judge, that authorizes and directs the police to search a particular place for certain property described in the warrant and also directs the police to bring that property to court. Generally, to get a search warrant, a police officer prepares a typed affidavit applying for the warrant and then personally appears before a judge. The judge reads the application; questions the officer, if necessary; and signs the warrant if he or she is in agreement with the officer that there is probable cause that certain property that may be evidence of a crime, proceeds from a crime, or is contraband (material that is illegal to possess, such as illegal drugs or illegal weapons) is present at a certain place.

Generally, a warrant can be executed only during daylight hours and only within a certain time period, although there are many exceptions. Officers executing a warrant generally must announce their presence before entering. At times, however, judges may add a "no knock" provision to the warrant, which allows the officers to enter without announcing their presence.

Most searches by police officers are not made with warrants because they are made on the street, where there is no time for an officer to proceed to court to obtain a warrant. Instead, most searches are made in accordance with one of the exceptions to the search warrant requirement—situations involving **exigent circumstances** (emergency situations). Exceptions to the warrant requirement will be discussed at length in the next section.

Often, the cases in which search warrants are used are lengthy investigations in which immediate action is not required. Also, warrants are often used in organized crime and other conspiracy-type investigations.

One of the major uses of warrants is after an informant has provided information to the police that certain people are engaged in continuous illegal acts, such as drug dealing. For example, a man tells the police that a person is a drug dealer and sells the drugs from her house. The police get as much information as they can from the informant and then dispatch a team of plainclothes officers to make undercover observations of the house. The officers do not see actual drug dealing because it is going on inside the house, but they see certain actions that go along with the drug trade, such as cars stopping at the house and people entering the house for a short time and then leaving and driving away. Based on these observations, the police can then go to court and request that a judge issue a search warrant. If the search warrant is issued, the police can enter and search the house.

The Supreme Court has had several standards by which to determine what evidence constitutes probable cause for a judge to issue a warrant. The first standard was a two-part (two-pronged) test that mandated that the police show (1) why they believed the informant and (2) the circumstances that showed that the informant had personal knowledge of the crime. This standard was articulated in two major Supreme Court cases, *Aguilar v. Texas* (1964) and *Spinelli v. United States* (1969). There were problems with this standard, however. For one thing, to show why the police believed the informant and how the informant had

Police officer and canine checking out a vehicle. A dog's positive alert alone generally constitutes probable cause to search a vehicle.

© Frances A. Miller/www.Shutterstock.com

obtained the information, the police had to identify the informant or show how the informant had been trustworthy in the past, or both. However, identifying the informant and the description of past tips could put the informant in danger.

In *Illinois v. Gates*, the Supreme Court in 1983 reversed the *Aguilar–Spinelli* two-pronged test and replaced it with the *totality of circumstances test*, which holds that an informant can be considered reliable if he or she gives the police sufficient facts to indicate that a crime is being committed and if the police verify these facts.

Exceptions to the Warrant Requirement

Many exigent circumstances arise in which the police cannot be expected to travel to court to obtain a search warrant. For example, the evidence might be destroyed by a suspect, the suspect might get away, or the officer might be injured. The following are the major exceptions to the search warrant requirement, and the rules established by the Supreme Court that govern these exceptions.

Plainclothes police officer submitting an affidavit for a search warrant to a judge

© Mikael Karlsson/Alamy

Incident to Lawful Arrest

In *Chimel v. California* (1969), the U.S. Supreme Court established guidelines regarding searches at the time of arrest. In this case, the Court ruled that incident to (at the time of) an arrest, the police may search the defendant and only that area immediately surrounding the defendant for the purpose of preventing injury to the officer and the destruction of evidence. This has become known as the "arm's reach doctrine."

On September 13, 1965, three police officers from the Santa Ana, California, police department arrived at Ted Chimel's house with a warrant to arrest him for the burglary of a coin shop. The police showed Chimel the arrest warrant and asked him if they could "look around." Chimel objected, but the officers told him they could search the house on the basis of the lawful arrest. The officers then searched the entire three-bedroom house for 45 minutes. They seized numerous items, including some coins. The coins were admitted into evidence, and Chimel was convicted at trial of burglary.

Upon appeal, the U.S. Supreme Court ruled that the warrantless search of Chimel's home was a violation of his constitutional rights. The Court thus established the "arm's reach doctrine." In 1973, however, in *United States v. Robinson*, the Court ruled that because a probable cause arrest is a reasonable Fourth Amendment intrusion, a search incident to that arrest requires no additional justification.

Field Interrogations (Stop and Frisk)

In 1968, the Supreme Court established the standard for allowing police officers to perform a **stop and frisk** (patdown) of a suspect in *Terry v. Ohio*. A stop and frisk is the detaining of a person by a law enforcement officer for the purpose of investigation (**field interrogation**), accompanied by a superficial examination by the officer of the person's body surface or clothing to discover any weapons, contraband, or other objects relating to criminal activity. In *Terry v. Ohio*, the Court ruled that a police officer could stop a person in a public place to make reasonable inquiries as to the person's conduct. It further ruled that when the following five conditions exist, a police officer is justified in patting down, or frisking, a suspect:

1. Where a police officer observes unusual conduct which leads him or her reasonably to conclude in light of his or her experience that criminal activity may be afoot . . .

2. . . . and that the person with whom he or she is dealing may be armed and dangerous . . .

A federal agent performs a stop-and-frisk in Arizona. **Terry v. Ohio** set five conditions under which an officer may frisk a suspect.

3. . . . where in the course of investigating this behavior he or she identifies himself or herself as a police officer . . .

4. . . . and makes reasonable inquiry . . .

5. . . . and where nothing in the initial stages of the encounter serves to dispel his or her reasonable fear for his or her own or other's safety . . .

he or she is entitled to conduct a carefully limited search of the outer clothing of such persons in an attempt to discover weapons that might be used to assault him or her. Such a search is a reasonable search under the Fourth Amendment, and any weapons seized may properly be introduced as evidence against the person from whom they were taken.

Exigent Circumstances Although the general rule on searches within a home and without a warrant is that such searches are presumptively unreasonable, the Supreme Court has established a few narrowly crafted exceptions to the warrant requirement. These exceptions allow the police to act when "the public interest requires some flexibility in the application of the general rule that a valid warrant is a prerequisite for a search." (*Arkansas v. Sanders*) The Court has thus recognized the following "exigent" or emergency circumstances as those in which there is insufficient time to obtain a search warrant:

1. To prevent escape
2. To prevent harm to the officers or others
3. To prevent the destruction of evidence

4. While in hot pursuit of a criminal suspect
5. To render immediate aid to a person in need of assistance

Consent Searches A police officer can also search without a warrant if consent is given by a person having authority to give such consent. Consent searches have some limitations, however. The request cannot be phrased as a command or a threat; it must be a genuine request for permission. The police must receive an oral reply; a nod of the head is not consent. Also, the search must be limited to the area for which consent is given. The following are some of the most important consent search decisions made by the Supreme Court.

In *Schneckloth v. Bustamonte* (1973), the Supreme Court ruled that a search conducted pursuant to lawfully given consent is an exception to the warrant and probable cause requirements of the Fourth Amendment; however, because a consensual search is still a search, the Fourth Amendment reasonableness requirement still applies. The court ruled that to determine whether an individual voluntarily consented to a search, the reviewing court should consider the totality of the circumstances surrounding the consent. In *United States v. Matlock* (1974), the Court ruled that for a consent search to be constitutionally valid, the consent must be voluntarily given by a person with proper authority. In this case, the Court ruled that a person sharing a room with another person had the authority to allow the police to search the room.

Two police officers interview a woman at her home. A police officer can search a home without a warrant if consent is given by a person having authority to give such consent.

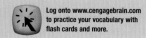
An example of a search that was considered unconstitutional is *Bumper v. North Carolina* (1968), in which the police searched a defendant's house by getting the permission of the defendant's grandmother, who also occupied the house. To get the grandmother's permission, the police told her that they had a lawful search warrant, which they did not actually have. During the search, the officers found a gun in the house, which was used as evidence in a rape case against the defendant, Bumper. The Court ruled that the government has the burden of proving that an individual voluntarily consented to the search, and in this case, the government did not have that proof. The Court also ruled that the officers' assertion that they had a search warrant was "coercive—albeit colorably lawful coercion," and the gun was thus suppressed as evidence.

Plain View Plain view evidence is unconcealed evidence inadvertently seen by an officer engaged in a lawful activity. If an officer is at a location legally

A police officer questions a suspect while another officer inspects the suspect's vehicle. The Carroll doctrine allows warrantless searches of vehicles under certain conditions.

doing police work and observes contraband or other plain view evidence, its seizure without a warrant is legal, according to the U.S. Supreme Court in *Harris v. United States* (1968). In *Arizona v. Hicks* (1987), the Court ruled that the evidence must indeed be in plain view—that is, without the police moving or dislodging objects to view the evidence.

Abandoned Property In *Abel v. United States* (1960), the U.S. Supreme Court established a standard regarding police searches of abandoned property. A hotel manager gave an FBI agent permission to search a hotel room that had been previously occupied by Abel. In searching the room, the agent found incriminating evidence in a wastepaper basket. Abel was then arrested and convicted based on this evidence. On appeal to the U.S. Supreme Court, the Court ruled that once Abel had vacated the room, the hotel had the right to give law enforcement agents the permission to search it.

Inventory In *Colorado v. Bertine*, the Supreme Court ruled in 1987 that the police may enter a defendant's automobile that they had impounded for safekeeping and were intending to return to the defendant after initial police and court processing, and may inventory its contents, without a warrant, to ensure that all contents are accounted for. In this case, Bertine had been arrested for driving while intoxicated. Upon making an inventory of his van's contents, the police found canisters of drugs. Bertine was thus additionally charged with violation of the drug laws. The Supreme Court ruled that the police action had not violated Bertine's constitutional rights.

Open Fields In *Hester v. United States* (1924), the Supreme Court established an "open fields exception" to the warrant requirement and said that fields not immediately surrounding a home do not have the protection of the Fourth Amendment and that no warrant is required to enter those fields and conduct a search.

The Automobile Exception Many students complain about the actions of police officers who search their automobiles. "Don't we have Fourth Amendment rights when we are in our cars?" they ask. "Yes," the professor answers, "but less than the rights you have in your house." The automobile exception to the search warrant requirement goes all the way back to 1925, in *Carroll v. United States*. In this case, the Supreme Court ruled that distinctions should be made among searches of automobiles, persons, and homes, and that a warrantless search of a vehicle, which can be readily moved, is valid if the police have probable cause to believe that the car contains the evidence they are seeking. This decision has become known as the **Carroll doctrine**.

In 1981, in *New York v. Belton*, the Supreme Court ruled that a search incident to a lawful arrest of the occupant of an automobile can extend to the entire passenger compartment of the automobile, including the glove compartment and suitcases or the clothing found in them. However, the Court reversed *Belton* in 2009 in *Arizona v. Gant*. In *Gant* the Court limited the authority to search the vehicle to situations in which the arrestee is within the reaching distance of the passenger compartment of the vehicle at the time of the search, or if it is reasonable to believe that the vehicle contains evidence of the offense of the arrest.

Border Searches A border search can be made without probable cause, without a warrant, and, indeed, without any articulable suspicion at all. In *United States v. Martinez-Fuerte* (1976), the Supreme Court ruled that border patrol officers do not need to have probable cause or a warrant to stop cars for brief questioning at fixed checkpoints.

Good Faith The Supreme Court established a "good faith" exception to the exclusionary rule in *United States v. Leon* (1984). It waived the exclusionary rule in cases in which the police act in reasonable reliance and good faith on a search warrant that is later ruled faulty or found to be unsupported by probable cause.

Searches by Private Persons In *Burdeau v. McDowell* (1921), the Supreme Court ruled that the Bill of Rights applies only to the actions of government agents; it does not apply to the actions of private security employees or private citizens not acting on behalf of, or with, official law enforcement agencies. The fact that private security personnel are not bound by the tenets of the Constitution and cannot obtain warrants, however, does not mean that they can indiscriminately violate the rights of offenders. If they do so, they can be sued at civil law and suffer severe financial damages.

LO5 Discuss the Police and Custodial Interrogation

FBI legal instructor Kimberly A. Crawford has written that the U.S. Supreme Court has recognized two constitutional sources of the right to counsel during interrogation. One source is the Court's interpretation in *Miranda v. Arizona* of the Fifth Amendment right against self-incrimination; the other is contained within the language of the Sixth Amendment. The impetus for the creation of the *Miranda* rights was the Supreme Court's concern that **custodial interrogations** are intrinsically coercive. However, the right to counsel contained within *Miranda* applies only when the subject of an interrogation is in custody.

In English common law, the lack of a confession was often viewed as a serious deficiency in the government's case, and was enough of a deficiency to cause a judge or jury to acquit an accused person. Although a confession is not required to prove guilt, the emphasis on securing a confession from a suspect remains today.

The Path to *Miranda*

The police have many crimes to investigate and often not enough resources to accomplish their mission. In many cases, there is not enough physical evidence or there are

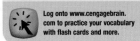

A felony suspect is questioned by a Santa Ana, California, police detective.

© Marmaduke St. John/Alamy

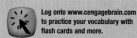
no eyewitnesses to assist the police in their investigation. Thus, police often must seek to gain a confession from a defendant, particularly in murder cases, in order to gain a conviction.

The history of methods used by the police to obtain confessions from suspects has been sordid, including beatings and torture that came to be known as "the third degree." From 1936 until 1966, the Supreme Court issued a number of rulings to preclude this misconduct and ensure compliance with due process as guaranteed by the Bill of Rights. The following landmark cases show the development of rules regarding custodial interrogation during those three decades.

End of the Third Degree

In *Brown v. Mississippi* (1936), the Supreme Court put an end to the almost official practice of brutality and violence (the **third degree**) then used by the police to obtain confessions from suspects. The case involved the coerced confessions, through beatings, of four men. The Supreme Court suppressed the confessions and emphasized that the use of confessions obtained through barbaric tactics deprives the defendants of their right to due process under the Fourteenth Amendment. The Court, in effect, said that coerced confessions are untrustworthy, unreliable, and unconstitutional.

Entry of Lawyers into the Station House

In 1964, the Supreme Court ruled in *Escobedo v. Illinois* that the refusal by the police to honor a suspect's request to consult with his lawyer during the course of an interrogation constituted a denial of his Sixth Amendment right to counsel and his Fifth Amendment right to be free from self-incrimination—rights made obligatory upon the states by the Fourteenth Amendment. The decision rendered any incriminating statement elicited by the police during such an interrogation inadmissible in court.

Ernesto Miranda in 1967.

© AP Photo

The Court also ruled that once a suspect becomes the focus of a police interrogation, is taken into custody, and requests the advice of a lawyer, the police must permit access to the lawyer.

The *Miranda* Ruling

The well-known case of *Miranda v. Arizona* (1966) was the culmination of many Supreme Court decisions focusing on the rights of individuals during police interrogations. The *Miranda* decision was actually a combination of cases involving four persons: Ernesto Miranda, arrested in Phoenix for kidnapping and rape; Michael Vignera, arrested in New York City for robbery; Carl Westover, arrested in Kansas City for robbery; and Roy Stewart, arrested in Los Angeles for robbery. What we now call the *Miranda* rules could instead have been called the *Vignera* or *Westover* or *Stewart* rules, but the Court decided to issue their ruling under Ernesto Miranda's case.

In *Miranda*, the Supreme Court ruled that confessions are by their very nature inherently coercive, and that custodial interrogation makes any statements obtained from defendants compelled and thus not voluntary. The Court thus felt that interrogations violate the Fifth Amendment, which guarantees that no one shall be compelled to be a witness against himself or herself in a criminal case, and that this guarantee is violated anytime a person is taken into custody and interrogated.

The Court then established the well-known **Miranda rules** or **Miranda warnings**, which state that prior to any interrogation of a person in custody, the police must do the following:

- Advise the suspect that he or she has the right to remain silent
- Advise the suspect that anything he or she says can and will be used in court against him or her
- Advise the suspect that he or she has the right to consult a lawyer and to have the lawyer present during questioning
- Advise the suspect that if he or she cannot afford an attorney, an attorney will be provided, free of charge

The Court further ruled that if, before or during the interrogation, the suspect in any way indicates a wish to

Miranda Rules

WARNING AS TO YOUR RIGHTS

You are under arrest. Before we ask you any questions, you must understand what your rights are.

You have the right to remain silent. You are not required to say anything to us at any time or to answer any questions. Anything you say can be used against you in court.

You have the right to talk to a lawyer for advice before we question you and to have him with you during questioning.

If you cannot afford a lawyer and want one, a lawyer will be provided for you.

If you want to answer questions now without a lawyer present you will still have the right to stop answering at any time. You also have the right to stop answering at anytime until you talk to a lawyer.

Photo © Fotoline/www.Shutterstock.com. Figure © 2013 Cengage Learning.

remain silent or to have an attorney, the interrogation may no longer proceed.

The *Miranda* rule applies to all custodial interrogations; this means, however, that not every police interview requires the warnings. The Supreme Court has made it clear that *Miranda* applies only when the suspect is *both* in custody *and* subject to interrogation.

When giving the *Miranda* warnings, officers must ensure, as a prerequisite to questioning, that a suspect makes a knowing, intelligent, and voluntary waiver of his or her rights. Also, if a suspect clearly indicates unwillingness to answer questions and invokes the right to silence, police must scrupulously honor that request. When a suspect makes a clear request to consult with an attorney, police must immediately cease any further questioning and may not contact the suspect about any crime unless a lawyer is present or unless the suspect initiates the contact with the police. The Court has also ruled that persons who cannot understand the *Miranda* warnings because of age, mental handicaps, or language problems cannot be legally questioned without an attorney present. In *Arizona v. Roberson* (1988), the Court held that the police may not avoid a suspect's request for a lawyer by beginning a new line of questioning, even if it is about an unrelated offense.

The Erosion of *Miranda*

In the aftermath of the *Miranda* decision, there was tremendous confusion in the legal community over its exact meaning. Consequently, a large number of cases were brought to the Court challenging and questioning *Miranda*. Eventually, the Supreme Court of the 1970s and 1980s under Chief Justice Warren E. Burger began to impose a series of exceptions to the *Miranda* decision.

The Court does recognize certain exceptions to *Miranda*. A sample of post-*Miranda* cases that have led to its weakening follow.

Harris v. New York In *Harris v. New York* (1971), the Court ruled that statements that are trustworthy, even when they are obtained without giving a defendant *Miranda* warnings, may be used to attack the credibility of the defendant when he or she takes the witness stand. In this case, the prosecutor accused Harris of lying on the stand and used statements obtained by the police, without *Miranda* warnings before the trial, to prove this dishonesty.

Justice Burger, speaking for the Court relative to the *Miranda* rule, wrote, "The shield provided by *Miranda* cannot be perverted into a license to use perjury by way of a defense, free from the risk of confrontation with prior inconsistent utterances. We hold, therefore, that petitioner's credibility was appropriately impeached by use of his earlier conflicting statements."

Michigan v. Mosley In *Michigan v. Mosley* (1975), the Court ruled that a second interrogation, held after the suspect had initially refused to make a statement, was not a violation of the *Miranda* decision. In the second interrogation, which was for a different crime, the suspect had been read the *Miranda* warnings.

Rhode Island v. Innis In *Rhode Island v. Innis* (1980), the Supreme Court clarified its definition of interrogation by ruling that the "definition of interrogation can extend only to words or actions on the part of police officers that *they should have known* [court's emphasis] were reasonably likely to elicit an incriminating response." In this case, a man told the police where he had left a shotgun he had used in a shooting—after the police had made remarks about the possibility of a disabled child finding it. (There was a home for disabled children nearby.)

New York v. Quarles In *New York v. Quarles* (1984), the Supreme Court created a "public safety" exception to the *Miranda* rule. In this case, a police officer, after arresting and handcuffing a man wanted in connection with a crime, and after feeling an empty shoulder holster on the man's body, asked him where the gun was without giving him the *Miranda* warnings. The gun was then suppressed as evidence because the officer's question had not been preceded by the warnings. The Supreme Court, however, overruled the state court and said that the officer's failure to read the *Miranda* warnings was justified in the interest of public safety.

Oregon v. Elstad In *Oregon v. Elstad* (1985), the Supreme Court ruled that the simple failure of the police to warn a suspect of his or her *Miranda* rights (with no indication of misbehavior or coercion on the part of the police) until after obtaining an incriminating statement or confession is not a violation of *Miranda*. In *Elstad*, law enforcement officers went to the home of a burglary suspect, Elstad, to take him into custody. The suspect's mother answered the door and led the officers to the suspect, who was in his bedroom. Before making the arrest, one of the officers waited for the suspect to get dressed and then accompanied him to the living room, while the other officer asked the suspect's mother to step into the kitchen, where he advised her that they had a warrant for her son's arrest on a burglary charge. The officer who remained with Elstad asked him if he was aware of why they were at his home to arrest him. Elstad replied that he did not know. The officer then asked him if he knew a person by the name of Gross (the subject of the burglary), and Elstad replied that he did and added that he had heard that there had been a robbery at the Gross house. The officer next told Elstad that he believed that he (Elstad) had been involved in the burglary, and Elstad stated to the officer, "Yes, I was there."

The police then brought Elstad to the police station, where he was advised of his *Miranda* rights and subjected to custodial interrogation. Elstad waived his rights and gave a full confession admitting to his role in the burglary. In court, Elstad's attorney made a motion to suppress his client's confession, arguing that the confession was "tainted" by the unwarned statement made in Elstad's living room. The trial court agreed and held that once the initial *Miranda* violation occurred, all that followed was tainted, including the station house confession, and therefore it was inadmissible. When it was appealed to the U.S. Supreme Court, however, the Court rejected the lower court's ruling and held that a simple failure to administer the *Miranda* warnings to a suspect—with no indication of behavior on the part of the law enforcement officer that could be interpreted as coercion, compulsion, or an effort to undermine the suspect's ability to exercise his or her free will—should not keep out a statement that the suspect makes that otherwise is voluntary.

The Court reasoned that events that are not known by a defendant have no bearing on his or her capacity to knowingly waive his or her rights.

Moran v. Burbine In *Moran v. Burbine* (1986), a murder case, the Supreme Court ruled that the police failure to inform a suspect undergoing custodial interrogation of his attorney's attempts to reach him does not constitute a violation of the *Miranda* rule. The Court reasoned that events that are not known by a defendant have no bearing on his or her capacity to knowingly waive his or her rights.

Illinois v. Perkins In *Illinois v. Perkins* (1990), the Supreme Court further clarified its *Miranda* decision. In the *Perkins* case, police placed an informant and an undercover officer in a cellblock with Lloyd Perkins, a suspected murderer incarcerated on an unrelated charge of aggravated assault. While planning a prison break, the undercover officer asked Perkins whether he had ever "done" anyone. In response, Perkins described at length the details of a murder-for-hire he had committed.

When Perkins was subsequently charged with the murder, he argued successfully to have the statements he had made in prison be suppressed because no *Miranda* warnings had been given before his conversation with the informant and undercover officer. On review, however, the Supreme Court reversed the order of suppression.

In rejecting Perkins's argument, the Supreme Court acknowledged that there are limitations to the rules announced in *Miranda*. The Court expressly declined to accept the notion that the *Miranda* warnings are required whenever a suspect is in custody in a technical sense and converses with someone who happens to be a government agent. Rather, the Court concluded that not every custodial interrogation creates the psychologically compelling atmosphere that *Miranda* was designed to protect against. When the compulsion is lacking, the Court found, so is the need for *Miranda* warnings.

The Court in *Perkins* also found the facts at issue to be a clear example of a custodial interrogation that created no compulsion. Pointing out that compulsion is determined from the perspective of the suspect, the Court noted that Perkins had no reason to believe that either the informant or the undercover officer had any official power over him, and therefore, he had no reason to feel any compulsion to make self-incriminating statements. On the contrary, Perkins bragged about his role in the murder in an effort to impress those he believed to be his fellow inmates. Basically, the Court said that *Miranda* was not designed to protect individuals from themselves.

The *Dickerson* Ruling

In a much-anticipated case, *Dickerson v. United States* (2000), the Supreme Court ruled that *Miranda* is a constitutional decision that cannot be overruled by an act of Congress. In this case, Charles Thomas Dickerson had been charged with conspiracy to commit bank robbery and other offenses. Before trial, he moved to suppress a statement he had made to the FBI, on the grounds that he had not received *Miranda* warnings before being interrogated. The district court suppressed the statement. The prosecution then appealed, arguing that two years after the Supreme Court's *Miranda* decision, Congress had passed a new federal criminal procedure and evidence law, 18 USC 3501—Admissibility of Confessions, providing that a confession shall be admissible in federal court if it is voluntarily given. The law does not require the reading of *Miranda* warnings to suspects in custody. The prosecution felt that Congress intended to overrule *Miranda* because the new law required merely voluntariness—not the four warnings as per *Miranda*—as the determining factor as to whether a statement or confession will be admissible.

After several appellate decisions, the U.S. Supreme Court finally ruled in *Dickerson* that *Miranda* is a constitutional decision—that is, a decision that interprets and polices the Constitution—and as such, cannot be overruled by an Act of Congress, such as 18 USC 3501—Admissibility of Confessions. Though conceding that Congress may modify or set aside the Court's rules of evidence and procedure that are not required by the Constitution, the Court emphasized that Congress may not overrule the Court's decisions, such as *Miranda*, that interpret and apply the Constitution.

The Court cited various other reasons for reaching its conclusion that *Miranda* is a constitutionally based rule. Among them, the Court noted that *Miranda* has become part of our national culture because the warnings are embedded in routine police practice. By holding *Miranda*

© David R. Frazier Photolibrary, Inc./Alamy

A sheriff deputy reads *Miranda* rights to a suspect.

to be a constitutional decision, the Court reaffirmed that *Miranda* governs the admissibility of statements made during custodial interrogation in both state and federal courts. Given the *Dickerson* decision, a violation of *Miranda* is now clearly a violation of the Constitution, which can result in suppression of statements in both federal and state courts.

Before *Dickerson*, some constitutional scholars had expected the Court to find a way to use the many cases just mentioned in the "Erosion of *Miranda*" section to overrule *Miranda*. In fact, the Court expressly declined to do so in *Dickerson*. Further, the Court's decision in this case did not attempt to find and defend an underlying rationale that would have reconciled *Miranda* with those previous relevant cases that threatened to undermine or erode *Miranda*.

PART 4 POLICE

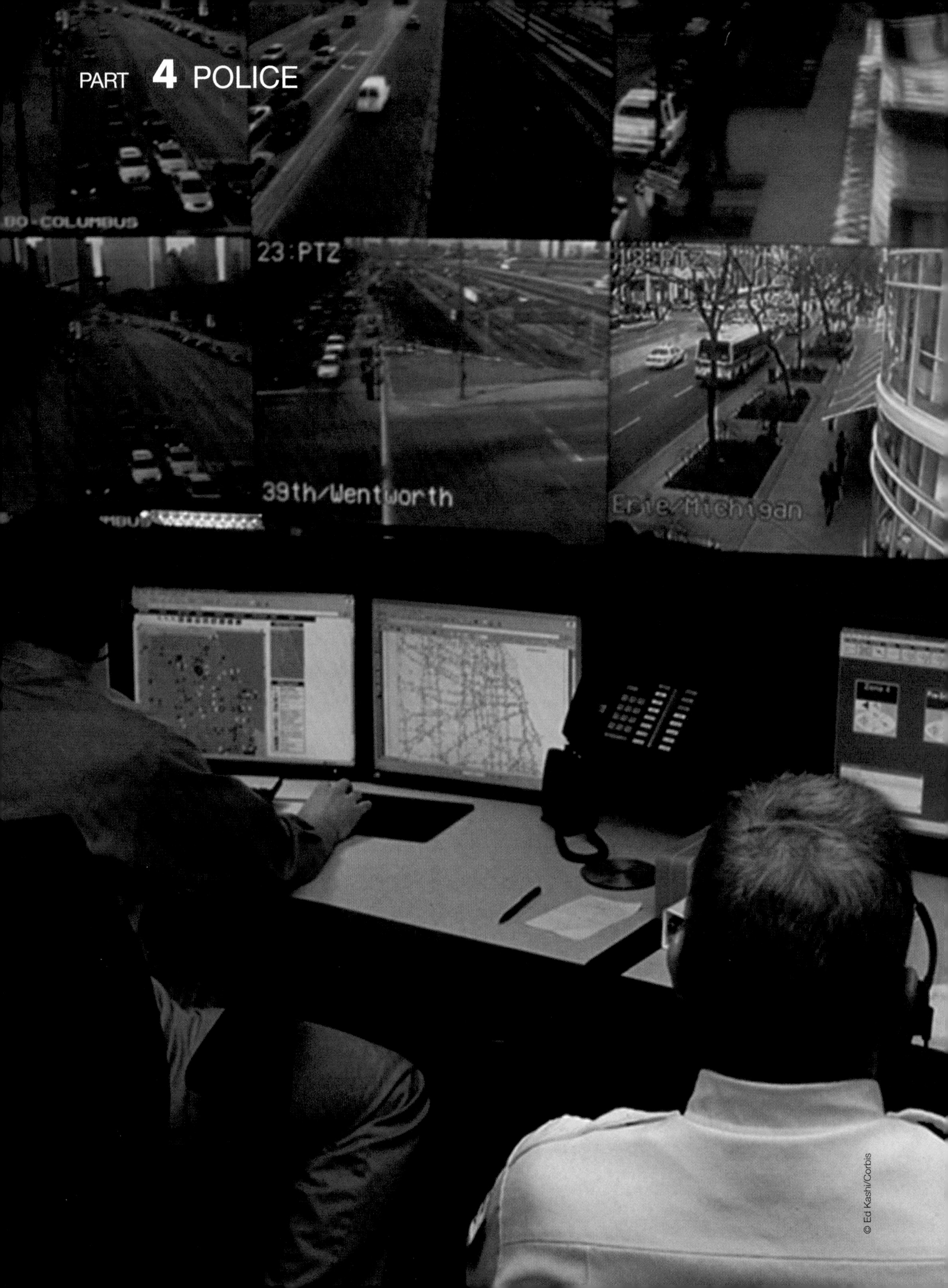

14

Computers, Technology, and Criminalistics in Policing

After studying this chapter, the student should be able to:

LO1 Describe computers in policing

LO2 Discuss fingerprint technology

LO3 Discuss modern forensics or criminalistics

LO4 Discuss DNA profiling (genetic fingerprinting)

LO1 Describe Computers in Policing

In 1964, St. Louis was the only city in the United States with a computer system for its police department. By 1968, 10 states and 50 cities had computer-based criminal justice information systems. Today, almost every law enforcement agency uses computers in many phases of their operations. Computer use in police work has thus increased exponentially since 1964.

The following sections discuss the most commonly used applications of computers in police work.

Computer-Aided Dispatch (CAD)

Before the computer revolution, the police communications system was slow and cumbersome. A citizen would call the police with a seven-digit telephone number. A police telephone operator would take the information, write it on an index card, and put the card on a conveyor belt, where it would travel to the dispatcher's desk. The dispatcher would then manually search maps and records for the police car that covered the area from which the call originated and then call that car, giving the officer all the information from the index card. All records were kept manually.

The 911 emergency telephone number system was introduced by American Telephone and Telegraph (AT&T) in 1968. The most recent available data indicate that 91 percent of local police departments and 94 percent of sheriff's offices participate in an emergency 911 system. In addition, 74 percent of local police departments and 71 percent of sheriff's offices have enhanced 911 systems capable of automatically displaying information such as a caller's phone number, address, and special needs. (U.S. Department of Justice, Bureau of Justice Statistics 2; Reaves, *Local Police Departments*, 2007 p. 15; Hickman and Reaves, *Sheriff's Offices* p. 1)

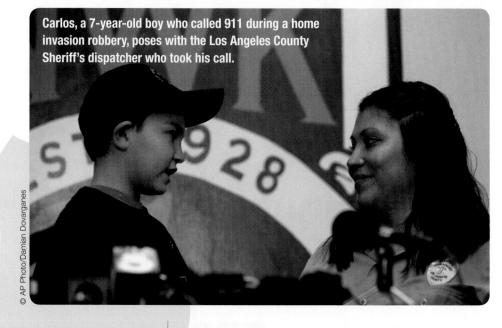

Carlos, a 7-year-old boy who called 911 during a home invasion robbery, poses with the Los Angeles County Sheriff's dispatcher who took his call.

© AP Photo/Damian Dovarganes

Today, **computer-aided dispatch (CAD)** allows almost immediate communication between the police dispatcher and police units in the field. Numerous CAD-system software packages are available for purchase by police departments. With typical CAD systems, after a 911 operator takes a call from a citizen, the operator codes the information into the computer, and the information immediately flashes on the dispatcher's screen. The CAD system prioritizes the calls on the dispatcher's screen, putting more serious calls (such as crimes in progress and heart attacks) above less serious calls (such as past crimes and nonemergency requests for assistance). The system verifies the caller's address and telephone number as well as determines the most direct route to the location. The system also searches a database for dangers near the location to which the officers are responding, calls from the same location within the last 24 hours, and any previous history of calls from that location. In addition, the CAD system constantly maintains the status of each patrol unit. In this way, the dispatcher knows which units are available and where all units are located. The system also determines which patrol unit is closest to the location needing police assistance.

Some CAD systems have automatic transponders within patrol units that enable dispatch personnel to monitor visually all patrol vehicles via a computer monitor and to assign units in coordination with this computer-generated information.

Enhanced CAD (Enhanced 911, or E911) The technology director for the National Emergency Number Association reports that 96 percent of the nation is covered by dispatch centers that have enhanced 911 capabilities. (Alford)

With an E911 system, when a person calls 911 for assistance, vital information is immediately flashed on a screen in front of the operator. The screen gives the exact address of the telephone being used; the name of the telephone subscriber; whether it is a residence, business, or pay telephone; the police patrol beat it is on;

Computer-aided dispatch allows detailed and almost immediate communication between the dispatcher and units in the field.

© Joel Gordon 2005

Mobile digital terminals (MDTs) allow the electronic transmission of messages between the police dispatcher and the officer in the field.

© Joel Gordon

determine which patrol units are nearest to a reported emergency incident and then dispatch the closest unit to the scene.

Cell Phone Technology Today, nearly half of all 911 calls are placed from a cell phone, and most sophisticated 911 systems have the ability to trace a cell phone call or determine the location from which the call is coming, which aids the police greatly. As an example, in July 2006, an 18-year-old woman was taken from the deserted streets of lower Manhattan in the early morning hours to a seedy hotel in Weehawken, New Jersey, where she was raped and murdered. The suspect stuffed the victim's body into a suitcase and dumped it into a trash bin behind an apartment building two blocks away. He then drove back to New York City and registered at another hotel. However, police were able to find the suspect because he had taken the victim's cell phone and used it to make some calls to his mother and his girlfriend. Police thus started their investigation by tracking the victim's cell phone, which led them to the people the killer had called because the cell phone number appeared on the caller IDs of the phones the killer had called. The police were then able to take him into custody shortly thereafter. (Baker A1, B5)

the nearest ambulance; and the closest fire department. This system also gives the police the ability to assist people at risk even if they cannot communicate because of illness, injury, or an inability to speak English. For example, if a sick or injured person initiates a call to 911 for assistance and then passes out or can no longer continue the conversation for some other reason, the police have the information in the computer and are still able to respond with assistance.

Some enhanced CAD and enhanced 911 systems use **mobile digital terminals (MDTs)** in each patrol unit. In systems using MDTs, voice communications are replaced by electronic transmissions that appear on an officer's MDT, a device put into a police vehicle that allows the electronic transmission of messages between the police dispatcher and the officer in the field. Officers receive messages via a computer screen and transmit messages via a keyboard.

The combination of geographic information systems (GIS), global positioning systems (GPS), and automatic vehicle location (AVL) with CAD and MDT software has increased the ability of departments to control and monitor their patrol functions. A department can quickly trace an officer's vehicle location when the officer is incapacitated and cannot verbally communicate his or her location. These systems also enable dispatchers to quickly

© Minerva Studio/www.Shutterstock.com

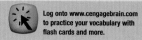
Reverse 911 (R911) R911 is a way for the police to contact the community in the event of an emergency or serious situation using a simple digital telephone click—which is much quicker and can cover a larger area than if the officers had to go door to door to notify residents. This technology was first used in DuPage County, Illinois, in 1996 and has been utilized by many municipalities since the terrorist attacks of September 11, 2001. In fact, it was used very successfully that day in Arlington, Virginia, following the terrorist attack on the Pentagon and enabled the rapid mobilization of off-duty officers. (Daigneau 44–45) During the California wildfires of October 2007, San Diego city officials implemented a reverse 911 system with automated calls going to residents and urging them to evacuate. (*Time* 35)

Automated Databases

As we have embarked on the beginning of the twenty-first century, computer technology is doing things in policing that were previously unimaginable, and the availability of automated databases has revolutionized police work. An automated database is an enormous electronic filing cabinet that is capable of storing information and retrieving it in any desired format.

The FBI created a major automated database, the **National Crime Information Center (NCIC)**, in 1967. The NCIC collects and retrieves data about people wanted for crimes anywhere in the United States; stolen and lost property, including stolen automobiles, license plates, and identifiable property, boats, and securities; and other criminal justice information. The NCIC also contains

National Crime Information Center (NCIC) servers.

© Photo Provided by FBI.

criminal history files and the status (prison, jail, probation, or parole) of criminals. The NCIC has millions of active records, which are completely automated by computer, and provides virtually uninterrupted operation day or night, seven days a week. Although the NCIC is operated by the FBI, local, state, and other federal agencies make approximately 70 percent of the record searches.

In 2000, the renaming of the NCIC as NCIC 2000 was combined with a major upgrade to the services mentioned above, which also extended these services down to the patrol car and the mobile officer. With this system, a police officer can quickly identify fugitives and missing persons using automated fingerprint identification system (AFIS) technology, which will be discussed later in this chapter. To make this identification, the officer places the subject's finger on a fingerprint reader in the patrol car, and the reader transmits the image to the NCIC computer. Within minutes, the computer forwards a reply to the officer. A printer installed in patrol cars allows officers to print out copies of a suspect's photograph, fingerprint image, signature, and tattoos, along with composite drawings of unknown subjects. The printer can also receive images of stolen goods, including cars. The new system additionally provides for enhanced name searches (based on phonetically similar names); prisoner, probation, and parole records; convicted sex offender registries; and other services.

Two other major automated forensic databases discussed later in this chapter are the Integrated Automated Fingerprint Identification System (IAFIS) and the Combined DNA Index System (CODIS).

Automated Crime Analysis (Crime Mapping)

Numerous software programs aid the police in **automated crime analysis**, or crime mapping. Crime analysis entails the collection and analysis of crime data (when, where, who, what, how, and why) to discern criminal patterns and assist in the effective assignment of personnel to combat crime. The most basic use of crime analysis is to determine where and when crimes occur so that personnel can be assigned to catch perpetrators in the act of committing the crime or to prevent them from committing it.

The forerunner in the use of modern, sophisticated automated crime analysis was the New York City Police Department's CompStat program. CompStat provides instant statistical updating of all reported crimes, arrests, and other police activities, such as traffic and other citations. This program and its movie screen–type visual displays provide the framework for the weekly crime analysis meetings at the headquarters of the New York City Police Department (NYPD), during which precinct commanders must account for all increases in crime and provide strategies to combat these crimes.

"Boltz," the Norman, Oklahoma, Hazardous Devices Unit's robot, carries a homemade explosive device. In addition to aiding investigations, technology can be used to help keep officers safe.

The keynote of the NYPD's reengineering program of the mid-1990s and the envy of police departments throughout the world, CompStat is a program that began to evolve in early 1994 when, after changes in the leadership of many of the NYPD's bureaus, disturbing information emerged. It appeared that the NYPD did not know most of its own current crime statistics and that there was a time lag of three to six months in the department's statistical reporting methods. Upon learning this, the department made a concerted effort to generate crime activity data on a weekly basis. CompStat has been credited with bringing about a drop in New York City crime to levels not seen since the 1960s. Numerous cities are now using CompStat programs and other forms of automated crime analysis and crime mapping.

© 3D Brained/www.Shutterstock.com

Computer-Aided Investigation (Computer-Aided Case Management)

Computer-aided investigation and **computer-aided case management** are revolutionizing the criminal investigation process.

Since the 1990s, British police have operated a computer-aided investigation system called the Home Office Large Major Enquiry System (HOLMES, which is a reference to the legendary fictional detective Sherlock Holmes). It is a sophisticated computer program developed for British investigators to aid them in managing complex investigations. (In Great Britain, an investigation is called

an enquiry.) HOLMES is a complete case management system that can retrieve, process, organize, recognize, and interrelate all aspects of information in a case. It also keeps track of ongoing progress, or the lack of it, in investigations. The system was created in response to the infamous Yorkshire Ripper case, in which 13 women were killed between 1974 and 1981. When the perpetrator was finally apprehended in 1981, it was discovered that he had been detained and questioned by at least six different police departments in connection with the attacks. However, because sharing information on related cases was so cumbersome for the neighboring forces at that time, the connection was never made. (Sutter 50–52)

Despite the computer's influence in the investigative process, it will never replace the investigator. The successful investigation of crimes and other police incidents will always primarily depend on the intelligence and hard work of investigators and police officers. As a prime example, recall the 2002 Beltway Sniper case, a series of random shootings that terrorized Washington, D.C., and its suburbs. The Beltway Snipers killed 10 people and wounded another three. Despite using geographic profiling and other computer models in one of the most intense manhunts in U.S. criminal history, the suspects were identified based on leads that one of the snipers provided about a seemingly unrelated case in Alabama. Moreover, despite the formation of a massive law enforcement dragnet for the suspects, they were caught after an alert motorist saw them sleeping in their car 50 miles from the closest crime scene. ("Predicting a Criminal's Journey" pp. 11–13)

Mobile Technology

The concept of mobile computing was introduced several decades ago with the development and use of CAD and MDTs (discussed earlier in this chapter), which supply officers with computer-aided dispatch data. Since then, mobile computerization and technology have expanded exponentially. Current systems give patrol officers the tools they need to function as if they were in an office while they remain out in the community performing police work. These systems provide patrol officers with records management systems (RMS), computer-aided dispatch, mobile data terminals, mobile wireless report entry (MRE), AVL/GPS mapping, and many other capabilities once available only in traditional offices. Mobile technologies also enable patrol officers to access real-time data and file reports via laptops

license plate recognition (LPR) technology
Employs cameras and computer software to discern the letters and numbers of vehicle license plates and then compares them with records contained in state and federal databases, including records from the department of motor vehicles and the NCIC.

inked prints (ten-prints)
Result of the process of rolling each finger onto a ten-print card.

latent prints
Fingerprint impressions left at a crime scene.

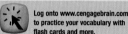

Log onto www.cengagebrain.com to practice your vocabulary with flash cards and more.

in patrol vehicles or through personal communication devices such as a personal digital assistant (PDA) or Black-Berry. Mobile technology thus minimizes the routine paperwork that must be done at the station house or police headquarters and reduces the amount of time that officers must be "out of service."

One of the latest mobile technological innovations is **license plate recognition (LPR) technology**. LPR technology can be used to search for stolen vehicles, vehicles listed in AMBER Alerts, or vehicles driven by wanted persons. This technology employs cameras and computer software to discern the letters and numbers of vehicle license plates and then compares them with records contained in state and federal databases, including records from the department of motor vehicles and the NCIC. Imaging cameras can be placed on the front or roof of a patrol vehicle or in its light bar. (Gordon and Wolf 8–13)

LPR technology was initially designed for use in parking lots (to record the time a vehicle entered), for access control (to allow authorized vehicles into a secure area), and for paying tolls. This technology is now also being used for border control and traffic fine enforcement.

LO2 Discuss Fingerprint Technology

Fingerprints have historically offered an infallible means of personal identification. Criminal identification by means of fingerprints is one of the most potent factors in apprehending fugitives who might otherwise escape arrest and continue their criminal

An officer uses the License Plate Recognition (LPR) technology in his vehicle. A bumper-mounted camera transmits passing cars' license plate information to the officer's dashboard computer.

activities indefinitely. This type of identification makes possible an accurate determination of a person's previous arrests and convictions, which results in the imposition of more equitable sentences by the judiciary. In addition, this system of identification enables the prosecutor to present his or her case in light of the offender's previous record. It also provides probation officers and parole board members with definite information upon which to base their judgments in dealing with criminals in their jurisdiction.

Fingerprints may be recorded on standard fingerprint cards or recorded digitally and transmitted electronically for comparison. By comparing fingerprints at the scene of a crime with the fingerprint record of a suspect, officials can establish absolute proof of the presence or identity of a person.

Basic Categories of Fingerprints

There are two basic categories of fingerprints: inked prints or ten-prints, and latent prints.

- **Inked prints** or **ten-prints** are the result of the process of rolling each finger onto a ten-print card (each finger is rolled onto a separate box on the card) using fingerprinting ink. Inked prints are kept on file at local police departments, state criminal justice information agencies, and the FBI. When a person is arrested, he or she is fingerprinted, and those inked prints are compared with the fingerprints on file of known criminals. Inked prints or ten-prints are also taken for numerous other types of investigations such as employment background and license applications.

- **Latent prints** are impressions left on evidence. These prints may be "lifted" and then compared with inked

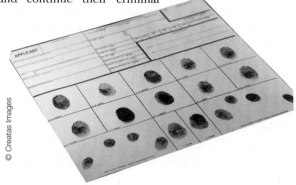

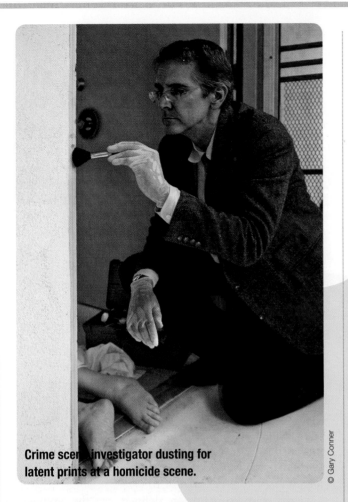

Crime scene investigator dusting for latent prints at a homicide scene.

© Gary Conner

prints on file to try to establish the identity of the perpetrator. Latent prints are impressions produced by the ridged skin on human fingers, palms, and soles of the feet. Latent print examiners analyze and compare latent prints to known prints of individuals in an effort to make identifications or exclusions. The uniqueness, permanence, and arrangement of the friction ridges allow examiners to positively match two prints and to determine whether an area of a friction ridge impression originated from one particular source to the exclusion of others. A variety of techniques, including the use of chemicals, powders, lasers, alternate light sources, and other physical means, are employed in the detection and development of latent prints. In instances where a latent print has limited quality and quantity of detail, examiners may perform microscopic examinations to make conclusive comparisons.

Automated Fingerprint Identification Systems

By the 1980s, **automated fingerprint identification systems (AFIS)** had begun to be developed. An AFIS enables a print technician to enter unidentified latent prints into the computer. The computer then automatically searches its files and presents a list of likely matches, which can be visually examined by a fingerprint technician in order to find the perfect match. Using AFIS technology, a person's prints can be taken and stored in memory without the use of the traditional inking and rolling techniques.

Until recently, AFIS technology was extraordinarily expensive and therefore was procured only by the largest agencies. Also, even though the technology provided excellent high-speed fingerprint matching once fingerprint databases became large enough, a drawback was that each system was stand-alone—that is, systems could not exchange information rapidly. But there are now software-based systems using open-system architecture, which means that any brand of computer based on the Unix operating system will work with the systems. These systems are also designed to exchange fingerprint and other data over the Internet with other criminal justice information systems, using the widely accepted Henry System of fingerprint classification.

These systems, designed for use in a booking facility, can use ink and paper fingerprints or can employ **Live Scan**, an optical fingerprint scanning system, to read a suspect's prints. The scanner uses electronic capture of the suspect's fingerprint pattern by means of electronic quality analysis and automatic image centering. The booking officer begins with a single-finger or dual-digit search by placing the suspect's finger on the scanner for reading. If the computer finds a possible match, the officer gets news of a "hit" within minutes. The computer selects the most likely matches, which then must be verified by a human operator. If there is no hit, the computer adds the fingerprint to its database automatically.

These systems also have image enhancement, and ten-print system capability. They can scan fingerprint cards, reduce them to electronic records, and store them for future reference. They can also produce fingerprint cards from electronically scanned Live Scan fingerprints. A latent fingerprint examiner can then link separate crime scenes using single latent prints, which can point to a common perpetrator or a pattern.

The use of Live Scan stations allows fingerprints and demographic information to be electronically captured, stored, and transmitted in minutes. Greater use of applicant fingerprints is among the many reasons why the use of ten-print Live Scan stations is increasing nationwide. Built-in quality control software helps reduce human errors. Because there is no ink, there is no smearing. If a mistake is made, a print can be retaken until a high-quality record is obtained. There is also no need to print a person again for local, state, and federal agencies because Live Scan can make copies. Further, higher-quality fingerprints mean a higher likelihood of the AFIS finding a match in its database without needing human verification.

Integrated Automated Fingerprint Identification System (IAFIS)

In 1999, the FBI began its Integrated Automated Fingerprint Identification System (IAFIS). This system has the capability to compare latent fingerprints against the largest criminal fingerprint repository in the world, which contains the fingerprints of almost 67.2 million individuals. This allows the FBI to make identifications, without the benefit of a named suspect, to help solve a variety of crimes.

IAFIS is primarily a ten-print system that searches an individual's fingerprints to determine whether a prior arrest record exists and maintains a criminal arrest record history for each individual. The system also offers significant latent print capabilities. Using IAFIS, a latent print specialist can digitally capture latent print and ten-print images and perform several functions with each, including enhancing it to improve image quality, comparing latent fingerprints against suspect ten-print records retrieved from the criminal fingerprint repository, searching latent fingerprints against the ten-print fingerprint repository when no suspects have been identified, doing automatic searches of new arrest ten-print records against an unsolved latent fingerprint repository, and creating special files of ten-print records to support major criminal investigations. (FBI, *Integrated Automated Fingerprint Identification System*)

As of 2011, IAFIS had almost 67.2 million records in its National Criminal History Record File, and it continues to set an international standard for providing fingerprints electronically. After a criminal ten-print search is submitted electronically, the FBI guarantees a response within two hours, and the prints are compared to those of anyone who has been arrested in the United States since the 1920s. (FBI, *Integrated*) IAFIS was instrumental in the capture of Lee Boyd Malvo, one of the two suspects in the 2002 Washington, D.C., area sniper case. A latent print entered into IAFIS matched Malvo's—his prints were in the system because he had been previously arrested by the INS. (Kanable, "Fingerprints" pp. 48, 50–53)

LO3 Discuss Modern Forensics or Criminalistics

The use of scientific technology to solve crime is generally referred to as **forensic science** or **criminalistics**. The terms *forensic science* and *criminalistics* are often used interchangeably. However, forensic science, the more general of the two terms, is that part of science applied to answering legal questions. According to Richard Saferstein, former chief forensic scientist of the New Jersey State Police laboratory and the author of nine editions of the leading textbook on forensic science and criminalistics, *Criminalistics: An Introduction to Forensic Science*, "Forensic science is the application of science to those criminal and civil laws that are enforced by police agencies in a criminal justice system." (Saferstein 2)

Criminalistics is actually just one of several branches of forensic science. Other branches include forensic medicine, forensic pathology, forensic toxicology, forensic physical anthropology, forensic odontology, forensic entomology, psychiatry, questioned documents, ballistics, tool work comparison, and serology. To simplify the information in this chapter for the nonscience student, however, the word *criminalistics* will be used interchangeably with *forensic science*. (See Table 14.1.)

Criminalistics has been defined as "the examination, evaluation, and explanation of physical evidence

© Dale a Stork/www.Shutterstock.com

TABLE 14.1	Forensic Specialties
Forensic pathology	Dead bodies
Forensic physical anthropology	Skeletal remains
Forensic odontology	Teeth formation
Forensic toxicology	Poisons
Forensic entomology	Insects at death scenes

An officer performs a ballistic test on a pistol retrieved from a crime scene.

Philippe Psaila/Photo Researchers, Inc.

related to crime." (Caplan and Anderson 2) Criminalistic evidence includes fingerprints, blood and blood stains, semen stains, drugs and alcohol, hairs and fibers, and firearms and tool marks. Forensic technicians, forensic scientists, and forensic chemists—or the more generic term, criminalists—generally specialize in one or more of the following areas: analysis of trace evidence, serology, drug chemistry, firearms and tool marks, and questioned documents. (See Tables 14.2 and 14.3.)

The purpose of criminalistics is to take physical evidence from a crime or a crime scene and to use it to (1) identify the person who committed the crime and (2) exonerate others who may be under suspicion. For example, was the revolver found on the suspect the one that had fired the bullet found in the body of the murder victim? If so, did the suspect fire it? Criminalistic evidence also can be used to establish an element of the crime and reconstruct how the crime was committed.

TABLE 14.3	Police Forensic Laboratories
Major Section	**Function**
Ballistics	Examination of guns and bullets
Serology	Examination of blood, semen, and other body fluids
Criminalistics	Examination of hairs, fibers, paints, clothing, glass, and other trace evidence
Chemistry	Examination of drugs and alcohol
Document analysis	Comparison of handwriting

In court, criminalistic evidence is presented via laboratory analysis by an expert prepared to interpret and testify to the scientific results, thus distinguishing forensic evidence from other forms of physical or tangible evidence such as stolen goods, articles of clothing, and other personal property.

In a study of criminalistic evidence and the criminal justice system, the National Institute of Justice discovered that the police are, on average, about three times more likely to clear (solve) cases when scientific evidence is gathered and analyzed, that prosecutors are less likely to agree to enter into plea negotiations if criminalistic evidence strongly associates the defendant with the crime, and that judges issue more severe sentences when criminalistic evidence is presented at trials. (Peterson)

TABLE 14.2	Services Provided by the FBI Laboratory
Forensic Analysis
Racketeering
Latent Print
Questioned Documents
Operational Response
Chemical Biological Sciences
Explosives
Evidence Response Team
Hazardous Material Response
Photographic and Imaging
Tedac (Terrorist Explosive Device Analytical Center)
Scientific Analysis
CODIS
Chemistry
DNA-Nuclear
DNA-Mitochondrial
Trace Evidence
Firearms/Tool Marks
Forensic Science
Counterterrorism and Forensic Science Research
Forensic Science Support
Forensic Facial Imaging
Evidence Control
Training
Classes

SOURCE: Adapted from FBI. *FBI Laboratory Services.* 11 March 2011, www.fbi.gov.

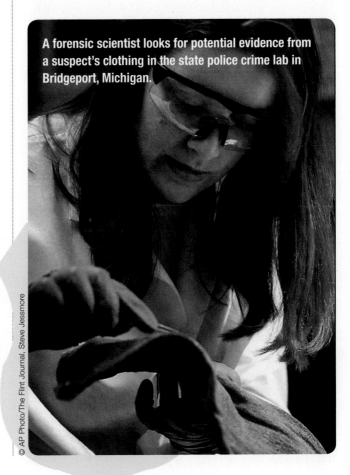

A forensic scientist looks for potential evidence from a suspect's clothing in the state police crime lab in Bridgeport, Michigan.

© AP Photo/The Flint Journal, Steve Jessmore

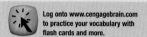
The Modern Crime Lab

Of the hundreds of public and private crime laboratories in the United States today, nearly 400 are publicly funded labs, including state or regional labs and county, municipal, and federal labs. The latest available statistics indicate that these public labs employ more than 11,900 full-time personnel, have total budgets exceeding $821 million, and receive nearly 2.7 million new cases each year. Most very large police departments operate their own police laboratories. Smaller departments may contract with large county crime labs or state police crime labs. Some departments use the services of the FBI lab. (Durose 1)

Private (nongovernment) labs are taking on greater importance in the U.S. legal system. Their analyses are increasingly being introduced into criminal and civil trials, often not only as evidence but also to contradict evidence presented by a prosecutor that was analyzed in a police lab.

LO4 Discuss DNA Profiling (Genetic Fingerprinting)

DNA profiling, also called **genetic fingerprinting** or **DNA typing**, has shown exponential progress in the last decade in helping investigators solve crimes and ensure that those guilty of crimes are convicted in court. According to the U.S. Department of Justice, "DNA evidence arguably has become the most well-known type of forensic evidence, probably because it can be uniquely identifying and because it is the genetic blueprint of the human body. For these reasons, DNA evidence has become a highly influential piece of the crime puzzle." (National Criminal Justice Reference Center)

The Science of DNA

Deoxyribonucleic acid (DNA) is the basic building code for all of the human body's chromosomes and is the same in each cell of an individual's body, including skin, bone, teeth, hair, organ, fingernail and toenail cells, and in all body fluids, including blood, semen, saliva, mucus, perspiration, urine, and feces. Every cell of the body contains DNA. Because the characteristics of certain segments of DNA vary from person to person, it is possible to analyze certain bodily substances and compare them with a sample from a suspect.

Forensic science consultant Richard Saferstein tells us that portions of the DNA structure are as unique to each individual as fingerprints. He writes that inside each of the 60 trillion cells in the human body are strands of genetic material called chromosomes. Arranged along the chromosomes, like beads on a thread, are nearly 100,000 genes. Genes, the fundamental units of heredity, instruct the body's cells to make proteins that determine everything from hair color to susceptibility to diseases. Each gene is actually composed of DNA specifically designed to carry out a single body function. Scientists have determined that DNA is the substance by which genetic instructions are passed from one generation to the next. (Saferstein 353–394)

DNA profiling has helped investigators solve crimes and ensure that those guilty of crimes are convicted in court. Profiling is the examination of DNA samples from a body substance or fluid to determine whether they came from a particular subject. For example, semen on a rape victim's clothing can be positively or negatively compared with a suspect's semen.

DNA technology in law enforcement has changed rapidly. The current procedure—**polymerase chain reaction-short tandem repeat (PCR-STR)**—has several distinct advantages for law enforcement over **restricted fragment length polymorphism (RFLP)**, an earlier DNA procedure. PCR-STR requires only pinhead-size samples,

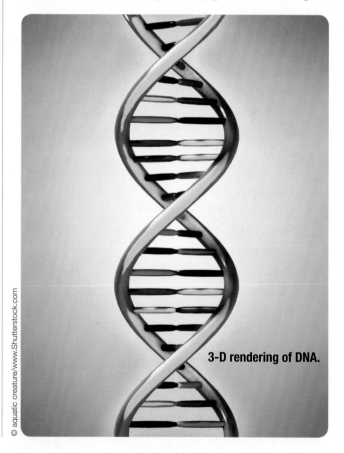

3-D rendering of DNA.

© aquatic creature/www.Shutterstock.com

rather than the dime-size samples needed for RFLP. With the PCR-STR process, samples degraded or broken down by exposure to heat, light, or humidity can still be analyzed.

The DNA Analysis Unit of the FBI laboratory analyzes body fluids and body fluid stains recovered as evidence in violent crimes. Examinations include the identification and characterization of blood, semen, saliva, and other body fluids using traditional serological techniques and related biochemical analysis. Once the stain is identified, it is characterized by DNA analysis using RFLP or PCR-STR techniques. The results of the analysis are compared with results obtained from known blood or saliva samples submitted from the victims or suspects. (FBI, *CODIS-NDIS Statistics*) At the same time that technological advances have made DNA more reliable and more efficient, the amount of time needed to determine a sample's DNA profile has dropped from between six and eight weeks to between one and two days.

The unit also uses **mitochondrial DNA (MtDNA) analysis**, which is applied to evidence containing very small or degraded quantities of DNA from hair, bones, teeth, and body fluids. The results of MtDNA analysis are then also compared with blood or saliva submitted from victims and suspects. Mitochondrial DNA isn't as useful for identification as nuclear DNA, but it doesn't break down as quickly—and that makes it vitally important in solving cold cases.

Another current DNA innovation is the **Combined DNA Index System (CODIS)**, or DNA databases. CODIS contains DNA profiles obtained from subjects convicted of homicide, sexual assault, and other serious felonies. Investigators are thus able to compare search evidence from their individual cases to the system's extensive national file of DNA genetic markers. By 2008, over 170 public law enforcement laboratories across the United States were participating in CODIS and the National DNA Index System (NDIS). Internationally, more than 40 law enforcement laboratories in over 25 countries use the CODIS software for their own database initiatives. (FBI, *NDIS Statistics*)

CODIS provides software and support services so that state and local laboratories can establish their own databases of convicted offenders, unsolved crimes, and missing persons. This software allows these forensic laboratories to exchange and compare DNA profiles electronically—thereby linking serial violent crimes, especially sexual assaults, to each other—and to identify

suspects by matching DNA from crime scenes to convicted offenders.

All 50 states have enacted DNA database laws requiring the collection of a DNA sample from specified categories of convicted offenders. Most currently take samples from convicted felons, but states vary on which types of felons. Some states are trying to pass legislation that will allow them to take samples from all persons charged with a felony; some are even considering collecting samples from people convicted of misdemeanors. Most federal, state, and local DNA analysts have received CODIS training. The **National DNA Index System (NDIS)**, the final level of CODIS, supports the sharing of DNA profiles from convicted offenders and crime scene evidence submitted by state and local forensic laboratories across the United States.

The current version of CODIS contains two indexes: a convicted offender index and a forensic index. The former index contains DNA profiles of those convicted of violent crimes, and the latter contains DNA profiles acquired from crime scene evidence. The CODIS is also separated into different segments, from the local to the national level. The system stores the information necessary to determine a match (a specimen identifier, the sponsoring laboratory's identifier, the names of the laboratory personnel who produced the profile, and the DNA profile). To ensure privacy, the system does not include such things as Social Security numbers, criminal history, or case-related information.

The FBI maintains the national database, whereas each state has its own designated database location and each participating locality maintains its own local database. Thus, it is possible for each locality to cross-reference a DNA profile against other DNA profiles around the country. Furthermore, it is likely that an international DNA database will be implemented, allowing law enforcement officials

DNA separation.

© Nicemonkey/www.Shutterstock.com

to identify suspects both nationally and internationally. As of 2011, NDIS had about 9.3 million offender profiles and about 356,000 forensic profiles from the scenes of unsolved crimes. In addition, as of 2011, CODIS had produced over 136,400 hits assisting in more than 131,300 investigations. (FBI, *CODIS-NDIS Statistics*)

DNA Databases

Initially, DNA fingerprinting or profiling was used to confirm the identity of an individual already suspected of having committed a specific crime; now, though, the use of offender DNA databases has altered the way a criminal investigation can proceed, and very small amounts of DNA recovered from a crime scene can be used to link an otherwise unknown suspect to the crime. The existing offender DNA databases have been upheld over Fourth Amendment challenges because of the minimal privacy expectations offenders have due to their status as offenders.

By 2006, every state had a DNA database statute that allows collection of DNA from specified offenders. All 50 states require DNA from sex offenders and murderers, and 46 states require DNA from all people who have committed violent crimes (including assault and battery and robbery). Over the past several years, a growing number of states have been expanding their databases to include people convicted of nonviolent felonies—45 states require DNA from people convicted of burglaries, 36 states require DNA from people convicted of certain drug felonies, and 31 states require DNA from all people convicted of a felony. (Cardwell)

Some believe that the growing practice of using voluntary DNA samples to link the donor to other unsolved crimes should be curbed. However, police and prosecutors defend the strategy, maintaining that it allows them to take full advantage of the technology to solve crimes. Darrell Sanders, chief of police in Frankfort, Illinois, says, "If we get someone's DNA legally, how can we justify giving him a free pass on something else he once did?" Defense attorneys such as Barry Scheck foresee the potential for abuse: "As it is, there's nothing to stop police from setting up a DNA base of 'the usual subjects.'" ("The Truth" p. 7)

Another issue is the implementation of a universal DNA database containing DNA fingerprints from every member of society. Some believe this would not withstand constitutional scrutiny because free persons have no diminished expectations of privacy as prisoners do. In addition, some feel that establishing a universal DNA

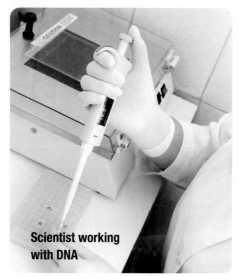

Scientist working with DNA

© Niderlander/www.Shutterstock.com

database would allow the government to intrude without suspicion on an individual's privacy.

A 2003 report by the Executive Office of the President of the United States praised DNA technology for becoming increasingly vital to identifying criminals, clearing suspects, and identifying missing persons. However, the report acknowledged that current federal and state DNA collection and analysis need improvement because crime labs are overwhelmed and ill-equipped to deal with the influx of DNA samples and evidence. The president proposed federal funding for the improvement of the use of DNA in these labs. Subsequently, Congress passed a five-year, $1 billion bill, the Justice for All Act of 2004. (Executive Office of the President)

Other Current DNA Issues

Backlog A major problem with DNA today is the growing backlog of DNA cases. In a 2006 article in the *Criminal Justice Policy Review*, Travis C. Pratt, Michael J. Gaffney, and Nicholas P. Lovrich, professors at Washington State University, and doctoral student Charles L. Johnson, also of Washington State University, revealed that as of 2003, there were 169,229 unsolved rape cases and 51,774 homicide cases that might contain biological evidence that had not yet been sent to a forensic laboratory for DNA testing. This meant that the evidence was just sitting around in police property rooms. State and local laboratories reported 57,349 backlogged cases of rape and homicide on hand waiting for DNA analysis. Thus, the combined estimate of rape and murder cases that still required DNA review was 278,352 throughout the nation. (Pratt, Gaffney, Lovrich, and Johnson 32–47)

The study estimated that as many as 264,371 property crime cases with possible biological evidence had also not yet been subjected to DNA analysis. This meant that there was a total backlog of 542,723 cases with the possibility of DNA evidence. The authors suggested that one reason so many unsolved cases had yet to be subjected to DNA analysis was police investigators' belief that forensic laboratories could not process such evidence quickly enough for it to be helpful. Pratt and colleagues also suggested that local and regional forensic laboratories could not afford the personnel, equipment, and facilities necessary to increase their volume of DNA analysis.

As of 2009, the U.S. Justice Department estimated a backlog of 600,000 to 700,000 DNA samples that remained untested. (Solomon Moore)

Contamination Another problem with DNA is the possibility of fingerprinting techniques contaminating DNA results. Testing reported in 2005 revealed the possibility that fingerprint brushes can accumulate DNA from surfaces with which they come into contact, and that they can redeposit this DNA-containing material onto a number of subsequently brushed objects. The chance of contamination occurring increases after powdering biological samples, such as blood, saliva, skin, or fresh prints. (van Oorschot, Treadwell, et al. 1417–1422)

Cold Hits A cold hit is a DNA sample collected from a crime scene that ties an unknown suspect to the DNA profile of someone in the national or a state's database.

A cold hit is not enough to close a case, however; an investigator from the jurisdiction where the original crime was committed has to reopen the case, then locate and apprehend the subject. Often, the subject is in prison, and the investigator has to go there to process him or her. The investigator also has to confirm the DNA sample and retest the subject to ensure accuracy.

DNA Warrants In 1999, the Milwaukee, Wisconsin, county prosecutor made an innovative legal move regarding DNA in an effort to prevent the statute of limitations from expiring in a case against an unknown person suspected in a series of kidnappings and rapes. The prosecutor filed a "John Doe" warrant, not an uncommon procedure in cases where a suspect's identity is unknown. What made this case different, though, was the means the prosecutor used to identify the suspect: The warrant identified the assailant as "John Doe, unknown male with matching deoxyribonucleic acid (DNA) at five locations." Since then, DNA warrants have been used a great deal. (Burke and Rexrode 121–124)

DNA Dragnets DNA dragnets are police requests of persons in an area to give voluntary DNA samples so that the police can compare these people's DNA with evidence found at the scene of a crime. DNA dragnets give police and grand juries limited authority to test the DNA of small groups of people based on a "reasonable suspicion"

© Neo Edmund/www.Shutterstock.com

standard of probability that each member of the group might be involved in a crime.

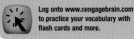
Familial DNA Searches Familial DNA analysis of the daughter of Dennis Rader, the BTK killer, was instrumental in his 2005 arrest for at least 10 homicides. (Shapiro) Familial DNA searches are common in Great Britain, and some researchers believe that close relatives of criminals are more likely than others to break the law. This technique has proven successful in several cases. (Weiss, "DNA of Criminals' Kin" p. A10) In one case, police retrieved DNA from a brick that was thrown from an overpass and smashed through a vehicle's windshield, killing the driver. A near-match of that DNA with someone in Britain's DNA database led police to investigate that offender's relatives, one of whom confessed to the crime when confronted with the evidence. However, Troy Duster, a sociologist at New York University, says familial searches would exacerbate already serious racial inequities in the U.S. criminal justice system because incarceration rates are eight times higher for blacks than they are for whites. Thus any technique that focuses on relatives of people in the databases will just expand that inequity. (Weiss, "Vast DNA Bank" p. A10)

Exonerations There have been numerous cases of persons who had been convicted of serious felonies and were later exonerated by DNA evidence. In 2003, Janet Reno, former U.S. attorney general, in a speech to the National Conference on Preventing the Conviction of Innocent Persons, stated that over the past 30 years, more than 100 people had been exonerated because of DNA or other tests. (Reno 163–165)

In the early 1990s, Scheck and Neufeld founded the first "Innocence Project," in conjunction with Cardozo Law School in New York. (Connors, Lundregan, Miller, and McEwen) The project began reviewing cases and assisting inmates from across the country who claimed they were innocent. By 2005, it was reported that the project had contributed to the exoneration of 162 persons who had been wrongly convicted and sentenced to death or long prison terms.

 Log onto www.cengagebrain.com for additional resources including videos, flash cards, games, self-quizzing, review exercises, web exercises, learning checks, and more.

15
Homeland Security

LO1 Define Homeland Security

The term **homeland security** has been used after the September 11 terrorism acts to describe defensive efforts within the borders of the United States. Officials use it to separate the U.S. Department of Homeland Security's (DHS) operations from those of the U.S. Department of Defense. (White 354) Following 9/11, the U.S. government prepared and published the *National Strategy for Homeland Security* to mobilize and organize the United States to secure its homeland from terrorist attacks.

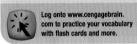

homeland security
Efforts made since the terrorist acts of September 11, 2001, to protect the United States against terrorist acts.

Log onto www.cengagebrain.com to practice your vocabulary with flash cards and more.

After studying this chapter, the student should be able to:

LO1 Define homeland security

LO2 Define terrorism

LO3 Discuss the post-9/11 response to terrorism and homeland defense

LO4 Discuss federal law enforcement efforts for homeland security

LO5 Discuss state and local law enforcement efforts for homeland security

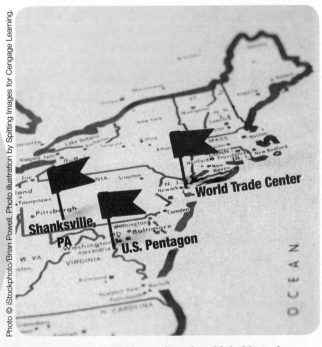

Photo © iStockphoto/Brian Powell. Photo illustration by Spitting Images for Cengage Learning.

On September 11, 2001, a series of unthinkable and incomprehensible events led to ultimate disasters in New York City, a grassy field near Shanksville, Pennsylvania, and the United States Pentagon in Northern Virginia.

The events of September 11, 2001, were an unprecedented challenge to the police officers who responded.

© Fabrik Studios/Photo Library

The objectives of the strategy are to prevent terrorist attacks against the United States, to reduce America's vulnerability to terrorism, and to minimize the damage and recover from attacks that do occur. The strategy provides direction to the federal government's departments and agencies that have a role in homeland security and suggests steps that state and local governments, private companies and organizations, and individual Americans can take to improve our security. (Office of the President)

Jonathan R. White, professor of interdisciplinary studies in the Brooks College at Grand Valley State University in Grand Rapids, Michigan, and a senior research associate for the Institute for Intergovernmental Research in Tallahassee, Florida, explains that *homeland security* simply means keeping the country safe. It protects lives, property, and infrastructure and is designed to secure the United States. (White 269)

LO2 Define Terrorism

Terrorism has many definitions. The Federal Bureau of Investigation (FBI) defines terrorism as "the unlawful use of force or violence against persons or property to intimidate or coerce a government, the civilian population, or a segment thereof, in furtherance of political or social objectives." The U.S. Defense Department defines it as "the unlawful use or threatened use of force or violence against individuals or property to coerce or intimidate governments or societies, often to achieve political, religious, or ideological objectives." Jonathan R. White sums up terrorism simply: "Terrorism uses violence or threatened violence against innocent people to achieve a social or political goal." (White 6–7) The National Counterterrorism Center defines terrorism as "premeditated, politically motivated violence perpetrated against noncombatant targets by subnational groups or clandestine agents." (National Counterterrorism Center)

The National Counterterrorism Center (NCTC) was created in 2004, under the Intelligence Reform and Terrorism Prevention Act (IRTPA), to serve as the primary organization in the U.S. government to integrate and analyze all intelligence pertaining to terrorism and counterterrorism and to conduct strategic operational planning by integrating all instruments of national power. The NCTC has the statutory mission to serve as the U.S. government's knowledge bank on international terrorism and to provide the Department of State with required statistical information. It is under the administrative control of the Office of the Director of National Intelligence (DNI). (National Counterterrorism Center)

In 2010, the NCTC reported that there were about 11,800 terrorist acts worldwide in 2008 that resulted in the deaths, injuries, and kidnappings of more than 54,000 noncombatants. Most fatalities were the result of conventional fighting methods, which included the use of bombs and small arms.

International Terrorism

According to John F. Lewis, Jr., retired assistant director of the FBI's National Security Division, the FBI divides the current international threat to the United States into three categories. (Lewis 3–10)

Terrorists use violence against innocent people to achieve a social or political goal.

© Ramzi Hachicho/www.Shutterstock.com

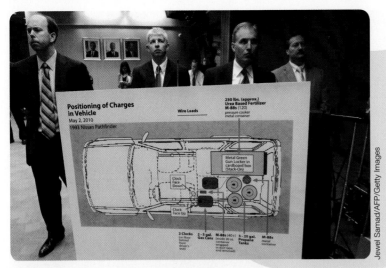

A diagram of the car bomb from the May 2010 Times Square, New York, car bombing attempt.

First, there are threats from foreign sponsors of international terrorism. These sponsors view terrorism as a tool of foreign policy. Their activities have changed over time. Past activities included direct terrorist support and operations by official state agents. Now these sponsors generally seek to conceal their support of terrorism by relying on surrogates to conduct operations. State sponsors remain involved in terrorist activities by funding, organizing, networking, and providing other support and instruction to formal terrorist groups and loosely affiliated extremists.

Second, according to Lewis, there are threats from formalized terrorist groups such as al-Qaeda, the Lebanese Hezbollah, the Egyptian al-Gama'a al-Islamiyya, and the Palestinian Hamas. These autonomous organizations have their own infrastructures, personnel, financial arrangements, and training facilities. They can plan and mount terrorist campaigns overseas as well as support terrorist operations inside the United States. Some groups use supporters in the United States to plan and coordinate acts of terrorism. In the past, these formalized terrorist groups engaged in such criminal activities in the United States as illegally acquiring weapons, violating U.S. immigration laws, and providing safe havens to fugitives.

Third, there are threats from loosely affiliated international radical extremists, such as those who attacked the World Trade Center in 1993. These extremists do not represent a particular nation. Loosely affiliated extremists may pose the most urgent threat to the United States at this time because they remain relatively unknown to law enforcement. They can thus travel freely, obtain a variety of identities, and

recruit like-minded sympathizers from various countries.

In 2005, the DHS reported that the threat of countries facilitating or supporting terrorism had diminished. It said that ideologically driven actors, particularly al-Qaeda, are the top terrorist threat against the United States today. The DHS also named several visual symbols such as the White House and the Statue of Liberty as the most likely targets of terrorism, and truck bombs and small explosives-laden boats as the most likely terrorism weapons. (Lipton A5)

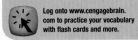
Domestic Terrorism

According to Lewis, **domestic terrorism** involves groups or individuals who operate without foreign direction, entirely within the United States, and target elements of the U.S. government or citizens. He states that the 1995 federal building explosion in Oklahoma City and the pipe bomb explosion in Centennial Olympic Park during the 1996 Summer Olympic Games underscore the ever-present threat that exists from individuals determined to use violence to advance their agendas. (Lewis 3)

Lewis reports that domestic terrorist groups today represent extreme right-wing, extreme left-wing, and special interest beliefs. The main themes espoused today by extremist right-wing groups are conspiracies having to do with the New World Order, gun control laws, and white supremacy. Many of these extremist groups also advocate antigovernment, antitaxation, or antiabortion sentiments and engage in survivalist training, their goal being to ensure the perpetuation of the United States as a white, Christian nation.

A bomb squad police officer searches a suspicious package in New York in July 2007.

In November 2009, a self-radicalized U.S. Army psychiatrist, Major Nidal Malik Hasan, facing deployment to one of America's war zones, killed 13 people and wounded 30 others in a shooting rampage with two handguns at the Fort Hood Army post in central Texas. Fort Hood is about 100 miles south of Dallas–Fort Worth and is the largest active-duty military post in the United States. (McFadden)

One particularly troubling element of right-wing extremism is the militia, or patriot, movement. Militia members want to remove federal involvement from various issues. They generally are law-abiding citizens who have become intolerant of what they perceive as violations of their constitutional rights. Membership in a militia organization is not entirely illegal in the United States, but certain states have legislated limits on militias, including on the types of training (for example, paramilitary training) that they can offer. The FBI bases its interest in the militia movement on the risk of violence or the potential for violence and criminal activity.

During the 1970s, leftist-oriented extremist groups posed the predominant domestic terrorist threat in the United States. Beginning in the 1980s, however, the FBI dismantled many of these groups by arresting key members for their criminal activities. The transformation of the former Soviet Union also deprived many leftist groups of a coherent ideology or spiritual patron. As a result, membership and support for these groups has declined.

Special interest terrorist groups are also domestic threats. They differ from both extreme left-wing and right-wing terrorist groups because their members seek to resolve specific interests rather than pursue widespread political change. Members of such groups include animal rights advocates, supporters of environmental issues, and antiabortion advocates. Although some consider the causes that these groups represent understandable or even worthy, these groups nevertheless remain separated from traditional law-abiding special interest groups because of their criminal activity. Groups such as the Animal Liberation Front (ALF) and the Earth Liberation Front (ELF) have used violent actions to attempt to force various segments of society, including the general public, to change their attitudes about issues they consider important.

These groups have released caged animals into the wild, targeted buildings where experimentation on animals has been conducted, damaged vehicles they feel are not environmentally friendly, and burned down new residential communities. In 1998, ELF

Detectives from the Fort Hood Directorate of Emergency Services respond to a November 2009 shooting rampage by self-radicalized U.S. Army psychiatrist, Major Nidal Malik Hasan.

members were linked to the destruction of the Vail Ski Resort in Colorado, a fire that caused $12 million in damage. ELF members were also charged with firebombing the University of Washington's Center for Urban Horticulture in 2001. In August 2003, several car dealerships in Southern California were targeted by ELF members who burned dozens of SUVs and an auto dealership warehouse and spray-painted vehicles with sayings such as "Fat, Lazy Americans." ELF has claimed responsibility for many arsons against commercial establishments that, the group says, damage the environment. (Associated Press, "1 Million" p. A4)

Radical, extremist, and hate groups have long presented a serious problem to U.S. society. Throughout a

It has been estimated that there are about 750 virulent hate groups in the United States, a number that is rising.

major part of our history, the Ku Klux Klan terrorized and killed thousands of citizens. In the 1960s and 1970s, radical hate groups such as the Black Panthers and the Black Liberation Army waged urban warfare against the police, maiming and killing scores of police officers. Also during that period of our history, militant student and antiwar groups caused tremendous problems for the police. Historically in our nation, radical groups have been involved in assassinations, bombings, terrorism, and other crimes and acts of violence to protest the policies of the United States and to attempt to impose their views on all members of our society.

Mark Potok of the Southern Poverty Law Center (SPLC), which tracks domestic hate and extremist groups, said there are currently about 926 virulent hate groups in the United States, and the number is rising. However, he also said that right-wing extremist activity has ebbed since its high-water mark in the 1990s, and there has been an erosion of these groups at the organizational level since the 2002 death of William Pierce, the founder and leader of the neo-Nazi National Alliance, and the incarceration of Matt Hale of the World Church of the Creator. (Potok 12–14) By 2006, the SPLC had tracked more than 844 cases of hate crimes that involved such hate groups as the Ku Klux Klan, neo-Nazi, Black Separatist, neo-Confederate, Racist Skinhead, and Christian Identity. (Phillips 64–71)

Furor over the illegal immigration issue in the United States has renewed attention on hate groups. "They think they've found an issue with racial overtones and a real resonance with the American public and they are exploiting it as effectively as they can." (Potok 36)

Anarchists also keep operating in the United States as they protest global and trade issues. Some of their members advocate violence and destruction of property and travel to trade meetings with the goal of disrupting the meetings and causing chaos and destruction in the streets.

Recently, attention has focused on homegrown terrorists who mirror violent Islamic extremism. In 2007, Willie T. Hulon, the executive assistant director of the National Security Branch of the FBI, after acknowledging that for the past decade, al-Qaeda has been the driving force of terrorism, wrote that he has increasingly seen the emergence of individuals and groups inspired by al-Qaeda that carry out attacks on their own soil:

> Homegrown terrorists or extremists, acting in concert with other like-minded individuals or as lone wolves, have become one of the gravest domestic threats we face. Largely self-recruited and self-trained, these terrorists may have no direct connection to al Qaeda or other terrorist groups. (Hulon 1)

LO3 Discuss the Post-9/11 Response to Terrorism and Homeland Defense

In the immediate aftermath of the 9/11 terrorist attacks, strict security procedures were instituted at airports, government buildings, cultural centers, and many other facilities.

The 9/11 terrorist acts were attributed to the multi-national terrorist group al-Qaeda (the Base) operated by Osama bin Laden, a known terrorist sheltered by the ruling Taliban government. On May 1, 2011, after spending almost 10 years as the world's most wanted terrorist, bin Laden was located and killed by U.S. Navy Seal commandos at his compound in Abbottabad, Pakistan.

Much has been written about the failure of U.S. law enforcement, particularly federal law enforcement, to deal with terrorism. Some report that the failure to follow up leads and analyze information have made the efforts of terrorists to commit terrorist attacks against America easier. Others reported that a major flaw of counterterrorism measures has been a lack of interagency cooperation and data sharing.

To address these concerns, on October 8, 2001, President Bush signed Executive Order 13228, which established the Office of Homeland Security. The office's mission was to develop and coordinate the implementation of a comprehensive national strategy to secure the United

Source: http://www.fbi.gov/wanted/topten/usama-bin-laden

Deceased

Former al-Qaeda leader Osama bin Laden was located and killed by U.S. Navy Seal commandos on May 1, 2011.

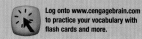

Log onto www.cengagebrain.com to practice your vocabulary with flash cards and more.

States from threats and attacks. To do so, the office coordinated the executive branch's efforts to detect, prepare for, prevent, and respond to terrorist attacks within this country.

On October 26, 2001, President Bush signed into law the **USA Patriot Act** (Uniting and Strengthening America by Providing Appropriate Tools Required to Intercept and Obstruct Terrorism) (Public Law No. 107-56), which gave law enforcement personnel new abilities to search, seize, detain, and eavesdrop in their pursuit of possible terrorists. The law expanded the FBI's wiretapping and electronic surveillance authority and allows nationwide jurisdiction for search warrants and electronic surveillance devices, including legal expansion of those devices to e-mail and the Internet. The Patriot Act also includes money-laundering provisions and set strong penalties for anyone harboring or financing terrorists. It established new punishments for possession of biological weapons and made it a federal crime to commit an act of terrorism against a mass transit system. The bill also allows law enforcement agents to detain terrorism suspects for up to seven days without filing charges against them.

In November 2001, the president signed into law the Aviation and Transportation Security Act, which established the Transportation Security Administration (TSA) within the Department of Transportation to protect the nation's transportation systems and ensure freedom of movement for people and commerce. This new agency assumed the duties formerly provided by the Federal Aviation Administration (FAA). The TSA recruited thousands of security personnel to perform screening duties at commercial airports and significantly expanded the federal air marshals program.

Later, in June 2002, the president proposed creating a new cabinet-level agency, the U.S. Department of Homeland Security (DHS), to replace the Office of Homeland Security. With the new cabinet agency, duties formerly belonging to other government agencies were merged, including border and transportation security; emergency preparedness and response; chemical, biological, radiological, and nuclear countermeasures; and information analysis and infrastructure protection. The new DHS went into effect in 2003.

In 2002, in response to public demand, the president and Congress appointed a blue-ribbon national commission to investigate the attacks. It was called the National Commission on Terrorist Attacks upon the United States,

popularly known as the 9/11 Commission. Its charge was to investigate how the nation had been unprepared for these terrorist attacks, how they had happened, and how the nation could avoid a repeat tragedy. Its final report, the *9/11 Commission Report: The Final Report of the National Commission on Terrorist Attacks Upon the United States*, was released in 2004.

LO4 Discuss Federal Law Enforcement Efforts for Homeland Security

The major federal law enforcement efforts for homeland security involve the Department of Homeland Security, the FBI, the Office of the Director of National Intelligence (ODNI), and some other federal agencies.

Department of Homeland Security (DHS)

After much debate, study, and planning in the aftermath of 9/11, the cabinet-level U.S. Department of Homeland Security was established in March 2003. (See Table 15.1.)

TABLE 15.1 U.S. Department of Homeland Security (DHS) Components and Agencies
Directorate for National Protection and Programs
Directorate for Science and Technology
Directorate for Management
Office of Policy
Office of Health Affairs
Office of Intelligence and Analysis
Office of Operations Coordination
Federal Law Enforcement Training Center
Domestic Nuclear Detection Office
Transportation Security Administration (TSA)
United States Customs and Border Protection (CBP)
United States Citizenship and Immigration Services
United States Immigration and Customs Enforcement (ICE)
United States Coast Guard
Federal Emergency Management Administration (FEMA)
United States Secret Service

SOURCE: U.S. Department of Homeland Security. 11 March 2011, www.dhs.gov.

The new agency merged 22 previously disparate domestic agencies into one department to protect the nation against threats to the homeland. The DHS incorporates the former duties of many agencies, including those of the Coast Guard, the U.S. Customs Service, the Secret Service, the Immigration and Naturalization Service, and the Transportation Security Administration, along with numerous other federal communications, science, and technology agencies. Although the DHS does not include the FBI, CIA, or National Security Agency, these agencies are required to share their data with the department's intelligence center. In 2011, it was estimated that the DHS had 230,000 employees and spent over $38 billion a year. (Department of Homeland Security, *Fact Sheet: Select*)

The Transportation Security Administration (TSA) protects the nation's transportation systems and ensures freedom of movement for people and commerce.

The department's first priority is to protect the nation from further terrorist attacks. The department's agencies thus analyze threats and intelligence, guard our borders and airports, protect our critical infrastructure, and coordinate the responses of our nation for future emergencies.

To understand the importance of the DHS to our homeland security, consider that 730 million people travel on commercial aircraft each year; more than 700 million pieces of baggage are screened for explosives; 11.2 million trucks and 2.2 million railcars cross into the United States; and 7,500 foreign flagships make 51,000 calls in U.S. ports annually. (Department of Homeland Security, *Fact Sheet: Border Security*)

The TSA is on the frontlines of the nation's efforts to secure air transportation from terrorism. Since 2002, federal rules have required the TSA to conduct security inspections of all air passengers and air travel. By 2011, the TSA had about 50,000 security officers, directors, inspectors, and air marshals. The TSA's air marshals are deployed on flights around the world. The number of marshals is classified, and they blend in with passengers and rely on their training, including investigative techniques, criminal terrorist behavior recognition, firearms proficiency, aircraft-specific tactics, and close-quarter self-defense measures to protect the flying public. Air marshals work in plainclothes, in teams of two or sometimes more. They board airplanes before passengers, survey the cabin, and watch passengers as they walk to their seats. (Transportation Security Administration)

U.S. Customs and Border Protection (CBP) is responsible for securing our borders while facilitating the flow of legitimate trade and travel. It protects 5,000 miles of border with Canada, 1,900 miles of border with Mexico, and 95,000 miles of shoreline. As of 2011, it employed about 57,519 employees, including the following enforcement personnel: 12,058 officers, 20,119 border patrol agents, 2.394 agriculture specialists, and 1,212 air and marine officers and pilots. The number of border patrol agents has doubled since 2001. (U.S. Customs and Border Protection)

In 2011, the DHS reported that every day in 2010 at U.S. ports of entry, CBP officers inspected more than 1 million travelers, including 271,000 vehicles; processed more than 58,000 truck, rail, and sea containers; seized more than 6,600 kilos of illegal narcotics; and intercepted more than 4,291 agricultural items and pests. (Department of Homeland Security, *Fact Sheet: Border Security*)

U.S. Immigration and Customs Enforcement (ICE) is responsible for enforcing the federal immigration laws, customs laws, and air security laws. It targets illegal immigrants; the people, money, and materials that support terrorism; and other criminal activities. As of 2011, ICE had about 19,000 employees in 400 offices in the United States and around the world. (U.S. Immigration and Customs Enforcement)

On the frontlines of our efforts in maritime security is the U.S. Coast Guard (USCG). The Coast Guard is a military branch of the United States Armed Forces and is involved in maritime law, mariner assistance, and search and rescue. The USCG patrols in any maritime region in which U.S. interests may be at risk, including international waters and America's coasts, ports, and inland waterways. It became part of the DHS in 2003. (United States Coast Guard)

The United States Coast Guard is on the front lines of our efforts in maritime security.

U.S. Navy photo by Chief Petty Officer Bill Mesta

Federal Bureau of Investigation (FBI)

counterterrorism
Enforcement efforts made against terrorist organizations.

Joint Terrorism Task Forces (JTTF)
Forces that make use of single-focused investigative units that meld personnel and talent from various law enforcement agencies.

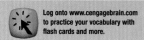
Log onto www.cengagebrain.com to practice your vocabulary with flash cards and more.

The Federal Bureau of Investigation (FBI) h traditionally been the lead federal agency in the response to and investigation of terrorism. In May 2002, in the wake of massive criticism that the FBI ha failed to properly handle information that could have led to the prevention of the September 11 attacks, FBI Director Robert S. Mueller completely reorganized the Bureau and created a new strategic focus for the agency that places the following as its three priorities: (1) protecting the United States from terrorist attack, (2) protecting the United States against foreign intelligence operations and espionage, and (3) protecting the United States against cyber-based attacks and high-technology crimes. The main organizational improvements Mueller implemented in the complete restructuring of the **counterterrorism** activities of the Bureau and the shift from a reactive to a proactive orientation were the development of special squads to coordinate national and international investigations; a reemphasis on the **Joint Terrorism Task Forces (JTTF)**; enhanced analytical capabilities along with personnel and technological improvements; a permanent shift of additional resources to counterterrorism; the creation of a more mobile, agile, and flexible national terrorism response; and targeted recruitment to acquire agents, analysts, translators, and others with specialized skills and backgrounds. (Federal Bureau of Investigation, 2002) In

2005, the FBI created its National Security Branch (NSB), which combines the missions, capabilities, and resources of the counterterrorism, counterintelligence, and intelligence elements of the FBI. (Federal Bureau of Investigation, *National Security Branch*)

Possibly the most important unit investigating terrorism in the United States is the FBI–Joint Terrorist Task Forces (JTTF). Before the establishment of these task forces, ad hoc task forces of local and federal authorities would be established to investigate each new terrorist case as it occurred and then disbanded after the investigation. The new concept ensures that the unit remains in place and becomes a close-knit, cohesive group capable of addressing the complex problems inherent in terrorism investigations. Because federal, state, and local law enforcement resources have been combined in these task forces, there is effective maximization of resources, provision of sophisticated investigative and technological resources, and linkages to all federal

IMMIGRATION

Enormous Resposbilities for U.S. Border Protection

- The United States has 5,525 miles of border with Canada and 1,989 miles with Mexico.

- The U.S. maritime border includes 95,000 miles of shoreline and a 3.4 million mile exclusive economic zone with 350 official ports of entry.

- Each year, more than 500 million people cross the borders into the United States, some 330 million of whom are noncitizens.

- More than 730 million people travel on commercial aircraft each year, and more than 700 million pieces of baggage are screened for explosives each year.

- Approximately 11.2 million trucks and 2.2 million rail cars cross into the United States each year.

- 7,500 foreign flagships make 51,000 calls in U.S. ports annually.

DATA SOURCE: U.S. Department of Homeland Security, 18 August 2006, www.dhs.gov.

Photo © iStockphoto/jamesbowyer. Figure © 2013 Cengage Learning.

FBI Priorities Post-9/11

- Protect the United States from terrorist attack.
- Protect the United States against foreign intelligence operations and espionage.
- Protect the United States against cyber-based attacks and high-technology crimes.
- Combat public corruption at all levels.
- Protect civil rights.
- Combat transnational and national criminal organizations and enterprises.
- Combat major white-collar crime.
- Combat significant violent crime.
- Support federal, state, local, and international partners.
- Upgrade technology to successfully perform the FBI's mission.

DATA SOURCE: Federal Bureau of Investigation, 21 August 2006, www.fbi.gov.

Photos © Kenneth Summers/www.Shutterstock.com; © ZIMMYTWS/www.Shutterstock.com; Figure © 2013 Cengage Learning.

government resources in the United States and worldwide. (Martin 23–27)

The objectives of these task forces are twofold: to respond to and investigate terrorist incidents or terrorist-related criminal activity (reactive measures), and to investigate domestic and foreign terrorist groups and individuals targeting or operating in the area for the purpose of detecting, preventing, and prosecuting their criminal activity (proactive measures).

The key to the success of the JTTF is the melding of personnel and talent from various law enforcement agencies into a single, focused unit. For example, the local police members bring the insights that come from years of living and working with the people in their area. They have usually advanced through their careers from uniformed precinct patrol to various detective duties before being assigned to the task force. Each of the other participating agencies similarly contributes its own resources and areas of expertise to the team. The integration of the many agencies, each bringing its own unique skills and investigative specialties to the task force, makes these units formidable in combating terrorism.

Other Federal Agencies

In addition to the DHS, the FBI, and the U.S. military, several other federal agencies are involved with crisis activities involving terrorism. One example is the Bureau of Alcohol, Tobacco, Firearms, and Explosives (ATF), which has special responsibilities in cases of arson and explosives.

LO5 Discuss State and Local Law Enforcement Efforts for Homeland Security

Although the previous section emphasized the role of our national government in responding to and combating terrorism and in providing homeland defense, we must remember that each act of terrorism is essentially a local problem that must be addressed by local authorities.

D. Douglas Bodrero, former commissioner of public safety for the state of Utah and a senior research associate with the Institute for Intergovernmental Research, writing in 1999, stated, "Every act of terrorism occurring within the United States remains local in nature...." (Bodrero, "Confronting" pp. 11–18) Writing again in 2002, Bodrero reiterated his emphasis that terrorism is primarily a concern for local governments:

> The planning or execution of terrorist acts on U.S. soil are the concern of every law enforcement agency, regardless of size or area of responsibility. Every terrorist event, every act of planning and preparation for that event, occurs in some local law enforcement agency's jurisdiction. No agency is closer to the activities within its community than the law enforcement agency that has responsibility and jurisdiction for protecting that community. (Bodrero, "Law Enforcement's New Challenge" pp. 41–48)

In a special edition of the *FBI Law Enforcement Bulletin* in December 2007, Willie T. Hulon, executive assistant director of the National Security Branch of the FBI, wrote:

> Local police officers, who are out on the streets, are the frontline of the war on terrorism.
>
> They often may be the first to detect potential terrorists. The vast jurisdiction of state, local, and tribal officers brings invaluable access to millions of people and resources, which can help protect the nation and its citizens. The information gathered on the street and in our communities is one of the most powerful tools we have. (Hulon 1–2)

A national counterterrorism instructor speaks to security, rescue, and police personnel on how to spot a suicide bomber at a mall. Local police are on the frontline of the war on terrorism.

In 2008, former Los Angeles Police Department (LAPD) chief William Bratton stated:

> The potential threat of terrorism is much more real now than it was in the 20th century. What is necessary is to actually police terrorism. That's where local police come in. There are 700,000 of us in local cities. (Bratton, as quoted in Uranga)

Although the FBI maintains the lead federal role in the investigation and prevention of domestic terrorism, every terrorist act, as Bodrero wrote, is essentially local. Thus local law enforcement officers will be the ones who respond first to a terrorist threat or incident and are the closest to sense the discontent among terrorist movements; they are also the officers who can monitor the activity of extremist causes, respond to hate crimes, and serve as the foundation of an effective assessment of threatening activities in their own communities.

In 2002, a four-day conference was held on the effect community policing has on homeland security. Conference speakers agreed that the community should be involved in countering any chronic crime problem facing the community, including terrorism. In the keynote address, former U.S. Attorney General John Ashcroft noted that the terrorists who committed the atrocities of 9/11 had lived in local communities for many months and moved unnoticed in neighborhoods and public places. He emphasized that citizens must become active stakeholders in securing their own safety and be trained by police agencies to become alert observers of dangerous signals, which can result in citizens supplying valuable information to aid law enforcement agencies' preventive efforts. (Terault 36–37)

In the aftermath of 9/11, state and local agencies have been asked to take roles as first responders to terrorist incidents and as intelligence gatherers. To this end, federal funding has been made available to state and local law enforcement for the development and enhancement of law enforcement information systems relating to terrorism, with an emphasis on information sharing. (Hickman and Reaves, "Local Police and Homeland Security" pp. 83–88)

Subsequent to the 2005 London bombings, many have stressed the importance of the local police in the war on terrorism. Former Los Angeles chief of police William Bratton noted:

> Terrorist cells seem cut off from al-Qaeda's headquarters. Now, rather than the well-financed groups of highly trained "professional" terrorists right out of bin Laden's camps, we are dealing with a new breed of young, educated men who are living among us in the United States and Europe. They are following al-Qaeda–influenced websites or heeding the calls to action by radical Imams. Without financing or logistical support from al-Qaeda, their attack plan may be whatever plan they can cobble together with imagination and Internet research. Because of

Since 9/11, state and local police officers have been asked to play an increased role in gathering intelligence.

that, now more than ever, it is more likely that the terrorist plot is going to be uncovered by the cop on the beat than a foreign intelligence source. (Bratton, "Responding" p. 2)

Commenting on the 2007 attempted bombings in London and Glasgow and the bombings of the Madrid and London transit systems, Sheri H. Mecklenburg, assistant U.S. attorney for the Northern District of Illinois, writes that the threat of terrorism now comes from local cells, thrusting local police into a role once thought of as the purview of international and federal agencies: that of antiterrorism combatants. She further writes that local law enforcement agencies will have to adapt their traditional policies and training to address the new dangers involved in confronting suicide bombers. (Mecklenburg 24–31)

As an example of local efforts to address the problems of terrorism, the New York City Police Department created two new deputy commissioner positions in 2002, a deputy commissioner for intelligence and a deputy commissioner for counterterrorism, and filled these positions with former high-ranking officials from the Central Intelligence Agency and the Marine Corps. The NYPD also created the Counter Terrorism Bureau (CTB) of 1,000 officers. The CTB consists of the Counter Terrorism Division as its intelligence and research arm and the JTTF as its investigative arm. New equipment, such as radiation-detection gear and biohazard suits, is now standard issue for all NYPD officers.

By 2011, about 1,000 NYPD employees were working directly on terrorism-related issues every day, including active investigations. The NYPD has its own liaison officers working full time in Britain, France, Israel, Canada, Singapore, Amman, the United Arab Emirates, Jordan, the Dominican Republic, and Australia who file daily reports on developments in each region, as well as a group of 80 highly trained civilians working on terrorism who build profiles of possible terrorists by drawing on confidential informants, surveillance, and links with other law enforcement agencies around the world. The civilians thus educate the department about terrorist tactics

and help search for threats in the city. In addition, the NYPD's CTB has Arabic and Farsi linguists and dozens of detectives and liaison officers from other city and state agencies. The department's telephone terrorist tip line receives about 150 calls a day. (Worth B1, B6)

In 2008, the NYPD, using federal funding, added to their counterterrorism strategy by assigning roving teams of NYPD officers to the NYC subway system, which carries nearly 5 million people a day along 656 miles of tracks. The subways have long been considered a potential target for terrorists. These teams, under a tactical plan known as Operation Torch, consist of officers from the Emergency Service Unit who are outfitted in heavy bullet-resistant vests and Kevlar helmets and carry automatic weapons, including M-4 rifles or MP5 submachine guns, and are accompanied by bomb-sniffing dogs.

After the July 2005 London transit bombings, NYPD officers began randomly inspecting train riders' backpacks and packages.

© AP Photo/Hiroko Masuike

After the July 2005 London bombings, NYPD officers began randomly inspecting train riders' backpacks and packages.

Since 9/11, the NYPD has had similar heavily armed officers patrol NYC's streets, particularly around Wall Street and landmarks such as the Empire State Building. As many as 100 police officers in squad cars from every precinct converge twice daily at randomly selected times and at randomly selected sites, like Times Square or the financial district, to rehearse their response to a terrorist attack. NYPD officials say that these operations are believed to be a crucial tactic to keep extremists guessing when and where a large police presence may materialize. (Baker, "New Operation")

By 2008, the Los Angeles Police Department (LAPD) had a counterterrorism unit of 300 members. In March 2008, the Los Angeles Police Department opened its National Counter-Terrorism Academy to teach local law enforcement about the roots of terrorism and how to combat it nationally. The five-month course takes mid-level managers from 30 local agencies, including Los Angeles fire and Long Beach police departments and the FBI, through the historical roots of terrorism and includes culturally sensitive interviewing techniques. Course lessons include religious extremism, homegrown terror

The philosophy behind the fusion center concept is that by integrating various forms of information and intelligence, law enforcement officials are better able to assess the risk of terrorist attack and are better able to respond to terrorist attacks and natural disasters.

groups, and the evolution of al-Qaeda. The objectives of the academy are to shift police officers away from the mind-set that they are only first responders and to train them in prevention techniques. (Uranga)

Since September 11, 2001, the California Highway Patrol (CHP) has spent more than a million hours in homeland security–related activities. Among CHP efforts are aggressive traffic enforcement, visible patrol, and investigations. (Brown and Maples 18–20)

The terrorist attacks of September 11, 2001, highlighted the inadequacy of information sharing among many law enforcement and intelligence agencies. Since 2004, state, local, and regional fusion centers have been formally established across the United States. The philosophy behind the fusion center concept is that by integrating various forms of information and intelligence, including intelligence from the federal government, governmental entities are better able to assess the risk of terrorist attack and will be better able to respond to both terrorist attacks and natural disasters. A fusion center is defined as a collaborative effort of two or more agencies that provide resources, expertise, and information to the center, with the goal of maximizing its ability to detect, prevent, investigate, and respond to criminal and terrorist activity. (Johnson 28–32)

The fundamental idea of the fusion centers was embraced by the September 11 Commission. Most centers are run by state police or other law enforcement agencies. Many also have representatives from a range of other agencies, such as the FBI and Department of Homeland Security and local fire and public works departments. The centers potentially can tap into state, local, and federal databases containing files on investigations, reports on suspicious incidents, and research material on terrorist weapons and tactics.

Because fusion centers also look at information regarding local-level criminal activity, they can analyze this information to determine whether any connection exists between low-level crime and terrorist activity. As one example, in 2005 a group of men engaged in a series of gas station robberies. Although these appeared to be typical local crimes, it was later discovered that these robberies had helped finance a terrorist plot to attack military and Jewish facilities. (Johnson 28–32)

In 2007 one leading law enforcement official, Chief John Batiste of the Washington State Patrol, reported that he saw a problem with maintaining an appropriate alert level in regard to potential terrorist threats. Batiste stated:

We are entering the seventh year since the Twin Towers fell. As time goes on, without another significant terrorist attack, it becomes increasingly challenging to convince the public and even our own personnel that risk still exists. (Batiste 39–40)

Now that we have passed the 10th anniversary of the September 11 attacks, the challenge continues.

 Log onto www.cengagebrain.com for additional resources including videos, flash cards, games, self-quizzing, review exercises, web exercises, learning checks, and more.

4LTR Press solutions are designed for today's learners through the continuous feedback of students like you. Tell us what you think about **POLICE2** and help us improve the learning experience for future students.

YOUR FEEDBACK MATTERS.

Complete the Speak Up
survey in CourseMate at
www.cengagebrain.com

 Follow us at
www.facebook.com/4ltrpress

References

Abel v. United States, 362 U.S. 217 (1960).

Aguilar v. Texas, 378 U.S. 108 (1964).

Alcohol and Highway Safety 2001: A Review of the State of Knowledge. National Highway Traffic Safety Administration. 2001. 28 November 2006. http://www.nhtsa.dot.gov/people/injury/research/alcoholhighway.

Alford, Roger. "24 Counties Have Only Basic 911 Service." *Associated Press,* 13 March 2006.

Alpert, Geoffrey and Patrick R. Anderson. "The Most Deadly Force: Police Pursuits." *Justice Quarterly* 3 (1986): 1–14.

American Indians and Crime: A BJS Statistical Profile, 1992–2002. Washington, D.C.: U.S. Department of Justice, 2004. NCJ#203097.

Arizona v. Gant, 129 U.S. 1710 (2009).

Arizona v. Hicks, 107 S.Ct. 1149 (1987).

Arizona v. Roberson, 486 U.S. 675 (1988).

Associated Press. "Man Guilty of Killing Girl." *Everett Herald* 18 November 2005. 25 July 2006. http://www.heraldnet.com.

---. "Many Villages in Alaska Lack Police." 7 February 2008. 7 February 2008. http://www.officer.com.

---. "1 Million in Luxury SUVs Destroyed in California Arson," *Everett Herald* 23 August 2003, p. A4.

Ayto, John. *Dictionary of Word Origins*. New York: Arcade, 1990.

Baker, Al. "New Operation to Put Heavily Armed Officers in Subways." *New York Times* 2 February 2008.

Batiste, John. "Police Executives Look to 2008." *Law and Order* December 2007: 39–40.

Bittner, Egon. *The Functions of the Police in Modern Society: A Review of Background Factors, Current Practices, and Possible Role Models*. Cambridge, Mass.: Oelgeschlager, Gunn, and Hain, 1979.

Blakeley, Tim. "Overcoming Lateral Transfer Training Issues." *Police Chief* December 2005: 92–96.

Bloch, Peter B. and Deborah Anderson. *Policewomen on Patrol: Final Report*. Washington, D.C.: Police Foundation, 1974.

Bodrero, D. Douglas. "Confronting Terrorism on the State and Local Level." *FBI Law Enforcement Bulletin* March 1999.

---. "Law Enforcement's New Challenge to Investigate, Interdict and Prevent Terrorism." *Police Chief* February 2002.

Bopp, W. J. "Year They Cancelled Mardi Gras: The New Orleans Police Strike of 1979." *Police at the Bargaining Table*. Ed. Charles A. Salerno. Springfield, Ill.: Charles C. Thomas, 1981. 201–221.

Brady v. Maryland, 373 U.S. 83 (1963).

Bratton, William. "Responding to Terror." *Subject to Debate* 7 (2005): 2.

Bratton, William J. and George L. Kelling. "There Are No Cracks in the Broken Windows." *National Review Online* 28 February 2006.

Broderick, John J. *Police in a Time of Change*. 2nd ed. Prospect Heights, Ill.: Waveland Press, 1987.

Brown, Jodi M. and Patrick A. Langan. *Policing and Homicide, 1976–1998: Justifiable Homicide by Police, Police Officers Murdered by Felons*. Washington, D.C.: National Institute of Justice, 2001.

Brown, Lee P. "The Role of the Sheriff." *The Future of Policing*. Ed. Alvin Cohn. Beverly Hills, Calif.: Sage, 1978. 237–240.

Brown, Michael K. *Working the Street*. New York: Russell Sage Foundation, 1981.

Brown v. Mississippi, 297 U.S. 278 (1936).

Brown, M. L. and L. D. Maples. "No Time for Complacency: Leadership and Partnerships Are Key in Homeland Security Efforts." *Police Chief* 3 (2006).

Bucqueroux, Bonnie. "What Community Policing Teaches Us about Community Criminal Justice." 29 August 2006. http://www.policing.com.

Buffa, Denise and Linda Massarella. "Suicide Teen Tricked Cops into Shooting Him: Dear Officer Please Kill Me." *New York Post* 17 November 1997: 3.

Bulman, Philip. "Police Use of Force: The Impact of Less-Lethal Weapons and Tactics." *NIJ Journal* 267 (March 2010).

Bumper v. North Carolina, 391 U.S. 543 (1968).

Burdeau v. McDowell, 256 U.S. 465 (1921).

Burke, Tod W. and Jason M. Rexrode. "DNA Warrants." *Law and Order* July 2000: 121–124.

Caldero, Michael A. and John P. Crank. *Police Ethics: The Corruption of Noble Cause*. 2nd ed. Cincinnati: Anderson, 2004.

Caplan, Mark H. and Joe Holt Anderson. *Forensic: When Science Bears Witness*. Washington, D.C.: National Institute of Justice, 1984.

Cardwell, Diane. "New York State Draws Nearer to Collecting DNA in All Crimes." *New York Times* 4 May 2006.

Carroll v. United States, 267 U.S. 132 (1925).

Cawley, Donald F., H. J. Miron, W. J. Aranjo, R. Wassserman, T. A. Mannello, and Y. Huffman. *Managing Criminal Investigations: A Manual*. Washington, D.C.: National Institute of Justice, 1977.

Centers for Disease Control and Prevention, U.S. Department of Health and Human Services. *HIV/AIDS Surveillance Report: HIV Infection and AIDS in the United States*. 19 March 2008. http://www.cdc.gov/hiv/topics/surveillance/basic.htm.

Chapman, Rob and Matthew C. Scheider. *Community Policing: Now More than Ever*. 2 May 2003. http://www.cops.usdoj.gov.

Chimel v. California, 395 U.S. 752 (1969).

Clark, M. Wesley. "Enforcing Criminal Law on Native American Lands." *FBI Law Enforcement Bulletin* April 2005: 22–31.

Colaprete, Frank A. "Knowledge Management in the Criminal Investigation Process." *Law and Order* October 2004: 82–89.

---. "The Case for Investigator Mentoring." *Police Chief* October 2004: 47–52.

Colorado v. Bertine, 479 U.S. 367 (1987).

Connors, E., T. Lundregan, N. B. Miller, and T. McEwen, *Convicted by Juries, Exonerated by Science: Case Studies in the Use of DNA Evidence to Establish Innocence After Trial*. Washington, D.C.: National Institute of Justice, 1996.

COPS website. 13 April 2010. http://www.cops.usdoj.gov.

Cordner, Gary W. "People with Mental Illness." *Department of Justice: Problem-Oriented Guides for Police, Guide #40*. Washington, D.C.: U.S. Department of Justice, May 2006.

---. "The Police on Patrol." *Police and Policing: Contemporary Issues*. Ed. Dennis Jay Kenney. New York: Praeger, 1989. 60–71.

Cordner, Gary W., Kathryn E. Scarborough, and Robert Sheehan. *Police Administration*. 6th ed. Cincinnati: Anderson, 2007.

Cox, Steven M. and Jack D. Fitzgerald. *Police in Community Relations*. 3rd ed. Madison, Wisc.: Brown and Benchmark, 1996.

Crawford, Kimberly A. "Constitutional Rights to Counsel During Interrogation: Comparing Rights Under the Fifth and Sixth Amendments," *FBI Law Enforcement Bulletin* (September 2002): 28–32.

Cross, Chad L. and Larry Ashley. "Police Trauma and Addiction: Coping with the Dangers of the Job." *FBI Law Enforcement Bulletin* October 2004.

Daigneau, Elizabeth. "Calling All Citizens: A Growing Number of Municipalities Are Using 'Reverse 911' to Alert Residents in the Event of an Emergency." *Governance* July 2002.

Delaware v. Prouse, 440 U.S. 648 (1979).

del Carmen, Rolando V. *Civil Liabilities in American Policing: A Text for Law Enforcement Personnel*. Englewood Cliffs, NJ: Prentice Hall, 1991.

Dempsey, John S. *Introduction to Investigations*. 2nd ed. Belmont, Calif.: Wadsworth, 2003.

Department of Homeland Security. *Fact Sheet: Select Department of Homeland Security 2007 Achievements*. 12 December 2007. 6 and 8 March 2008. www.dhs.gov.

Department of Homeland Security. *Fact Sheet: Border Security and Immigration Enforcement*. 10 March 2011. www.dhs.gov.

Department of Homeland Security. *Protecting Travelers and Commerce*. 10 March 2011. www.dhs.gov.

Department of Homeland Security website. 13 April 2010. www.dhs.gov/files/programs.

Dickerson v. United States, 530 U.S. 428 (2000).

"Dispatches." *On Patrol* Summer 1996: 25.

Drunk Driving: Problem-Oriented Guides for Police. Problem-Specific Guides Series #36. Washington, D.C.: U.S. Department of Justice, 2006.

Dulaney, W. Marvin. *Black Police in America*. Bloomington: Indiana University Press, 1996.

Durose, Matthew R. *Census of Publicly Funded Forensic Crime Laboratories, 2005*. Washington, D.C.: National Institute of Justice, 2008.

Durose, Matthew R., Erika L. Smith, and Patrick A. Langan. *Contacts between Police and the Public, 2005*. Washington, D.C.: Bureau of Justice Statistics, U.S. Department of Justice, 2007. NCJ#215243.

Eck, John E. *Managing Case Assignments: The Burglary Investigation Decision Model Replication*. Washington, D.C.: Police Executive Research Forum, 1979.

Elgin Police Department website. 21 May 2008. http://www.cityofelgin.org.

Escobedo v. Illinois, 378 U.S. 478 (1964).

Executive Office of the President of the United States. *Advancing Justice through DNA Technology*. Washington, D.C.: National Institute of Justice, 2003.

Fahri, Paul. "Dateline' Pedophile Sting: One More Point" Washington Post, April 9, 2006.

Falcone, David N. *Dictionary of Criminal Justice, Criminology and Criminal Law*. Upper Saddle River, N.J.: Pearson/Prentice Hall, 2005.

Falk, Kay. "Indian Country—Where Wide Open Spaces and Boundaries Blur." *Law Enforcement Technology* February 2006: 17–22.

FBI homepage. Federal Bureau of Investigation. 10 March 2011. http://www.fbi.gov.

Federal Bureau of Investigation. 2002. http://www.fbi.gov/pressrel/speeches/speech052902.htm.

---. *CODIS-NDIS Statistics*. 11 March 2011. www.fbi.gov.

---. *FBI Laboratory Services*. 11 March 2011. www.fbi.gov/hq/lab/labhome.htm.

---. *Federal Law Enforcement Officers Killed and Injured—2009*. Washington, D.C.: Federal Bureau of Investigation, 2011. 10 March 2011. http://www.fbi.gov.

---. *Indian Country Crime*. 9 June 2006. http://www.fbi.gov.

---. *Integrated Automated Fingerprint Identification System (IAFIS)*. 10 March 2010. www.fbi.gov/hq/cjisd/iafis.htm.

---. *Law Enforcement Officers Accidentally Killed—2009*. Washington, D.C.: Federal Bureau of Investigation, 2011. 10 March 2011. http://www.fbi.gov.

---. *Law Enforcement Officers Assaulted—2009*. Washington, D.C.: Federal Bureau of Investigation, 2011. 10 March 2011. http://www.fbi.gov.

---. *Law Enforcement Officers Feloniously Killed—2010*. Washington, D.C.: Federal Bureau of Investigation, 2011. 10 March 2011. http://www.fbi.gov.

---. *National Security Branch*. 22 February 2008. www.fbi.gov/hq/nsb/nsb.htm.

---. *NDIS Statistics*. 23 February 2008. www.fbi.gov/hq/lab/codis/clickmap.htm.

---. *Uniform Crime Reports*, 2007. 21 October 2008. www.fbi.gov.

---. *Uniform Crime Reports*, 2008.

---. *Uniform Crime Reports*, 2009. 8 March 2010. http://www.fbi.gov.

---. *Uniform Crime Reports*, 2010.

---. *Uniform Crime Reports*, "Crime in the United States," 29 July 2006. http://ww.fbi.gov.

Fooksman, Leon. "Detectives from Different Agencies in Palm Beach County Team Up to Tackle Violence." *South Florida Sun-Sentinel* 2 June 2006.

Forst, Linda. *The Aging of America: A Handbook for Police Officers*. Springfield, Ill.: Charles C. Thomas, 2000.

French, Laurence. "Law Enforcement in Indian Country." *Criminal Justice Studies* 18 (2005): 69–80.

Gaines, Larry and Victor Kappeler. *Policing in America*. 5th ed. LexisNexis, 2005.

Gaines, Larry K., John L. Worrall, Mittie D. Southerland and John E. Angell, *Police Administration*, 2nd ed. (New York: McGraw-Hill, 2003) p. 367

Garner, Joel H. and Christopher D. Maxwell. *Understanding the Prevalence and Severity of Force Used by and Against the Police, Executive Summary*. Washington, D.C.: National Institute of Justice, 2002.

Goldstein, Herman. *Police Corruption: A Perspective on its Nature and Control*. Washington, D.C.: Police Foundation, 1975.

---. *Policing a Free Society*. Cambridge, Mass.: Ballinger, 1977.

---. *Problem-Oriented Policing*. New York: McGraw-Hill, 1990.

Gonzalez, Daniel. "Illegal-Immigration Foes Want Police to Change Rules." *Arizona Republic* 4 November 2007. 5 November 2007. http://www.azcentral.com.

Gordon, Arthur and Ross Wolf. "License Plate Recognition Technology: Innovation in Law Enforcement Use." *FBI Law Enforcement Bulletin* March 2007.

Greenwood, Peter W. and Joan Petersilia. *The Criminal Investigation Process, Volume I: Summary and Policy Implications*. Santa Monica, Calif: Rand Corporation, 1975.

Griggs v. Duke Power Company, No. 401. U.S. 424 (1971).

Hampton v. United States, 425 U.S. 484 (1976).

Harris v. New York, 401 U.S. 222 (1971).

Harris v. United States, 390 U.S. 234 (1968).

Harrison, Bob. "Gamers, Millennials, and Generation Next: Implications for Policing." *Police Chief*. October 2007. 1 February 2008. http://www.theiacp.org.

Hedlund, Karey and Tod W. Burke. "Reserve Officers: A Valuable Resource." *FBI Law Enforcement Bulletin* December 2006: 12.

Hemmens, Craig, John L. Worrall, and Alan Thompson. *Significant Cases in Criminal Procedure*. Los Angeles: Roxbury, 2004.

Henry, Nicholas. *Public Administration and Public Affairs*. 9th ed. Upper Saddle River, N.J.: Pearson Education, Inc., 2004.

Hester v. United States, 265 U.S. 57 (1924).

Hibberd, James. "Police Psychology." *On Patrol* Fall 1996.

Hickman, Matthew J. and Brian A. Reaves. "Local Police and Homeland Security: Some Baseline Data." *Police Chief* October 2002.

---. *Local Police Departments, 2003*. Washington, D.C.: Bureau of Justice Statistics, 2006. NCJ#2101118.

---. *Sheriff's Offices, 2003*. Washington, D.C.: Bureau of Justice Statistics, 2006.

---. *State and Local Law Enforcement Training Academies, 2002*. Washington, D.C.: Bureau of Justice Statistics, 2004. NCJ#203350.

Hoffman, John. "Rural Policing." *Law and Order* June 1992: 20–24.

Holzman, Arnold and Mark Kirschner. "Pre-Employment Psychological Evaluations." *Law and Order* September 2003: 85–87.

Hoover, Jerry. "The Reno Model Police Training Officer (PTO) Program." *NAFTO News* December 2004.

Housing and Urban Development website. 13 April 2010. http://www.hud.gov/buying/.

Hughes, Kristen A. *Justice Expenditure and Employment in the United States, 2003*. Washington, D.C.: Bureau of Justice Statistics, 2006.

Hulon, Willie T. "Focus on Terrorism." *FBI Law Enforcement Bulletin* December 2007.

Huston, H. Range, M. D., and Diedre Anglin, M. D. "Suicide by Cop." *Annals of Emergency Medicine* 6 (1998).

IACP website. *2009 Community Policing Awards*. 13 April 2010. http://www.theiacp.org.

Illinois v. Gates, 462 U.S. 213 (1983).

Illinois v. Perkins, 110 S.Ct. 2394 (1990).

International Association of Chiefs of Police (IACP). "The Future of Women in Policing: Mandates for Action." November 1998. 24 April 2004. http://www.theiacp.org/pubinfo/researchcenterdox.htm.

---. "What Do Victims Want? Effective Strategies to Achieve Justice for Victims of Crime." May 2000. 28 April 2004. http://www.theiacp.org.

Isaacs, H. H. "A Study of Communications, Crimes, and Arrests in a Metropolitan Police Department." President's Commission on Law Enforcement and Administration of Justice, *Task Force Report: Science and Technology*. Washington, D.C.: U.S. Government Printing Office, 1967.

Jacob, Herbert. *Urban Justice*. Boston: Little, Brown, 1973.

Jacoby, Jeff. "A Tale of 2 Stories about Anti-Semitism." *Boston Globe* 6 August 2006.

Jensen, Carl J. III. "Consuming and Applying Research: Evidence-Based Policing." *Police Chief* 2 (2006): 98–101.

Johnson, Bart R. "A Look at Fusion Centers: Working Together to Protect America." *FBI Law Enforcement Bulletin* December 2007.

Jones, Richard Lezin. "New York Police Officers Face Counseling on September 11 Events." *New York Times* 30 November 2001.

Kanable, Rebecca. "Fingerprints Making the Case: AFIS and IAFIS Are Helping Find Matching Prints, but There Are More to Be Found." *Law Enforcement Technology* March 2003.

Kansas City Police Department. *Response Time Analysis: Executive Summary*. Washington, D.C.: U.S. Government Printing Office, 1978.

Kappeler, Victor. *Critical Issues in Police Civil Liability*. 3rd ed. Prospect Heights, Ill.: Waveland Press, 2001.

Kelling, George L. *"Broken Windows" and Police Discretion*. Washington, D.C.: U.S. Department of Justice, 1999.

Kelling, George L., Tony Pate, Duane Dieckman, and Charles E. Brown. *The Kansas City Preventive Patrol Experiment: A Summary Report*. Washington, D.C.: Police Foundation, 1974.

Kelly, Patricia and Rich Martin. "Police Suicide Is Real." *Law and Order* 3 (2006).

Kenny, Dennis Jay, ed. *Police and Policing: Contemporary Issues*. New York: Praeger, 1989.

Khashu, Anita. *Role of the Local Police: Striking a Balance Between Immigration Enforcement and Civil Liberties*. Washington, D.C.: Police Foundation, 2009.

Kindschi-Gosselin, Denise. *Heavy Hands: An Introduction to the Crimes of Family Violence*. 2nd ed. Upper Saddle River, N.J.: Prentice Hall, 2003.

Kirkham, George L. "A Professor's Street Lessons." *Order Under Law*. Eds. R. Culbertson and M. Tezak. Prospect Heights, Ill.: Waveland Press, 1981. 81.

Kirkham, George L. and Laurin A. Wollan, Jr. *Introduction to Law Enforcement*. New York: Harper & Row, 1980.

Kissinger, Meg. "Milwaukee Department Hit Hard by Officer Suicides." *Milwaukee Journal Sentinel* 22 January 2008. 23 January 2008. http://www.officer.com.

Klein, Allison. "D.C. Has Weekend Free of Shootings." *Washington Post* 11 December 2007: B1.

Klinger, David. "Police Responses to Officer-Involved Shootings." *National Institute of Justice Journal* 253 (2006).

Klockars, Carl B. "The Dirty Harry Problem." *Annals of the American Association of Political and Social Science* November 1980: 33–47.

---. *Idea of Police*. Thousand Oaks, Calif.: Sage, 1985.

---. "The Modern Sting." *Thinking about Police: Contemporary Readings*. Ed. Carl B. Klockars. New York: McGraw-Hill, 1983.

Knapp Commission. *Report on Police Corruption*. New York: Braziller, 1973.

Krause, Kevin. "Police Agencies Mellow on Applicant's Drug Use." *South Florida Sun-Sentinel* 11 December 2002.

Lee, Natasha. "Chief Rethinks Community Policing Policy." *Stamford Advocate* 10 April 2006.

Legel, C. "Evaluating an Entry-Level Exam." *Law and Order* December 2005: 66–69.

Lewis, John F. Jr. "Fighting Terrorism in the 21st Century." *FBI Law Enforcement Bulletin* March 1999.

Lipton, Eric. "Homeland Report Says Threat from Terrorist-List Nations Is Declining." *New York Times* 31 March 2005: A5.

Mapp v. Ohio, 367 U.S. 643 (1961).

Martin, Robert A. "The Joint Terrorism Task Force: A Concept That Works," *FBI Law Enforcement Bulletin* (March 1999) 23–27.

McFadden, Robert D. "Army Doctor Held in Ft. Hood Rampage." *New York Times* 6 November 2009. www.nytimes.com.

McGuire, Robert J. "The Human Dimension in Urban Policing: Dealing with Stress in the 1980s." *Police Chief* November 1979.

McManamy, Rob. "Study Authors Find Cracks in 'Broken Windows.'" *University of Chicago Chronicle* 30 March 2006.

Mecklenburg, Sheri H. "Suicide Bombers: Are You Ready." *Police Chief* September 2007: 24–31.

Michigan v. Mosley, 423 U.S. 96. (1975).

Mieth v. Dothard, 418 F. Supp. 1169 (1976).

Milanovich, Clement. "The Blue Pressure Cooker." *Police Chief* 47 (1980): 20.

Miranda v. Arizona, 384 U.S. 436 (1966).

Mitchell, Allison. "A Night on Patrol: What's Behind Police Tensions and Discontent." *New York Times* 19 October 1992: B1, B2.

Moore, Mark H. and Robert C. Trojanowicz. *Corporate Strategies for Policing, Perspectives on Policing, no. 6*. Washington, D.C.: National Institute of Justice, 1988.

Moore, Solomon. "In a Lab, an Ever-Growing Database of DNA Profiles." *New York Times* 12 May 2009. www.nytimes.com.

Moran, Robert. "City Voters Approve Anticrime Cameras." *Philadelphia Inquirer* 17 May 2006.

Moran v. Burbine, 475 U.S. 412 (1986).

Morash, Merry and Jack Greene. "Evaluating Women on Patrol: A Critique of Contemporary Wisdom." *Evaluation Review* 10 (1986): 230–255.

Morash, Merry and J. Kevin Ford, eds. *The Move to Community Policing: Making Change Happen*. Thousand Oaks, Calif.: Sage Publications, 2002.

Mothers Against Drunk Driving. "Ignition Interlock Legislative Success." 2006. 29 April 2010. www.madd.org.

"Mugged by Reality." *Policy Review* 84 (1 July 1997). http://www.hoover.org/publications/policy-review/article/7500.

Mumola, Christopher J. *Arrest-Related Deaths in the United States, 2003–2005*. Washington, D.C.: Bureau of Justice Statistics, 2007.

Murphy, Gerard R. and Chuck Wexler. *Managing a Multijurisdictional Case: Identifying Lessons Learned from the Sniper Investigation*. Washington, D. C.: Police Executive Research Forum (PERF), 2004. www.ojp.usdoj.gov/BJA/pubs/SniperRpt.pdf.

National Advisory Commission on Civil Disorders. *Report*. Washington, D.C.: U.S. Government Printing Office, 1968.

National Advisory Commission on Criminal Justice Standards and Goals. *Police*. Washington, D.C.: U.S. Government Printing Office, 1973.

National Center for Victims of Crime. *A Police Guide to First Response: Domestic Violence, Residential Burglary and Automobile Theft*. Washington, D.C.: U.S. Department of Justice, 2002.

National Center for Women and Policing. *Police Family Violence Fact Sheet*. 22 February 2008. http://www.womenandpolicing.org.

National Commission on Terrorist Attacks upon the United States. *9/11 Commission Report: The Final Report of the National Commission Terrorist Attacks upon the United States.* New York: Norton, 2004.

National Counterterrorism Center. 10 March 2011. www.nctc.gov.

National Criminal Justice Reference Center. *In the Spotlight: Forensic Science: Summary.* 27 July 2006. www. ncjrs.gov/spotlight/forensic/Summary.html.

National Highway Traffic Safety Administration. *2008 Traffic Safety Annual Assessment—Highlights.* June 2009. www.nrd.nhtsa.dot.gov/pubs/811172.pdf.

National Highway Traffic Safety Administration website. http://www.nhtsa.gov.

---. *Study of Deaths Following Electro Muscular Disruption: Interim Report.* Washington, D.C.: National Institute of Justice, 2008.

New York v. Belton, 453 U.S. 454 (1981).

New York v. Quarles, 104 S.Ct. 2626 (1984).

Niederhoffer, Arthur. *Behind the Shield: The Police in Urban Society.* Garden City, N.Y.: Doubleday, 1967.

Office of the President, Office of Homeland Security. *National Strategy for Homeland Security.* Washington, D.C.: Office of the President, 2002.

O'Hara, Patrick. "Why Law Enforcement Organizations Fail: Mapping the Organizational Fault Lines in Policing." *Crime and Justice International* March/April 2006: 23–26.

Ohlemacher, Stephen. "Minority Population Increasing in States." *Newsday* 15 August 2006.

Quijas, Louis F. 13 December 2006. www.cops.usdoj.gov.

"On-the-Job Stress in Policing—Reducing It, Preventing It." *National Institute of Justice Journal* January 2000: 18–24.

Oregon v. Elstad, 470 U.S. 298 (1985).

Palmiotto, Michael J. *Police Misconduct: What Is It?* Upper Saddle River, NJ: Prentice Hall, 2001.

Parent, Richard B. "Aspects of Police Use of Deadly Force in British Columbia: The Phenomenon of Victim-Precipitated Homicide." MA thesis, Simon Fraser University, 1996.

Payton v. New York, 445 U.S. 573 (1980).

Perez, Douglas and J. Alan Moore. *Police Ethics: A Matter of Character.* Belmont, CA: Wadsworth, 2002.

Perin, Michele. "Police Suicide." *Law Enforcement Technology* 9 (2007).

Perry, Steven W. *Census of Tribal Justice Agencies in Indian Country, 2002.* Washington, D.C.: U.S. Department of Justice, 2005.

Peterson, Joseph L. *Use of Forensic Evidence by the Police and Courts.* Washington, D.C.: National Institute of Justice, 1987.

Phillips, Amanda. "Skinheads in America," *Law Enforcement Technology* 64 (2007): 64–71.

Phoenix Police Department website. 13 April 2010. www.phoenix.gov/police.

Pittaro, Michael. "Police Occupational Stress and Its Impact on Community Relations." *Police Forum: Academy of Criminal Justice Sciences* 1 (2008).

Pitts, Steve, Ronald Glensor, and Kenneth Peak. "The Police Training Officer Program: A Contemporary Approach to Postacademy Recruit Training." *Police Chief* 8 (2007). 31 January 2008. http://www.theiacp.org.

"Police Arrest Same Man 416 Times" *WKRN, Nashville, Tennessee* 25 February 2008. 25 February 2008. http://www.wkrn.com.

Police Executive Research Forum (PERF). "2002 Herman Goldstein Award Winners." 2 September 2006. http://www.policeforum.org.

Pollock, Joycelyn. *Ethical Dilemmas and Decisions in Criminal Justice.* 5th ed. Belmont, CA: Thomson/Wadsworth, 2007.

Pomfret, John. "Police Finding It Hard to Fill Jobs." *Washington Post* 27 March 2006.

Potok, Mark. Cited in Michael A. Gips "Whither Domestic Terrorists?" *Security Management* (March 2004): 12–14.

Pratt, Travis C., Michael J. Gaffney, Nicholas P. Lovrich, and Charles L. Johnson. "This Isn't CSI: Estimating the National Backlog of Forensic DNA Cases and the Barriers Associated with Case Processing." *Criminal Justice Policy Review* 1 (2006).

"Predicting a Criminal's Journey to Crime." *National Institute of Justice Journal* 253 (January 2006).

President's Commission on Law Enforcement and Administration of Justice. *The Challenge of Crime in a Free Society.* Washington, D.C.: U.S. Government Printing Office, 1967.

---. *Task Force Report: Science and Technology.* Washington, D.C.: U.S. Government Printing Office, 1967.

Preston, Julia. "Report Faults Training of Local Officers in Immigration Enforcement Program." *New York Times* 2 April 2010. 3 April 2010. http://www.nytimes.com.

Problem Oriented Guides for Police, Response Series, Guide # 6: Sting Operations. #2005CKWXK001, October 2007. Department of Justice, Office of Community Oriented Policing Services. http://www.usdoj.gov.

Rafky, David. "My Husband the Cop." Police Chief August 1984.

Rand, Michael R. and Erika Harrell, "Crimes against People with Disabilities, 2007" Bureau of Justice Statistics: Special Report (Washington D.C.: U.S Department of Justice, October 2009)

Reaves, Brian A. Census of State and Local Law Enforcement Agencies, 2004. Washington, D.C.: Bureau of Justice Statistics, 2007.

---. Federal Law Enforcement Officers, 2004. Washington, D.C.: Bureau of Justice Statistics, 2006.

---. Local Police Departments, 2007. Washington, D.C.: Bureau of Justice Statistics, 2010.

Reichers, Lisa M. and Roy Roberg. "Community Policing: A Critical Review of Underlying Assumptions." Journal of Police Science and Administration June 1990: 110.

Reiner, G. H., T. J. Sweeney, R. V. Waymire, F. A. Newton III, R. G. Grassie, S. M. White, and W. D. Wallace. Integrated Criminal Apprehension Program: Crime Analysis Operations Manual. Washington, D.C.: Law Enforcement Assistance Administration, 1977.

Reno, Janet. "Preventing the Conviction of the Innocent: A Compelling and Urgent Need." Judicature 4 (2004).

Rhode Island v. Innis, 446 U.S. 291 (1980).

Riley, Michael. "Promises, Justice Broken." Denver Post 13 November 2007. 14 November 2007. http://www.denverpost.com.

Rochin v. California, 342 U.S. 165 (1952).

Roth, Jeffrey A. and Joseph F. Ryan. "The Cops Program after 4 Years: National Evaluation." Research in Brief August 2000: 1.

Saferstein, Richard. Criminalistics: An Introduction to Forensic Science. 8th ed. Upper Saddle River, N.J.: Pearson/Prentice Hall, 2004.

Schneckloth v. Bustamonte, 412 U.S. 218 (1973).

Schobel, Gary B., Thomas A. Evans, and John L. Daly. "Community Policing: Does It Reduce Crime, or Just Displace it?" Police Chief August 1997: 64–71.

Schulz, Dorothy Moses. Breaking the Brass Ceiling: Women Police Chiefs and Their Paths to the Top. Westport, Conn.: Praeger, 2004. 29.

---. From Social Worker to Crimefighter: Women in United States Municipal Policing. Westport, Conn.: Praeger, 1995.

Scrivner, Ellen. "Helping Families Cope with Stress." Law Enforcement News 15 June 1991: 6.

---. Innovations in Police Recruitment and Hiring: Hiring in the Spirit of Service. Washington, D.C.: Department of Justice, 2006. NCJ#212981.

Shapiro, Ari. "Police Use DNA to Track Suspects through Family." 12 December 2007. www.npr.org.

Sheehan, Robert and Gary W. Cordner. Introduction to Police Administration. 2nd ed. Cincinnati: Anderson, 1989.

Sherman, Lawrence. "Evidence-Based Policing." Ideas in American Policing. Washington, D.C.: Police Foundation, 1998.

Sherman, Lawrence W., ed. Police Corruption: A Sociological Perspective. Garden City, NY: Doubleday, 1974.

Sherman, Lawrence W. and Richard A. Berk. The Minneapolis Domestic Violence Experiment. April 1984. http://www.policefoundation.org/pdf/minneapolisdve.pdf.

Sichel, J. L., L. N. Freeman, J. C. Quint, and M.E. Smith. Women on Patrol—A Pilot Study of Police Performance in New York City. Rockville, MD: National Institute of Justice, 1978.

Siegel, Larry J. and Joseph J. Senna. Introduction to Criminal Justice. 10th ed. Belmont, Calif.: Thomson/Wadsworth, 2005.

Siegel, Larry J., Dennis Sullivan, and Jack R. Greene. "Decision Games Applied to Police Decision Making." Journal of Criminal Justice Summer 1974.

Silverthorne Lumber Co. v. United States, 251 U.S. 385 (1920).

"Sir Robert Peel's Nine Principles of Policing." 28 August 2008. http://www.newwestpolice.org.

Skolnick, Jerome. Justice without Trial: Law Enforcement in a Democratic Society. New York: Wiley, 1966.

"Special Report/Wildfires." Time 5 November 2007: 35

Spelman, William and D. K. Brown. Calling the Police: Citizen Reporting of Serious Crime. Washington, D.C.: Police Executive Research Forum, 1981.

Spinelli v. United States, 393 U.S. 410 (1969).

Stevens, Dennis J. Applied Community Policing in the 21st Century. Boston: Allyn & Bacon, 2003.

Sullivan, John. "Taking Back a Drug-Plagued Tenement, Step One: The Dealers Out." New York Times 16 August 1997: 25–26.

Sutter, Sharon Hollis. "Holmes...Still Aiding Complex Investigations." *Law and Order* November 1991.

Swanson, Charles R., Leonard Territo, and Robert W. Taylor. *Police Administration*. 5th ed. Upper Saddle River, N.J.: Prentice Hall, 2001.

Taylor, B., B. Kubu, L. Fridell, C. Rees, T. Jordan, and J. Cheney. *Cop Crunch: Identifying Strategies for Dealing with the Recruiting and Hiring Crisis in Law Enforcement*. Washington, D.C.: U.S. Department of Justice, National Institute of Justice, 2005.

Taylor, Marisa. "Local Police Split Over Immigration Enforcement." *McClatchy Newspapers* 6 December 2007.

Tennessee v. Garner, 471 U.S. 1 (1985).

Terault, Mike. "Community Policing: Essential to Homeland Security." *Sheriff* September/October 2002.

Terry, W. Clinton. "Police Stress: The Empirical Evidence." *Journal of Police Science and Administration* 9 (1981).

Terry v. Ohio. 392 U.S. 1 (1968).

Thibault, Edward, Lawrence W. Lynch, and R. Bruce McBride. *Proactive Police Management*. Englewood Cliffs, N.J.: Prentice Hall, 1985.

Thompson, R. Alan. *Career Experiences of African American Police Executives: Black in Blue Revisited*. New York: LFB Scholarly, 2003.

Transportation Security Administration. "Who We Are." 22 April 2011. www.tsa.gov.

Trojanowicz, Robert C. "Building Support for Community Policing: An Effective Strategy." *FBI Law Enforcement Bulletin* May 1992: 7–12.

Trojanowicz, Robert, Victor E. Kappeler, Larry K. Gaines, and Bonnie Bucqueroux. *Community Policing: A Contemporary Perspective*. 2nd ed. Cincinnati: Anderson Publishing, 1998.

"The Truth Is in Your Genes." *Law Enforcement News* 15 and 31 December 2000.

United States Coast Guard. "About Us." 8 March 2008. www.uscg.mil.

United States v. Leon, 468 U.S. 897 (1984).

United States v. Martinez-Fuerte, 428 U.S. 543 (1976).

United States v. Matlock, 415 U.S. 164 (1974).

United States v. Place, 462 U.S. 696 (1983).

United States v. Robinson, 414 U.S. 218 (1973).

United States v. Russell, 411 U.S. 423 (1973).

Uranga, Rachel. "LAPD Fights Terror," *Daily Breeze,* March 19, 2008.

U.S. Census website. www.census.gov.

U.S. Commission on Civil Rights. *Who Is Guarding the Guardians? A Report on Police Practices*. Washington, D.C.: U.S. Government Printing Office, 1981.

U.S. Customs and Border Protection. "Protecting Our Borders Against Terrorism." 22 April 2011. www.cbp.gov.

U.S. Department of Justice. *A Resource Guide on Racial Profiling Data Collection Systems: Promising Practices and Lessons Learned*. Washington, D.C.: Department of Justice, 2000. NCJ#184768.

U.S. Department of Justice, Bureau of Justice Statistics. *State and Local Law Enforcement Statistics*. Washington, D.C.: Bureau of Justice Statistics, 2006.

U.S. Department of Justice, Community Relations Service. *Twenty Plus Things Law Enforcement Agencies Can Do to Prevent or Respond to Hate Incidents against Arab-Americans, Muslims, and Sikhs*. Washington, D.C.: U.S. Department of Justice. 18 August 2006. http://www.usdoj.gov/crs/twentyplus.htm.

U.S. Department of Justice, Office of Community Oriented Policing. *Criminal Intelligence Sharing: A National Plan for Intelligence-Led Policing At the Local, State and Federal Levels*. U.S. Department of Justice. August 2002. http://www.ncirc.gov/documents/public/supplementaries/intel_sharing_report.pdf.

U.S. Government Accountability Office. *Taser Weapons: Use of Tasers by Selected Law Enforcement Agencies*. Washington, D.C.: U.S. Government Accountability Office, 2005.

U.S. Immigration and Customs Enforcement. "About Us." 3 March 2011. www.ice.gov.

Van Maanen, John. "Observations on the Making of a Policeman." *Order Under Law*. Eds. Culbertson and Tezak. Prospect Heights, Ill: Waveland Press, 1981.

van Oorschot, Roland A. H., Sally Treadwell, et al. "Beware of the Possibility of Fingerprinting Techniques Transferring DNA." *Journal of Forensic Sciences* 6 (2005).

---. *Tired Cops: The Importance of Managing Police Fatigue*. Washington, D.C.: Police Executive Research Forum, 2000.

Violanti, John M. "What's Killing America's Cops? Mostly Themselves, According to New Study." *Law Enforcement News* 15 November 1996: 1.

Volk, Daniel C. "Police Join Feds to Tackle Immigration." 28 November 2007. http://www.stateline.org.

Walker, Samuel and Charles M. Katz. *Police in America: An Introduction.* 6th ed. New York: McGraw-Hill, 2008.

Weeks v. United States, 232 U.S. 383 (1914).

Weich, Susan. "Suicide by Cop Takes Toll on Police." *St. Louis Post-Dispatch* 6 February 2006.

Weigand, Charles H. "Combining Tactical and Community Policing Considerations." *Law and Order* May 1997: 70–71.

Weisburd, David, Cody W. Telep, Joshua C. Hinkle, and John E. Eck, "Is Problem-Oriented Policing Effective in Reducing Crime and Disorder? Findings from a Campbell Systematic Review." *Criminology and Public Policy* 9 (1 February 2010).

Weiss, Rick. "DNA of Criminals' Kin Cited in Solving Cases." *Washington Post* 12 May 2006.

---. "Vast DNA Bank Pits Policing vs. Privacy." *Washington Post* 3 June 2006.

Westley, William, *Violence and the Police: A Sociological Study of Law, Custom, and Morality.* Cambridge, Mass.: MIT Press, 1970.

White, Jonathan R. *Terrorism and Homeland Security.* 5th ed. Belmont, Calif.: Thomson/Wadsworth, 2006.

Wilson, James Q. *Varieties of Police Behavior: The Management of Law and Order in Eight Communities* Cambridge, Mass.: Harvard University Press, 1968.

Wilson, James Q. and George L. Kelling. "'Broken Windows': The Police and Neighborhood Safety." *Atlantic Monthly* March 1982: 29–38.

Wolf v. Colorado, 338 U.S. 25 (1949).

Womack, Charissa L. "A National Survey of Police Practices Regarding the Criminal Investigations Process: Twenty-five Years After Rand." Cited in *Criminal Investigations: The Impact of Patrol Officers on Solving Crime*, MA thesis. University of North Texas, 2007. 23 April 2008. http://digital.library.unt.edu/permalink/meta-dc-3594:1.

Worth, Robert F. "In a Quiet Office Somewhere, Watching Terrorists." *New York Times* 23 February 2005.

Wuestewald, Todd and Brigitte Steinheider. "Shared Leadership: Can Empowerment Work in Police Organizations," *Police Chief* January 2006.

Youth Crime Watch of America website. 4 May 2010. www.ycwa.org.

Zhao, Jihong "Soloman" and Quint Thurman. *Funding Community Policing to Reduce Crime: Have Cops Grants Made a Difference from 1994 to 2000?* U.S. Department of Justice, Office of Community Oriented Policing Services. July 2004.

Index

Italic page numbers indicate material in tables or figures.

A

AARP, 159
abandoned property, 170, 186
Abel v. United States (1960), 186
abortion, 180
administrative liability, 118
administrative license revocation (ALR), 135
administrative units, 50
administrators, police, 48, 91, 102, 132
Admissibility of Confessions, 191
adverse impact, 59, 99
affirmative action, 100
AFIS. *See* automated fingerprint identification system
African Americans, 7–8. *See also* minorities
　1960s urban riots, 11–12, 155
　challenges facing, 104–105
　discrimination against, 8, 98–99
　double marginality and, 99
　friendly fire and, 105
　job performance of, 101–102
　police hiring of, 8, 19, 21, 101–103
　police relationship to, 155–156
　racial profiling of, 114, 155–156
　representation of, 102–103
　Rodney King incident, 13–14
　tokenism, 104–105
age requirements, 54
aggressive driving, 135–136
aggressive patrol, 132, 173
aging population, 159
Aguilar v. Texas (1964), 183–184
AIDS (acquired immune deficiency syndrome), 95

Air Force Office of Special Investigations (OSI), 29
air marshals, 213
Alaska, 21
alcohol testing unit, 50
alcohol use
　ATF and, 27
　drunk driving, 68, 135
　illegal sales of, 49
　by police officers, 90
　prohibition of, 9, 10, *10*
Alfred the Great, 4
All Hands on Deck patrol, 132
al-Qaeda, 209, 211, *211*, 216, 217
alternative vehicle deployment, 133
AMBER alert system, 146
ambiguity, in police role, 68–70, 154
American Association of Retired Persons, 159
American Colonies, 6–8, 77
American Federation of Labor (AFL), 9, 45
American frontier, policing of, 8–9
American Indians. *See* Native Americans
American Institute of Stress, 87
American Law Institute, 77, 151
analysis. *See* crime; DNA; SARA process
Animal Liberation Front (ALF), 210
animals, illegal trafficking, 29
Arab Americans, 157. *See also* minorities; Muslims
Aristotle, 107
Arizona, 8, 22–23
Arizona Rangers, 8
Arizona v. Gant (2009), 187
Arizona v. Hicks (1987), 186
Arizona v. Roberson (1988), 189
Arlington, Virginia, 196
Arlington, Washington, 23
arm's reach doctrine, 184
arrests. *See also* probable cause; warrants

　analysis of, 68
　authority to arrest, 41, 181–182
　discretion in, 73–75
　false, 119
　by female police officers, 101
　jurisdiction on tribal lands, 22–23
　to maintain order, 71
　mandatory, 161
　Miranda rights, 187–191
　police injuries/fatalities during, 93–95
　of protestors/rioters, 10–12, 14
　statistics on, 13, 68, *69*, 77, 132
　from sting operations, 149–151
　types of, 68
arson, 27, 214–215
Ashcroft, John, 216
Ashley, Larry, 90
Asian Americans, 103, 156. *See also* minorities
assassinations and attempted assassinations, 9, 11, 40, 210
assaults, in line of duty, 94–95
assessment (SARA), 168–169
ATF. *See* Bureau of Alcohol, Tobacco, Firearms, and Explosives
Atlanta, Georgia, 7–8
Atlanta Police Department, 7–8
audio recorders, 149
Augustus, Caesar, *3*, 4
Austin, Stephen, 8
authority, in policing, 84
automated fingerprint identification system (AFIS), 196, 199–200
automatic vehicle location (AVL), 195
automobile exception, 186–187
auxiliaries, 44
auxiliary services units, 50
Aviation and Transportation Security Act (2001), 212

attention to lawsuits by, 119

crime prevention campaigns by,
162–163

Dateline "To Catch a Predator" sting,
149

portrayal of police by, 89, 109, 120,
141, 154

medical examination, 62

medical model, 167

mentally ill, 161, 170–171

mentoring, 143

merit employment, 41

methods of operation (MOs), 144

metropolitan law enforcement, 18, 19

Metropolitan Police Act (1829), 5

Michigan v. Mosley (1975), 189

Mieth v. Dothard (1976), 100

military, 37

military police agencies, 29

militia, 209–210

Minneapolis Domestic Violence Experiment,
161

minorities

adverse impact in selection of, 59, 99

bias-based policing and, 114–115,
155–156

challenges facing, in policing, 104–105

civil rights movement and, 11–12

discrimination after Civil War, 8

federal employees of, 25

performance review of, 101–102

physical agility testing and, 60

police-community relations and,
10–14, 23, 155–158

police shootings of, 12, 13–14, 76

recruitment of, 56

status in policing today, 102–104

Miranda, Ernesto, 188, *188*

Miranda rights, 187–191

Miranda rules (warnings), 188–189, *189*

Miranda v. Arizona (1966), 109, 179, 187

mitochondrial DNA (MtDNA) analysis, 203

mobile digital terminals (MDTs), 195

modus operandi, 144

morals. *See* ethics

Moran v. Burbine (1986), 190

Morash, Merry, 173

mortgage lending crash, 170

Mothers Against Drunk Driving (MAAD), 135

motorized patrol, 126–127

The Move to Community Policing (Morash
& Ford), 173

Mueller, Robert S., 26–27, 214

Muhammad, John Allen, 145

multiculturalism, 155

murder, 181, 190–191, 195

Murray, Jim, *148*

Muslims, 103, 114, 157. *See also* minorities

mutual pledge, 4

MySpace, 147

N

Namath, Joe, 37

National Advisory Commission on Criminal
Justice Standards and Goals, 125, 142

National Center for Community Policing, 167

National Clandestine Laboratory Registry,
145

National Commission on Terrorist Attacks
upon the United States, 212

national commissions, overseeing police,
109

National Conference on Preventing the
Conviction of Innocent Persons, 205

National Counter-Terrorism Academy, 217

National Counterterrorism Center (NCTC),
208

National Crime Information Center (NCIC),
196

National Crime Victimization Survey, 159

National Criminal History Record File, 200

National DNA Index System (NDIS),
203–204

National Guard, *9*, 12, 14, 15

National Highway Traffic Safety
Administration (NHTSA), 133–134,
135, 136

National Institute of Justice (NIJ), 22,
172, 201

National Institute of Justice report, 76,
78, 90

National Park Service, 28

National Prohibition, 9, 10, *10*

National Sheriff's Association (NSA), 159

*National Survey of Police Practices
Regarding the Criminal Investigations
Process*, 140

Native Americans. *See also* minorities

American frontier policing and, 8

Bureau of Indian Affairs, 22, 28, 156

police relations and, 156

tribal law enforcement and, 22–23

natural disaster, 15

Naval Criminal Investigative Service (NCIS),
29

NBC *Dateline* sting, 149

neck restraints, 77–78

negligence, 119

neighborhoods, 166–167, *167*, 171

Neighborhood Watch, *162*, 162–163

neo-Nazi National Alliance, 211

Newark (N.J.) Police Department, 7

New Mexico Mounted Patrol, 8

New Orleans Police Department (NOPD)

founding of, 7

Hurricane Katrina, 15, 87

strikes of, 45

New World Order, 209

New York City Police Department (NYPD)

CompStat and, 13, 14, 196–197

corruption in, 12, 109

founding of, 7

subway systems and, 217

terrorism and, 217

wild cat strike of, 45

New York v. Belton (1981), 187

New York v. Quarles (1984), 189

Nicomachean ethics, 107

night watch system, 5, 6–7

911

calls from cell phones, 195

differential response to, 129

enhanced 911 system, 195

origin of, 193

rapid response to, 123, 125–126

reverse 911 system, 130, 196

311 system and, 129

9/11 Commission Report, 212

noble cause corruption, 111

noncriminal regulations, enforcing, 71

nonsworn personnel, 41–42

norms, 82, 84

O

oath of office, 108

Office of Homeland Security, 211

Officer Next Door (OND) program,
171–172

Oklahoma City Federal Building bombing,
13, 81, 91, 209

Old West, 8

omnipresence, 71, 148

one-way radio, 9

open fields exception, 186

open fire, 148

operational stress, 88

operational styles, police, 72

operational units, 49

training unit, 50

transparency, police, 170

Transportation Security Administration (TSA), 28, 212, 213, *213*

transportation vehicles, 9, *9*, 131, 132–133

Triad program, 159, *159*

tribal law enforcement, 22–23

Trojanowicz, Robert C., 167

Truman, Harry S., 28

tuition reimbursement, 55

Twitter, 147

287(g) program, 24

two-pronged test, 183–184

two-way radio, 9

Tzu, Lao, 37

U

undercover investigation, 149–151

uniformed tactical operations, 131–132

unions, police, 9–10, 45–46

United States v. Leon (1984), 187

United States v. Martinez-Fuerte (1976), 187

United States v. Matlock (1974), 185

United States v. Place (1983), 182

United States v. Robinson (1973), 184

units, of police departments, 49–51

unity of command, 39

Unix system, 199

unknown problems/disturbances, 92

Urban Cohort, 4

Urban Homestead Initiative, 171–172

urban riots, 11–12, 155

U.S. armed forces, 25

U.S. Army, 22, 29

U.S. Census, 155, 156

U.S. Coast Guard, 15, 28, 213, *214*

U.S. Commission on Civil Rights, 91

U.S. Constitution, 25, 86, 108
    Fourth Amendment to, 180–187, 204
    Fifth Amendment to, 85, 181, 187, 188
    Fourteenth Amendment to, 99, 178–180, 188
    Eighteenth Amendment to, 10
    Twenty-first Amendment to, 10
    Amendments governing criminal justice system, 177–191, *178*

U.S. Criminal Code, 25

U.S. Customs Service, 28

U.S. Government Accountability Office, 77

U.S. Marines, 14, 217

U.S. Marshals, 26, 27

U.S. Navy Seals, 211, *211*

U.S. Park Police, 28

U.S. Postal Service, 29

U.S. Secret Service, 28

U.S. Supreme Court, 10, 108, 135, 151, 178–187

USA Patriot Act, 15, 212

V

Vanguard Justice Society v. Hughes (1979), 100

Varieties of Police Behavior (Wilson), 72

vice unit, 49

victims of crime
    domestic violence, 160–161
    Hispanic Americans as, 169
    people with disabilities as, 159
    relationship of criminal to, 74
    relationship of police officer to, 74
    senior citizens as, 159
    women as, 157

video recorders, 149

Vietnam War demonstrations, 10, 11

vigilantism, 8

Vigiles, 4

Vignera, Michael, 188

Violent Crime Control and Law Enforcement Act (Crime Bill), 22, 172

Virginia Tech shootings, 130

vision requirements, 54

voice stress analyzer, 60–61

Volstead Act, 10

volunteer officers, 44

W

Walker, Samuel, 110–111

walking a beat, 124–125

war, demonstrations against, 11

Ward, William Arthur, 37

war on drugs, 27

war on terror, 56

warrants, *180*, 180–187, 205

Washington D.C. Police Department, 132, 144–145, 197, 200

Washington State Patrol, 218

Washington (state) Stillaguamish Tribal Police, 23

watch and ward, 5

watchman style, 72

watchmen, 5, 6–7, 72

weapons, tracing, 27

Weber, Max, 34

Weeks v. United States (1914), 178, 180

weight requirements, 54

Wells, Alice Stebbins, 98

Westley, William, 83

Westover, Carl, 188

White, Jonathan R., 208

white-collar crime, 143, 150

white male backlash, 100–101

wildlife law enforcement agents, 29

Wilson, James Q., 126, 166–168

Wilson (N.C.) Police Department, 170

Wilson's operational styles, 72

Wolfgang, Marvin, 145

Wolf v. Colorado (1949), 180

women. *See also* minorities
    adverse impact in selection, 59, 99
    challenges facing, 104
    discrimination against, 97–98, 100
    domestic violence and, *75*, 113–114, 160–161
    hiring of, 21, 98–99, 101–102
    job performance of, 101
    physical agility testing and, 60
    representation of, 102
    as victims/offenders, 157

Women on Patrol (LEAA), 101

wooden clubs, 77

work environment, police, 88, 90

Working the Street (Brown), 82

World Church of the Creator, 211

World Trade Center
    1993 bombing of, 13, 209
    2001 9/11 attack on, 14–15, *15*

written entrance examination, 59–60

Wuestewald, Todd, 37–38, 39, 40

Wyoming, 21

Y

Yorkshire Ripper case, 197

youth, 49, 149, 159–160

Youth Crime Watch of America, 160

YouTube, 147

Z

zero-tolerance policing, 13, 173

Zhao, Jihong "Solomon," 173

NOTES

NOTES

NOTES

NOTES

Your Chapter in Review cards are explained here. Turn the page to see the review card for Chapter 1.

CHAPTER 1 | IN REVIEW
Police History

Chapter Summary

LO1 Discuss the Early Police

- The word police comes from the Latin word *politia*, which means "civil administration." Etymologically, the police can be seen as those involved in the administration of a city.

- The police represent the civil power of government, rather than the military power of government.

- Maintaining order and dealing with lawbreakers had previously been a private matter.

- At about the time of Christ, special, highly qualified members of the military formed the Praetorian Guard and could be considered the first group of police officers. Their job was to protect the palace and the emperor.

- Augustus established the Praefectus Urbi (Urban Cohort) and the Vigiles of Rome. Both groups had law enforcement responsibilities.

LO2 Discuss English Policing: Our English Heritage

- The American system of law and criminal justice was borrowed from the English.

- England's king, Alfred the Great, established a system of "society control" for citizens to group together and protect each other.

> **The chapter summary highlights important points from the chapter.**

- [...]r established a rudimentary criminal justice system [...] for law enforcement remained with the people [...]tablished (1) the watch and ward; (2) the hue and [...] the requirement that all males keep weapons in their homes for use in maintaining the public peace.

- Seventeenth-century English policing system was a form of individual, private police similar to the bounty hunter of the American West.

- In 1828, Sir Robert Peel, England's home secretary, drafted the first police bill, the *Act for Improving the Police in and near the Metropolis (the Metropolitan Police Act)*, which established the first large-scale, uniformed, organized, paid, civil police force in London. Peel has become known as the founder of modern policing, and early police were guided by his nine principles.

Sir Robert Peel.

© Photo By Time Life Pictures/Mansell/Time Life Pictures/ Getty Images

- The London Metropolitan Police was organized around the "beat system," in which officers were assigned to relatively small permanent posts and were expected to become familiar with them and the people residing there.

LO3 Discuss American Policing: The Colonial Experience

- By the seventeenth century, northern colonies started to institute a civil law enforcement system closely matching the English model with the county sheriff as the most important law official.

- In cities, the town marshal was the top law enforcement official with help from constables and night watchmen.

(continued on reverse)

Glossary Terms

> **Log onto www.cengagebrain.com to practice your vocabulary with flash cards and more.**

> **Find flash cards and more at www.cengagebrain.com. The shortcut box provides a quick reminder of the web address.**

[...]also patrolled Rome's streets to protect citizens.

LO2

mutual pledge A form of community self-protection developed by King Alfred the Great in the latter part of the ninth century in England.

hue and cry A method developed in early England for citizens to summon assistance from fellow members of the community.

constable An offici[...] [...]ned to keep the pe[...] system in En[...]

> **Glossary terms and definitions are grouped by the learning objective under which they appear.**

shire-reev[...] placed in ch[...] part of the s[...] evolved into[...] sheriff.

watch an[...] form of polic[...] against crim[...] men were required to serve on it.

thief-takers Private English citizens with no official status who were paid by the king for every criminal they arrested. They were similar to the bounty hunter of the American West.

Peel's Nine Principles Basic guidelines created by Sir Robert Peel for the London Metropolitan Police in 1829.

beat system System of policing created by Sir Robert Peel for the London Metropolitan Police in 1829 in which officers were assigned to relatively small permanent posts.

(continued on reverse)

Glossary Terms (continued)

LO3

slave patrols Police-type organizations created in the American South during colonial times to control slaves and support the southern economic system of slavery.

LO4

posse comitatus A common-law descendent of the old hue and cry. If a crime spree occurred or a dangerous criminal was in the area, the U.S. frontier sheriff would call upon the posse comitatus, a Latin term meaning "the power of the county."

LO5

Volstead Act (National Prohibition, Eighteenth Amendment) Became law in 1920 and forbade the sale and manufacture of alcohol.

CompStat Weekly crime strategy meetings, featuring the latest computerized crime statistics and high-stress brainstorming; developed by the New York City Police Department in the mid-1990s.

Rodney King incident The 1991 videotaped beating of an African American citizen by members of the Los Angeles police department.

terrorist attacks against the United States of America on September 11, 2001 The terrorist attacks committed by al-Qaeda.

Department of Homeland Security Federal cabinet department established in the aftermath of the terrorist attacks of September 11, 2001.

USA Patriot Act Public Law No. 107-56 passed in 2001 giving law enforcement new abilities to search, seize, detain, or eavesdrop in their pursuit of possible terrorists; full title of law is Uniting and Strengthening America by Providing Appropriate Tools Required to Intercept and Obstruct Terrorism.

Chapter Summary (continued)

- The southern colonies developed a formal system of social control to maintain the

Glossary terms and chapter summary points continue on the back of every card.

...Policing: Eighteenth and Nineteenth Centuries

- During the eighteenth century, the most common form of American law enforcement was the system of constables in the daytime and the watch at night.

- The first organized American police department was created in Boston in 1838, followed by New York City, Philadelphia, Chicago, New Orleans, Cincinnati, Baltimore, and Newark.

- In the American South, the former slave patrols eventually evolved into formal local police departments.

- On the frontier, early settlers faced many problems and formal law enforcement was rare. What little law enforcement existed consisted mainly of the sheriff and the town marshal.

- Some states and territories created their own police organizations. The Texas Rangers served as a border patrol for the Republic of Texas.

- The growing use of technology had a profound effect on American police departments from 1900 to 1960.

- The Boston police strike of 1919 increased interest in police reform and was a significant event in the history of policing along with National Prohibition.

LO5 Discuss American Policing: Twentieth and Twenty-First Centuries

- The 1960s and 1970s were probably the most turbulent era for policing in U.S. history. Numerous social problems permeated these decades, and the police were right in the middle of each problem.

- The 1980s and 1990s saw many positive developments ...mputers, a re... ...cepts of ... ...g po...

Key images from each chapter are highlighted on the Chapter in Review cards.

- As the world welcomed a new millennium, some of the same issues continued to dominate the police landscape: police misconduct, corruption, and brutality. There were also many positives for the police as the crime rate decline that had started in the 1990s continued into the 2000s, and as local, state, and federal law enforcement agencies reorganized and reengineered themselves to address the concerns of the new millennium.

Plane striking the World Trade Center on September 11, 2001.

© Photo By Peter C. Brandt/Getty Images

- The September 11, 2001, terrorist attacks on the United States changed policing to a degree that we cannot yet imagine. The demands ... ...e and disorder problems they face on the ... all the social problems they confront there, ...rotect citizens from terrorist attacks.

Additional resources are available at www.cengagebrain.com. Log in to access videos, flash cards, crossword puzzles and more.

...ed to the realization that local, state, and ... ...creation of the Department of Homeland Security, we...ll-equipped to handle a major natural disaster.

Log onto www.cengagebrain.com for additional study tools including videos, flash cards, games, self-quizzing, review exercises, web exercises, learning checks, and more.

Chapter Summary

LO1 Discuss the Early Police

- The word police comes from the Latin word *politia*, which means "civil administration." Etymologically, the police can be seen as those involved in the administration of a city.

- The police represent the civil power of government, rather than the military power of government.

- Maintaining order and dealing with lawbreakers had previously been a private matter.

- At about the time of Christ, special, highly qualified members of the military formed the Praetorian Guard and could be considered the first group of police officers. Their job was to protect the palace and the emperor.

- Augustus established the Praefectus Urbi (Urban Cohort) and the Vigiles of Rome. Both groups had law enforcement responsibilities.

LO2 Discuss English Policing: Our English Heritage

- The American system of law and criminal justice was borrowed from the English.

- England's king, Alfred the Great, established a system of "society control" for citizens to group together and protect each other.

- In 1285 c.e., the *Statute of Winchester* established a rudimentary criminal justice system in which most of the responsibility for law enforcement remained with the people themselves. The statute formally established (1) the watch and ward; (2) the hue and cry; (3) the parish constable; and (4) the requirement that all males keep weapons in their homes for use in maintaining the public peace.

- Seventeenth-century English policing system was a form of individual, private police similar to the bounty hunter of the American West.

- In 1828, Sir Robert Peel, England's home secretary, drafted the first police bill, the *Act for Improving the Police in and near the Metropolis (the Metropolitan Police Act)*, which established the first large-scale, uniformed, organized, paid, civil police force in London. Peel has become known as the founder of modern policing, and early police were guided by his nine principles.

Sir Robert Peel.

© Photo By Time Life Pictures/Mansell/Time Life Pictures/ Getty Images

- The London Metropolitan Police was organized around the "beat system," in which officers were assigned to relatively small permanent posts and were expected to become familiar with them and the people residing there.

LO3 Discuss American Policing: The Colonial Experience

- By the seventeenth century, northern colonies started to institute a civil law enforcement system closely matching the English model with the county sheriff as the most important law official.

- In cities, the town marshal was the top law enforcement official with help from constables and night watchmen.

(continued on reverse)

Glossary Terms

LO1

Praetorian Guard Select group of highly qualified members of the military established by the Roman emperor Augustus to protect him and his palace.

Vigiles Early Roman firefighters who also patrolled Rome's streets to protect citizens.

LO2

mutual pledge A form of community self-protection developed by King Alfred the Great in the latter part of the ninth century in England.

hue and cry A method developed in early England for citizens to summon assistance from fellow members of the community.

constable An official assigned to keep the peace in the mutual pledge system in England.

shire-reeve Early English official placed in charge of shires (counties) as part of the system of mutual pledge; evolved into the modern concept of the sheriff.

watch and ward A rudimentary form of policing, designed to protect against crime, disturbances, and fire. All men were required to serve on it.

thief-takers Private English citizens with no official status who were paid by the king for every criminal they arrested. They were similar to the bounty hunter of the American West.

Peel's Nine Principles Basic guidelines created by Sir Robert Peel for the London Metropolitan Police in 1829.

beat system System of policing created by Sir Robert Peel for the London Metropolitan Police in 1829 in which officers were assigned to relatively small permanent posts.

(continued on reverse)

Glossary Terms (continued)

LO3

slave patrols Police-type organizations created in the American South during colonial times to control slaves and support the southern economic system of slavery.

LO4

posse comitatus A common-law descendent of the old hue and cry. If a crime spree occurred or a dangerous criminal was in the area, the U.S. frontier sheriff would call upon the posse comitatus, a Latin term meaning "the power of the county."

LO5

Volstead Act (National Prohibition, Eighteenth Amendment) Became law in 1920 and forbade the sale and manufacture of alcohol.

CompStat Weekly crime strategy meetings featuring the latest computerized crime statistics and high-stress brainstorming; developed by the New York City Police Department in the mid-1990s.

Rodney King incident The 1991 videotaped beating of an African American citizen by members of the Los Angeles police department.

terrorist attacks against the United States of America on September 11, 2001 The terrorist attacks committed by al-Qaeda.

Department of Homeland Security Federal cabinet department established in the aftermath of the terrorist attacks of September 11, 2001.

USA Patriot Act Public Law No. 107-56 passed in 2001 giving law enforcement new abilities to search, seize, detain, or eavesdrop in their pursuit of possible terrorists; full title of law is Uniting and Strengthening America by Providing Appropriate Tools Required to Intercept and Obstruct Terrorism.

Chapter Summary (continued)

- The southern colonies developed a formal system of social control to maintain the institution of slavery.

LO4 Discuss American Policing: Eighteenth and Nineteenth Centuries

- During the eighteenth century, the most common form of American law enforcement was the system of constables in the daytime and the watch at night.

- The first organized American police department was created in Boston in 1838, followed by New York City, Philadelphia, Chicago, New Orleans, Cincinnati, Baltimore, and Newark.

- In the American South, the former slave patrols eventually evolved into formal local police departments.

- On the frontier, early settlers faced many problems and formal law enforcement was rare. What little law enforcement existed consisted mainly of the sheriff and the town marshal.

- Some states and territories created their own police organizations. The Texas Rangers served as a border patrol for the Republic of Texas.

- The growing use of technology had a profound effect on American police departments from 1900 to 1960.

- The Boston police strike of 1919 increased interest in police reform and was a significant event in the history of policing along with National Prohibition.

LO5 Discuss American Policing: Twentieth and Twenty-First Centuries

- The 1960s and 1970s were probably the most turbulent era for policing in U.S. history. Numerous social problems permeated these decades, and the police were right in the middle of each problem.

- The 1980s and 1990s saw many positive developments including better use of computers, a reduction in violent crime, and new concepts of community policing and problem-solving policing.

Plane striking the World Trade Center on September 11, 2001.

© Photo By Peter C. Brandt/Getty Images

- As the world welcomed a new millennium, some of the same issues continued to dominate the police landscape: police misconduct, corruption, and brutality. There were also many positives for the police as the crime rate decline that had started in the 1990s continued into the 2000s, and as local, state, and federal law enforcement agencies reorganized and reengineered themselves to address the concerns of the new millennium.

- The September 11, 2001, terrorist attacks on the United States changed policing to a degree that we cannot yet imagine. The demands on the police to confront the serious crime and disorder problems they face on the streets, as well as to attempt to ameliorate all the social problems they confront there, have been increased with new duties to protect citizens from terrorist attacks.

- The disaster caused by Hurricane Katrina led to the realization that local, state, and federal government agencies, despite the creation of the Department of Homeland Security, were ill-equipped to handle a major natural disaster.

 Log onto www.cengagebrain.com for additional study tools including videos, flash cards, games, self-quizzing, review exercises, web exercises, learning checks, and more.

Chapter Summary

LO1 Explain the U.S. Public Security Industry

- For the latest reporting year, local, state, and federal agencies spent approximately $185 billion for criminal justice agencies, including police, corrections, and judicial services—an increase of 418 percent from 20 years ago.

LO2 Discuss Local Law Enforcement

- The term local law enforcement or local police refers to the vast majority of all the law enforcement employees in the United States.

Municipal or city governments operate the vast majority of the nearly 12,575 local police departments in the United States.

© iStockphoto.com/Stuartb

LO3 Describe State Law Enforcement

- 49 of the 50 U.S. states have primary state law enforcement agencies. State police departments were developed to deal with growing crime in nonurban areas of the country.

Many small, remote towns and villages cannot afford to hire local police officers and often rely on state troopers.

© Ronald Karpilo/Alamy

(continued on reverse)

Glossary Terms

Log onto www.cengagebrain.com to practice your vocabulary with flash cards and more.

LO1

local control The formal and informal use of local or neighborhood forms of government and measures to deter abhorrent behaviors.

LO3

centralized model of state law enforcement Combines the duties of major criminal investigations with the patrol of state highways.

decentralized model of state law enforcement A clear distinction between traffic enforcement on state highways and other state-level law enforcement functions.

TABLE 2.3 Major Federal Law Enforcement Agencies

Department of Justice

Federal Bureau of Investigation

Drug Enforcement Administration

U.S. Marshals Service

Bureau of Alcohol, Tobacco, Firearms, and Explosives

Department of the Treasury

Internal Revenue Service—Criminal Investigation Division

Executive Office for Asset Forfeiture

Executive Office for Terrorist Financing and Financial Crime

Office of Foreign Assets Control

Financial Crimes Enforcement Network

Department of Homeland Security (See Chapter 15)

Department of the Interior

National Park Service

Fish and Wildlife Service

U.S. Park Police

Bureau of Indian Affairs

Bureau of Land Management

Bureau of Reclamation

Department of Defense

Army Criminal Investigation Division

Naval Criminal Investigative Service

Air Force Office of Special Investigations

U.S. Postal Service

Postal Inspections Service

Department of Agriculture

U.S. Forest Service

Department of Commerce

Bureau of Export Enforcement

National Marine Fisheries Administration

Department of Labor

Office of Labor Racketeering

Department of State

Diplomatic Security Service

Other Federal Law Enforcement Agencies

Amtrak Police

Bureau of Engraving and Printing Police

U.S. Capitol Police

U.S. Mint Police

U.S. Supreme Court Police

Library of Congress Police

National Gallery of Art Police

Veterans Health Administration

SOURCE: Reaves, Brian A. *Federal Law Enforcement Officers, 2004.* Washington, D.C.: Bureau of Justice Statistics, 2006.

Chapter Summary (continued)

LO4 Discuss Federal Law Enforcement

- Federal law enforcement agencies employed more than 105,000 full-time federal law enforcement personnel authorized to make arrests and carry firearms.

LO5 Explain International Police

- The International Criminal Police Organization (Interpol) was established for the development of cooperation among nations regarding common police problems.

- Interpol's mission is to track and provide information that may help other law enforcement agencies apprehend fugitives, thwart criminal schemes, exchange experience and technology, and analyze international criminal activity trends.

Some Interesting FACTS about Sheriffs' Offices Today

25% of departments use foot patrol routinely.

10% use regular bicycle patrol.

94% participate in a 911 emergency system compared with **28%** in 1987, and **71%** employ enhanced 911.

36% have officers assigned full time to a special unit for drug enforcement, and nearly a quarter assign officers to a multi-agency drug task force.

10% maintain a written community policing plan, and **51%** use full-time community policing officers.

60% have problem-solving partnerships or written agreements with community groups.

47% use full-time school resource officers.

Nearly all have a written policy on pursuit driving, and about half of them restrict vehicle pursuits according to specific criteria.

97% have a written policy on the use of deadly force, and **89%** have a policy on the use of nonlethal force.

Nearly half have a written plan specifying actions to be taken in a terrorist attack.

96% authorize use of chemical agents such as pepper spray, up from **52%** in 1990.

Two-thirds use video cameras in patrol cars.

SOURCE: Hickman, Matthew J. and Brian A. Reaves, *Sheriff's Offices, 2003.* Washington, D.C.: Bureau of Justice Statistics, 2006, pp. iii, iv.

 Log onto www.cengagebrain.com for additional study tools including videos, flash cards, games, self-quizzing, review exercises, web exercises, learning checks, and more.

Chapter Summary

LO1 Define the Major Managerial Concepts of Organizing a Police Department

- The major managerial concepts common to most organizations are division of labor, managerial definitions, leadership, organizational model and structure, chain of command (hierarchy of authority), span of control, delegation of responsibility and authority, unity of command, and rules, regulations, and discipline.

FIGURE 3.3

Chain of Command from Chief to Patrol Officer

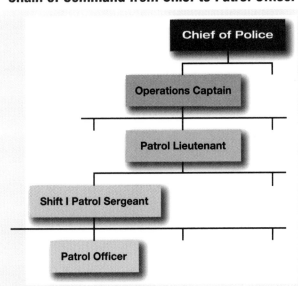

SOURCE: Sheehan, Robert and Cordner, Gary W. Adapted from *Introduction to Police Administration*, 2nd ed., p. 189. Matthew Bender & Company, Inc., 1998. Reprinted by permission of the authors.

LO2 Discuss Alternative Organizations, Models, and Structures for Organizing a Police Department

- Most police organizations use quasi-military or military models of organization, which has led to the professionalization of the police but resulted in a lack of participation by the rank and file. This has also caused a paradox of leadership in policing since most decisions in policing are actually made by police officers acting autonomously on the street.

LO3 Describe Methods of Organizing a Police Department by Personnel

- The civil service system has resulted in eliminating much political influence, favoritism, nepotism, and bias in police employee management.

(continued on reverse)

Glossary Terms

LO1

organization A deliberate arrangement of people doing specific jobs, following particular procedures to accomplish a set of goals determined by some authority.

bureaucracy An organizational model marked by hierarchy, promotion on professional merit and skill, the development of a career service, reliance on and use of rules and regulations, and impersonality of relationships among career professionals in the bureaucracy and with their clientele.

management The process of running an organization so that the organization can accomplish its goals.

PODSCORB Acronym for the basic functions of management: planning, organizing, directing, staffing, coordinating, reporting, and budgeting.

leadership An influential relationship among leaders and followers who intend real changes that reflect their mutual purposes.

quasi-military organization An organization similar to the military along structures of strict authority and reporting relations.

chain of command Managerial concept stating that each individual in an organization is supervised by and reports to only one immediate supervisor.

span of control The number of officers or subordinates a superior can supervise effectively.

unity of command A managerial concept that specifies that each individual in an organization is directly accountable to only one supervisor.

LO2

shared leadership Power-sharing arrangement in which workplace influence is shared among individuals who are otherwise hierarchical unequals.

(continued on reverse)

Glossary Terms (continued)

L○3

civil service system A method of hiring and managing government employees that is designed to eliminate political influence, favoritism, nepotism, and bias.

Pendleton Act A federal law passed in 1883 to establish a civil service system that tested, appointed, and promoted officers on a merit system.

sworn members Police employees given traditional police powers by state and local laws, including penal or criminal laws and criminal procedure laws.

nonsworn (civilian) members Police employees without traditional police powers generally assigned to noncritical or nonenforcement tasks.

squad A group of officers who generally work together all the time under the supervision of a particular sergeant.

platoon All of the people working on a particular tour or shift.

civilianization The process of removing sworn officers from noncritical or nonenforcement tasks and replacing them with civilians or nonsworn employees.

reserve officer Either part-time compensated or noncompensated sworn police employees who serve when needed.

lateral transfers The ability and opportunity to transfer from one police department to another.

blue flu Informal job actions by officers in which they refuse to perform certain job functions in an attempt to win labor concessions from their employers.

L○4

beat The smallest geographical area an individual officer can patrol.

precinct/district/station The entire collection of beats in a given geographic area; the organizational headquarters of a police department.

Chapter Summary (continued)

L○4 Explain Methods of Organizing a Police Department by Area

- The size of the geographic area many police agencies cover forces them to subdivide the area into smaller areas of responsibility, such as beats.

L○5 Describe Methods of Organizing a Police Department by Time

- Because of the responsibility of being available 24 hours a day, 7 days a week, the police often employ a three-tour system.

L○6 Discuss Methods of Organizing a Police Department by Function or Purpose

- The functions the police are charged with performing are complex and diverse: maintain order, enforce the law, and provide services to citizens. These functions are generally charged to a department's operational units—primarily patrol, criminal investigations, traffic, and community services units. The police also perform administrative duties and auxiliary services.

TABLE 3.1 Organizing a Police Department by Function or Purpose

Operations	Administration	Auxiliary Services
Patrol	Personnel	Records
Traffic	Training	Communications
Criminal investigations	Planning and analysis	Property
Vice	Budget and finance	Laboratory
Organized crime	Legal assistance	Detention
Juvenile services	Public information	Identification
Community services	Clerical/secretarial	Alcohol testing
Crime prevention	Inspections	Facilities
Community relations	Internal affairs	Equipment
	Intelligence	Supply
		Maintenance

SOURCE: Used with permission from Robert Sheehan and Gary W. Cordner, *Introduction to Police Administration*, 2nd ed., pp. 114–115. Copyright 1998 Matthew Bender & Company, Inc., a member of the LexisNexis Group. All rights reserved.

 Log onto www.cengagebrain.com for additional study tools including videos, flash cards, games, self-quizzing, review exercises, web exercises, learning checks, and more.

Chapter Summary

LO1 Find Information on Jobs in Law Enforcement

- Many jobs are available in policing at the federal, state, and local levels, including a growing number of civilian positions. The most convenient way to find out about law enforcement jobs, department standards, and the testing process is through law enforcement websites.

Job Hunt
- ☐ papers
- ☐ human resources/personnel offices
- ☐ agency websites
- ☐ law enforcement websites
- ☐ discoverpolicing.org
- ☐ officers I see on the street
- ☐ career fairs
- ☐ high school / college placement offices

© Kevin Renes/www.Shutterstock.com

LO2 Explain the Standards in the Police Selection Process

- The standards for hiring police officers have changed in recent years to facilitate the inclusion of more females and minorities. The police standards cover physical, age, and education requirements, as well as criminal record restrictions.

LO3 Discuss the Recruitment Process

- The recruitment process that law enforcement employers use has changed over the years to address the evolving challenges.

 Log onto www.cengagebrain.com to practice your vocabulary with flash cards and more.

Glossary Terms

LO2

tuition reimbursement Money a police department will pay officers to reimburse them for tuition expenses while they are employed by the police department and are pursuing a college degree.

LO3

recruitment process The effort to attract the best people to apply for the police force.

police cadet A nonsworn law enforcement position for young adults age 18 and over. Generally, these positions are part-time, paid, education-oriented positions in police departments, and the targeted candidates are college students interested in moving into a law enforcement career.

civilianization Replacing sworn positions with civilian employees. Some positions that are often civilianized include call takers, dispatchers, front desk personnel, crime analysts, crime prevention specialists, accident investigators, crime scene technicians, public information officers, and training personnel.

LO4

job analysis Identifies the important tasks that must be performed by police officers, and then identifies the knowledge, skills, and abilities necessary to perform those tasks.

knowledge, skills, and abilities (KSAs) Talents or attributes necessary to do a particular job.

job-related Concept that job requirements must be necessary for the performance of the job a person is applying for.

LO5

selection process The steps or tests an individual must progress through before being hired as a police officer.

emotional intelligence The ability to interpret, understand, and manage one's own and others' emotions. This encompasses the competencies

(continued on reverse)

(continued on reverse)

Glossary Terms (continued)

valued in law enforcement such as self-awareness, self-control, conflict management, and leadership.

adverse impact A form of de facto discrimination resulting from a testing element that discriminates against a particular group, essentially keeping members of that group out of the applicant pool.

physical agility test A test of physical fitness to determine if a candidate has the needed strength and endurance to perform the job of police officer.

polygraph Also called a lie detector test; a mechanical device designed to ascertain whether a person is telling the truth.

background investigation The complete and thorough investigation of an applicant's past life, including education, employment, military service, driving record, criminal history, relationships, and character. This includes verification of all statements made by the applicant on the background form and the evaluation of detected and undetected behavior to make a determination if the candidate is the type of person suited to a career in law enforcement.

LO6

police academy The initial formal training that a new police officer receives to learn police procedures, state laws, and objectives of law enforcement. The academy gives police officers the KSAs to accomplish the police job.

field training An on-the-job training program that occurs after the police academy under the direction of an FTO.

field training officer (FTO) An experienced officer who mentors and trains a new police officer.

Hogan's Alley A shooting course in which simulated "good guys" and "bad guys" pop up, requiring police officers to make split-second decisions.

in-service training Training that occurs during a police officer's career, usually on a regular basis and usually within the department; often required by department policy or state mandate.

probationary period The period in the early part of an officer's career in which the officer can be dismissed if not performing to the department's standards.

Chapter Summary (continued)

LO4 Define and Explain the Job Analysis

- A job analysis is conducted by the law enforcement agency to determine the knowledge, skills, and abilities (KSAs) needed for the job, and these are incorporated into the selection process.

LO5 Explain the Police Selection Process

- The selection process is lengthy and usually involves a series of examinations, interviews, and investigative steps designed to select the best candidate to appoint to a police department from the many who apply.

FIGURE 4.1

Screening methods used in the selection of new officer recruits in local police departments across the nation.

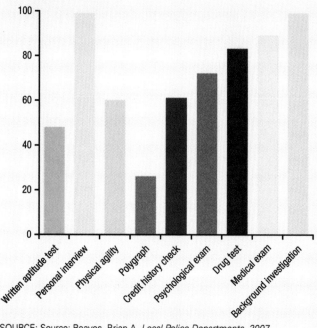

SOURCE: Source: Reaves, Brian A. *Local Police Departments, 2007.* Washington, D.C.: Bureau of Justice Statistics, 2010.

LO6 Explain the Police Training Process, the Probationary Period, and In-Service Training

- Recruit training consists of training in a police academy followed by field training.

- Recruits will then complete a probationary period usually lasting from 12 to 18 months. Police training will continue throughout an officer's career.

 Log onto www.cengagebrain.com for additional study tools including videos, flash cards, games, self-quizzing, review exercises, web exercises, learning checks, and more.

Chapter Summary

LO1 Define the Police Role and the Ambiguity of the Police Role

- The two major ways of looking at the police role are the crime-fighting role (law enforcement) and the order maintenance role (peacekeeping and providing social services). The police role is very ambiguous, but thinking about the role of the police has increased since September 11, 2001.

LO2 Discuss the Goals and Objectives of Policing

- The two primary goals and objectives of police departments are maintaining order and protecting life and property. Secondary goals include preventing crime, arresting and prosecuting offenders, recovering stolen and missing property, assisting sick and injured people, enforcing noncriminal regulations, and delivering services not available elsewhere in the community.

An officer responds to a call by neighbors about children left at home alone. Protecting life is one of the primary goals of police departments.

© Joel Gordon

LO3 Explain Police Operational Styles

- Many researchers suggest that police officers adopt a police operational style in thinking about their role in society and how they should do their jobs.

LO4 Discuss Police Discretion

- An important aspect of a police officer's job is the exercise of discretion, what it means, how and why it is exercised, what factors influence the use of discretion by the police, and how police departments can attempt to control discretion.

Glossary Terms

Log onto www.cengagebrain.com to practice your vocabulary with flash cards and more.

LO1

police role The concept of "what do the police do."

order maintenance Major view of the role of the police that emphasizes keeping the peace and providing social services.

crime-fighting role A major view of the role of the police that emphasizes crime-fighting or law enforcement.

ambiguous Not clearly defined; having several possible interpretations.

LO2

omnipresence A concept that suggests that the police are always present or always seem to be present.

LO3

police operational styles Styles adopted by police officers as a way of thinking about the role of the police and law in society.

LO4

discretion Freedom to act or decide a matter on one's own.

(continued on reverse)

(continued on reverse)

Glossary Terms (continued)

LO5

deadly force Force that can cause death.

fleeing felon doctrine Doctrine widely followed prior to the 1960s that allowed police officers to use deadly force to apprehend a fleeing felon.

Tennessee v. Garner U.S. Supreme Court case that ended the use of the fleeing felon rule.

defense of life standard Doctrine allowing police officers to use deadly force against individuals using deadly force against an officer or others.

less-than-lethal weapons Innovative alternatives to traditional firearms, such as batons, bodily force techniques, chemical irritant sprays, and Tasers or stun guns.

Chapter Summary (continued)

LO5 Discuss Police Discretion and Police Shootings and the Use of Deadly Force

- Despite common perceptions, police rarely use force. Police shootings or the use of deadly force by the police might be the ultimate use of discretion by the police.

A police officer knocking a suspect off his feet using a new weapon. The weapon's effect is causing the fence behind him to appear distorted.

© Pascal Goetgheluck/Photo Researchers, Inc.

Log onto www.cengagebrain.com for additional study tools including videos, flash cards, games, self-quizzing, review exercises, web exercises, learning checks, and more.

Chapter Summary

LO1 Define the Police Culture or Subculture and the Police Personality

- The police culture or police subculture is a combination of shared norms, values, goals, career patterns, lifestyles, and occupational structures that is somewhat different from the combination held by the rest of society, and is characterized by clannishness, secrecy, and isolation from those not in the group.

POLICE CULTURE

▶ honor

▶ loyalty

▶ individuality

Photo © Medicanela/dreamstime.
Figure © 2013 Cengage Learning.

LO2 Explain Police Stress

- Stress is the body's reaction to internal or external stimuli that upset the body's normal state. The body's reaction to highly stressful situations is known as the flight-or-fight response.

- Police have higher rates of divorce, suicide, alcoholism and other manifestations of stress than other professions.

Flight-or-fight response.

© AP Photo/The Wilson Daily Times, Grant Roberson

Glossary Terms

LO1

police culture or police subculture A combination of shared norms, values, goals, career patterns, lifestyles, and occupational structures that is somewhat different from the combination held by the rest of society.

blue wall of silence A figurative protective barrier erected by the police in which officers protect one another from outsiders, often even refusing to aid police superiors or other law enforcement officials in investigating wrongdoing of other officers.

blue curtain A concept developed by William Westley that claims police officers trust only other police officers and do not aid in the investigation of wrongdoing by other officers.

police personality Traits common to most police officers. Scholars have reported that this personality is thought to include such traits as authoritarianism, suspicion, hostility, insecurity, conservatism, and cynicism.

police cynicism An attitude that there is no hope for the world and a view of humanity at its worst.

***Dirty Harry* problem** A moral dilemma faced by police officers in which they may feel forced to take certain illegal actions to achieve a greater good.

LO2

flight-or-fight response The body's reaction to highly stressful situations in which it is getting prepared for extraordinary physical exertion.

suicide by cop The phenomenon in which a person wishing to die deliberately places an officer in a life-threatening situation, thus resulting in the officer using deadly force against that person.

(continued on reverse)

(continued on reverse)

Glossary Terms (continued)

LO3

police suicide The intentional taking of one's own life by a police officer.

LO4

AIDS Acquired immune deficiency syndrome.

Chapter Summary (continued)

LO3 Discuss Police Suicide

- The suicide rate for police officers is three times that of the general population, and three times as many officers kill themselves compared with the number of officers killed by criminals in the line of duty.

LO4 Discuss Police Danger

- In 2010, 128 state and local law enforcement officers were feloniously slain or accidentally killed in the line of duty.

- In 2009, over 57,368, assaults were committed against state and local police officers.

Police officers perform necessary and often dangerous tasks.

© Lilac Mountain/www.Shutterstock.com

Chapter Summary

LO1 Describe the History and Problems of Minorities in Policing and How It Impacted Their Ability to Obtain Jobs and Promotions in Law Enforcement

- Law enforcement agencies in the United States have a long history of discrimination against minorities resulting in women not being given full patrol duties until the 1970s and African American officers often being restricted in the types of functions they could perform.

LO2 Discuss the Provisions of the U.S. Legal System that Enabled Minorities to Overcome Job Discrimination

- The fight for equality was facilitated by the 1964 Civil Rights Act, which barred discrimination on the basis of gender, race, color, religion, or national origin yet despite recommendations by national commissions, minorities were forced to take their cases to the U.S. courts.

The Path to Equality: Court Cases

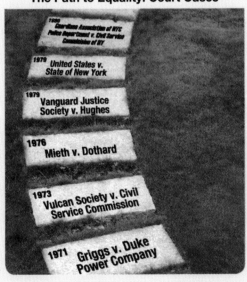

1980 Guardians Association of NYC Police Department v. Civil Service Commission of NY

1979 United States v. State of New York

1979 Vanguard Justice Society v. Hughes

1976 Mieth v. Dothard

1973 Vulcan Society v. Civil Service Commission

1971 Griggs v. Duke Power Company

Photo © iStockphoto/Hsing-Wen Hsu. Photo illustration by Spitting Images for Cengage Learning.

LO3 Discuss the Issue of White Male Backlash

- Affirmative action programs and quotas gave rise to white male backlash.

LO4 Introduce the Academic Studies Reviewing the Performance of Minorities in Police Work

- Academic studies indicated that minorities could perform the duties involved in the patrol function.

LO5 Describe the Status of the Various Minority Groups in Law Enforcement Today

- Minorities are now making their way into administrative positions in law enforcement agencies.

(continued on reverse)

Glossary Terms

 Log onto www.cengagebrain.com to practice your vocabulary with flash cards and more.

LO1

job discrimination Unequal treatment of persons in personnel decisions on the basis of their race, religion, national origin, gender, or sexual orientation.

double marginality The expectation by white officers that African American officers will give members of their own race better treatment and the simultaneous hostility from the African American community that black officers are traitors to their race.

LO2

Fourteenth Amendment Amendment to the U.S. Constitution passed in 1868 that guarantees "equal protection of the law" to all citizens of the United States; frequently used to govern employment equality in the United States.

Civil Rights Act of 1964 Prohibits job discrimination based on race, color, religion, sex, or national origin.

Equal Employment Opportunity Act of 1972 (EEOA) Extended the 1964 Civil Rights Act and made it applicable to state and local governments.

de facto discrimination The indirect result of policies or practices that are not intended to discriminate, but do, in fact, discriminate.

affirmative action An active effort to improve employment or educational opportunities for minorities. This includes ensuring equal opportunity as well as redressing past discrimination.

(continued on reverse)

Glossary Terms (continued)

quota Numbers put in place as part of goals and objectives in affirmative action plans.

reverse discrimination The label often attached to the preferential treatment received by minority groups.

Chapter Summary (continued)

LO6 Examine Some of the Current and Emerging Challenges Faced by Minorities in Law Enforcement in Current Times

- Challenges remain to achieve appropriate representation of underrepresented groups in law enforcement.

CHALLENGES facing women today

- Women's perception of the job
- Recruitment
- Acceptance by coworkers
- Workplace harassment
- Dating and relationships
- Pregnancy
- Family issues

Photo © iofoto/www.Shutterstock.com. Figure © 2013 Cengage Learning.

CHALLENGES facing African Americans and other minorities

- Recruitment
- Acceptance by coworkers
- Workplace harassment
- Competition from the private sector
- Tokenism
- Job assignments
- Friendly fire incidents

Photo © David Hiller/Jupiter Images. Figure © 2013 Cengage Learning.

Log onto www.cengagebrain.com for additional study tools including videos, flash cards, games, self-quizzing, review exercises, web exercises, learning checks, and more.

Chapter Summary

LO1 Define and Describe Ethics

- Ethics is defined as the study of what is good or bad conduct and is critical in understanding and confronting police misconduct.

LO2 Discuss the Various Ways Police Actions Are Reviewed

- Police corruption has been around for many years, and several high-profile incidents have led to the formation of commissions to study the problem.

National Commissions overseeing the Police

1931	National Commission on Law Observance and Enforcement (Wickersham Commission)
1967	President's Commission on Law Enforcement and Administration of Justice
1968	National Advisory Commission on Civil Disorders
1973	National Advisory Commission on Criminal Justice Standards and Goals
1982	Commission on Accreditation for Law Enforcement Agencies

© 2013 Cengage Learning.

LO3 Identify the Various Definitions, Types, and Extent of Police Corruption and Explore the Reasons for Police Corruption

- A police officer is corrupt when he or she is acting in his or her official capacity and receives a benefit or something of value (other than a paycheck) for doing something or for refraining from doing something.

© Dave L. Ryan/Photolibrary

There is an ongoing debate as to whether accepting a free cup of coffee is a form of corruption.

(continued on reverse)

Glossary Terms

LO1

ethics The study of what constitutes good or bad conduct.

corruption Acts involving misuse of authority by a police officer in a manner designed to produce personal gain for the officer or others.

LO2

Knapp Commission Commission created in 1970 to investigate allegations of widespread, organized corruption in the New York City Police Department.

judicial review Process by which the actions of the police in areas such as arrests, search and seizure, and custodial interrogation are reviewed by the court system to ensure their constitutionality.

LO3

grass-eaters Police officers who participate in the more passive type of police corruption by accepting opportunities of corruption that present themselves.

meat-eaters Officers who participate in a more aggressive type of corruption by seeking out and taking advantage of opportunities of corruption.

gratuities Items of value received by someone because of his or her role or job rather than because of a personal relationship.

bribe Payment of money or other contribution to a police officer with the intent of subverting the aim of the criminal justice system.

"rotten apple" theory Theory of corruption in which it is believed that individual officers within the agency are bad, rather than the organization as a whole begin bad.

noble cause corruption Stems from ends-oriented policing and involves police officers bending the rules to achieve the "right" goal of putting a criminal in jail.

(continued on reverse)

Glossary Terms (continued)

LO4

police deception Form of misconduct that includes perjury and falsifying police reports.

LO5

biased-based policing Any police-initiated activity that relies on a person's race or ethnic background rather than on the person's behavior as a basis for identifying that individual as being involved in criminal activity.

LO7

internal affairs division The unit of a police agency that is charged with investigating police corruption or misconduct.

integrity test Proactive investigation of corruption in which investigators provide opportunities for officers to commit illegal acts.

citizen oversight Also referred to as civilian review or external review. A method that allows for the independent citizen review of complaints filed against the police through a board or committee that independently reviews allegations of misconduct.

LO8

civil liability Potential liability for payment of damages as a result of a ruling in a lawsuit.

criminal liability Being subject to punishment for a crime.

Chapter Summary (continued)

LO4 Describe Other Forms of Police Misconduct Including Drug-Related Corruption, Police Deception, Sex-Related Corruption, and Domestic Violence

- Other forms of police misconduct include drug-related corruption, sleeping on duty, police deception, sex-related corruption, and domestic violence in police families.

LO5 Define and Discuss Biased-Based Policing

- Biased-based policing is an issue that has been addressed in the last two decades and most departments collect data to examine the issue in their jurisdiction.

LO6 Discuss the Definition, Types, and Extent of Police Brutality

- Although use of force is a necessary part of the job, it must be reasonable and appropriate. When officers cross the line, force becomes excessive.

LO7 Explore Various Responses to Police Corruption

- There are many different responses to police corruption, including investigations, discipline, and termination. Preventive actions can also be taken to minimize the occurrences of corruption and misconduct.

RESPONSES TO CORRUPTION
- investigation
- discipline
- termination
- decertification

Photo © Patrick Hermans/www.Shutterstock.com. Figure © 2013 Cengage Learning.

LO8 Discuss the Issue of Liability and the Effects of Lawsuits on Police Officers and Police Agencies

- Police may be held liable for their actions through the state courts or the federal courts.

Chapter Summary

LO1 Understand the Traditional Methods of Doing Police Work and Examine Their Effectiveness

- The three cornerstones of traditional police work are random routine patrol, rapid response to calls by citizens to 911, and retroactive investigation of past crimes by detectives.

LO2 Discuss the Activities Involved in the Patrol Function

- Many activities comprise patrol operations including enforcing laws and keeping the peace.

ACTIVITIES OF A PATROL OFFICER:

- Enforcing laws
- Deterring crime
- Maintaining order
- Keeping the peace
- Enforcing traffic laws
- Keeping traffic flowing
- Investigating accidents
- Conducting preliminary investigations
- Responding to calls for assistance
- Assisting vulnerable populations

LO3 Describe the Findings of the Kansas City Patrol Study

- The Kansas City study indicated that the amount of random patrol had no effect on crime or the citizens' fear of crime.

LO4 Examine the Issue of Rapid Response to Citizens' 911 Calls

- Rapid police response to calls was found to be not as critical as once thought because of delays outside the police control.

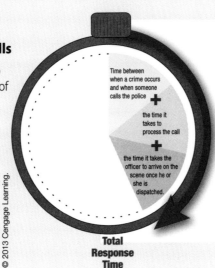

Time between when a crime occurs and when someone calls the police **+** the time it takes to process the call **+** the time it takes the officer to arrive on the scene once he or she is dispatched.

Total Response Time

© 2013 Cengage Learning.

(continued on reverse)

Glossary Terms

 Log onto www.cengagebrain.com to practice your vocabulary with flash cards and more.

LO1

random routine patrol Officers driving around a designated geographic area.

rapid response to citizens' calls to 911 Officers being dispatched to calls immediately, regardless of the type of call.

retroactive investigation of past crimes by detectives The follow-up investigation of crimes by detectives that occurs after a crime has been reported.

LO2

foot patrol Police officers walk a beat or assigned area rather than patrolling in a motor vehicle.

LO3

Kansas City patrol study The first study conducted to test the effectiveness of random routine patrol.

LO5

evidence-based policing Using available scientific research on policing to implement crime-fighting strategies and department policies.

LO6

directed patrol Officers patrol specific locations at specific times to address a specific crime problem.

split-force patrol A method in which the patrol force is split; half responds to calls for service and the other half performs directed patrol activities.

differential response to calls for service The police response to calls for service varies according to the type and severity of the call.

(continued on reverse)

Glossary Terms (continued)

LO8

saturation patrol Assigning a larger number of uniformed officers than normal to an area to deal with a particular crime problem.

bike patrol Officers patrol an assigned area on bicycle rather than in a patrol car.

LO9

red light cameras Automated cameras mounted on poles at intersections. The cameras are triggered when a vehicle enters the intersection after the light has turned red. The camera records the violation and the license plate number. A citation and the photos are sent to the owner of the vehicle along with instructions on how to pay the fine or contest the ticket.

police pursuits The attempt by law enforcement to apprehend alleged criminals in a moving motor vehicle when the driver is trying to elude capture and increases speed or takes evasive action.

police pursuit policies Policies regulating the circumstances and conditions under which the police should pursue or chase motorists driving at high speeds in a dangerous manner.

LO10

police paramilitary unit (PPU) A term popularized in the late 1990s to refer to police units organized in a more militaristic manner (such as SWAT teams), with their primary function being to threaten or use force collectively.

Chapter Summary (continued)

LO5 Discuss Some of the Innovative Ways of Performing the Patrol Function

- Departments should use evidence-based policing and other innovative ideas in an effort to work smarter.

LO6 Describe Some of the Innovative Ways of Responding to 911 Calls and Crime Problems in the Community

- Police can better manage their resources by responding to calls based on the severity and importance of the calls and employing differential response alternatives.

LO7 Examine New Methods of Resource Allocation

- Police agencies are exploring the most effective ways of allocating their personnel.

LO8 Discuss New Tactical Approaches to Patrol Operations

- Police officers can use a variety of methods to fight crime and serve their community, including vehicle patrol, foot patrol, bicycle patrol, mounted patrol, and other innovative methods, such as scooters, multi-terrain vehicles, and mobile substations.

© Michael Rubin/www.Shutterstock.com

LO9 Describe New Efforts to Combat the Drunk Driving Problem and Efforts Targeting Aggressive Driving

- Law enforcement is using more innovative techniques in an effort to attack the DUI and aggressive driving problems.

LO10 Discuss Special Operations, Including SWAT Teams, Emergency Service Units, and K-9 Units

- SWAT teams, ESUs, and K-9 units supplement the patrol mission in fighting crime.

 Log onto www.cengagebrain.com for additional resources including videos, flash cards, games, self-quizzing, review exercises, web exercises, learning checks, and more.

Chapter Summary

LO1 Discuss Traditional Detective Operations

- The Rand study, *The Criminal Investigation Process*, revealed that a lot of detectives' time was spent unproductively and, consequently, investigations were not being efficiently conducted.

LO2 Describe the Activities of a Detective in a Police Agency

- Detective units may be organized on a decentralized or centralized basis.

Photo of "All Felonies" detective courtesy John Kruse, Wenatchee Police Dept. Photo of "Burglary," Homicide" and "Auto Theft" detectives courtesy M.J. Rose Images. Photo of "All Felonies" desk plaque © Alaettin YILDIRIM/ www.Shutterstock.com. Photo of remaining desk plaques © zimmytws/www.Shutterstock.com. Photo illustration by Spitting Images for Cengage Learning.

LO3 Introduce Alternatives to Retroactive Investigation of Past Crimes by Detectives

- Alternatives to traditional retroactive investigation of past crimes by detectives include improved case management, mentoring and training of detectives, and improved crime analysis and information management.

LO4 Discuss the Importance of Crime Analysis and Information Management

- Analyzing and sharing information through the use of multi-agency task forces, repeat offender programs, cold-case squads, surveillance cameras, and the Internet has led to improved case clearance.

(continued on reverse)

Glossary Terms

 Log onto www.cengagebrain.com to practice your vocabulary with flash cards and more.

LO2

detective mystique The idea that detective work is as glamorous, exciting, and dangerous as it is as depicted in the movies and on television.

LO3

Managing Criminal Investigations (MCI) Proposal recommended by the Rand study regarding a more effective way of investigating crimes, including allowing patrol officers to follow up on cases and using solvability factors to determine which cases to follow up.

solvability factors Factors considered in determining whether or not a case should be assigned for follow-up investigation.

mentoring Filling a role as teacher, model, motivator, coach, or advisor in someone else's professional job growth.

LO4

crime analysis The use of analytical methods to obtain pertinent information on crime patterns and trends that can then be disseminated to officers on the street.

investigative task forces A group of investigators working together to investigate one or more crimes. These investigators are often from different law enforcement agencies.

repeat offender programs (ROPs) Enforcement efforts directed at known repeat offenders through surveillance or case enhancement.

cold-case squads Investigative units that reexamine old cases that have remained unsolved. They use the passage of time coupled with a fresh set of eyes, to help solve cases that had been stagnant for years and often decades.

(continued on reverse)

Glossary Terms (continued)

L○5

decoy operations Operations in which officers dress as and play the role of potential victims in the hope of attracting and catching a criminal.

blending Plainclothes officers' efforts to blend into an area in an attempt to catch a criminal.

sting operations Undercover police operations in which police pose as criminals in order to arrest law violators.

civil liability (or code) enforcement teams Teams used in jurisdictions to address the crime problem through the enforcement of civil laws and building and occupational codes.

L○6

undercover investigations Covert investigations involving plainclothes officers.

L○7

entrapment A legal defense that holds that police originated the criminal idea or initiated the crimal action.

Chapter Summary (continued)

L○5 Describe the Proactive Tactics Being Used by Investigators

- Proactive tactics in police investigations include decoy operations, stakeout operations, sting operations, and code enforcement teams.

Retired Police Chief Jim Murray regularly patrols the Internet in the persona of a 13-year-old girl and his work has resulted in many arrests of men making online solicitations for sex.

L○6 Describe Undercover Operations, Including Undercover Drug Operations

- Other traditional proactive techniques include undercover operations.

L○7 Define Entrapment and Show How It Relates to Police Tactical and Undercover Operations

- The legal concept of entrapment and how it affects undercover operations and proactive tactics is an important concept for officers to understand.

 Log onto www.cengagebrain.com for additional resources including videos, flash cards, games, self-quizzing, review exercises, web exercises, learning checks, and more.

Chapter Summary

LO1 Illustrate the Meaning of Police–Community Relations and Their Importance to the Safety and Quality of Life in a Community

• Positive relationships between the police and the public are crucial.

LO2 Define Human Relations, Public Relations, and Community Relations

• Human relations, public relations, and community relations are all important to the police-community relationship.

LO3 Explore Public Attitudes Regarding the Police and Efforts Undertaken Around the Nation to Improve Public Perceptions

• The public's perception of the police is fundamental to the relationship between the police and their community.

LO4 Describe Various Minority Populations and Some of Their Issues Regarding Police Interactions

• Police departments are reaching out to their various minority communities in an effort to build bridges and enhance relationships.

Los Angeles police officers pray at the Islamic Center of Southern California.

Ann Johansson for The New York Times/Redux

Glossary Terms

 Log onto www.cengagebrain.com to practice your vocabulary with flash cards and more.

LO2

human relations Everything done with each other as human beings in all kinds of relationships.

police public relations Activities performed by police agencies designed to create a favorable image of themselves.

police–community relations The relationships involved in both human relations and public relations between the police and the community.

International Association of Chiefs of Police (IACP) An organization composed of police leaders from across the United States that is very influential in setting standards for police departments throughout the country. IACP publishes *Police Chief* magazine, conducts research, and writes publications to assist law enforcement.

LO5

Triad A joint partnership between the police and senior citizens to address specific problems seniors encounter with safety and quality-of-life issues.

Drug Abuse Resistance Education (DARE) The most popular antidrug program in which police officers teach students in schools about the dangers of drug use.

Gang Resistance Education and Training (GREAT) An educational program modeled after DARE that addresses the issue of gangs.

Police Explorers A program for young adults between the ages of 14 and 20 in which they work closely with law enforcement and explore the police career.

(continued on reverse)

(continued on reverse)

Glossary Terms (continued)

Police Athletic League (PAL) A large sports program involving police officers and youth.

Minneapolis Domestic Violence Experiment An experiment conducted in Minneapolis, Minnesota, to examine the deterrent effect of various methods of handling domestic violence, including mandatory arrest.

LO6

Neighborhood Watch Crime prevention programs in which community members participate and engage in a wide range of specific crime prevention activities, as well as community-oriented activities.

citizen patrols A program that involves citizens patrolling on foot or in private cars and alerting the police to possible crimes or criminals in the area.

Operation Identification Engraving identifying numbers onto property that is most likely to be stolen.

police storefront station or mini-station A small satellite police station designed to serve a local part of the community and facilitate the community's access to police officers.

Crime Stoppers A program where a cash reward is offered for information that results in the conviction of an offender.

citizen police academies Academies provided by the police department for the citizens of a community to enhance their understanding of the workings of their police department.

Community Emergency Response Team (CERT) A program in which civilians are trained in basic emergency response, first aid, and search and rescue.

Chapter Summary (continued)

LO5 Explore the Challenges Various Populations—Including the Aging Population, Youth, Crime Victims, Victims of Domestic Violence, the Mentally Ill, and the Homeless—Face When Interacting with the Police

- The many groups that make up our communities have specific and varying needs that the police need to be aware of and make efforts to address to build and strengthen their relationships.

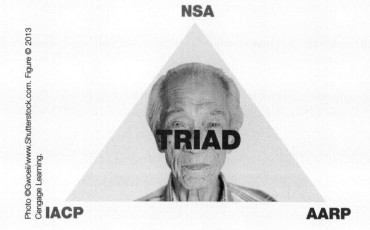

Photo ©Gwoeii/www.Shutterstock.com. Figure © 2013 Cengage Learning.

LO6 Discuss Some Innovative Community Crime Prevention Programs That Focus on Crime Reduction and Improving the Quality of Life in Communities

- Community crime prevention programs, including Neighborhood Watch, National Night Out, citizen patrols, citizen volunteer programs, home security surveys, police storefront stations, Crime Stoppers, mass media campaigns, chaplain programs, citizen police academies, and other programs are designed to assist in the fight against crime and improve the quality of life in U.S. communities.

LO7 Describe the Latest Trends in the Police–Business Relationship

- The business community is a valuable asset and partner in the crime fight, though not one without controversy.

 Log onto www.cengagebrain.com for additional resources including videos, flash cards, games, self-quizzing, review exercises, web exercises, learning checks, and more.

Chapter Summary

LO1 Discuss the Current Thinking about Corporate Strategies for Policing, Including Strategic Policing, Community Policing, and Problem-Solving Policing

- The three corporate strategies for modern policing are strategic policing, community policing, and problem-solving policing.

LO2 Explore the Philosophy and Genesis of the Current Corporate Strategies of Community Policing and Problem-Solving Policing

- Community policing and problem-solving policing have been practiced for over 20 years, and some say they have been tremendously popular and successful.

LO3 Discuss the Effect of Community Policing on Current Policing

- There are many ways to implement community policing; it is flexible and can be implemented to address the particular problems that an agency faces.

LO4 Explain the Process of Implementing Problem-Solving Policing

- Problem-oriented or problem-solving policing involves the process of scanning, analysis, response, and assessment (SARA).

Photo by Robert Nickelsberg/Getty Images

The Baltimore Police Department is working on reducing its crime rate by analyzing when and where incidents are occurring and developing a proactive approach to the bigger crime problem.

Glossary Terms

 Log onto www.cengagebrain.com to practice your vocabulary with flash cards and more.

LO1

strategic policing Involves a continued reliance on traditional policing operations.

community policing Philosophy of empowering citizens and developing a partnership between the police and the community to work together to solve problems.

problem-solving policing Analyzing crime issues to determine the underlying problems and addressing those problems.

LO2

James Q. Wilson and George L. Kelling The authors of the seminal March 1982 *Atlantic Monthly* article entitled "Broken Windows: The Police and Neighborhood Safety," which came to be called the broken windows model of policing.

broken windows model Theory that unrepaired broken windows indicate to others that members of the community do not care about the quality of life in the neighborhood and are unlikely to get involved; consequently, disorder and crime will thrive.

LO3

Robert C. Trojanowicz Founded the National Center for Community Policing in East Lansing, Michigan.

LO4

Herman Goldstein First mentioned the concept of "problem-solving or problem-oriented policing" in 1979.

(continued on reverse)

(continued on reverse)

Glossary Terms (continued)

LO6

resident officer programs Programs through which officers live in particular communities to strengthen relations between the police and the community.

Officer Next Door (OND) program A plan initiated in 1997 that allows police officers to receive 50 percent discounts and low-cost loans to purchase homes in "distressed" areas nationwide. It is under the umbrella Good Neighbor Next Door program, which also includes teachers, firefighters, and emergency medical technicians.

Crime Bill of 1994 The Violent Crime Control and Law Enforcement Act, signed by President Clinton in 1994.

Office of Community Oriented Policing Services (COPS) Established to administer the grant money provided by the 1994 Crime Bill and to promote community policing.

Regional Community Policing Institutes (RCPIs) Part of the COPS program, the more than 30 RCPIs provide regional training and technical assistance to law enforcement around the country regarding community policing.

LO7

fusion center An organization composed of individuals from various federal, state, country, and municipal law enforcement agencies in an area. These individuals facilitate the gathering and sharing of intelligence information and the evaluation of this information. The primary goal of these organizations is strengthening homeland security.

Chapter Summary (continued)

LO5 Describe Some Successful Examples of Problem-Oriented Policing

- There are many examples of successful problem-oriented policing around the country.

LO6 Examine the Status of Community Policing Today

- The programs aimed at working with various populations to serve them better are examples of community policing. Most departments use a variety of programs to demonstrate their community policing philosophy.

Photo © iStockphoto/Andy Dean. Photo of police cap © iStockphoto/Michelle Milliman. Photo illustration by Spitting Images for Cengage Learning.

Many communities are adopting resident officer programs because of the belief that resident officers provide a high-profile presence that helps to prevent crime.

LO7 Discuss How Community Policing Strategies Can Be Useful in the Fight against Terror

- The future of community policing, in particular in the areas of terrorism, was discussed as well as the role that community policing can play in homeland security.

Chapter Summary

LO1 Describe the Police and the United States Constitution

- The primary law regulating life in the United States is the U.S. Constitution, including its many amendments. The U.S. criminal justice system is based on the Bill of Rights, the first 10 amendments to the U.S. Constitution. The U.S. Supreme Court, through its policy of judicial review, has made a significant impact on the way the police do their job.

TABLE 13.1 U.S. Constitution: Amendments Governing the U.S. Criminal Justice System	
First Amendment	Congress shall make no law respecting an establishment of religion, or prohibiting the free exercise thereof; or abridging the freedom of speech, or of the press; or the right of the people peaceably to assemble, and to petition the government for a redress of grievances.
Fourth Amendment	The right of the people to be secure in their persons, houses, papers, and effects against unreasonable searches and seizures, shall not be violated, and no warrants shall issue, but upon probable cause, supported by oath or affirmation, and particularly describing the place to be searched, and the persons or things to be seized.
Fifth Amendment	No person shall be held to answer for a capital, or otherwise infamous crime, unless on a presentment or indictment of a grand jury, except in cases arising in the land or naval forces, or in the militia, when in actual service in time of war or public danger; nor shall any person be subject for the same offense to be twice put in jeopardy of life or limb; nor shall be compelled in any criminal case to be a witness, against himself, nor be deprived of life, liberty, or property, without due process of law; nor shall private property be taken for public use, without just compensation.
Sixth Amendment	In all criminal prosecutions, the accused shall enjoy the right to a speedy and public trial, by an impartial jury of the State and district wherein the crime shall have been committed, which district shall have been previously ascertained by law, and to be informed of the nature and cause of the accusation; to be confronted with the witnesses against him; to have compulsory process for obtaining witnesses in his favor, and to have the assistance of counsel for his defense.
Eighth Amendment	Excessive bail shall not be required, nor excessive fines imposed, nor cruel and unusual punishments inflicted.
Fourteenth Amendment (Section 1)	All persons born or naturalized in the United States and subject to the jurisdiction thereof, are citizens of the United States and of the State wherein they reside. No State shall make or enforce any law which shall abridge the privileges or immunities of citizens of the United States; nor shall any State deprive any person of life, liberty, or property, without due process of law; nor deny to any person within its jurisdiction the equal protection of the laws.

(continued on reverse)

Glossary Terms

 Log onto www.cengagebrain.com to practice your vocabulary with flash cards and more.

LO1

judicial review Process by which actions of the police in areas such as arrests, search and seizure, and interrogations are reviewed by the U.S. Court system at various levels to ensure the constitutionality of these actions.

exclusionary rule An interpretation of the U.S. Constitution by the U.S. Supreme Court that holds that evidence seized in violation of the U.S. Constitution cannot be used in court against a defendant.

silver platter doctrine Legal tactic that allowed federal prosecutors to use evidence obtained by state police officers that had been obtained through unreasonable searches and seizures.

LO2

arrest The initial taking into custody of a person by law enforcement authorities to answer for a criminal offense or violation of a code or ordinance.

probable cause Evidence that may lead a reasonable person to believe that a crime has been committed and that a certain person committed it.

reasonable suspicion The standard of proof that is necessary for police officers to conduct stops and frisks.

LO3

search and seizure Legal concept relating to the searching for and confiscation of evidence by the police.

LO4

search warrant A written order, based on probable cause and signed by a judge authorizing police to search a specific person, place, or property to obtain evidence.

(continued on reverse)

Glossary Terms (continued)

exigent circumstances One of the major exceptions to the warrant requirement of the Fourth Amendment. Exigency may be defined as "emergency."

stop and frisk The detaining of a person by law enforcement officers for the purpose of investigation, accompanied by a superficial examination of the person's body surface or clothing to discover any weapons, contraband, or other objects relating to criminal activity.

field interrogation Unplanned questioning of an individual who has aroused the suspicions of an officer.

plain view evidence Evidence seized without a warrant by police who have the right to be in a position to observe that evidence.

Carroll doctrine The legal doctrine that automobiles have less Fourth Amendment protection than other places. Arose from the landmark 1925 U.S. Supreme Court case *Carroll v. United States.*

LO5

custodial interrogation The questioning of a person in police custody regarding his or her participation in a crime.

third degree The pattern of brutality and violence used by the police to obtain confessions from suspects.

Miranda rules (*Miranda* warnings) Rules established by the U.S. Supreme Court in the landmark case *Miranda v. Arizona* (1966) that require the police to advise suspects confronting custodial interrogation of their constitutional rights.

Chapter Summary (continued)

LO2 Discuss the Police and Arrest

- The police authority to arrest an individual is controlled by the Fourth and Fifth Amendments.

LO3 Discuss the Police and Search and Seizure

- Police searches are governed by the Fourth Amendment, which prohibits all unreasonable searches and seizures and requires that all warrants be based on probable cause and particularly describe the place to be searched and the persons or things to be seized.

LO4 Describe the Warrant Requirement and the Search Warrant

- Most of the arrests made by the average police officer do not involve a warrant, because most crimes on the street necessitate immediate action. The general rule regarding search and seizure is that law enforcement officers must obtain a search warrant before they conduct a search.

© REUTERS/John Gress /Landov

A police officer executes a search warrant for marijuana at a Kalamazoo, Michigan home. Under the exclusionary rule, any evidence from this search would be inadmissible in court if the evidence was seized in violation of the U.S. Constitution.

LO5 Discuss the Police and Custodial Interrogation

- The U.S. Supreme Court has recognized two constitutional sources of the right to counsel during interrogation: the Court's interpretation in *Miranda v. Arizona* of the Fifth Amendment right against self-incrimination and the Sixth Amendment.

Chapter Summary

LO1 Describe Computers in Policing

- Computers have enabled the police to dispatch officers immediately to any calls for service. They have also aided the police in the investigation process by enabling officers to feed descriptions and MOs into the computer and to receive almost instantaneous printouts on possible suspects.

LO2 Discuss Fingerprint Technology

- The computer has also caused a revolution in the processing of fingerprints through automated fingerprint identification system (AFIS) terminals.

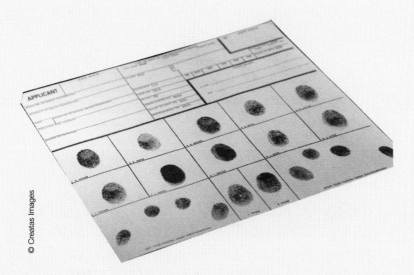

© Creatas Images

LO3 Discuss Modern Forensics or Criminalistics

- The use of scientific technology to solve crime is generally referred to as forensic science or criminalistics.

TABLE 14.1 Forensic Specialties

Forensic pathology	Dead bodies
Forensic physical anthropology	Skeletal remains
Forensic odontology	Teeth formation
Forensic toxicology	Poisons
Forensic entomology	Insects at death scenes

(continued on reverse)

Glossary Terms

 Log onto www.cengagebrain.com to practice your vocabulary with flash cards and more.

LO1

computer-aided dispatch (CAD) System that allows almost immediate communication between the police dispatcher and police units in the field.

mobile digital terminal (MDT) A device put into a police vehicle that allows the electronic transmission of messages between the police dispatcher and the officer in the field.

National Crime Information Center (NCIC) Computerized database of criminal information maintained by the FBI.

automated crime analysis The automated collection and analysis of crime data (when, where, who, what, how, and why) to discern criminal patterns and assist in the effective assignment of personnel to combat crime.

computer-aided investigation (computer-aided case management) The use of computers to perform case management and other functions in investigations.

license plate recognition (LPR) technology Employs cameras and computer software to discern the letters and numbers of vehicle license plates and then compares them with records contained in state and federal databases, including records from the department of motor vehicles and the NCIC.

LO2

inked prints (ten-prints) Result of the process of rolling each finger onto a ten-print card.

latent prints Fingerprint impressions left at a crime scene.

automated fingerprint identification system (AFIS) Fingerprinting innovation developed in the 1980s in which a print technician can enter unidentified latent fingerprints into a computer. The computer then automatically searches its files and presents a list of likely matches.

(continued on reverse)

Glossary Terms (continued)

Live Scan The electronic taking and transmitting of fingerprints, as opposed to traditional ink methods.

Integrated Automated Fingerprint Identification System (IAFIS) A system for searching an individual's fingerprints against a computerized database of fingerprints.

LO3

forensic science That part of science applied to answering legal questions.

criminalistics A branch of forensic science that deals with the study of physical evidence related to crime.

LO4

DNA profiling, genetic fingerprinting, DNA typing The examination of DNA samples from a body fluid to determine whether they came from a particular subject.

deoxyribonucleic acid (DNA) The basic building code for all of the human body's chromosomes.

polymerase chain reaction-short tandem repeat (PCR-STR) One of the latest DNA technology systems; requires only pinhead-size samples rather than the dime-size samples needed for RFLP.

restricted fragment length polymorphism (RFLP) Traditional method of DNA technology analysis.

mitochondrial DNA (MtDNA) analysis DNA analysis applied to evidence containing very small or degraded quantities of DNA from hair, bones, teeth, and body fluids.

Combined DNA Index System (CODIS) Database that contains DNA profiles obtained from subjects convicted of homicide, sexual assault, and other serious felonies.

National DNA Index System (NDIS) The final level of CODIS, which supports the sharing of DNA profiles from convicted offenders and crime scene evidence submitted by state and local forensic laboratories across the United States.

cold hit A DNA sample collected from a crime scene that ties an unknown suspect to the DNA profile of someone in the national or a state's database.

Chapter Summary (continued)

LO4 Discuss DNA Profiling (Genetic Fingerprinting)

- DNA profiling, also called genetic fingerprinting or DNA typing, has shown exponential progress in the last decade in helping investigators solve crimes and ensure that those guilty of crimes are convicted in court.

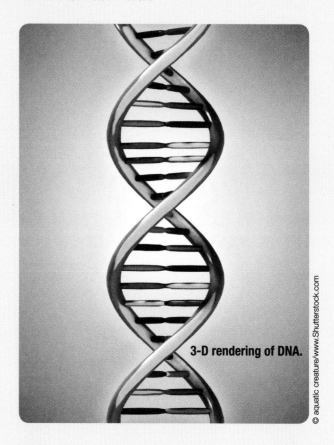

3-D rendering of DNA.

© aquatic creature/www.Shutterstock.com

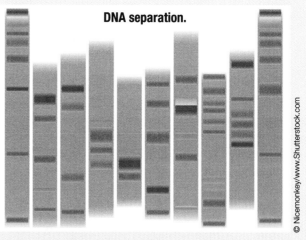

DNA separation.

© Nicemonkey/www.Shutterstock.com

 Log onto www.cengagebrain.com for additional study tools including videos, flash cards, games, self-quizzing, review exercises, web exercises, learning checks, and more.

Chapter Summary

LO1 Define Homeland Security

- The term homeland security has been used after the September 11 terrorism acts to describe defensive efforts within the borders of the United States. Officials use it to separate the U.S. Department of Homeland Security's (DHS) operations from those of the U.S. Department of Defense.

LO2 Define Terrorism

- There are many definitions of terrorism. Terrorists target civilian populations—noncombatants.

LO3 Discuss the Post-9/11 Response to Terrorism and Homeland Defense

- In October of 2001, the Office of Homeland Security was established and the USA Patriot Act was signed into law.

LO4 Discuss Federal Law Enforcement Efforts for Homeland Security

- The first DHS priority is to protect the nation against further terrorist attacks. The department's agencies analyze threats and intelligence, guard our borders and airports, protect our critical infrastructure, and coordinate the responses of our nation for future emergencies.

TABLE 15.1 U.S. Department of Homeland Security (DHS) Components and Agencies
Directorate for National Protection and Programs
Directorate for Science and Technology
Directorate for Management
Office of Policy
Office of Health Affairs
Office of Intelligence and Analysis
Office of Operations Coordination
Federal Law Enforcement Training Center
Domestic Nuclear Detection Office
Transportation Security Administration (TSA)
United States Customs and Border Protection (CBP)
United States Citizenship and Immigration Services
United States Immigration and Customs Enforcement (ICE)
United States Coast Guard
Federal Emergency Management Administration (FEMA)
United States Secret Service

SOURCE: U.S. Department of Homeland Security. 11 March 2011, www.dhs.gov.

Glossary Terms

 Log onto www.cengagebrain.com to practice your vocabulary with flash cards and more.

LO1

homeland security Efforts made since the terrorist acts of September 11, 2001, to protect the United States against terrorist acts.

LO2

terrorism Premeditated, politically motivated violence perpetrated against noncombatant targets.

domestic terrorism Terrorism committed by citizens of the United States in the United States.

LO3

USA Patriot Act Public Law No. 107-56, passed in 2001, giving law enforcement new abilities to search, seize, detain, and eavesdrop in their pursuit of possible terrorists; full title of law is USA Patriot Act—Uniting and Strengthening America by Providing Appropriate Tools Required to Intercept and Obstruct Terrorism.

LO4

counterterrorism Enforcement efforts made against terrorist organizations.

Joint Terrorism Task Forces (JTTF) Forces that make use of single-focused investigative units that meld personnel and talent from various law enforcement agencies.

(continued on reverse)

Chapter Summary (continued)

LO5 Discuss State and Local Law Enforcement Efforts for Homeland Security

- State and local law enforcement officers will be the ones who respond first to a terrorist threat or incident and serve as the foundation of an effective assessment of threatening activities in their communities.

A national counterterrorism instructor speaks to security, rescue, and police personnel on how to spot a suicide bomber at a mall. Local police are on the frontline of the war on terrorism.